Christ Jesus and the
Jewish People Today

About the cover art

In his final letter, the Apostle Paul described the relationship of Gentiles in the church to the Jewish tradition as akin to a wild olive branch being grafted into a domesticated olive tree (Rom. 11: 17-24). It was impossible for him to know that a few years after his death the Roman Empire would destroy the Temple in Jerusalem, that in the following centuries the church would effectively become a thoroughly Gentile community, and that rabbinic Judaism would become normative for the Jewish people. The cover's olive tree thus illustrates the two traditions growing out of the trunk of biblical Israel: Christianity and rabbinic Judaism, whose branches have historically and theologically intertwined as history unfolded.

Christ Jesus and the Jewish People Today

New Explorations of
Theological Interrelationships

Edited by

Philip A. Cunningham,
Joseph Sievers,
Mary Boys,
Hans Hermann Henrix &
Jesper Svartvik

WILLIAM B. EERDMANS PUBLISHING COMPANY
GRAND RAPIDS, MICHIGAN / CAMBRIDGE, U.K.

GREGORIAN & BIBLICAL PRESS

Published 2011
in the United States of America by
Wm. B. Eerdmans Publishing Co.
2140 Oak Industrial Drive N.E., Grand Rapids, Michigan 49505 /
P.O. Box 163, Cambridge CB3 9PU U.K.
www.eerdmans.com
and in Italy by
Gregorian and Biblical Press
Piazza della Pilotta, 35, 00187 Rome
www.gbpress.net

Printed in the United States of America

16 15 14 13 12 11   7 6 5 4 3 2 1

Library of Congress Cataloging-in-Publication Data

Christ Jesus and the Jewish people today : new explorations of theological interrelationships /
    edited by Philip A. Cunningham ... [et al.].
        p.   cm.
    Includes bibliographical references.
    Eerdmans ISBN 978-0-8028-6624-0 (pbk.: alk. paper)
    GBPress ISBN 978-88-7839-186-4
    1. Christianity and other religions — Judaism.   2. Judaism — Relations — Christianity.
    3. Salvation — Christianity — History of doctrines.   4. Salvation — Judaism.
    5. Covenants — Religious aspects — Christianity.   6. Covenants — Religious aspects —
    Judaism.   7. Jesus Christ — Jewish interpretations.   I. Cunningham, Philip A.

BM535.C5234   2011
261.2′6 — dc22

                                                            2010046699

Dedicated to the memory of
Rabbi Dr. Michael Signer
Abrams Professor of Theology at the University of Notre Dame

researcher, colleague, friend,
pioneer in "translating" between
the Catholic and Jewish cultures of discourse

May his name be for a blessing
May the perpetual light shine upon him

Contents

Foreword

Walter Cardinal Kasper

In 2010, the official dialogue between the Jewish people and the Catholic Church celebrated two anniversaries: a fiftieth anniversary, for on September 18, 1960, Pope John XXIII gave Augustin Cardinal Bea the task of conducting dialogue with Jews; and a forty-fifth anniversary, for on October 28, 1965, Pope Paul VI solemnly promulgated Vatican II's *Nostra Aetate*, the declaration that is fundamental for this dialogue. I am glad that the present volume can appear on this occasion, and I would like to express my deepest thanks to all who were involved in its realization.

In this foreword I would like to set the present volume into the context of the recent history of Jewish-Christian relations and then to make some fundamental points about the relationship between Judaism and the church from my perspective.

The history of Jewish-Christian relations is complex and difficult. In addition to some better times, as when bishops took Jews under their protection against pogroms by mobs, there were dark times that have been especially impressed upon the collective Jewish consciousness. The Shoah, the state-sponsored organized murder of approximately six million European Jews, based on a primitive racial ideology, is the absolute low point in this history. The Holocaust cannot be attributed to Christianity as such, since it also had clear anti-Christian features. However, centuries-old Christian theological anti-Judaism contributed as well, encouraging a widespread antipathy for Jews, so that ideologically and racially motivated antisemitism could prevail in this terrible way, and the resistance against the outrageous inhuman brutality did not achieve the breadth and clarity that one should have expected.

Unfortunately, it required the unprecedented crime of the Shoah for a fundamental rethinking to come about. This happened after 1945 in all the mainline churches. On the Catholic side the declaration of Vatican II, *Nostra Aetate,* was the decisive turning point. It is — as Benedict XVI made absolutely clear once again during his visit to the Roman synagogue on January 17, 2010 — irrevocable. It is irreversible because of the plain fact that the decisive theological arguments of the declaration *Nostra Aetate* are firmly established in two higher-ranking conciliar constitutions, the Dogmatic Constitution on the Church (nos. 6, 9, 16) and the Dogmatic Constitution on Divine Revelation (nos. 3, 14).

In the declaration *Nostra Aetate* two statements are of special importance. Fundamental is the recognition of the Jewish roots of Christianity and its Jewish heritage. Based on these common roots and common heritage, as Pope John Paul II said during his visit to the Roman synagogue on April 13, 1986, Judaism is not external but internal to Christianity; Christianity is in a unique relationship with it. This overrode the old anti-Judaism. The second important statement concerns the condemnation of antisemitism. In the declaration, the church deplores "all outbreaks of hatred, persecution, displays of antisemitism that have been directed at any time and by anyone against the Jews." Both statements have been explicitly confirmed by Popes John Paul II and Benedict XVI several times, particularly during their visits to the Roman synagogue and to Auschwitz, among other occasions.

The Council's statement has not remained a dead letter: since then many decisive things have happened in order to translate the declaration into life and into reality. Above all, the visits of Pope John Paul II and Pope Benedict XVI to the Roman synagogue and to the Holy Land, and likewise the visits to Rome by high-level Jewish delegations, have eloquently expressed the newly grown relationship and have strengthened it further. Thus, mutual estrangement has been reduced, and trust, cooperation, and friendship have been built. Furthermore, the recognition of the State of Israel by the Holy See and the establishment of formal diplomatic relations in 1993 were only possible on the basis of *Nostra Aetate.*

In 1974, Pope Paul VI established the Commission for Religious Relations with the Jews with the task of promoting relations and cooperation with Jews. Through the International Catholic Jewish Liaison Committee (ICJLC) it conducts regular international dialogues with the International Jewish Committee for Interreligious Consultations (IJCIC), a consortium of a number of major Jewish organizations. The Commission has published important documents for the understanding and application of

Nostra Aetate (*Guidelines and Suggestions for Implementing the Conciliar Declaration* Nostra Aetate, *4* [1974]) and *Notes on the Correct Way to Present Jews and Judaism in Preaching and Catechesis in the Roman Catholic Church* (1985), as well as concerning the Shoah (*We Remember: A Reflection on the Shoah*, 1998). In addition, since 2003 the Commission has conducted in an extremely warm and friendly atmosphere a fruitful dialogue with the Chief Rabbinate in Jerusalem.

Furthermore, in all concerned bishops' conferences there are committees and dialogues on the national level, and fruitful cooperation has grown in theology and in many other areas. "Weeks of Brotherhood," *Nostra Aetate* anniversaries, etc. seek to keep alive the concern of reconciliation and dialogue with Judaism in a broader public sphere. The documents on just this subject that were published up until the year 2000 fill two thick volumes totaling about 1,800 pages.[1] It is virtually impossible to keep track of the abundance of publications in book form and in individual articles, as in the form of essay collections. Thus, treatises *Pro Judaeis* have replaced the old *Adversus Judaeos* tractates. This all shows that a new and fundamentally different situation has emerged.

It was obvious in these national and international dialogues that coming to grips with the past and the reestablishment of confidence were the first priority. The remembering of what was will remain an important task — particularly in the education of young generations — as a warning for the future as well. But since the ICJLC meeting in Buenos Aires (2004) on the topic "*Tzedeq* and *Tzedaqah* — Justice and Charity," attention focuses more on our common responsibility for the present and for the future. It is a matter of cooperating in the building of a world in which such terrible events as the Shoah are no longer possible.

Of course, after such a long history of estrangement and in view of the remaining fundamental differences between Judaism and Christianity, it was inevitable that misunderstandings and controversies would arise and continue to arise. They included, among other things, the newly formulated intercession for the extraordinary rite of the Good Friday liturgy, the assessment of the attitude of Pope Pius XII to the Shoah during the Second World War, and the question of the mission to the Jews.

1. See Rolf Rendtorff and Hans Hermann Henrix, eds., *Die Kirchen und das Judentum.* Volume I: *Dokumente von 1945 bis 1985* (Paderborn/Gütersloh: Bonifatius/Gütersloher Verlagshaus, 2001), which contains 746 pp.; and Hans Hermann Henrix and Wolfgang Kraus, eds., *Die Kirchen und das Judentum.* Volume II. *Dokumente von 1986 bis 2000* (Paderborn/Gütersloh: Bonifatius/Gütersloher Verlagshaus, 2001), which has 1,036 pp.

Being in the best interest of both parties, letters and conversations on the official level could relatively rapidly clarify and settle to some extent the occasionally heated controversies because of the confidence that had grown in the meantime. These controversies draw attention again to the differences between Judaism and Christianity that are fundamental for both communities. They transcend the issues of the day and until now have been little treated and processed. This involves such key issues as the Christian confession of Jesus as the Christ (i.e., messiah) and the Son of God, which is directly related to the trinitarian understanding of biblical monotheism, the universal salvific significance of Jesus Christ, his death and his resurrection, freedom from the law, and much else.

Of course, there can be no question of dissolving the deep-seated differences on these issues in favor of some sort of syncretism, or of relativizing them. Most definitely, this discussion may not involve any covert proselytism. The basis for dialogue must rather be the realization that Jews and Christians differ on these issues and must respect and appreciate each other in their otherness. But precisely for the sake of mutual respect and appreciation, in the newly generated climate of trust it must be a primary goal to actively reduce old misunderstandings and develop possible approaches to understanding each other's positions. At first, this exploration of core issues should take place between specialists on an academic level and not be part of the official dialogues. An initial commendable attempt, albeit one that was discussed critically from various sides, was made by Jewish scholars with "*Dabru Emet:* To Speak the Truth" (2000). Subsequently, at the suggestion of the Commission for Religious Relations with the Jews, an informally convened international group of Christian theologians began meeting in 2006; individual Jewish specialists and friends were invited to participate as critical observers. Their work studied the specific question of how to relate the universal saving significance of Jesus Christ to Israel's ongoing covenantal life with God.

The Commission suggested and encouraged this conversation, and it was kept informed about its progress, although it was not officially engaged itself. To my great joy, the working group can now set forth its results in this volume. These are not the products of an official dialogue but the results of a conversation on the academic level. As in every academic conversation, each author bears the responsibility for his or her own ideas. However, their contributions have arisen from the conversations among these Christian scholars and with Jewish friends and are to be understood in this deliberative context. Their publication now presents an invitation for other interested parties to join in this discussion critically and constructively and to advance it further.

Whoever peruses the contributions collected in this volume will quickly recognize that this conversation is by no means completed. We stand only at the beginning of a new beginning. Many exegetical, historical, and systematic questions are still open, and presumably there will always be such questions. There will also always be different positions on all of these questions. Thus, there is to date no conclusive theory that is more or less generally accepted about the relationship of Judaism and Christianity, if there ever will be.

From my point of view, though, there are already today a few trajectories that can be drawn out, without any claim to comprehensiveness. I confine myself to six points, which I can only present in this context in broad strokes. All six points are developed out of a Christian perspective and are not made with the expectation that our Jewish conversation partners can agree to all of them.

1. Israel is the divinely chosen and beloved people of the covenant, which was never revoked or terminated (Rom. 9:4; 11:29). That is why Israel cannot be collectively described as an accursed people cast off by God. It also cannot be said that the covenant with Israel has been replaced by the New Covenant. The New Covenant for Christians is not the replacement (substitution), but the fulfillment of the Old Covenant. Both stand with each other in a relationship of promise or anticipation and fulfillment. This relationship must be understood in the context of the whole history of the covenant. The whole history of God with his people takes place in a sequence of various covenants with Abraham, Moses, Joshua, and Ezra; in the end, the prophet Jeremiah promises a new covenant (Jer. 31:31). Each of these covenants takes up the previous covenant and at the same time reinterprets it anew. Thus the New Covenant is the final reinterpretation promised by the prophets of the Old Covenant. It is the definitive yes and amen to all of God's promises (2 Cor. 1:20), but not their suspension or abolition.

2. The problem is not only the relationship of the Old and New Covenants, but the different problem of the relationship of post-biblical rabbinic and Talmudic Judaism — which arose only after the destruction of the Second Temple in the year 70 C.E. — with the church. The canons and structures of both formed in parallel. Therefore the New Testament can give us no clear and above all no uniform answer to the question just posed. Paul wrestled with it again and again, but in a sense, the situation was still open in his lifetime. The schism between Judaism and Christianity

that continues until today is already clearly discernible in the Fourth Gospel with, on the one hand, the exclusion of Christians from the synagogue (John 9:22; 16:2), and on the other hand, the polemics of the Christians against "the Jews" (John 5:16, 18; 7:1, etc.). Nevertheless, the Gospel of John cannot be interpreted to be anti-Jewish in the latter sense; it also knows that salvation is from the Jews (John 4:22). Likewise for the Letter to the Hebrews. Although a long-standing reading of Hebrews contends that it declares the Old Covenant to be obsolete and fading away (Heb. 8:13), it would be anachronistic to project the distinction between Judaism and Christianity back already into the first century. This letter is written to the Hebrews and not possibly written against the Hebrews. So the text does not seek to devaluate Judaism as such, but questions the value of the Levitical priesthood and its sacrificial rites.

After the destruction of the Second Temple, a rabbinic Jewish and a Christian interpretation of the Old Testament developed in parallel and in interaction, both based on their respective religious presuppositions. The document of the Pontifical Biblical Commission, *The Jewish People and Their Sacred Scriptures in the Christian Bible* (2001), however, explicitly notes that both are possible interpretations of the Old Testament text (§22). In this regard, the statement of *Nostra Aetate* receives its full weight, that the Jews, according to the testimony of the Apostle, "are still beloved of God for their fathers' sake, for his gifts of grace are irrevocable." Even the invitation and the call for dialogue can be fully appreciated only against this background.

3. If one takes the last statement seriously, then post-biblical Judaism and the church are not two covenant peoples: they are the one covenant people. They do not represent, therefore, two parallel ways of salvation. Rather, God has spoken through Jesus Christ his definitive yes and amen to all the promises of salvation (2 Cor. 1:20). From a Christian perspective, the death and resurrection of Christ also mean salvation for the Jews. Between Judaism and Christianity, therefore, is a differentiation that is neither simply a parallel coexistence, nor an opposition. Rather, Paul has shown in his insights concerning salvation history in Romans 9–11 that the two are dialectically related to each other in their difference. This relationship can hardly be reduced to a formula or a catchy phrase. It is, as Paul says, ultimately a mystery (Rom. 11:33-36). If one wishes, one can try to describe this mystery in a similar way to the formula of the Council of Chalcedon (451 C.E.) and define the relationship of both with a double negation: without confusion and without separation.

4. Perhaps more helpful than a conceptual clarification is the image that Paul uses in the Letter to the Romans for the relationship between Judaism and Christianity. He speaks of the root of Israel into which the wild branches of the Gentiles have been implanted (Rom. 11:16-20). This image, going back to the prophet Isaiah (Isa. 11:1), expresses the sense of distinction within unity in two ways. On the one hand, it is said that the engrafted wild branches have not grown from the rootstock itself and cannot be derived from it. The grafting is something new: it is God's own irreducible act. The church is thus not simply a branch, a fruit, or an offshoot of Israel. On the other hand, the church must draw its vigor and strength from the rootstock of Israel. If the engrafted branches are cut off from the root, they become withered, weak, and eventually die. Thus, cutting itself off from its Jewish roots for centuries weakened the church, a weakness that became evident in the altogether too feeble resistance against the persecution of Jews.

But the reverse is also true. Without the engrafted branches the root remains a barren stump. The engrafted branches give the rootstock new vitality and fertility. Thus the church has spread universally among the nations the monotheism of Israel and the Ten Commandments as the core of the Mosaic law, and has thereby contributed to the fact that the promise given to Abraham that he would be a blessing to all nations (Gen. 12:3; 18:18; etc.) has come true. Israel without the church is in danger of becoming too particularistic and reclusive, while the church without Israel, as the example of Marcionism makes clear, is in danger of losing its historical grounding and becoming ahistorical and Gnostic. Israel and the churches need each other and therefore are dependent on each other. A true ecumenism without Israel is not possible.

5. A well thought-out determination of the relationship of Israel and the church is fundamental to answering the question of Christian mission among the Jews. Every Christian reflection on this delicate subject must proceed from the universal salvific significance of Jesus Christ as well as from the universal mission of the church. This was, of course, natural for Paul, too; this is why on his missionary journeys he went first (Rom. 1:16) to the Jews in the synagogue, and only after he met opposition did he then turn to the Gentiles. It is nonetheless true that Jews are not pagans; they do not repent of false and dead idols to turn to the true and living God (1 Thess. 1:9). This means that command for mission is as valid for Jews as for pagans, but it must be put into effect differently among Jews than pagans.

This difference has not always been observed, and unfortunately there has been a history of forced conversions of Jews. In principle, though, the church takes this difference into account. In contrast to some fundamentalist movements, the Catholic Church sponsors no specific institutional missionary work aimed at Jews. This is more than a mere fact; it is an important ecclesial reality. It should not be ruled out that some Jews, such as Edith Stein, may convert to Jesus Christ just as in reverse there are Christians who turn to the Jewish faith. However, these are personal decisions of conscience, which must be respected by both sides, but from neither side are they a strategic goal.

According to Paul, "all Israel will be saved" (Rom. 11:26ff.). This relates to the Pontifical Biblical Commission's observation that "Jewish messianic expectation is not in vain" and therefore that at the end of time both Jews and Christians will recognize the "One who is to come," the eschatological messiah (PBC 2001, §21). This does not mean that the church and Christians should behave passively in the meantime and simply sit on their hands. The exclusion of a targeted institutional mission does not prohibit, but rather implies that Christians and the church are generally required to give Jews witness to their faith in Jesus Christ now. Such Christian witness will be, especially after the Shoah, discreet and humble, must avoid any appearance of triumphalism, and show respect and esteem for the conviction of the Jewish partner. Humility admittedly may not be mistaken for sycophancy or even cowardice. To be a witness *(martyr)* according to the Scriptures is no small thing and should be done with candor.

6. The common heritage of Jews and Christians includes the joint vocation to a common witness to the one God and his commandments. This includes the unmasking and prophetic criticism of the new false gods and idols of our time, and a shared commitment to human dignity, to justice and peace in the world, to the dignity and worth of the family, and to the integrity of creation. Not least, Jews and Christians can together give witness to the dialogue, cooperation, and reconciliation that are possible even after a difficult and complex history. Likewise, they can stand together for *teshuvah,* i.e., for repentance and reconciliation. Moreover, with the celebration of the Sabbath or Sunday, they perform an indispensable service for the freedom of people: they are showing that in this world there should be a sacred time dedicated to God and that being human should not be reduced to labor, economics, business, and pleasure.

Above all, Jews and Christians look to the future: they give witness together — in the midst of the many dilemmas and instances of hopelessness in the world — to the hope for the perfect justice and the universal *shalom* that God alone will usher in at the end of time. Thus they contribute to build a just and humanitarian world in which such a terrible event as the Shoah cannot be repeated. That the dialogue in the not-too-distant future may also help to promote a peace process in the Middle East is, unfortunately, thus far an unrealized wish of all parties.

No one could have foreseen forty-five years ago where we are today in the relationship between Jews and Christians. We have advanced farther than we could have imagined back then. But today we also see more clearly that the road to each other and with each other is not complete and still has a long way to go. *Nostra Aetate* is far from being a finished agenda. It is my hope that this volume will both show us where we stand today and also encourage us to continue on the path and to tackle the many questions that are still waiting.

Introduction

1. The Origins of the Christ and the Jewish People Consultations

On October 28, 1965, Pope Paul VI promulgated one of the most influential documents of the Second Vatican Council: the Declaration on the Relationship of the Church to Non-Christian Religions, *Nostra Aetate*. Although in the course of its composition the declaration had been expanded to discuss all religions of the world, its original subject — the unique relationship of the Catholic Church to Judaism and the Jewish people — remained at the heart of the final document. By repudiating the presentation of Jews "as rejected or accursed by God" and by insisting that "God holds the Jews most dear," *Nostra Aetate* reversed previously unchallenged presuppositions that had shaped Christian attitudes and theologies for centuries. It thus paved the way for an unprecedented era of increasingly positive relations between Catholics and Jews.

Forty years later, in September 2005, hundreds of scholars from dozens of countries gathered at the Pontifical Gregorian University in Rome to consider the impact of *Nostra Aetate* on interreligious relations.[1] In

---

1. The conference, "*Nostra Aetate* Today: Reflections Forty Years after Its Call for a New Era of Interreligious Relationships," occurred on September 25-28, 2005, and was sponsored by the Institute for the Study of Religions and Cultures with the Cardinal Bea Centre for Judaic Studies at the Pontifical Gregorian University in Rome in collaboration with the following institutions in the United States: Georgetown University, Washington, DC; the Joseph Cardinal Bernardin Center at Catholic Theological Union, Chicago; the Center for Christian-Jewish Learning at Boston College; and the Center for Christian-Jewish Understanding of Sacred Heart University, Fairfield, CT. The conference included many scholars from other world religions, but we focus here on the Catholic-Jewish relationship.

terms of Catholic-Jewish relations, many crucial developments had occurred in the intervening four decades. These included:

- The establishment of the Pontifical Commission for Religious Relations with the Jews, which published three defining statements of the
  Roman Catholic magisterium's evolving understanding of its new relationship with Jews and Judaism.[2]
- The flowering of extensive dialogue between Catholics and Jews on
  several continents among both leaders and ordinary members of both
  communities.
- An intensive promotion of Catholic-Jewish relations during the long
  pontificate of John Paul II, including many theologically groundbreaking papal addresses[3] and the enormously influential actions of
  visiting the Great Synagogue of Rome, praying at Auschwitz, establishing formal diplomatic relations with the State of Israel, and, perhaps
  most iconically, praying for God's forgiveness for Christian sins
  against Jews and committing the church to fellowship with them, both
  at the Vatican and at the Western Wall.[4]
- The composition of numerous statements by national bishops' conferences that fostered positive relations locally.
- Extensive research into biblical, historical, theological, and other as-

2. These are "Guidelines and Suggestions for Implementing the Conciliar Declaration,
Nostra Aetate, 4" (1974); "Notes on the Correct Way to Present Jews and Judaism in
Preaching and Teaching in the Roman Catholic Church" (1985); and "We Remember: A Re-
flection on the Shoah" (1998). The Commission is hereafter referred to as CRRJ.

3. See Eugene J. Fisher and Leon Klenicki, eds., *Spiritual Pilgrimage: Pope John Paul II:
Texts on Jews and Judaism, 1979-1995* (New York: Crossroad, 1995). See also the online collection   at: http://www.ccjr.us/dialogika-resources/documents-and-statements/roman-
catholic/pope-john-paul-ii.

4. John Paul II has had an enormous international influence on theological scholarship
in Christian-Jewish reflections. As a small sample, see Marie-Thérèse Hoch and Bernard
Dupuy, eds., *Les Églises devant le Judaïsme. Document officiels 1948-1978* (Paris: Cerf, 1980);
International Catholic-Jewish Liaison Committee, ed., *Fifteen Years of Catholic-Jewish Dia-
logue 1970-1985. Selected Papers* (Vatican: Vaticana, 1988); Rolf Rendtorff and Hans Hermann
Henrix, eds., *Die Kirchen und das Judentum. Band I: Dokumente von 1945 bis 1985* (Pader-
born/Gütersloh: Bonifatius/Gütersloher Verlagshaus, 2001); Hans Hermann Henrix and
Wolfgang Kraus, eds., *Die Kirchen und das Judentum. Band II: Dokumente von 1986 bis 2000*
(Paderborn/Gütersloh: Bonifatius/Gütersloher Verlagshaus, 2001); Pier Francesco Fuma-
galli, ed., *Fratelli Prediletti. Chiesa e Popolo ebraico. Documenti e fatti: 1965-2005* (Milano:
Mondadori, 2005); Ernst Fürlinger, ed., *Der Dialog muss weitergehen. Ausgewählte vatika-
nische Dokumente zum interreligiösen Dialog* (Freiburg: Herder, 2009).

pects of interfaith relations by Jewish and Christian scholars. Some of this research was collaborative.

• Local dialogue groups, often with support from diocesan and Jewish agencies, have worked to foster strong bonds between Jews and Christians.

• Perseverance in maintaining communications and positive relations even when embroiled in heated controversy and disagreement.

These and other factors informed the scholarly exchanges at the 2005 *Nostra Aetate* anniversary conference. The papers and discussions at that event made it clear that the conciliar declaration had given rise to challenging and still unresolved theological questions. Foremost among these questions were those concerning the relationships among Jesus Christ, the covenantal status of the Jewish people, and understandings of salvation. Papers that explored these topics seemed to the conference organizers to draw some similar conclusions, suggesting an emerging consensus.

To explore this possibility, professors at four Catholic universities[5] collaborated in arranging a theological consultation on October 19-22, 2006, with about two dozen scholars from eight countries. The participants were primarily Catholics because the purpose of the consultation, titled "Christ and the Jewish People," was to pursue a core question for Christian theology from within a Catholic perspective. However, the group also included a few Lutheran and Jewish scholars. Our Lutheran colleagues greatly enriched our deliberations and assured an ecumenical dimension. Jews participated in this Christian endeavor as "consultants," whose role was to ensure the accuracy of any references to Jewish concepts and teachings. They also offered very helpful insights from within their own tradition. This first meeting of the "Christ and the Jewish People" initiative took place at the Casa Divin Maestro in Ariccia, Italy, where the original drafters of *Nostra Aetate* had done some of their work in the 1960s.

The group focused its attention on this "meta-question" confronting Christian, and particularly Catholic, theology today:

5. They were the Cardinal Bea Centre for Judaic Studies at the Pontifical Gregorian University; the Joseph Cardinal Bernardin Center at Catholic Theological Union, Chicago; the Center for Christian-Jewish Learning at Boston College; and the Katholieke Universiteit Leuven in Belgium.

How might we Christians in our time reaffirm our faith claim that Jesus Christ is the savior of all humanity, even as we affirm Israel's[6] covenantal life with God?

The Ariccia discussions enabled the organizers to map out the contours of the meta-question. They also identified considerable areas of agreement, though there were, naturally, divergences as well. Walter Cardinal Kasper attended part of the Ariccia consultation, and has offered his support throughout the process as it unfolded. We are grateful for his encouragement and for the foreword that he has composed for this volume.

To pursue certain subsidiary questions, the steering committee decided to convene a number of smaller sessions, which met over the next few years at the Katholieke Universiteit Leuven in Belgium, at the University of Notre Dame in the United States, and, with the support of Lund University in Sweden, at the Swedish Theological Institute in Jerusalem.[7]

As our conversation deepened, several related questions were explored:

- What is the significance of the belief that the Word of God became incarnate as a Jew?
- How do we understand "salvation"?
- What is the relationship between covenant and salvation?
- How is Jesus Christ constitutive of salvation?
- How does the Shoah (Holocaust) challenge how Christians think of Christ as savior?

Ultimately, the steering committee decided to publish this collection of essays reflecting our discussions of these and interrelated questions. Most of the authors have been involved in one or more of our consultations, though a few additional scholars were invited to contribute their specialized expertise.

As our consultations unfolded, it gradually became clear that our thinking was converging on a number of basic principles. For the most

6. Unless otherwise modified, such as in "State of Israel," "Israel" in this essay refers collectively to the Jewish people today and through history. It is their most frequent biblical, rabbinic, and liturgical self-designation. It is the name given to the patriarch Jacob, whose descendants were henceforth called the "children of Israel."

7. In addition to the various host institutions, these conferences were supported by the universities listed in note 5, later joined by the Institute for Jewish-Catholic Relations of Saint Joseph's University in Philadelphia, USA.

part, these perspectives informed the composition of this volume, and readers will perceive them throughout the pages that follow.

2. Principles When Theologizing about the Church of Christ and the People of Israel

A. *There Is a Need for Profound Humility*

As we pursued many relevant interconnected questions, we were struck by the realization that a profound humility must guide Christian theologians who engage the question of how Christ as universal savior relates to the covenantal life of the Jewish people. We saw several reasons for this.

First, since it is God who has initiated relationships with Israel and with the church, calling them both to participate in the unfolding of the divine will for creation, God's transcendence and freedom must always be acknowledged. Although God reveals Godself to both Israel and the church, there are limits to the abilities of human minds to fathom the Holy One.

Second, both the church and Israel are "mysteries," in the theological sense of that word.[8] This does not mean that they cannot be comprehended or discussed, but rather that there is a transcendent aspect to their existence that humans cannot fully grasp. The God who is Mystery, "whose ways are not our ways" (cf. Isa. 55:8), called both Israel and the church into being and sustains them in relationship. Our conversations often evoked the exclamation of the Apostle Paul, who, after also pondering the interrelationship between the two mysteries of Israel and God's people in Christ, exclaimed, "O the depth of the riches and wisdom and knowledge of God! How unsearchable are his judgments and how inscrutable his ways!" (Rom. 11:33).

Third, we recognized that there are limits to what human language is able to express about transcendent realities. In his essay, "A Realm of Differences: The Meaning of Jewish Monotheism for Christology and Trinitarian Theology," Gregor Maria Hoff writes that theologians must therefore often resort to "tensive language" — language characterized by

---

8. N.B. CRRJ, "Guidelines" (1974), conclusion: "The problem of Jewish-Christian relations concerns the Church as such, since it is when 'pondering her own mystery' that she encounters the mystery of Israel."

paradoxical, contradictory, or not entirely compatible concepts. For example, the christological formula of the Council of Chalcedon describes the human and divine natures of Christ as united but unmixed; inseparable but distinct. Hoff suggests that this tensive formulation might well be used to describe, from the Christian viewpoint, the mysterious relationship between the church and Israel: united but discrete. Similarly, he advances the seemingly paradoxical argument that Christian trinitarianism, far from compromising Judaism's exclusive monotheism, actually preserves it in the face of the incarnation of God's Word.

Fourth, theological humility is also necessary because the Holy One has not fully revealed to either Israel or the church everything that God might be doing within the other community. Christian theologians should recognize that they have certain "blind spots" with regard to the Jewish people's covenantal life with God since they do not experience God in the exact same ways that Jews do. Essential in this regard is the Vatican's injunction "to learn by what essential traits Jews define themselves in the light of their own religious experience."[9]

Finally, it should be noted that theological humility prompted us to decide not to explore beyond the boundaries of the Christian-Jewish relationship to the relationship of Christians with the other religions and ways of life in the world.

B. History Is Essential for the Work of Christian Theology and the Bible Must Be Interpreted with Historical and Literary Critical Methods

We are acutely conscious of the shameful history of the Christian vilification, oppression, and marginalization of Jews that precedes our work. This awareness is indeed a fifth reason for theological humility. Therefore, we are all convinced that history is essential for the work of Christian theology. Similarly, we recognize that the interpretation of the Bible demands the use of historical criticism and of literary analysis.[10] This is made clear

9. N.B. CRRJ, "Guidelines" (1974), preamble.

10. Pontifical Biblical Commission, "The Interpretation of the Bible in the Church" (1993): "The historical-critical method is the indispensable method for the scientific study of the meaning of ancient texts. Holy Scripture, inasmuch as it is the 'word of God in human language,' has been composed by human authors in all its various parts and in all the sources that lie behind them. Because of this, its proper understanding not only admits the use of this method but actually requires it" (I,A). See also: "Catholic exegesis freely makes use of

by the persistent deicide charge leveled against Jews of almost every century, which Pope John Paul II noted was based on "erroneous and unjust interpretations of the New Testament relative to the Jewish people and their presumed guilt."[11]

We know that the persistent Christian denial of theological validity to Jewish spiritual life contributed to the subjugation of Jews in European Christendom. We know the tragic consequences of theological triumphalism and arrogance, and are particularly challenged by the horrors of the Shoah. The Vatican's Commission for Religious Relations with the Jews asks: "Did anti-Jewish sentiment among Christians make them less sensitive, or even indifferent, to the persecution launched against the Jews by National Socialism when it reached power?"[12] We believe, therefore, that efforts to relate our faith in Jesus Christ as the universal savior to the enduring relationship between God and Israel must unfold with sincere respect for the Jewish people and with remorse and humility for our "past errors and infidelities."[13]

Four essays in this collection directly address this subject. In "Historical Memory and Christian-Jewish Relations," John T. Pawlikowski insists that theology must reckon with its effects in history, both positively and negatively. Concerning the impact of Christianity on European Jews, he urges that the components and legacy of Christian antisemitism be honestly confronted, especially with regard to the Shoah. Mary C. Boys traces the historical consequences of the long-lived assertion that Jews were collectively cursed by God for all time because of the crucifixion of Jesus. In "Facing History: The Church and Its Teaching on the Death of Jesus," she demonstrates how Jewish life was regularly battered by this perennial notion, and concludes that attention needs to be paid today to how the Gospel passion narratives might be carelessly construed, almost out of habit, to unwittingly delegitimize Judaism after the time of Jesus. In "Reading the Epistle to the Hebrews Without Presupposing Supersessionism," Jesper

---

the scientific methods and approaches which allow a better grasp of the meaning of texts in their linguistic, literary, socio-cultural, religious and historical contexts, while explaining them as well through studying their sources and attending to the personality of each author" (III).

11. John Paul II, "Address to Participants in the Vatican Symposium on 'The Roots of Anti-Judaism in the Christian Milieu,'" October 21, 1997.

12. CRRJ, "We Remember: A Reflection on the Shoah" (1998), IV.

13. John Paul II, "Introductory Letter to the Document 'We Remember: A Reflection on the Shoah,'" March 2, 1998.

Svartvik studies one New Testament text that came to be read as declaring that the "Old Covenant" had been rendered obsolete by the coming of Christ. Instead of being a letter *to* the Hebrews, it became a letter *against* the Hebrews. Svartvik examines several crucial exegetical questions and concludes "that a reading of Hebrews as arguing that Christianity has replaced or superseded Judaism is anachronistic, and therefore is incorrect." Daniel J. Harrington discusses "The Gradual Emergence of the Church and the Parting of the Ways." He reviews the New Testament books in terms of how their authors variously understood themselves in relation to Judaism, judging that although these texts contain the seeds of an eventual split into two religious communities, none of them definitively reject the Jewish tradition but instead see themselves as connected to it. Thus, understood in its historical context, the New Testament can help Christians today move forward with Jews as partners in God's unfolding plans.

C. Salvation Is Relational, Eschatological, and Intertwined with Covenant

Naturally, the topic of salvation was extensively discussed in our consultations. We noted how too often this rich concept is reduced, especially in popular discourse, to only one meaning: getting to heaven. In fact, the concept is so multilayered and textured that the Catholic Church has never specified a formal definition. In the Christian tradition, the experience and anticipation of salvation has been richly described in terms of redemption, reconciliation, sanctification, and incorporation into the divine life, or as being freed from sin, oppression, meaninglessness, or death. In our deliberations, it seemed important to stress two dimensions of salvation that are often overlooked: (1) salvation involves relationship with God, as both individuals and communities; and (2) salvation leads toward the Reign of God, which is mysteriously experienced as both "already" and "not yet."

In this context, we also discussed the biblical concept of "covenant." Christians and Jews both speak of their relationship with God as "covenantal" — a sharing in life with mutual responsibilities. It is through this covenantal life with God that Israel and the church experience, serve, and anticipate the fullness of God's saving will. Although Israel and the church have both known God's saving power in their histories, especially at their respective foundational events of Exodus-Sinai and the Death-Resurrection of Jesus, they also both recognize that creation is awaiting the fullness of salvation in the future.[14] In different ways, both Jews and Christians understand themselves as having entered into covenant with the Holy One in order to be of service to the coming of God's Reign. Jews and Christians also see their covenantal relationship as unceasing because God is always faithful, despite the waywardness of the human partner, "for God's gift and call are irrevocable" (Rom. 11:29).

These substantial degrees of similarity between Jewish and Christian thinking today should be pondered. After all, in the early centuries, as the emerging Gentile church sought to distinguish itself from Israel, it came to reject the possibility that both Jews and Christians could be in covenant with God. Sociological factors weighed heavily in this rejection, which was, however, expressed theologically[15] and was related to the deicide charge.[16] This delegitimation of Israel's covenantal life dominated Christian thought until the twentieth century, and was not officially critiqued in the Catholic Church until *Nostra Aetate*. Even today, some Catholic theologians find it necessary to fall back into replacement theology, questioning whether the Jewish Torah-centered covenant is still valid, fearing that if it is, the universal saving significance of Christ would be compromised.[17]

In our consultations, we discussed the recurring question of whether Israel and the church abide in two completely different covenants with God, whether the Sinai covenant and the church's covenant in Christ are simply two instances among the numerous covenants mentioned in the Bible, or whether Israel and the church both participate in one Covenant (upper case "C") with God, in distinct yet related ways.

---

14. See the rich discussion in CRRJ, "Notes" (1985), II, 8-11.

15. See the *Epistle of Barnabas* 4:6: "Take heed for yourselves and do not be like some, adding largely to your sins, and saying, 'The covenant is both theirs and ours.'"

16. See, for example, Augustine of Hippo's *Reply to Faustus the Manichean*: "Here no one can fail to see that in every land where the Jews are scattered they mourn for the loss of their kingdom, and are in terrified subjection to the immensely superior number of Christians. . . . [Like Cain, the Jews may not be killed] for whoever destroys them in this way shall suffer sevenfold vengeance, that is, shall bring upon himself the sevenfold penalty under which the Jews lie for the crucifixion of Christ. So to the end of the seven days of time, the continued preservation of the Jews will be a proof to believing Christians of the subjection merited by those who, in the pride of their kingdom, put the Lord to death" (XII, 12).

17. See, e.g., Avery Cardinal Dulles: "The Second Vatican Council, while providing a solid and traditional framework for discussing Jewish-Christian relations, did not attempt to answer all questions. In particular, *it left open the question whether the Old Covenant remains in force today*" (italics added) ("The Covenant with Israel," *First Things* [November 2005]: 17).

Participants noted that in official Catholic teaching since *Nostra Aetate* there is a recurring recognition of an innate spiritual bond between Christianity and Judaism. As Pope John Paul II expressed it: "The Church of Christ discovers her 'bond' with Judaism by 'searching into her own mystery' (cf. *Nostra Aetate*, 4). The Jewish religion is not 'extrinsic' to us, but in a certain way is 'intrinsic' to our own religion. With Judaism therefore we have a relationship which we do not have with any other religion."[18] This unique relationship means that the "Church and Judaism cannot, then, be seen as two parallel ways of salvation,"[19] as if they were completely unrelated covenantal communities. Rather, Israel and the church are distinct communities in the Covenant, in profound relationship with the God who saves, living out their covenantal duties in their distinct Torah-centered and Christ-centered ways.

Therefore, we saw a connection between salvation and being in covenant, or perhaps better, between covenant and the history of salvation.[20] Christian Rutishauser's "'The Old Unrevoked Covenant' and 'Salvation for All Nations in Christ': Catholic Doctrines in Contradiction?" explores how the structure of God's covenant with Israel was "doubled" by the Christ event, launching a new epoch in salvation history by opening up the covenant's universal meaning. He argues that the unfolding of salvation history is predicated upon Sinai's distinction between Israel and the nations, a covenantal structure that must necessarily endure until the fulfillment of salvation in God's Reign.

18. John Paul II, "Address at the Great Synagogue of Rome," April 13, 1986.

19. CRRJ, "Notes" (1985), I, 7.

20. Walter Cardinal Kasper has expressed this connection between covenant and salvation history in this way: ". . . But whilst Jews expect the coming of the Messiah, who is still unknown, Christians believe that he has already shown his face in Jesus of Nazareth whom we as Christians therefore confess as the Christ, he who at the end of time will be revealed as the Messiah for Jews and for all nations. The universality of Christ's redemption for Jews and for Gentiles is so fundamental throughout the entire New Testament (Eph 2:14-18; Col 1:15-18; 1 Tim 2:5 and many others) and even in the . . . Letter to the Romans (Rom 3:24; 8:32) that it cannot be ignored or passed over in silence. So from the Christian perspective the covenant with the Jewish people is unbroken (Rom 11:29), for we as Christians believe that these promises find in Jesus their definitive and irrevocable Amen (2 Cor 1:20) and at the same time that in him, who is the end [or goal] of the law (Rom 10:4), the law is not nullified but upheld (Rom 3:31). This does not mean that Jews in order to be saved have to become Christians; if they follow their own conscience and believe in God's promises as they understand them in their religious tradition they are in line with God's plan, which for us comes to its historical completion in Jesus Christ" ("Christians, Jews and the Thorny Question of Mission," *Origins* 32, no. 28 [December 19, 2002]: 463-64).

D. The Totality of the "Christ Event"
Reveals the Word of the Saving God

The tendency to flatten the rich multiple facets of "salvation" into a single dimension is related to a similar tendency, especially in Western Christianity, to conceive of Christ as savior in a constricted or narrow way. We discussed the widespread pattern of thinking of salvation as realized only by the sufferings of the crucified Jesus to the exclusion of the incarnation, of his deeds and teachings, and of the resurrection. Alternatively, some Christians focus myopically on one aspect or the other of the story of Jesus. For instance, an exclusive stress on Jesus' parables and ethical teachings can devalue the significance of the incarnation of God's Word in Jesus.

We agreed that a Christian theology of salvation should be rooted in all aspects of the "Christ event": the incarnation of God's Word in the first-century Jew, Jesus; the ministry of Jesus as a faithful son of Israel, making the Reign of God tangibly present among his people and exemplifying life in Covenant; his execution in service to the coming of God's Reign; and his resurrection to transcendent life, which brought the church into being as an assembly sustained in the Covenant through the Spirit of the Living Christ present in its midst. For Christians, human interrelationship with the divine has achieved an enhanced transparency through God's integration into humanity in and through Jesus, with consequences for the deepening, continuing divine Reign in human salvation history.

Naturally, the significance of the Jewishness of Jesus was a major theme in the consultation's work. Hans Hermann Henrix and Barbara U. Meyer explore the many ramifications of this historical fact in their respective essays, "The Son of God Became Human as a Jew: Implications of the Jewishness of Jesus for Christology" and "Jesus Christ: The Dogmatic Significance of Christ Being Jewish." Henrix urges the necessity of specifying that the Word became *Jewish* flesh, and not just some sort of generic human being. Therefore, "Jesus Christ confirms, reaffirms, or reinforces Jewish covenantal life, since [he] is obedient to the Torah and fulfills it." He goes on to develop the image of Jesus as the "Torah Incarnate," arguing that this understanding mediates Christ's salvation to the Jewish people. Meyer begins by observing that Christians seem to find it difficult to develop the idea that Jesus lived as a Jew, perhaps because the realization can disturb Christian identification with Jesus and the striving to imitate him. After presenting Jesus as a true *Mensch* and considering whether Jesus could have been turned into a *Muselmann*, a destroyed human being, she concludes that in his Jewishness, Jesus Christ binds Christians to the living God of the living Covenant. "The memory of Jesus being Jewish brings with it a re-membering of this Jew to his fellow Jews. . . . [W]ithout conversion or confusion, Christians are inseparably and indivisibly responsible to the Jewishness of the one Jew and for that of other Jews."

E. The Christian Trinitarian Tradition Pertains to the Relationship of Christ and the Church to Israel

We also discussed the tendency in Western Christianity to deemphasize the trinitarian tradition and to restrict God's saving activity in the world to Jesus Christ. In an extreme form, a fixation on the Second Person to the exclusion of the tri-unity of God becomes christomonism.

The Christian conviction that everything God does involves all three divine "subsistents" was seen to be essential for theologies of the relationship of the church to the Jewish people. Elizabeth Groppe explores this connection in "The Tri-Unity of God and the Fractures of Human History," proposing that the renewal in Catholic trinitarian theology offers many possibilities for conversation with Jews. Drawing on the work of the Catholic theologian Catherine Mowry LaCugna and the Jewish scholar Abraham Joshua Heschel, she sketches a trinitarian narrative of salvation history in which "person, not substance, is the ultimate ontological category and God's to-be is to-be-in-communion." Philip A. Cunningham and Didier Pollefeyt also invoke trinitarian theology to discuss how Christ's salvation is — from a Christian perspective — operative within Israel's covenantal life today. If Jews dwell in covenant with God, then — from a Christian viewpoint — they must be in an enduring relationship with the triune God, including God's Word, which is inseparably united with the now-glorified Jew, Jesus.

F. Nostra Aetate Has Implications for All Branches of Christian Theology and Life

The interweaving of many theological disciplines in our consultations confirmed our impression that *Nostra Aetate* (in tandem with other conciliar and postconciliar documents) has ramifications for all aspects of Christian self-understanding and life. In addition to other essays in this collection, those by Thomas Norris and Liam Tracey, respectively, focus on ecclesiology and liturgy. In "The Jewish People at Vatican II: The Drama of a Development in Ecclesiology and Its Subsequent Reception in Ireland and Britain," Norris compares the preconciliar situation with Vatican II's sacramental understanding of the church and its description of the church as the people of God. This latter approach, in particular, opened up new vistas for seeing the Jewish people of God as related to the church in a vital, living way. These, in turn, generated new insights into the nature of the church itself. Tracey, in "The Affirmation of Jewish Covenantal Vitality and the Church's Liturgical Life," surveys whether Catholic worship has been much affected by the reform in understandings of Judaism inaugurated by *Nostra Aetate*. He concludes that much further study, reflection, and discussion are needed, especially with regard to the theological underpinnings of the liturgy. Might it be time, for example, to investigate how the paschal mystery could be enacted liturgically so as to better celebrate the whole saving work of God from creation to its fulfillment?

G. Christian Theology Can No Longer Ignore the Jewish Religious Experience

The work of the "Christ and the Jewish People" consultations has been a predominantly Catholic endeavor concerned with issues of Christian theology, engaging our meta-question with reference to Catholic teaching documents and developments. Nonetheless, our deliberations have been greatly enriched by the vital participation of two Lutheran scholars at most of our gatherings.

In addition, all the Christian theologians benefited from the invaluable contributions of Jewish colleagues. The role of these consultants was primarily to ensure the accuracy of statements made about the Jewish tradition or history, but the secondary activity of informing our theological work with Jewish insights was perhaps even more helpful. As our work unfolded we became more and more convinced of the need to encounter Judaism in all its complexity on its own terms, and not, as Christian theologians have tended to do, with a Judaism as imagined and constructed by Christians. This was true not only because the consultation was dealing directly with Jewish topics, but also because Christian theology is organically related to Judaism, as noted by John Paul II in his remarks about the intrinsic relationship of Judaism to the church cited above.

This practice of collaborating with Jewish colleagues even on an essentially Christian project continues in this volume. At various points in the collection, Tamara Cohn Eskenazi, Adam Gregerman, Edward Kessler, Ruth Langer, and Marc Saperstein offer observations and reactions to a number of the essays written by the Christian authors. While the diverse Christian and Jewish perspectives do not always converge, the differing viewpoints provide an essential and enriching stimulus that advances mutual understanding.

3. Further Thanks

The editors would like to take this opportunity to thank Dr. John Cavadini and the Theology Department at the University of Notre Dame for hosting one of our consultations. Thanks, too, to Dr. Maria Brutti for preparing the volume's index.

4. Dedication

One Jewish colleague and friend is sadly absent from this book. Michael Signer, an energetic and vital participant in many of our consultations, died before the initial drafts of these essays were completed. He had dedicated much of his professional life to promoting understanding between Jews and Christians, offering crucial insights that will be sorely missed. We therefore dedicate this volume to him, and launch this compilation with an essay by his close friend, Hanspeter Heinz, "'Your Privilege: You Have Jewish Friends': Michael Signer's Hermeneutics of Friendship."

"Your Privilege: You Have Jewish Friends":
Michael Signer's Hermeneutics of Friendship

Hanspeter Heinz

1. Introduction

Michael Signer is one of my best friends and my best Jewish friend. He remains my friend and companion even beyond his death. When I am searching for orientation regarding difficult theological questions, when I reflect from time to time on the practice of my faith and prayer, when I work for better Christian-Jewish relations — especially when stumbling blocks lie once again in the way — then Michael inspires me with his ideas, and he encourages me with his perceptible presence. And, Betty, his wife, is always there as well.

For almost forty years, my meetings and close theological collaboration with Jews, especially in the discussion group "Jews and Christians" of the Central Committee of German Catholics,[1] have been and continue to be a unique gift. Over the decades, I have become even more convinced that Christians cannot theologize well without Jewish colleagues. Most of all, I owe this conviction to Michael. Working with him as a friend and rabbi has enriched my own Christian identity and has deepened my own work as a theologian and pastor.

While I am writing this essay, Michael is looking at me. For on my desk is a picture of him from the University of Notre Dame's website. When I look at it, I think of the words that Rabbi David Ellenson, president of the Hebrew Union College–Jewish Institute of Religion, spoke in his eulogy for Michael:

---

1. See Hanspeter Heinz and Michael Signer, eds., *Coming Together for the Sake of God: Contributions to Jewish-Christian Dialogue from Post-Holocaust Germany* (Collegeville, MN: Liturgical Press, 2007).

I think the most amazing thing about Michael, as Betty has observed, is that he did not know how amazing — how very special — he really was. There is a telling picture of Michael on the Notre Dame website where a smiling Michael looks like an enthusiastic boy who cannot believe his good fortune in being where he is. It is this trope that informed him his entire life, and when he and Betty traveled throughout Europe and the United States savoring vintage wines and gourmet cheeses and sausages, when he lectured and taught at leading universities throughout the entire world, when he inspired and challenged his students at HUC and Notre Dame, in Berlin, and at the Vatican, when he led academic and religious conferences at Notre Dame and elsewhere, when he came to Israel and dialogued at Tantur with Jews, Christians, and Muslims or at Hartman or at Hebrew University, he seized and affirmed life and I think part of him could never fully believe that his spiritual and academic quests, his intellectual brilliance and warm and open manner, had brought him to these settings and allowed him to achieve such a prominent, even paramount, role in all these places. Michael modeled so many things for me. However, foremost among them was that profound scholarship is linked to the deepest existential commitments that a person possesses.[2]

2. A Unique Friendship

Michael and I thought often of our first meeting in July 1989 in Augsburg. Jakob J. Petuchowski, whom I had known well for years, came with his students, David Ellenson and Michael Signer, to the second Sol and Arlene Bronstein colloquium on the topic "Atonement in the Liturgy." In a brilliant talk, Michael gave an exegesis of Leviticus 16. Hans Hermann Henrix remembers: he "surprised his Christian colleagues that he was familiar both with Jewish exegeses between 1100 and 1300 (Rashi, Abraham ben Meir ibn Esra, Mose ben Nachman) and with the exegeses of the Church Fathers and the representatives of medieval scholasticism (Origines, Hrabanus Maurus, Rupert of Deutz, Ralph of Flaix). It was not only in the Augsburg symposium that Michael was a living commentary of reconciliation."[3]

But, the bridge between us had already been built three days prior to

---

2. www.huc.edu/newspubs/pressroom/article.php?pressroomid=170.

3. Hans Hermann Henrix, "A Visionary from Across the Atlantic" http://www.ccjr.us/news/in-memoriam/michael-signer/tribute-to-michael-signer?start=50.

Michael's talk. My research assistant at the time, Peter Klasvogt, and I had picked up our three guests from the train station and invited them to dinner in a Greek restaurant. After the first glass of wine, German academic politeness was overcome, and we talked with each other in the American way, with our first names and without reference to titles. Later in the evening, we all celebrated the Shabbat gathered around the kitchen table in our *vita communis* (common living) accommodations in Ottmaring. On the next day, Peter accompanied our guests to Dachau, where a sadist devised most of the methods of torture later practiced in Auschwitz and other concentration camps. These experiences laid the cornerstone for our friendship. Even David, who had come to Germany with serious concerns and who had made his first trip to Germany despite warnings from his homeland, soon felt relaxed. He showed the same humor as Michael and delighted in his nickname "Coca-Cola rabbi," which we had jokingly given him after noticing that he preferred this drink at all times of the day.

My last encounter with Michael and Betty, twenty years later in South Bend, sealed our friendship forever. I was lucky to have been able to visit Michael in the first days of December when he was still well enough to enjoy my being there. Our three days together brought us much joy, and it was good to be able to say goodbye. We talked about his illness, of course, but soon everything had been said about it. His "first breakfast" consisted of numerous medications which Betty prepared. Prior to taking each pill, he recited a *berakhah* (blessing) "so that it works well," as he put it. He inquired in great detail about our mutual friends and wanted to know how the Christian-Jewish dialogue was going in Germany. He was especially honored by an advance copy of his festschrift that Franklin Harkins had given to him a few days earlier. He had already read it in its entirety. I was most touched by our last Shabbat dinner together. The next day he gave me his blessing and asked for mine. We both knew that this was our farewell, even if we did not speak of it. Only two days after my departure, the last phase of Michael's suffering began — a constant back and forth between home and hospital.

Since 1989, Michael and I had seen each other at least once a year when he was passing through Germany on his way to or from Israel or when he came to conferences or lectures in Germany. It was his talent for language that made him so daring as to hold two lectures in German in 2007! Together with Betty, our "chief rabbi" and coordinator, we held international seminars with Jewish and Christian participants at Auschwitz, Krakow, Nuremberg, and Lublin. Our main goal was always to interest students,

3

graduates, and scholars in Jewish-Christian dialogue and to educate them about the important topics that come with this dialogue. They are our hope for making Christian-Jewish dialogue prosper in the generations to come.

The joy that we shared as friends was no less important than our projects together. We often ate fish or pasta asciutta together in my kitchen — Betty admired her husband's new talents as a cook, for our dishes tasted good to her as well. During our long walks in the vicinity of the village of Bachern, where I have been active as country priest for twenty-six years, we regularly lost our way because we were so absorbed in our discussions. At some point, we would let someone pick us up in a car and return us to the village. We did some crazy things in our parish. Rabbi Michael allowed himself to be convinced by his friend Hanspeter to take part in a blessing of a motor vehicle for the first time: we dedicated the village's new fire truck in both German and Hebrew. Even the mayor was deeply impressed. There, we also experienced a jamboree ox race. It was quite an adventure because these "racing animals" run or buck according to their own whims and hardly let themselves be disciplined.[4] After the celebration of high mass the next day with Auxiliary Bishop Losinger, who comes from the parish, Michael asked him lightheartedly: "Bishop, do you think that it was a coincidence that the winning ox is named Anton as you are?"

We even took part in some holy mischief with one another. A highlight occurred on Michael's 60th birthday, which we celebrated together with Betty. My colleagues, Alois Halder and Heinz-Günther Schöttler, and I presented our world-famous rabbi, supposedly on behalf of the Holy Father, a "certificate of appointment" as the first Jewish cardinal of the Catholic Church. Together with this certificate we presented him not with a pectoral, the ceremonial chain for bishops, but instead with an ephod: two pewter vessels attached to a silver chain, one of them filled with oil for blessings, the other with incense to drive away demons. The document, adorned with the papal coat of arms and a forged signature of the pope, subsequently found a special place in Michael's office at Notre Dame.

Like overgrown boys, we played games that often oscillated between fun and seriousness. While packing his suitcase one day, Michael could find neither his *kippah* nor his invaluable diary. In order to calm his anxiety, I offered: "As a good Catholic, in such situations I successfully turn to St. Anthony, the patron saint of lost things. If you would like, I could turn to him for you." And, sure enough, when Michael was unpacking his suit-

4. http://www.amperanzeiger.de/sport.htm.

case on the next station of his trip, the lost things were there again! One time, I sent an e-mail to Michael: "My Rhineland humor and your Jewish humor are truly gifts of nature." Michael replied: "It is not quite that simple. For you Rhinelanders, humor may be a gift of God that makes life easier. For us Jews, God has forced us to have humor because without it we could not have survived our history." Indeed, our free time together and our correspondence brought us much more than relaxation. Without our deep theological discussions, our friendship would have surely lacked seriousness and depth. With that observation, I have finally come to the actual topic of this essay.

3. Discoveries in Faith

"Most theologians and bishops operate with a different hermeneutics than you do," Michael once wrote me. "They rely on historical texts of the biblical era and the Christian tradition. You, on the other hand, have Jewish friends — this is your privilege — and you rely on dialogue with living Judaism when you do theology. You thus work on differing levels and come to differing results."

To a far lesser degree, I wondered if this insight was at work in my correspondence with Walter Cardinal Kasper in 2005 concerning our discussion group's declaration *Jews and Christians in Germany: Responsibility in Today's Pluralistic Society* (April 13, 2005).[5] Michael was a member of our discussion group until his death.

In his letter, Cardinal Kasper agreeably posed a number of critical questions about the paragraph in the declaration titled, "No more missionizing of Jews!" His objections can be summarized in the following: How does this bold theory hold up with the Christian belief of the universality and singularity of Jesus Christ, the redeemer of all of humanity? In my response, I referred to my experiences with post-biblical, rabbinic Judaism, the kind of Judaism that characterizes the Jewish religion since the first centuries of the church. These experiences have relieved me of any doubt that the God of Israel — who is also the God of Jesus Christ and the church — is as equally real and present in Michael and in other Jewish friends as in the authentic witnesses of Christianity.

---

5. http://www.zdk.de/data/erklaerungen/pdf/Jews_and_Christians_in_Germany_2005 _04_13_1132840406.pdf.

The spiritual perception of the presence of God, of holiness, in the Jewish or Christian other compels us to reject any claims that either of us are God's enemies. Demeaning religious disputes from the past have nothing to do with us and our times.

For Michael and me, conversation and dialogue have both a religious and an ethical meaning. They have a religious meaning because the Word of God demands our existential consent. To speak in terms of Christianity, this means a yes to faith. They also have an ethical meaning because of God's instruction. To speak in terms of Judaism, this means the Torah, which empowers us to act and which strives to change our lives. In this sense, when we spoke of persons such as the pope or of occurrences such as the Second Vatican Council, our hermeneutical formula read: the mostly hidden, inner driving force *(ipsissima intentio)* reveals more than the authentic wording *(ipsissima vox)*. In other words, what brings someone to become agitated against something or to engage oneself for something? What brings someone to give warning about someone or to invite someone into their midst? Where do we see the God of the Bible at work, and where do we see Diabolos, the tempter, at work? And, what do these discoveries mean for our life and actions? The terms for valuable discoveries in faith, which I have found by use of this hermeneutical formula, include most prominently *blessing, prayer, Torah, and history.*

Through his visits and activities with me, Michael knew many people and families in Bachern, and he occasionally accompanied me to church services. One day, I asked him if he would speak during Sunday services and bless our parish. The echo in the congregation was heard loud and clear: "The rabbi and our pastor are friends! He even gave us his blessings. He belongs to us now." Michael's spontaneous reaction: "I'm glad to belong. Now, I have finally found a congregation, and I am your rabbi from now on." He often repeated these sentiments publicly. This is not only merely a well-meaning anecdote, for it was the beginning of a friendship between a Christian congregation and a rabbi, one that only became more enriching as the years went by. It was thus a matter of course that our congregation prayed for Michael's recovery and for Betty every Sunday since the onset of his illness.

Another "blessed" experience occurred at the end of a daylong interreligious seminar. My colleague Klaus Kienzler, who had belonged to our group of friends since the Augsburg symposium in 1989, was presiding at a Eucharistic celebration. Michael was in attendance. At the beginning of the service, Klaus asked Michael whether he would like to give us his blessing as he had done with the congregation in Bachern. Michael replied that he could only decide at the end of this service. When the time came, he stood up and said: "What I experienced during this hour impressed me as much as a good Jewish service. God truly lives among you! How could I refuse my friend Klaus's request that I give you my blessings?" As in Bachern, Christians experienced firsthand that this blessing is very special. It is still talked about with joy today. Even more special was the blessing that Michael gave me upon our most recent farewell, for this blessing is his personal legacy. He could not give anything more or greater. For me, the moment of his blessing was cut from the same cloth as the blessings that Abraham, Isaac, and Jacob gave their descendants.

As with these blessings, I discovered through my interactions with Jews a new spiritual and theological meaning of the Word of God: an encounter with the holiness of God. During one of our last international Jewish-Christian seminars in Nuremberg in 2005, we visited a nearby country synagogue that serves today as a museum.[6] There, a Torah scroll was on exhibit in the middle of the room. An impassioned discussion broke out among the Jewish professors and students about the fact that every visitor to the museum could touch the Torah scroll with their hands. This is unacceptable! And, the scroll is damaged as well. One should repair it or bury it with dignity! Cannot one of you take care of this so that this undignified situation is rectified? As we were leaving on the bus, I said to Michael: "When you were discussing the fate of the Torah scroll so seriously, the thought came to me that I would react in the same way upon seeing a consecrated host being passed around to tourists in a church or a museum which had previously been a Catholic Church. And, regarding your concerns about the damage to the scroll, another idea came to me: I would react similarly if an injured person were lying on the street in need of help." Michael found my associations to be apt, and he rejoiced with me about my discovery.

Again and again in our seminars, we Christians experienced through Michael the holiness of the Torah. He included us in his efforts to take the wording of the text seriously and to thoughtfully explore its meaning through personal questions and in light of the antagonistic interpretations in our traditions. And, at the end of our discussions, the deciding question was always posed regarding how the old biblical text moves us personally, spiritually, and existentially, perhaps how it unsettles us, but always how it

6. http://fsmt.de/index.php?option=com_content&task=blogcategory&id=15&Itemid=33.

obligates us. Studying the Bible and reflecting upon theological questions require no less than the exertion of our whole being. Michael and I were in full accord about this. Even when approaching a topic for the first time, Michael placed great value in the interplay between life and thought. This approach was much more than a didactic instrument on the part of a gifted teacher. In his eulogy, David Ellenson quotes John Cavidini, the chairperson of the Department of Theology at Notre Dame: "Michael had a special gift for creating opportunities for spiritual exchange of great depth. He allowed (and even encouraged) people to engage with their own starting point and with their own temperament and never expected people to enter into dialogue or scholarship from a point of view that was not their own. He therefore gave people space to think and to feel, and that is a great spiritual gift."[7]

Michael always retained his inquiring eye, even when an interpretation or insight seemed convincing. When one of us was discussing a new insight, we would always conclude with the question: "And, how do you see it?" Open questions aimed toward exploring new horizons were more important to Michael than finished answers that grow old quickly. In one seminar, Michael once made especially clear the great importance of the Torah for Jews when exploring new horizons: "For Jews, studying is worshiping. If you are really interested in Jews and Judaism, you must thoroughly study our tradition." Perhaps by learning from Judaism, Catholic professors, bishops, and priests would experience for themselves that for Christians, too, studying the Bible is an act of worship.

"More than theology, it is the church's long history of alienation and hostility against the Jews which separates Christians and Jews." This was one of Ernst Ludwig Ehrlich's fundamental theses.[8] Ehrlich, who passed away in 2007, was a cofounder and the most senior Jewish member of our discussion group of the Central Committee of German Catholics. Michael and I wholeheartedly agreed with him. Accordingly, we chose locations for our international seminars where the horrors of history and efforts toward a new beginning could be grasped. Among them: Auschwitz, Nuremberg, and Lublin. As a wise saying goes, we were convinced that "a place of guilt should also be a place of grace." During Michael's first visit to the concen-

---

7. See note 2.
8. See Hanspeter Heinz and Hans Hermann Henrix, eds., *"Was uns trennt, ist die Geschichte": Ernst Ludwig Ehrlich — Vermittler zwischen Juden und Christen* (München/Zürich/Wien: Verlag Neue Stadt, 2008).

tration camp at Auschwitz-Birkenau, I experienced how much the sufferings of their people burden Jews. After a long trip in an unheated Polish train to Krakow, Michael and his three Augsburg colleagues arrived at our destination. We went to the concentration camp the next day together with a Polish friend. We spoke hardly a word with each other, neither on the way there nor during the tour. In the barracks in which the prisoners' hair, glasses, shoes, and suitcases are piled, Michael suddenly became weak and almost collapsed. Klaus Kienzler attentively took Michael's arm and placed his other arm around his shoulder. They stood still for a time quietly sobbing until Michael, supported by Klaus, continued slowly and silently onward. The shock is still with me today. How immeasurably heavy does the burden of history weigh down a Jewish friend, even when neither he himself nor close members of his family were direct victims of the Shoah! I wanted to sink into the ground with shame, for it was "my people" who had done this. This experience only strengthened our discussion group's view that Auschwitz is also a problem for Germans and Christians. Of course, it is a completely different problem than for Jews and it therefore requires a completely different kind of sorrow. But, the truth remains vivid that we can — and must — assist each other and search with one another for the way through the depths of history into the future.

During my last visit to South Bend, I gratefully spoke to Michael about these mutual experiences in faith, through which he had opened new horizons for my Christian existence. When I asked whether he too had a new existential experience, after some hesitation he replied: "Prayer." What I already knew from previous e-mails was that he found great support in the prayers that so many people all over the world had spoken for him, his family, and his doctors in the months prior. He was especially affected by his students' prayers at the Lourdes Grotto at Notre Dame, who prayed daily for him the words of Psalm 23: "Though I walk through the valley of the shadow of death, I will fear no evil, for you are at my side." The energizing power of such prayer was new to him, and it did not disturb him that the Catholic devotion to Mary and the religious aesthetics of the Lourdes Grotto were foreign to him. What counted for him was the thesis of *Dabru Emet,* which he co-authored, "Christians and Jews worship the same God." We agreed that God indeed knows the "exchange rates" of our prayers, how to convert them from one mode of expression to another.

At this point, I must mention my recent experiences of Michael's prayers, of which until then I had only read about in the literature. "On Yom Kippur," as Betty wrote in one of her e-mails, "I heard Michael singing liturgical prayers in the shower. I couldn't believe it because he had been so sick for weeks!" My spontaneous reply in my next e-mail: "See how God treats his faithful servant. He inflicts him with the worst pain, and what is the pious rabbi's response? He stands under the shower and sings the praises of God. Truly biblical!" I promptly received Betty's reply: "That's a great insight. So it is."

He who, like Beethoven, composes a world-famous violin concerto is a genius. He who, like Menuhin, interprets such concertos in a brilliant way is also a genius. Michael was such a genius of interpretation. For students and colleagues, and occasionally for bishops as well, he was always able to make Jewish and Christian sources accessible in a way that opened eyes and hearts to the treasures of both traditions. He was able to elicit and ask thorny questions that required his listeners to no longer be satisfied with their prior answers. The most important discoveries of faith, for which I thank my Jewish friends and especially Michael, and which provoke in me the healthy unrest of theological reflection, are my experiences of blessing and Torah and history and prayer.

4. Violations of Love

On a long walk, Michael once told me: "The Song of Songs is for me the most important book of the Bible. It is the key that opens everything." This is an interesting insight, since this short book addresses neither the people or land of Israel, nor hardly the God of Israel, but rather the love of a young couple! More important, it concerns searching and finding, dialogue and meeting, and relationships and love. Are these not of most importance between heaven and earth, among Jews and Christians, and for relations with all people? Our experiences in Jewish-Christian dialogue confirm this insight. The other side of the coin is that nothing hurts biblical people more than violations of love.

When *Dabru Emet* was published, we were at an international Jewish-Christian seminar in Auschwitz. Michael's extensive efforts toward the realization of this document were well known. *Dabru Emet* bravely entered uncharted waters in that it invited Jews to take part in a previously neglected *theological dialogue* with the church. This Jewish statement "catapulted Michael to international fame and attention."[9] However, I never

9. Ellenson, see note 2.

saw Michael so upset and downcast as on that day. For on the same day, the Vatican published its document *Dominus Iesus*. Michael burst out: "Our whole tedious work of reconstruction after the Council has been shattered with one blow. Jewish-Christian relations are in shambles!" The quotations from *Dominus Iesus* reported by the media appalled Michael's Christian colleagues as much as they did himself. We also reacted against the Catholic teaching that Christianity represents the only fully valid path to salvation among the religions. How can one claim that one holds Judaism in high regard and that one loves the Jews when, at the same time, one also devalues the grandeur of the Sinai Covenant — a covenant never revoked by God — by deeming this covenant to be inferior? It is a testament to Michael's strength and love to his students and colleagues that he continued on with our seminar after this affront.

Another painful setback for Michael and his Jewish and Christian partners in the United States was Mel Gibson's film, *The Passion of the Christ*. It was less the film itself, the nature of which was already known months before its first showing, but rather the widespread apathy to its problems in the Catholic community. In our congregation's parish newsletter, I formulated my criticism: "What kind of terrible God is this, who needs such a victim in order to be reconciled with humanity? This is not the God of the Bible, but instead a pagan, bloodthirsty God of revenge. In this film there are only the holy and the brutish; neither then nor today is this a true picture of humanity. (President Bush also separated the world in the axis of evil and the axis of good. We know the murderous consequences of this.) Mel Gibson's orgy of violence numbs the senses, while the Good Friday liturgy opens the heart toward Jesus' suffering and for that of all people." Michael's reaction to the newsletter: "I would have expected such clear words from at least a few bishops."

In spite of all the setbacks and especially of all violations of love, Michael always overcame the temptation to sink into resignation. He remained a pioneer of Christian-Jewish dialogue until the end. For me, our friendship is a sacred obligation to continue down the path of dialogue and reconciliation.

5. Boundaries of Thought

Michael was a sharp thinker. Therefore, he never allowed himself to be satisfied with a tempting intuition or a moving event without argumentatively seeking out the grounds or legitimacy behind them. For instance, does a comparison between the holiness of the Torah for Jews and the holiness of the Eucharist for Christians stand up to argumentative examination? We never understood the axiom that "faith is a mystery" as one that prohibits thinking, for faith does not call on our hearts, hands, and feet alone. It also calls on our brains. There were other boundaries of thought that marked a watershed in our dialogue.

Often, after a certain amount of trust was developed, our Christian students ventured out with their most important question: "Professor, what do you think of Jesus?" The response from the otherwise humorous and friendly rabbi was always rather brusque: "Nothing at all." After a pause, he would then continue: "God does not direct this question to me, but instead to you. Thus, it interests me greatly what Jesus Christ means to you, whether and how he changes your lives, whether, for example, he turns your hearts toward us Jews." Once, I asked him afterward: "But, if I let myself be circumcised, would you also think about your baptism?" We laughed in mutual understanding.

"That is not a concern of mortals!" We raised this distinction between God and humanity again and again in our discussions to illustrate the boundaries of the loquaciousness and verbosity of theologians. Our convictions tell us that the revelation of God teaches us only how we should live before him so that he can say to us as he said to Abraham: "Walk before me and be whole" (Gen. 17:1). In the reverse this would mean: God does not tell us of things that carry no consequences for our life, and thus we should not ask ourselves of them. Only nonsense comes of this. As a biblical source for this argument, I cited the question posed by the apostles on the day of ascension: "So when they met together, they asked him, 'Lord, are you at this time going to restore the kingdom to Israel?' He said to them: 'It is not for you to know the times or dates the Father has set by his own authority'" (Acts 1:6-7; see also Mark 13:32). It is even not for the risen Christ to know, but for God alone! Neither Jesus nor the apostles needed this knowledge for their mission. For me, it is clear that the messiah at the end of time will be Jesus; Michael was convinced of the opposite. But despite this, we were united by the question regarding which one of us will be surprised most when the messiah comes.

I am firmly convinced that we live on after death as individuals because our life lasts as long as the love of God, which does not die; Michael says that he does not know, that he leaves this to God. In both cases, finding out the true answers to these questions of the messiah and of eternal life would have changed nothing in our lives. Our yes to God and to humanity was identical. What separates us in belief justifies in no way heated words or arguments. In accord with good rabbinical tradition, Michael cited in such situations Psalm 62:11: "One thing God has spoken, two things have I heard." Jews and Christians hear the revelation of the same God clearly in differing ways, but that means not that we should accuse each other of being hard of hearing, intellectually sluggish, obdurate, or anything else.

It is different when crossing the boundaries of faith, where our traditions have stood still, where no authorities have ventured. One example: in our discussion group, a question of importance for our Christian members arose again and again, namely, "Who are we Christians for you Jews? Do you believe that we also have a special relationship with the God of Israel?" In general, the answer was: "According to Jewish tradition, everyone who holds himself to the Noahide Covenant is considered to be righteous among the peoples and will be able to have a share in the coming world." This, however, did not satisfy us because we as Christians, in contrast to other religions, believe that we are in covenant with the God of Israel, who is also the God of Jesus Christ. Finally, I asked Michael for his personal answer to this question at our discussion group's retreat in Munich in 2006. In his talk there, titled "Jews, Christians, and Verus Israel," he addressed the question in a completely new way. By means of the Halakhah, he transcended the Halakhah and came to the conclusion: "For me, you are brothers, not others," when you fulfill the fundamental demands of the Halakhah, such as the love of God and of the people and land of Israel. During the following discussion, all of the Jewish participants agreed with this border transgression!

While Michael, via his photograph on my desk, looks at me, I realize the legacy of our two-decades-long friendship: that I will always be sworn to work for the future of Christian-Jewish dialogue and for a theology in dialogue. At the same time, before my eyes is the way in which Michael, who for sixty-three years had never been sick but had then been afflicted with his first and yet fatal illness, fought for life and retained an open heart for others until his last day, accompanied by Betty and his many friends. When the life and death of my friend Michael passes before my eyes, I think of a sentence from the New Testament, a sentence that is also cited in the fourth Eucharistic Prayer: "having loved His own who were in the world, He loved them unto the end" (John 13:1) — *eis to telos:* to the last breath, to the outermost possibility.

Historical Memory and Christian-Jewish Relations

John T. Pawlikowski

1. "The Turn toward History" and Christian Antisemitism

One of the most important developments in Christian theology over the past several decades has been what David Tracy has termed "the turn toward history."[1] The Second Vatican Council is one example of this turn. For the Council was not satisfied in issuing a statement on the church couched in more classical theological language but insisted on a companion document, *Gaudium et Spes*, which established the church's location within human history as a foundation for ecclesial understanding. History has now become an indispensable "font" for theological reflection in our day. As a result, any theological reflection on the relationship of the church and the Jewish people must be rooted in historical awareness. Bernard Lonergan and Charles Curran[2] have both highlighted this important methodological shift in Catholic theology coming out of the Council, particularly such documents as *Gaudium et Spes* (the Church in the Modern World) and *Dignitatis Humanae* (the Declaration on Religious Liberty).

In terms of relations with Jews, a theology shaped by a historical consciousness must recognize the church's centuries-long record of contemptuous teachings against Jews[3] based on the two interrelated pre-

---

1. See Elisabeth Schüssler Fiorenza and David Tracy, "The Holocaust as Interruption and the Christian Return to History," in Elisabeth Schüssler Fiorenza and David Tracy, eds., *The Holocaust as Interruption. Concilium* 175 (Edinburgh: T. & T. Clark, 1984).

2. See Charles E. Curran, *Catholic Social Teaching 1891–Present: A Historical, Theological and Ethical Analysis* (Washington, DC: Georgetown University Press, 2002), pp. 58-60.

3. Christianity's original negative view of the Jews and Judaism tended to be primarily in the theological realm. But in subsequent centuries it evolved into a perspective rooted in

mises: (a) that Jews bore responsibility for the death of Christ; and (b) that, as a result, they were expelled from their former covenantal relationship with God and replaced in that relationship by the Christian church. This theological understanding was not confined to academic realms but had terrible practical consequences for members of the Jewish community throughout much of European history. While we must continue to maintain a transcendental dimension in ecclesiology since the church is the Mystical Body of Christ, we cannot totally divorce the church as sacrament from the church as an incarnate historical institution. The two are profoundly interrelated. Hence the ultimate integrity of the church is tied to how it has manifested itself concretely throughout human history. And here is where the church's treatment of the Jews matters profoundly.

I will not rehearse here the well-documented history of Christian antisemitism. That has been done by various scholars such as Edward Flannery,[4] and Frederick Schweitzer and Marvin Perry.[5] What is significant about this history is the shadow it places over ecclesiology. No authentic theology of the church can be put forth today without an honest and thorough confrontation with this dark side of the church's life. Because a "historical consciousness" approach to theological reflection will not permit a sharp separation between what is spoken of by some as "the church as such," i.e., the church as mystical communion, and the institutional manifestation of the church, this longstanding shadow affects the definition of the church at its very heart. The church cannot enter into a fully authentic dialogue with the Jewish community, nor present itself and its teaching as a positive moral voice in contemporary society until it has cleansed its soul of its role in contributing to antisemitism.

Our present question must now be: How far has the church gone in coming to grips with the consequences of its antisemitic legacy based on its theological claim of covenantal expulsion of the Jews and their substi-

---

the outright hatred we call antisemitism rather than the original anti-Judaism based on theological objections.

4. Edward H. Flannery, *The Anguish of the Jews: Twenty-Three Centuries of Antisemitism*, revised and updated edition, foreword by Philip A. Cunningham, A Stimulus Book (New York/Mahwah, NJ: Paulist, 2004).

5. Marvin Perry and Frederick M. Schweitzer, *Antisemitism: Myth and Hate from Antiquity to the Present* (New York/Houndmills, UK: Palgrave/Macmillan, 2002). Also cf. my essay, "Religion as Hatred: Antisemitism as a Case Study," *Journal of Hate Studies* 3, no. 1 (2003-4): 37-48.

tution by the Christian community in that covenantal relationship? The answer is, not far enough.

2. The Second Vatican Council and the Repudiation of Contempt

In what Gregory Baum has termed the most radical change in the ordinary magisterium of the church pronounced by Vatican II,[6] its Declaration on Non-Christian Religions, *Nostra Aetate,* rejected the notion of widespread Jewish culpability for the death of Jesus and affirmed continued Jewish covenantal inclusion after the Christ event. Its principal argument for this major theological about-face was based on the teaching of St. Paul in Romans 9–11.

But in my judgment history also played a part, even if behind the scenes. For one, scholars had come to the conclusion that there existed no genuine historical evidence for general Jewish culpability (that some individual Jewish leaders may have had a role remains open for further discussion), while the evidence was strong for the primary responsibility of Pilate and the Roman imperial authorities. But more recent history, namely, the experience of the Holocaust, also had an impact. Once more the church had compelling evidence of the continuing influence of its classic antisemitic tradition. Many of those who most strongly promoted the passage of *Nostra Aetate* had direct contact with Christian resistance movements during the Nazi era and became convinced that this antisemitic tradition had to be removed from the church once and for all. Pope John XXIII, who began the process that led to *Nostra Aetate,* was no doubt motivated to place the Jewish question on the conciliar agenda because of his personal experiences in Turkey and France during the war and as a result of his moving encounter with French Jewish historian and survivor Jules Isaac. Historical reality had hit home during the Council. There was simply no way the church could continue to proclaim Jewish covenantal exclusion, having now witnessed the genocidal actions that such a theology could abet.

The late Avery Cardinal Dulles and some other church leaders have argued in recent years that in undertaking this profound theological change at Vatican II, the bishops ignored the full evidence of the New Testament. He appealed to the Epistle to the Hebrews, which he understood as pro-

---

6. Gregory Baum, "The Social Context of American Catholic Theology," *Proceedings of the Catholic Theological Society of America* 41 (1986): 87.

claiming the end of the Jewish "old" covenant.[7] In retrospect it probably would have been better if the Council had confronted these texts from Hebrews directly. I would posit that historical evidence may have played some role in their sidelining. Having known and experienced the negative effect of such theological claims, there was simply no way the drafters could continue to use them as defining texts for the theology of the Christian-Jewish relationship. So I would want to argue that historical consciousness may have been an important factor in moving the theology of the church's relationship with the Jewish people to a base in Paul rather than in Hebrews.

It should be noted, however, that many important biblical scholars have questioned the classical interpretation of Hebrews as arguing for the abolition of the Jewish covenant after Christ. Both Alan Mitchell[8] and Luke Timothy Johnson,[9] in major recent volumes on Hebrews, have argued that it is a letter directed exclusively to Christians to sustain their faith and does not discuss the ongoing validity of the Jewish covenant per se. This biblical scholarship disallows the attempt by Cardinal Dulles to interject Hebrews back into a discussion of the theology of the Christian-Jewish relationship over against Vatican II's reliance on Romans 9–11.[10]

Recent years have seen some notable efforts on the part of Christians, including Christian leaders, to deal with the history of antisemitism. During the 1990s some nine hierarchies in various parts of Europe and in the United States issued statements that acknowledged a measure of culpability.[11] The strongest declaration by far came from the French Catholic bishops in September 1997. They clearly saw their admission of responsibility as a necessary step of cleansing and healing in preparation for the new millennium. "[I]t is a well-proven fact," say the French bishops,

7. Avery Cardinal Dulles, "Evangelization and the Jews," with a response by Mary C. Boys, Philip A. Cunningham, and John T. Pawlikowski, *America* 187, no. 12 (October 21, 2002): 8-16. See also Albert Cardinal Vanhoye, "The Plan of God Is a Union of Love with His People," Address to the World Synod of Bishops, October 6, 2008; Rome: ZENIT News Service. A preliminary English translation is also at http://www.vatican.va/news_services/press/sinodo/documents/bollettino_22_xii-ordinaria-2008/02_inglese/b05_02.html.

8. Alan Mitchell, *Hebrews,* Sacra Pagina Series 13, Daniel J. Harrington, S.J., ed., A Michael Glazier Book (Collegeville, MN: Liturgical Press, 2007), pp. 25-28.

9. Luke Timothy Johnson, *Hebrews, a Commentary,* New Testament Library (Louisville: Westminster/John Knox, 2006).

10. See also elsewhere in this volume the essay by Jesper Svartvik, "Reading the Epistle to the Hebrews Without Presupposing Supersessionism."

11. These documents can be found in *Catholics Remember the Holocaust* (Washington, DC: United States Catholic Conference, 1998).

that for centuries, up until Vatican Council II, an anti-Jewish tradition stamped its mark in different ways on Christian doctrine and teaching, in theology, apologetics, preaching, and in the liturgy. It was on such ground that the venomous plant of hatred for the Jews was able to flourish. Hence, the heavy inheritance we still bear in our century, with all its consequences.[12]

The document clearly admits the failure of church authorities to challenge this antisemitic shadow on Christian theology and practice:

For the most part, those in authority in the Church, caught up in a loyalism and docility that went far beyond the obedience traditionally accorded civil authorities, remained stuck in conformity, prudence, and abstention. This was dictated in part by their fear of reprisals against the Church's activities and youth movements. They failed to realize that the Church, called at that moment to play the role of defender within a social body that was falling apart, did in fact have considerable power and influence, and that in the face of the silence of other institutions, its voice could have echoed loudly by taking a definitive stand against the irreparable.[13]

Pope John Paul II, who brought a historical-consciousness orientation to Catholic self-understanding even though, as Charles Curran has rightly noted, not to the same extent as Paul VI, did turn to *Gaudium et Spes* on many occasions for his vision of the church and saw the necessity for the church to expose and atone for its failings in several areas at the dawn of a new millennium. He forthrightly addressed the issue of the church's deeply flawed outlook on Jews and Judaism during the liturgical ceremony he sponsored in Rome in March 2000 and then again during his historic visit to Israel, where he placed the same admission of guilt in the Western Wall in Jerusalem.

3. Discomfort with Confronting History

John Paul II also approved the publication in March 1998 of the statement on the Holocaust, *We Remember,* for which he wrote an introduction.[14]

---

12. *Catholics Remember the Holocaust,* p. 34.
13. *Catholics Remember the Holocaust,* p. 32.
14. The text of *We Remember,* can be found at http://www.vatican.va/roman_curia/pontifical_councils/chrstuni/documents/rc_pc_chrstuni_doc_16031998_shoah_en .html.

This statement was not without some controversy, largely because of certain revisions imposed by the Vatican Secretariat of State headed by Angelo Cardinal Sodano upon the original version of the text that had been prepared by Edward Idris Cardinal Cassidy, then president of the Holy See's Commission for Religious Relations with the Jews.[15] These controversial alterations exaggerated the number of Christians who spoke out against Nazism and risked their lives to save Jews, and presented only the positive efforts of Pope Pius XII on behalf of Jews, without addressing lingering problematic issues. But this document *did* make it quite clear that many Christians failed in their responsibilities during the Holocaust. Furthermore, as Cardinal Cassidy clarified in subsequent presentations on *We Remember,* the document did not exempt the highest ecclesiastical authorities from such failures of responsibility.

Theologically, a pivotal statement in *We Remember* has to do with how Christian responsibility is described. Culpability is basically assigned to a group of "wayward Christians" who by implication deviated from what the church clearly taught about Jews and Judaism. First of all, it is hard to accept the notion that culpability resided exclusively within a group of Christian deviants who were somehow led astray by false preachers. Scholarship has clearly established how central the anti-Jewish teachings were in Christian preaching and church art for centuries and in more recent centuries in basic educational materials. So to lay Christian culpability only on a group of marginal members of the Christian community is to falsify the historical record.

The deeper theological challenge comes from the strict separation in *We Remember* between the so-called "church as such" and the actual historical institution. Clearly this indicates a distancing from an ecclesiology that regards the manifestation of the sacramental church in a concrete historical institution present in *Gaudium et Spes* and in the writings of Paul VI. Here is an example of the ambiguity in the thought of John Paul II who, as Charles Curran has stressed, did in the main continue the historical orientation of Paul VI but moved away from that perspective at certain critical moments. This is one such critical moment. Francis Cardinal George, in a public conference in Chicago on *We Remember,* relayed details

15. These controversial aspects of *We Remember* were discussed in a conference at the Catholic Theological Union in Chicago cosponsored by the school's Cardinal Bernardin Center and the Tanenbaum Center of New York. The papers from this conference can be found in Judith H. Banki and John T. Pawlikowski, eds., *Ethics in the Shadow of the Holocaust: Christian and Jewish Perspectives* (Franklin, WI/Chicago: Sheed & Ward, 2001).

of a personal conversation he had with John Paul II on this point. Cardinal George indicated that the pope was adamant that "the church as such" could never be implicated in any way in the evil of the Holocaust.[16]

During his pontificate Pope Benedict XVI has seemed to be moving away from the historical consciousness of Paul VI and retained in part by John Paul II. For instance, he seldom draws on *Gaudium et Spes* in his writings and statements. Though he has on several occasions promised to continue to walk on the path laid out by John Paul II, we in fact see him taking a quite different road on the question of Christian responsibility during the Holocaust.

The first social encyclical from Benedict XVI issued on June 29, 2009. *Caritas in Veritate* does show some thrust on his part toward recognizing history as a font for theological understanding. Benedict XVI also recognizes that social/political institutions influence basic spirituality. But one also senses a certain tension within the encyclical with his more common emphasis on theological truth that remains unaffected by history. The number of times that *truth* is highlighted in the document is striking. Unlike Paul VI, who proclaimed an open and potentially changing perspective on the Catholic approach to social institutions, Benedict XVI leaves the impression that the ideal social institutions have been defined by natural law and are in place for the duration of human history.[17] I think the encyclical shows him struggling to mesh his newfound and genuine commitment to social justice with his longstanding commitment to unchanging theological truths.

Despite his unfortunate rescinding in 2009 of the excommunication of four bishops belonging to the Priestly Society of Saint Pius X, including the noted Holocaust denier Bishop Richard Williamson, Pope Benedict XVI never belittles the significance of the Holocaust. In his visit to the synagogue in Cologne during World Youth Day in the summer of 2005 and in his statement at the Birkenau extermination camp in late May 2006, he certainly acknowledged the horrors of the Holocaust. He made his own the January 2005 words of John Paul II that marked the sixtieth anniversary of the liberation of the Auschwitz camp, of which Birkenau is considered an integral part: "I bow my head before all those who experienced this

16. For a further discussion of this issue, cf. the essays by Robert Schreiter and Irving Greenberg in Banki and Pawlikowski, eds., *Ethics in the Shadow of the Holocaust*, pp. 51-80.

17. For an English text of *Caritas in Veritate*, cf. *Origins*, 39, no. 9 (July 16, 2009): 1291-1359; http://www.vatican.va/holy_father/benedict_xvi/encyclicals/documents/hf_ben-xvi_enc_20090629_caritas-in-veritate_en.html.

manifestation of the *mysterium iniquitatis.* The terrible events of that time," the pope continued, "must never cease to rouse consciences, to resolve conflicts, to inspire the building of peace."[18] There is little doubt that Pope Benedict XVI views the Holocaust as one of the darkest moments in European history. In his remarks to a general audience on November 30, 2005, he termed the Holocaust an "infamous project of death." And on the occasion of the seventieth anniversary of Kristallnacht, he once again expressed horror over the sufferings endured by Jews under Hitler and rededicated himself to combating any continued manifestation of antisemitism.[19] This statement was significant because the pope spoke directly in a significant way to the Jewish character of the Holocaust rather than describe it in more generic terms as an attack on all humanity. He reiterated this in his February 2009 message to American Jewish leaders, a message spoken with intensity according to Rabbi David Rosen, the then chair of the International Jewish Committee for Interreligious Consultation (IJCIC), who was present at the meeting: "The entire human race feels deep shame at the savage brutality shown to your people at that time."[20]

But when we come to a discussion of the root causes of the Holocaust, Pope Benedict XVI tends to avoid John Paul II's approach. In part this may be due to their differing personal experiences of the Holocaust. But it is also probably rooted to an even greater extent in their considerably different ecclesiological perspectives, with Benedict XVI strongly emphasizing the transcendent understanding of the church as basically unaffected by events in human history. As Cardinal Ratzinger, Benedict XVI did give some indication of an understanding of the link between traditional Christian antisemitism and the ability of the Nazis to carry out their program of Jewish extermination. In a front-page article in *L'Osservatore Romano* (December 19, 2000), he argued that "it cannot be denied that a certain insufficient resistance to this atrocity on the part of Christians can

18. Pope Benedict XVI, "Visit to Cologne Synagogue," *Origins* 35, no. 12 (September 1, 2005): 206; http://vatican.va/holy_father/benedict_xvi/speeches/2005/august/documents/hf_ben-xvi_spe_20050819_cologne-synagogue_en.html.

19. See under the dates November 30, 2005, and November 9, 2008, at http://www.ccjr.us/dialogika-resources/documents-and-statements/roman-catholic/pope-benedict-xvi/; cf. the Message to the president of the Holy See's Commission for Religious Relations with Jews on the Occasion of the 40th Anniversary of the Declaration *Nostra Aetate,* October 26, 2005, at the same website.

20. Pope Benedict XVI, "Meeting with American Jewish Leaders," *Origins* 38, no. 38 (March 5, 2009): 598.

be explained by the inherited anti-Judaism in the hearts of not a few Christians."[21] But this remains a rather isolated text in his overall corpus. And in comparison to several of the episcopal conference texts cited earlier (especially the French) it appears quite weak. Pope Benedict XVI has tended to present the Holocaust as primarily, even exclusively, a neo-pagan phenomenon that had no roots in Christianity but instead constituted a fundamental attack on all religious belief, including Christianity.

No reputable scholar on the Holocaust would deny its neo-pagan roots or its fundamental opposition to all religious perspectives, and I count myself among them. But equally, they would insist on surfacing the Holocaust's significant links with classical Christian antisemitism. The Holocaust succeeded in a culture that supposedly was deeply impacted by Christian values for centuries. Much of the Nazi anti-Jewish legislation replicated laws against Jews existing in "Christendom" since medieval times. I have always opposed drawing a simple straight line between classical Christian antisemitism and the Holocaust. Clearly the Nazi program depended on modern philosophy and pseudo-scientific racist theories. But we cannot obfuscate the fact that traditional Christianity provided an indispensable seedbed for the widespread support, or at least acquiescence, on the part of large numbers of baptized Christians during the Nazi attack on the Jews and other marginalized groups. Christian antisemitism definitely had a major role in undergirding Nazism in its plan for Jewish extermination and perhaps also in the Nazi treatment of other victim groups such as the disabled, the Roma and Sinti (i.e., gypsies), and gay people.

In his Cologne and Birkenau addresses, Pope Benedict XVI seemed to be supporting an interpretation of the Holocaust that presents it solely as an attack on religion in all its forms rather than a phenomenon that drew strongly on a previous antisemitic base in the heart of Christianity. His remarks can leave the impression, intended or not, that the Holocaust was simply the result of secularizing modern forces in Europe at the time of the Nazis and not dissimilar to the secularizing modern forces that affect Europe today, forces that Benedict XVI has assailed for many years. The fact that neither in the Cologne nor the Birkenau addresses is there any reference made to the official 1998 Vatican document on the Holocaust, *We Re-*

---

21. As quoted in Edward Idris Cardinal Cassidy, *Ecumenism and Interreligious Dialogue — Unitatis Redintegratio, Nostra Aetate (Rediscovering Vatican II)* (New York/Mahwah, NJ: Paulist, 2005), p. 249.

member, nor to the earlier national bishops' statements, tends to confirm this interpretation of Pope Benedict's perspective. Meira Scherer-Edmunds, in an article in *U.S. Catholic,* described the papal visit to the synagogue in Cologne as a "milestone" but also a "missed opportunity" because of the pope's failure to deal forthrightly with Christian culpability during the Nazi era.[22] The editors of *Commonweal* offered a similar critique of the pope's address at Birkenau,[23] a critique I subsequently supported in a published letter to the magazine.[24] Finally, in his initial response to the controversy caused by the remarks of Bishop Richard Williamson of the Priestly Society of St. Pius X regarding the Holocaust, the pope, while condemning the Holocaust in no uncertain terms, once again spoke of it in general terms and made no reference to the collaboration of Catholics in carrying out Hitler's genocidal attack against the Jews.

In dealing with the question of the church and history in light of the Holocaust we must take up the issue raised by Austrian philosopher Friedrich Heer (1916-83). For Heer, Catholicism's failure to confront adequately the Holocaust is symptomatic of how Catholicism has reacted to all other evils, especially to war and to the possibility of a nuclear holocaust. For him, the main problem stems from the church's withdrawal from history:

> The withdrawal of the church from history has created that specifically Christian and ecclesiastical irresponsibility towards the world, the Jew, the other person, even the Christian himself, considered as a human being — which was the ultimate cause of past catastrophes and may be the cause of a final catastrophe in the future.[25]

For Heer, antisemitism has been the historical manifestation of a much deeper cancer in Christianity that was manifested in classical Christianity. The disregard of the fate of the Jewish people throughout history, especially between 1918 and 1945, can only be understood, he claims, as part of a general disregard for humanity and the world. He primarily attributes this disregard to the dominance in Christian theology of the so-

---

22. Meinrad Scherer-Edmunds, "Never Again! The Pope's Visit to the Cologne Synagogue Was Both a Milestone and a Missed Opportunity," *U.S. Catholic* 70, no. 11 (November 2005): 50.

23. *Commonweal* 133, no. 12 (June 16, 2006): 5.

24. *Commonweal* 133, no. 13 (July 16, 2006): 2.

25. Friedrich Heer, *God's First Love* (New York: Weybright & Talley, 1970), p. 406.

called "Augustinian principle," which views the world under the aspect of sin and which ultimately leads to a sense of fatalism and despair about the world.[26] According to Heer in a work originally published in 1967, this fatalistic tendency is as great a danger as it was in the period of the incubation of Nazism, especially from 1933 to 1945. He writes: "There is a straight line from the church's failure to notice Hitler's attempt at a 'Final Solution' of the Jewish problem to her failure to notice today's and tomorrow's endeavors to bring about a 'Final Solution' to the human problem."[27] While Heer had nuclear warfare in mind when penning these words, he might well apply them today to the ecological challenge in global society. The only cure for this centuries-long pattern in Christianity, according to Heer, is to abandon the "Augustinian principle" and replace it with a return to the Hebrew Bible's roots of Christ's own piety and to even older roots — namely, to the original faith in which people felt themselves to be both God's creatures and responsible partners. In other words, to the strongly responsibility-based spirituality found in the Hebrew scriptures. Pope John Paul II's use of the term "co-creators" for the human community in his encyclical *Laborem Exercens* might in fact be seen as an important example of such a return to this spirituality.

4. Rethinking Christian Theologies

To my mind there is little question that the greatest challenge posed to Christians in dialogue with Judaism is coming to grips with the history of antisemitism. The late Pope John Paul II defined antisemitism as a sin on several occasions.[28] Therefore, the church will need to commit itself to a complete and honest evaluation of its record in this regard. We do have a model for such ecclesial self-examination, one praised by the late Joseph Cardinal Bernardin in his major address at Hebrew University on March

26. Recently there have been some efforts to take another look at Augustine's writings. Paula Fredriksen has done this regarding Judaism in *Augustine and the Jews: A Christian Defense of Jews and Judaism* (New York/London: Doubleday, 2008). It is possible we may have to make some distinction between Augustine himself and later Augustinianism in this area.

27. Friedrich Heer, "The Catholic Church and the Jews Today," *Midstream* 17 (May 1971): 29.

28. Pope John Paul II, "The Sinfulness of Antisemitism," *Origins*, 23, no. 13 (September 5, 1991): 204; *Crossing the Threshold of Hope*, ed. Vittorio Messori (New York: Alfred A. Knopf, 1994), p. 96.

23, 1995.[29] Bernardin highlighted the effort undertaken by the Archdiocese of Lyon, France, for a thorough investigation by respected scholars of archdiocesan records during the Nazi period. Bernardin insisted that such investigations were crucial for the church to enter dialogue with Jews with credibility as well as for its ability to speak to major issues of our day in global society.

Cardinal Bernardin's words remain prophetic. It certainly will not prove easy for institutional Catholicism to undertake such a comprehensive self-examination. But it has little choice in my judgment. What occurred in Lyon must become commonplace, including at the level of the Vatican, if the church is to have an authentic moral voice in society.

In light of the experience of the Holocaust, ecclesiological understanding in Catholicism needs revamping. Scholars such as Johann-Baptist Metz have begun this.[30] Such revamping needs to take seriously the point made by Donald Dietrich in his volume *God and Humanity: Jewish-Christian Relations and Sanctioned Murder*. Dietrich argues that "the Holocaust has reemphasized the need to highlight the person as *the* central factor in the social order to counterbalance state power."[31] Put another way, any authentic notion of ecclesiology after the experience of the Holocaust must make human rights a central component. The vision of the church that must direct post-Holocaust Christian thinking is one that sees the survival of all persons as integral to the authentic survival of the church itself. Jews, Poles, the Roma, gays, and the disabled should not have been viewed as "unfortunate expendables" during the Nazi period — and there is no place for any similar classification today. There is no way for Christianity, or any other religious tradition, to survive meaningfully if it allows the death or suffering of other people to become a byproduct of its efforts at self-preservation. Surely for Christians a communal sense of ethics must accompany the commitment to personal human rights. But no communal ethical vision can ever remove personal human rights from the center of its concern.

Other areas of systematic theology must be rethought in light of the

---

29. Joseph Cardinal Bernardin, "Anti-Semitism: The Historical Legacy and the Continuing Challenge for Christians," in *A Blessing to Each Other: Cardinal Joseph Bernardin and the Jewish-Catholic Dialogue* (Chicago: Liturgy Training Publications, 1996), p. 159.

30. See Johann-Baptist Metz, "Facing the Jews: Christian Theology after Auschwitz," in Fiorenza and Tracy, eds., *The Holocaust as Interruption*, pp. 26-33.

31. Donald Dietrich, *God and Humanity in Auschwitz: Jewish-Christian Relations and Sanctioned Murder* (New Brunswick, NJ/London: Transaction, 1995), p. 269.

Holocaust. One is our understanding of God and the divine-human rela-tionship. Theologians such as Rebecca Chopp and David Tracy have ar-gued that historical realities such as the Holocaust force us to restate basic doctrinal beliefs. Dogma, following upon Donald Dietrich's assertions, needs to become "person-centered." It is not possible to give a detailed treatment of this topic in this essay. I have addressed both the God ques-tion after the Holocaust and its implications for the foundation for Chris-tian ethics and the issue of Christology in other published writings.[32] Suf-fice it to say here that all dogmatic formulations after the Holocaust must include a "response" dimension within the ongoing historical process. Dogma and history must be integrated, with each influencing the other, as was argued by several scholars, including myself, in an issue of the interna-tional theological publication *Concilium* titled "The Holocaust as Inter-ruption."[33] A movement in this direction can also be found in the Decem-ber 1999 declaration from the Vatican's International Theological Commission (promulgated in March 2000), which was in fact commis-sioned by the then Joseph Cardinal Ratzinger, who headed the Congrega-tion for the Doctrine of the Faith at that time.[34]

The philosopher Hannah Arendt's critical question in *On Revolution* as to whether Christianity can be "revolutionary" needs to receive an affir-mative response from the church.[35] Only in this way can Friedrich Heer's legitimate concern about Christianity's withdrawal from history be allevi-ated. Christological interpretation cannot eliminate the possibility of "newness" in human history.

32. See John T. Pawlikowski, "God: The Foundational Ethical Question after the Holo-caust," in Jack Bemporad, John T. Pawlikowski, and Joseph Sievers, eds., *Good and Evil after Auschwitz: Ethical Implications for Today* (Hoboken, NJ: KTAV, 2000), pp. 53-66; and John Pawlikowski, "Christology after the Holocaust," in T. Merrigan and J. Haers, eds., *The Myr-iad Christ: Plurality and the Quest for Unity in Contemporary Christology* (Leuven: Leuven University Press and Peeters, 2000), pp. 381-97.

33. Fiorenza and Tracy, eds., *The Holocaust as Interruption*.

34. See Section #4 ("Historical Judgment and Theological Judgment") of the December 1999 document (promulgated March 2000) from the Vatican's International Theological Commission, *Memory and Reconciliation: The Church and the Faults of the Past*. It can be found at: http://www.ccjr.us/dialogika-resources/documents-and-statements/roman-catholic/vatican-curia/281-memory; also see Fiorenza and Tracy, eds., *The Holocaust as In-terruption*, pp. 26-33.

35. Hannah Arendt, *On Revolution* (New York: Viking, 1963), p. 20.

5. The Parting of the Ways

The final issue I would raise in this paper regarding the history-theology link has to do with the profound reimaging of the separation between Judaism and Christianity. Over the last decade or more biblical and historical scholarship, some of it associated with what has been termed "The Parting of the Ways" research, has shown us how much Jesus himself and "the followers of the Way" remained integrated within the Jewish community of their time and how gradual and protracted the eventual separation really was. Can we continue to present the church as a distinct, separate institution founded by Jesus prior to his death? I frankly do not think we can, even though we continue to proclaim that message on Holy Thursday in particular. Our theological assertions in this regard must become far more nuanced in light of the new historical research.[36] Admittedly such a reformulation will test the faith of many in the church. And it will also increasingly face a methodological challenge as certain Catholic leaders increasingly insist that the tradition of the church must take precedence over new scientific evidence. While I would agree that faith is not totally or exclusively dependent on scientific research, neither can contemporary faith expression ignore the results of new scholarship, especially when such new information significantly undercuts previous faith narratives.

Since the question of Jesus' dealings with his Jewish contemporaries is being treated in other essays, I will take up that issue only insofar as it affects how we perceive the initial Jewish-Christian relationship at its origins. And there is no question that historical scholarship on the first centuries of the Jewish-Christian interaction is altering our understanding of that relationship in profound ways. To emphasize this point, one impor-

---

36. On a related note, already in the early 1980s Karl Rahner had pointed out that in light of historical-critical exegesis, some aspects of speaking of Jesus as "instituting" the church had been shown to be problematic: "Our real problem, however, and our real theme is the question: What can we say and how can we speak of an institution of the Church by Jesus or its provenance from him, if and although he proclaimed this imminence of the kingdom of God?" (*Theological Investigations XIX: Faith and Ministry* [London: Darton, Longman & Todd, 1983], p. 29). Therefore, he preferred the institution of the church to be understood in the sense that the church draws its origin from Jesus. Of course, the significance of the Jewishness of Jesus and the early church for this question had not yet come to the forefront at that time. See also the essays in this volume by Daniel Harrington, Hans Hermann Henrix, and Barbara Meyer.

tant collection of essays looking at this question has been titled *The Ways That Never Parted.*[37]

Several biblical scholars began a major reconsideration of how early Christians related to Jews even before the emergence of the "Parting of the Ways" scholarship. Robin Scroggs and the late Anthony Saldarini were two prominent examples of this movement toward a fundamental reinterpretation of the separation of the church and the Jewish community.

In the mid-1980s Scroggs published his distillation of where the new historical research on early Christian-Jewish relations was moving.[38] He summarized developments under four headings: (a) The movement begun by Jesus and continued after his death in Palestine can best be described as a reform movement within Judaism. There is little extant evidence during this period that Christians had an identity separate from Jews. (b) The Pauline missionary movement, as Paul understood it, was a Jewish mission that focused on the Gentiles as the proper object of God's call to his people. (c) Prior to the end of the Jewish war with the Romans that ended in 70 C.E., there was no such reality as Christianity. Followers of Jesus did not have a self-understanding of themselves as a religion over against Judaism. A distinctive Christian identity only began to emerge after the Jewish-Roman war. And (d) the later sections of the New Testament all show some signs of a movement toward separation, but they also generally retain some contact with their Jewish matrix.

Anthony Saldarini added to the emerging picture painted by Scroggs. In various essays he underlined the continuing presence of the "followers of the Way" within the wide tent of Judaism in the first centuries of the Common Era. Saldarini especially underscored the ongoing nexus between Christian communities and their Jewish neighbors in Eastern Christianity, whose theological outlook is most often ignored in presentations about the early church within Western Christian theology.[39]

37. Adam H. Becker and Annette Yoshiko Reed, eds., *The Ways That Never Parted: Jews and Christians in Late Antiquity and the Early Middle Ages,* Texts and Studies in Judaism #95 (Tübingen: Mohr Siebeck, 2003). Also see Matt Jackson-McCabe, ed., *Jewish Christianity Reconsidered: Rethinking Ancient Groups and Texts* (Minneapolis: Augsburg Fortress, 2007); Fabian Udoh, ed., *Redefining First-Century Jewish and Christian Identities: Essays in Honor of Ed Parish Sanders* (Notre Dame: University of Notre Dame Press, 2008).

38. Robin Scroggs, "The Judaizing of the New Testament," *Chicago Theological Seminary Register* (Winter 1986): 1.

39. Anthony J. Saldarini, "Jews and Christians in the First Two Centuries: The Changing Paradigm," *Shofar* 10 (1992): 32-43; "Christian Anti-Judaism: The First Century

The initial scholarship on this issue by Scroggs and Saldarini was eventually reaffirmed by John Meier in the third volume of his comprehensive study of New Testament understandings of Jesus. Meier argues that from a careful examination of the New Testament evidence, Jesus must be seen as presenting himself to the Jewish community of his time as an eschatological prophet and miracle worker in the likeness of Elijah. He was not interested in creating a separatist sect or a holy remnant along the lines of the Qumran sect. But he did envision the development of a special religious community within Israel. The idea that this community "within Israel would slowly undergo a process of separation from Israel as it pursued a mission to the Gentiles in this present world — the long-term result being that his community would become predominantly Gentile itself — finds no place in Jesus' message or practice."[40] And a scholar within the "Parting of the Ways" movement, David Frankfurter, has insisted that within the various "clusters" of groups that included Jews and Christian Jews there existed a "mutual influence persisting through *late antiquity*. There is evidence for a degree of overlap that, all things considered, threatens every construction of an historically distinct 'Christianity' before at least the mid-second century."[41]

The growing number of biblical scholars who have become engaged in this "Parting of the Ways" discussion all stress the great difficulty in locating Jesus within an ever-changing Jewish context in the first century. Some speak of "Judaisms" and "Christianities" in the period, almost all involving some mixture of continued Jewish practice with new insights drawn from the ministry and preaching of Jesus. For scholars such as Paula Fredriksen, even speaking of "the parting of the ways" is unhelpful because it implies two solid blocks of believers.[42] The various groups in fact were entangled for at least a couple of centuries. So, as Daniel Boyarin has rightly insisted, we cannot speak of Judaism as the "mother" or the "elder brother" of

---

Speaks to the Twenty-First Century," the Joseph Cardinal Bernardin Jerusalem Lecture 1999 (Chicago: Archdiocese of Chicago, the American Jewish Committee, Spertus Institute of Jewish Studies, and the Jewish United Fund/Jewish Community Relations Council, 1999).

40. John P. Meier, *A Marginal Jew: Rethinking the Historical Jesus*, vol. 3, *Companions and Competitors* (New York: Doubleday, 2001), p. 251.

41. David Frankfurter, "Beyond 'Jewish-Christianity': Continuing Religious Sub-Cultures of the Second and Third Centuries and Their Documents," in Becker and Reed, eds., *The Ways That Never Parted*, p. 132.

42. Paula Fredriksen, "What 'Parting of the Ways'? Jews, Gentiles, and the Ancient Mediterranean City," in Becker and Reed, eds., *The Ways That Never Parted*, pp. 35-64.

Christianity.[43] Rather, what eventually came to be known as Judaism and Christianity in the Common Era resulted from a complicated "co-emergence" over an extended period of time during which various views of Jesus became predominantly associated with one or two focal points. Many factors contributed to this eventual differentiation, including Roman retaliation against "the Jews" for the late first-century revolt against the occupation of Palestine and the development of a strong "against the Jews" *(adversus Judaeos)* teaching during the patristic era. The "conversion" of Emperor Constantine also proved decisive for the eventual split into two distinctive religious communities.

Clearly this new scholarship poses considerable challenges for two central aspects of Christian theology: christology and ecclesiology. How do we integrate a profoundly Jewish Jesus into christological understanding, and how do we articulate the origins of the church? Surely we can no longer glibly assert that "Christ founded the church" in his own lifetime if we take seriously, as I believe we must, that the church evolved out of Judaism quite gradually over a couple of centuries and that there was no distinct religious body called "church" in Jesus' own lifetime and for decades thereafter. Taking history seriously indeed forces us to reexamine our Christian identity in fundamental ways. Some may advise that we should ignore such implications and continue with traditional expressions of belief. I cannot walk that path. While I would never say my faith is premised solely and exclusively on historical data, neither can my expression of faith suppress such data. My fundamental understanding of christology and ecclesiology, as well as my perspective on the theological dimensions of the Christian-Jewish relationship, has been strongly impacted by the historical data spoken of in this essay. And I remain glad it has. Indeed, it could be said that all of the articles in this volume are to varying degrees founded on the principle that history is important for the process of doing Christian theology. It is, in fact, recent history that has given rise to the meta-question of this book: how Jewish covenantal life relates to the saving work of Jesus Christ throughout time.

43. Daniel Boyarin, "Semantic Differences; or 'Judaism'/'Christianity,'" in Becker and Reed, eds., *The Ways That Never Parted*, pp. 65-85.

Facing History: The Church and Its Teaching on the Death of Jesus

Mary C. Boys

1. Introduction

On October 28, 1965, the Second Vatican Council released its declaration, *Nostra Aetate,* that spoke of the "ray of truth" revealed by other religious traditions.[1] This modest statement was nonetheless remarkable, marking the first time an ecumenical council had spoken positively of other religions. Yet it seems unlikely that the Council participants could have anticipated an event just forty years later when the Pontifical Gregorian University hosted a conference on *Nostra Aetate (NA)* that included Buddhist scholars from Sri Lanka, Japan, and Turkey; Hindu scholars from India and the United States; Muslim scholars from Lebanon, Scotland, Egypt, and Malaysia; and Jewish and Christian scholars from Europe, Israel, and North America.

The presence of scholars from diverse religious traditions engaging one another with respect and seriousness on topics generated by a brief conciliar declaration symbolized the magnitude of what it had initiated. Yet the advance of dialogue since 1965 that would have left our ancestors in faith incredulous did not resolve a major theological tension in the decla-

---

1. "So, too, other religions which are found throughout the world attempt in their own ways to calm the hearts of men by outlining a program of life covering doctrine, moral precepts and sacred rites.

"The Catholic Church rejects nothing of what is true and holy in these religions. She has a high regard for the manner of life and conduct, the precepts and doctrines, which, although differing in many ways from her own teaching, nevertheless often reflect a ray of that truth which enlightens all men." *Nostra Aetate* §2, in *Vatican Council II: The Conciliar and Post-Conciliar Documents* (rev. ed.), ed. Austin Flannery, O.P. (Collegeville, MN: Liturgical Press, 1984). I will use the Flannery edition for all citations of *NA*.

ration. Even as the Catholic Church "rejects nothing of what is true and holy in these religions," it nonetheless is "duty bound to proclaim without fail, Christ who is the way, the truth and the life (Jn. 14:6) . . . in whom God reconciled all things to himself (2 Cor. 5:18-19)," and thus the one in whom "men [all people] find the fullness of their religious life."[2]

This tension between an ancient formula of Christian faith — Jesus Christ as the savior of all — and new perspectives engendered by profound engagement with persons of other religious traditions has inspired extensive scholarship.[3] It is at issue in a singular way in the relationship between Judaism and Christianity. Christians who recognize the enduring quality of the covenant between God and the Jewish people are wrestling with how to hold together both claims. Are not Jews covenanted with the God who saves?

Nostra Aetate §4, the section devoted to the church's relationship with Judaism, overturned nearly two millennia of preaching and teaching in its claim that responsibility for the death of Jesus ought not to be ascribed to all Jews. Yet this same section is filled with ambiguities that are not fully resolved in subsequent documents pertaining to the relationship of the church with Jews. Given the centrality of ecclesial teaching that Jesus has saved humankind through his death, one wonders whether church authorities are somewhat hesitant to confront some troubling aspects of the New Testament's accounts of the crucifixion.

Nevertheless, *NA* has made a tremendous difference in formal relations between the Catholic Church and the Jewish people. As the foundational text of dialogue — its Ur-text, as it were — *NA* has prompted initiatives that would have amazed our ancestors in faith: diplomatic relations between the Holy See and the State of Israel, visits by two popes to Auschwitz and Yad Vashem, establishment of centers for Jewish-Catholic dialogue and chairs in Jewish Studies at Catholic colleges and universities, and sponsorship of innumerable meetings and conferences intended to deepen learning about the religious other and to foster reconciliation with a people the church had estranged over the centuries. Various statements from the Commission for Religious Relations with the Jews, the Pontifical Biblical Commission (PBC), and bishops' conferences have refined and expanded its claims. While its effect on the larger Catholic theological scene

2. The citation is from *Nostra Aetate* §2. In the Latin original, the term translated as "men" is the more inclusive *homines* (human beings) rather than *viri* (male persons).

3. See the fine survey by Paul F. Knitter, *Introducing Theologies of Religion* (Maryknoll, NY: Orbis Books, 2002).

has developed more slowly, *NA* has given rise to volumes of commentary and served as a stimulus to other Christian traditions in the arduous process of rethinking their relationship with Judaism. Frequently cited in pastoral resources, *NA* became the basis for revision of religious textbooks in Europe and North America.[4]

And yet on the ground too little has changed. For the vast majority of the world's Catholics who will never encounter a living Jewish community, *NA* §4 may well seem both esoteric and irrelevant. Even Catholics in a North American, European, or Australian context, who may have a greater sense of comity between their church and Jews, are unlikely to know what *NA* and any of the subsequent texts actually say, let alone what prompted them.

Moreover, the significance of one of *NA*'s central assertions — "neither all Jews indiscriminately at that time, nor Jews today, can be charged with the crimes committed during [Christ's] passion" — is overshadowed, if not lost, amidst the proclamation of the passion narratives twice-yearly on Passion or Palm Sunday (according to one of the Synoptic Gospels) and Good Friday (according to the Gospel of John). The passion narratives are proclaimed as part of a powerful liturgical drama. Given the importance of ritual to religious identity, the Gospel lections about the death of Jesus occupy a central place in how Christians understand their faith.[5] Congregants hear, generally without commentary to the contrary, that Jews were responsible for the death of Jesus, whether the "chief priests, scribes, and elders," as rendered in the Synoptic Gospels, or simply "the Jews," as in the Fourth Gospel. Jewish responsibility for the death of Jesus is reiterated on a number of the Sundays after Easter in which excerpts from the Acts of the Apostles are read.[6]

---

4. See Claire Huchet Bishop, *How Catholics Look at Jews: Inquiries into Italian, Spanish and French Teaching Materials* (New York and Ramsey, NJ: Paulist, 1974); Eugene J. Fisher, *Faith without Prejudice: Rebuilding Christian Attitudes toward Judaism* (New York and Ramsey, NJ: Paulist, 1977); Philip A. Cunningham, *Education for Shalom: Religion Textbooks and the Enhancement of the Catholic and Jewish Relationship* (Philadelphia: American Interfaith Institute, 1995).

5. On the power of ritual to form identity, see Paul Connerton, *How Societies Remember* (Cambridge: Cambridge University Press, 1989).

6. Two of the Eastertide Sundays in Year B have problematic readings from Acts. The Third Sunday of Easter has Acts 3:13-15, 17-19, in which Peter accuses the people: "You denied the Holy and Righteous One. . . . The author of life you put to death." The Fourth Sunday of Easter has Acts 4:8-12, in which Peter, "filled with the Holy Spirit," addresses the "leaders of the people and elders" concerning "Jesus Christ the Nazorean, whom you crucified."

Such concerns suggest the importance of pursuing ways of integrating *NA* and related texts into the church's life. If the insights provided by *NA* are to enrich the church, a substantial enhancement in understanding and interpreting biblical texts, particularly those dealing with the passion and death of Jesus, is prerequisite. As I will show, *NA* and many of the subsequent documents shy away from a clear and candid admission of the way in which the accusation that the Jews were responsible for the death of Jesus has been the substratum of the church's anti-Jewish teaching for nearly two millennia — with deadly consequences for Jews. Moreover, developments in biblical studies now offer possibilities for understanding and interpreting the events surrounding Jesus' crucifixion in important new ways.

My essay has three sections. In an initial section, I trace the charge of "Christ-killers," showing how it stands at the center of the "tormented" history of the church's relations with Jews.[7] By so doing, I intend to provide documentation that might serve as background for a much less ambiguous confession by the church. It is the history we must face; it is the history we must remember as we proclaim the passion of Christ. In the second section I examine how *NA* and subsequent Vatican documents deal with the death of Jesus.[8] While the later documents offer refinements and greater detail, further *attention to the historical context and clear interpretational strategies* would contribute significantly to thinking in the church. Thus, in the final section, I delineate aspects of this historical context and propose some principles by which we might more adequately approach the passion as it is rendered in the canonical Gospels.[9]

---

7. See the 1998 document, *We Remember: A Reflection on the Shoah,* by the Commission for Religious Relations with the Jews, ch. 3: "The history of relations between Jews and Christians is a tormented one" (http://www.vatican.va/roman_curia/pontifical_councils/chrstuni/documents/rc_pc_chrstuni_doc_16031998_shoah_en.html).

8. For reasons of space, I have limited my analysis to Vatican documents (i.e., from the Second Vatican Council, the Commission for Religious Relations with the Jews, and the Pontifical Biblical Commission).

9. Many other NT passages deal with the death of Jesus, but I am limiting my focus here to the Gospels. Notable among problematic texts beyond the Gospels is 1 Thessalonians 2:14-16. On this, see Didier Pollefeyt and David Bolton, "Paul and the Wrath of God: A Hermeneutical Approach to 1 Thes 2:14-16," paper given at the symposium, "Paul in His Jewish Matrix," Pontifical Gregorian University and Pontifical Biblical Institute, Rome, Italy, 20-May 22, 2009. After reviewing numerous strategies to account for this passage, they argue that interpreters must seek a wider redemptive horizon of this text; it must be recontextualized in light of the overall emphasis in 1 Thessalonians on God's salvific will.

1. The Jews as "Christ-Killers": Accepting Responsibility for Church Teaching

What lies behind the church's recent concern that the Jews as a people not be blamed for the crucifixion? Without question, *NA*'s assertion that "what happened in His passion cannot be charged against all the Jews, without distinction, then alive, nor against the Jews of today" bears historical significance. Yet it fails to confess that for nearly two millennia the church preached and taught exactly this, and, as a consequence, Jews suffered gravely. Politically, it may well be that the drafters could not go farther than they did in 1965, given the culture of the church and the controversies the various drafts engendered.[10] Today, however, a frank admission of just how deadly this accusation has been would reveal a church accepting responsibility for its past.

Rivalry Between Church and Synagogue

The charge that the Jews killed Jesus became a crucial component of the rhetoric of Christian identity formation. It was a key element in its rivalry with the synagogue in the complex and protracted "partings of the way" by which Christianity ultimately separated from Judaism.[11] As a fundamental dimension of the "us/them" binary, it stood at the center of the assertion that the Way of Christ, the crucified Savior, was the *only* faithful way to God and that the followers of Christ had become God's people. By implication, God now rejected the Jews, the former people of God, because of their infidelity in killing Jesus.

Alleged Jewish responsibility for the crucifixion was by no means limited to the canonical Gospels, but became part of apocryphal literature, such as the *Gospel of Peter* and the *Acts of Pilate*— both of which exculpate Pilate.[12] In the early church an entire literature developed among the liter-

---

10. The drafting process of *NA* was highly contentious. For a vivid account of the Council, see John W. O'Malley, *What Happened at Vatican II* (Cambridge, MA: Belknap Press/Harvard University Press, 2008). See also Alberto Melloni, "*Nostra Aetate* and the Discovery of the Sacrament of Otherness," in *The Catholic Church and the Jewish People: Recent Reflections from Rome,* ed. Philip A. Cunningham, Norbert J. Hofmann, and Joseph Sievers (New York: Fordham University Press, 2007), pp. 129-51.

11. See, in this volume, Daniel J. Harrington, "The Gradual Emergence of the Church and the Partings of the Ways."

12. See the text (fragments, rather than a complete work) and discussion in Christian Mauer and Wilhelm Schneemelcher, "The Gospel of Peter," in *New Testament Apocrypha*, vol. 1,

ary elite that a later age categorized as *Adversus Judaeos* (against Jews).[13] In this rhetorical realm, certain themes formed a constellation of charges. The north star of the constellation was the claim that the Jews are Christ-killers; surrounding this were accusations of their faithlessness, blindness, carnality, and legalism. These tropes resonated through theological commentary, pastoral exhortation, and popular culture. They have not entirely disappeared, though they appear less often now, especially in the churches of the West that have sought to repair relations with Jews.

This is a lengthy and tragic history, too long to examine in detail. Hence, my focus on three aspects: Judas as an archetype of Jews, the violence associated with the charge that Jews had killed Christ, and the role of the Christ-killer charge in the Shoah.

Judas, the Quintessential Jew

A principal way of heaping opprobrium on Jews was by associating Judas with the grotesque, with Satan/the devil, and with avarice/thievery. It provided ample inspiration for Christian imagination. Tragically, too often these negative depictions contributed to a portrait of Judas as the "quintessential Jew," an association abetted by linguistic similarities: *Ioudas,* in the LXX, a translation from the Hebrew *Yehûdâh,* Judas (the fourth of the

---

ed. W. Schneemelcher, trans. R. McL. Wilson (Louisville: Westminster/John Knox, 1991, paperback reprint 2006), pp. 216-27. The date of this text and whether it influenced the composition of the passion narratives of the canonical Gospels is debated. Cf. J. Dominic Crossan, *The Cross That Spoke* (San Francisco: Harper & Row, 1988), who argues that a shorter form of the *Gospel of Peter* (the "Cross Gospel") was a source for the passion narratives of the canonical gospels, and Raymond E. Brown, *The Death of the Messiah,* vol. 2 (New York: Doubleday, 1994), pp. 1317-49, for a detailed refutation of Crossan's thesis and an argument that the author of the *Gospel of Peter* likely had access to the oral tradition stemming from the Gospels of Luke and John. Dating of the *Acts of Pilate* is uncertain. The oldest extant copy is a twelfth-century Greek manuscript, and there are two basic editions (with the older edition translated into many languages), and a number of variations. One section may have been composed by the late second century. For an English translation, see F. Scheidweiler, in *New Testament Apocrypha,* vol. 1, pp. 505-26.

13. See Guy G. Stroumsa, "From Anti-Judaism to Antisemitism in Early Christianity?" in *Contra Iudaeos: Ancient and Medieval Polemics between Christians and Jews,* ed. Ora Limor and Guy G. Stroumsa (Tübingen: J. C. B. Mohr, 1996), pp. 7-9. On this topic, see also the massive work of Heinz Schreckenberg, *Die christlichen Adversus-Judaeos-Texte und ihr literarisches und historisches Umfeld* (Frankfurt: Peter Lang), vol. 1: *1.–11. Jh.* (4th rev. ed. 1999 [795 pages]); vol. 2: *11.–13. Jh.: Mit einer Ikonographie des Judenthemas bis zum 4. Lateran-konzil* (3rd enlarged ed. 1997 [739 pages]); vol. 3: *13.–20. Jh.* (1994 [774 pages]).

twelve sons of Jacob-Israel; Gen. 29:35). So Judas is related etymologically to "Jew" (i.e., *Yehûdî,* Hebrew; *Ioudaios,* Greek). But the relationship is more than linguistic. As Augustine of Hippo (354-430) wrote in his *Expositions on the Psalms,* just as Peter symbolizes the church, so does Judas the Jews (109: 17, 20).[14] John Chrysostom used Judas as an object lesson in the "tyranny of covetousness," as one who neither enjoyed the money nor the present, and missed the life to come.[15] Chrysostom believed that Judas in his greed was like all Jews: "Shall I tell you of their plundering, their covetousness, their abandonment of the poor, their thefts, their cheating in trade?"[16]

Over the centuries, Judas became an even more malevolent figure. Ekbert of Schönau, a twelfth-century Benedictine abbot, expanded Matthew's account of Judas's kiss of Jesus in his meditation on the passion, *Stimulus amoris:*

> How willing your spirit was for the Passion, good Jesus, you showed clearly when you met of your own accord those bloody men coming with your betrayer, seeking your soul in the night with lanterns and axes and arms, and you revealed yourself at a sign which they received from the leader of the shameful act. For you did not turn away from the bloodthirsty beast approaching for a kiss of your mouth, but the mouth in which no deceit was found, you applied sweetly to the mouth which abounded in malice. O innocent lamb of God, why you and that wolf? What linking of God to Belial?[17]

Ekbert has dehumanized Judas; he is a "bloodthirsty beast" and a "wolf." Moreover, Ekbert's focus on the mouth-to-mouth kiss may be read, as

14. Augustine, *Expositions on the Psalms,* 109: "For as some things are said which seem peculiarly to apply to the Apostle Peter, and yet are not clear in their meaning, unless when referred to the Church, whom he is acknowledged to have figuratively represented, on account of the primacy which he bore among the Disciples; as it is written, I will give unto you the keys of the kingdom of heaven, Matthew 16:19 and other passages of the like purport: so Judas does represent those Jews who were enemies of Christ, who both then hated Christ, and now, in their line of succession, this species of wickedness continuing, hate Him." See http://www.newadvent.org/fathers/1801109.htm (accessed December 10, 2008).

15. Homily 85 on the Gospel of Matthew (Matt. 26:67-68). See http://www.newadvent .org/fathers/200185.htm (accessed December 10, 2008).

16. See Paul W. Harkins, *St. John Chrysostom: Discourses against Judaizing Christians* (Washington, DC: Catholic University of America Press, 1979), *Discourse* 1.7.1.

17. Latin text and English translation in Thomas H. Bestul, *Texts of the Passion: Latin Devotional Literature and Medieval Society* (Philadelphia: University of Pennsylvania Press, 1996), p. 84. Bestul dates this meditation sometime between 1155 and 1184.

does Thomas Bestul, as a dramatization of a confrontation between Christian and Jew that "instantiates the special apprehensions of the late twelfth-century Christian society in regard to Jews."[18] Judas has transgressed the social hierarchy in the feudal world in which such a kiss signaled equality. The bloodthirsty beast's kiss expresses Ekbert's disgust at the defilement of bodily contact with Jews — a contact that ecclesiastical authorities sought to minimize, even eliminate, in forthcoming rulings.

Ekbert was a major influence on Bonaventure's (ca. 1217-74) allegorical treatise *Lignum vitae* (Tree of Life). For the Franciscan monk Bonaventure, "The first thing that occurs to the mind of anyone who would contemplate devoutly the passion of Christ is the perfidy of the traitor."[19] Like his predecessor, Bonaventure emphasized the horror of the betrayer's kiss on Jesus' mouth: "His face which fills the heavens with joy, was defiled by spittle from impure lips, struck by impious and sacrilegious hands, and covered in derision with a veil."[20]

Dante Alighieri (1265-1321) memorably placed Judas Iscariot *(Giuda Scarïotto)* in the ninth and lowest circle of hell, the circle of treachery. Having begun their descent into the Inferno on Good Friday, Dante and his guide Virgil ended their journey in Judecca *(Giudecca)*, the innermost zone of the ninth circle where they found Judas being eternally eaten by Lucifer, his head inside Lucifer's central mouth (Brutus and Cassius are in his two other mouths) and his back raked by the devil's claws:

> Within each mouth he used it like a grinder.
> With gnashing teeth he tore to bits a sinner
> so that he brought much pain to three at once.
>
> The forward sinner found that biting nothing
> When matched against the clawing, for at times
> his back was stripped completely of its hide.
>
> "That soul up there who has to suffer most,"
> my master said: "Judas Iscariot
> his head inside, he jerks his legs without."[21]

18. Bestul, *Texts*, pp. 84-85.

19. Bonaventure, *The Works of Bonaventure*, vol. 1, trans. José de Vinck (Paterson, NJ: St. Anthony Guild Press, 1964), p. 116.

20. Cited in Bestul, *Texts*, p. 96.

21. *The Divine Comedy of Dante Alighieri: Inferno*, trans. Allen Mandelbaum (New York: Bantam, 1980), Canto 34.55-63.

Dante's placement of Judas in the lowest circle of hell fostered popular imagination about Judas's traitorous character. Medieval passion plays of the fourteenth and fifteenth centuries added avarice to his depiction. As Kim Paffenroth observes, in these plays Judas "both conforms to and perpetuates the stereotype of the obscenely greedy Jew."[22]

The Turn to Violence Against the "Christ-Killers"

The Crusades heralded a tragic turn to violence against Jews in the twelfth and thirteenth centuries. In addition to their reputation as "Christ-killers," Jews were further stereotyped as usurers, bribers, and secret killers. "It had become easier to think of Jews as less than fully human and to treat them accordingly"; they were even depicted as imaginary monsters.[23] Bestul argues that the formation of attitudes that intensified hostility toward Jews in the later Middle Ages was both reflected in and actively supported by the way narratives on the passion treated Jews.[24] He shows that from about the middle of the twelfth century the role of Jews was magnified in accounts of the passion. In part this arose from a more affective piety that followed upon the theological reinterpretation of the meaning of the incarnation and redemption among eleventh- and twelfth-century theologians. Greater focus on the humanity of Christ in turn led to greater focus on his suffering — and thereby on those regarded as responsible for his crucifixion, the Jews.

The highly graphic and detailed descriptions of the torture visited upon the suffering Jesus correlated with the revival of Roman juridical practice that had fallen into disuse after the empire's fall. The shifts in narrative art from the latter half of the thirteenth century paralleled the restoration of judicial torture in the civil realm. This was matched in the ecclesiastical world. Various papal documents expressed contempt for the "treason" of heresy; *Ad extirpanda* of Innocent IV in 1252 permitted the

22. Paffenroth, *Judas*, p. 40.

23. Gavin I. Langmuir, *Toward a Definition of Antisemitism* (Berkeley: University of California Press, 1990), p. 306. The "Jews," Langmuir argues, functioned as symbols that allowed Christians to repress fantasies about crucifixion and cannibalism, doubts about the real presence of Christ in the Eucharist, and "unbearable doubts and fears about God's goodness and the bubonic bacillus that imperceptibly invaded people's bodies. By attacking 'Jews,' individuals who were poorly integrated in their societies and within themselves could express the tensions they felt as a conflict between good and bad people, between Christians and Jews" (p. 306).

24. Bestul, *Texts* p. 69.

torture of heretics.[25] Bestul argues that the religious intentions of the passion narratives were subverted; they promoted "values and beliefs about torture and punishment"; they supported "an outlook that certain ways of behaving" were "expected and legitimate."[26] The passion narratives sanctioned the construction of categories of persons on the margins of society and subject to persecution and violence:

> These victims of violence are not Christ, but they can be seen as forming a context, even a necessary context, against which we are meant to measure the magnitude of Christ's suffering for us. *That is, the suffering of Jews, heretics and lepers provides a reference point in the contemporary material world that helps the Christian to reconstruct imaginatively, as much as it is humanly possible to do so, the immeasurably greater and finally inexpressible pain that Christ endured in the cause of human salvation.*[27]

Other examples, more numerous than can be mentioned here, serve as clues to the extent to which the NT accounts of the passion of Jesus were taken up in imaginative but dangerous ways in church and European culture via Latin devotional literature (e.g., Ekbert's *Stimulus amoris* and Bonaventure's *Lignum vitae*), late twelfth-century French romances (e.g., *Le Roman de l'Estoire dou Graal*, a poem on Joseph of Arimathea, in which Jews are "base-born people"); mystical literature (e.g., *The Book of Margery Kempe*); hagiography (e.g., *The Life and Passion of Saint William the Martyr of Norwich*); literature (e.g., Chaucer's "Prioress's Tale"); and passion plays. The latter reached their apotheosis in the production of the Bavarian village of Oberammergau that continues to the present. First performed in 1634, the Oberammergau Passion play has been staged virtually every decade since 1680.[28] The perfidy of the Jews has been a constant in

25. Latin text and an English translation of this document may be consulted at http://userwww.sfsu.edu/~draker/history/Ad_Extirpanda.html.

26. Bestul, *Texts*, p. 157.

27. Bestul, *Texts*, p. 159. Emphasis added.

28. The *Tablet*, a Catholic weekly journal published in London, has been carrying advertisements for the 2010 production, which is scheduled for 102 performances between May 15 and October 3, 2010. For analysis of various versions, see Saul S. Friedman, *The Oberammergau Passion Play: A Lance against Civilization* (Carbondale: Southern Illinois University Press, 1984). Interventions have been made by Jewish and Christian officials to make changes to the play; see James Shapiro, *Oberammergau: The Troubling Story of the World's Most Famous Passion Play* (New York: Vintage, 2000); and A. James Rudin, "Oberammergau: A Case Study of Passion Plays," in *Pondering the Passion: What's at Stake*

the various productions, although some attempts have been made in recent years to ameliorate some of most offensive portrayals.

Given the emphasis on Jewish villainy, it is not surprising that Adolf Hitler praised the play. Hitler first attended Oberammergau's play in 1930, and then came as the führer on August 13, 1934, for the 300th anniversary.[29] In 1942 Hitler said that it was vital the play be continued, since it provided "knowledge of the menace of Jewry." Oberammergau outshone all others, in Hitler's judgment:

> Never has the menace of Jewry been so convincingly portrayed as in the presentation of what happened in the times of the Romans. There one sees in Pontius Pilate a Roman racially and intellectually so superior that he stands out like a firm, clean rock in the middle of the whole muck and mire of Jewry.[30]

The Influence of Interpretations of the Passion in the Shoah

What role did these troubling tellings of the passion story play in the Shoah? Certainly, multiple causal factors were behind this genocide; many had nothing or little to do with theology. The chaos of postwar Germany after its defeat in World War I and the signing of the Treaty of Versailles in 1919 left the nation vulnerable to political unrest and economic devastation, with forces on the left and right contending for power. Nationalist passions were aroused, sustained by the romantic mythology of the German *Volk* and propaganda about "race science." The rise of modernism and the cultural *Zeitgeist* of the 1920s alarmed many of a more conservative bent. A formidable leader seemed necessary to stabilize the country and restore its rightful place among world powers. Many regarded Adolf Hitler and his National Socialist German Workers Party (NSDAP) — Nazi Party — as the answer to their nation's crises. Appointed as chancellor in

---

for Christians and Jews? ed. Philip A. Cunningham (Lanham, MD: Rowman & Littlefield, 2004), pp. 97-108.

29. The villagers of Oberammergau sent Hitler a special set of mounted photographs of the play and actors with the inscription, "To our Führer, the protector of the cultural treasures of Germany, from the Passion village of Oberammergau." Cited in James Bentley, *Oberammergau and the Passion Play: A Guide and a History to Mark the 350th Anniversary* (New York: Penguin, 1984), p. 38.

30. Cited in Friedman, *The Oberammergau Passion Play,* p. 117. There was no production in 1940; the play resumed in 1950.

January 1933, Hitler pursued Nazi ideology with demonic zeal. As dictator, he brutally suppressed dissent, removed all legal rights from Jews, remilitarized the country, and propounded the myth of Aryan supremacy.

Catholic priest and scholar Philip Haeuser (1876-1960) appropriated this mythology in his depiction of Jesus as a warrior to a group of Nazi Party members in December 1930: Jesus was a soldier who had engaged in battle against the Pharisees: "Only because of this will to do battle, because of his courage to do battle, was he fated to be whipped and crucified."[31] God sent this militant Jesus to establish a church purified of Jewish tradition. Haeuser, who had written his doctoral dissertation on the *Epistle of Barnabas* and translated Justin Martyr's *Dialogue with Trypho* — two staples of the *Adversus Judaeos* literature — was a prominent antisemite whose views were widely circulated through public appearances and publications. Christ, he wrote, campaigned against Jewish leaders, "against the scribe, the Jewish preachers, the representatives of Jewish law, and the inhabitants of Jerusalem." Jews had "condemned their Messiah to death in their blindness, stubbornness, and depravity. . . . The Jewish people ceased once and for all to be an instrument of divine grace and mercy."[32] Hitler was a modern savior. In a 1936 address, Haeuser proclaimed that "Christ emphasizes the great law of life . . . he leads the struggle against inaction, against the synagogue — Hitler does the same thing today." Christ was unable to finish his task because he was crucified. "Hitler will see his task through."[33]

Given Haeuser's rightwing views, his adulation of Hitler, and his antisemitism, it is not surprising that his negative depiction of Jews included holding them responsible for the death of Jesus and thus rejected by God. Haeuser never retracted his views. In contrast, Romano Guardini (1885-1968), a priest and scholar who taught at the University of Berlin until the Nazis forced him to retire, wrote a book in 1937 with the goal of turning people away from devotion to Hitler and back to worship of Jesus. Still in print (and with an introduction to the 1997 edition by then-Cardinal Josef Ratzinger), *The Lord* became well known. No friend of Nazi ideology, Guardini nevertheless harshly portrayed the Jews in *The Lord*.[34]

31. Cited in Kevin P. Spicer, *Hitler's Priests: Catholic Clergy and National Socialism* (DeKalb: Northern Illinois University Press, 2008), p. 117. Spicer notes that Haeuser, unlike Grundmann and his colleagues, did not deny that Jesus had been born a Jew (p. 107).

32. Cited in Spicer, *Hitler's Priests*, p. 107.

33. Cited in Spicer, *Hitler's Priests*, p. 129.

34. Guardini wrote four books critical of Nazi ideology. See Robert A. Krieg, *Catholic Theologians in Nazi Germany* (New York: Continuum, 2004), pp. 107-30.

By crucifying Jesus, the Jews precipitated humankind's second Fall as Adam's sin had the first. They had rejected the Lord because they had been preoccupied with the details of the Mosaic law; their hearts had become hardened, and their sacrifices at the Temple were mere ritualism rather than true worship. Jesus preached the message of grace. "But the Jewish people did not believe. They did not change their hearts, so the kingdom did not come as it was to have come."

> The Jewish people, the Pharisees and Scribes and high priests, how "grown up" they are! The whole heritage of sin with its harshness and distortion looms at us. How old they are! Their memory reaches back more than one and a half millennia, back to Abraham — a historical consciousness not many nations can boast. Their wisdom is both a divine gift and fruit of long human experience; knowledge, cleverness, correctness. They examine, weigh, differentiate, doubt; and when the Promised One comes and prophecy is fulfilled, their long history about to be crowned, they cling to the past with its human traditions, entrench themselves behind the Law and the Temple, are sly, hard, blind — and their great hour passes them by. God's messiah must perish at the hands of those who "protect" his law. From his blood springs young Christianity, and Judaism remains prisoner of its hope in the coming of One who has already come.[35]

The Lord became a bestseller; it was even passed around in bomb shelters as a way of maintaining people's hope that Jesus Christ was the savior, not the self-proclaimed Führer Hitler. Yet its negative representation of Judaism reinforced the longstanding view of Jews as Christ-killers and Judaism as a desiccated religion that had given way to Christianity. Guardini later expressed regret for what he had written about Jewish responsibility for the death of Jesus, and urged Germany to assume moral responsibility for the Holocaust.[36] Yet the fact that a scholar and priest of such learning and integrity, as well as a critic of Nazi ideology, espoused such views, shows how deeply embedded that charge had become in Christianity.

In reviewing the work of theologians supportive of the Third Reich, both Protestant and Catholic, it is evident that alleged Jewish responsibil-

35. Cited by Robert A. Krieg, "German Catholic Views of Jesus and Judaism, 1918-1945," in *Antisemitism, Christian Ambivalence, and the Holocaust*, ed. Kevin P. Spicer (Bloomington: Indiana University Press, 2007), pp. 50-75, citation 67.

36. Krieg, "German Catholic Views," p. 27.

ity for the death of Jesus was but one element in the vilification of Judaism that permeated society. Judaism was degenerate; Jews were foreigners; they constituted a separate race inferior to Aryans that nonetheless sought world domination. Jews were avaricious; they polluted German society. They were inhuman, and thus expendable.

Without dismissing the influence of these views or underestimating the force of Nazi propaganda and the ruthlessness with which they enforced their regime, it seems undeniable that the teachings of Christianity about Judaism played their own nefarious role. And at the heart of Christian teaching about Judaism was the accusation that Jews had killed Jesus and thus rejected God. To claim, as did Catholic theologian Bernhard Bartmann, that by killing Jesus the Jews had rejected God was to provide a religious buttress for Nazi race hatred. "Jerusalem had not wanted salvation, and it was no longer able to receive it. Israel now lacked God's grace, for God no longer gave it to Israel."[37]

Interpretations of the passion were not limited to the ecclesial realm. It is clear that the Nazis drew significantly on the Christ-killer myth in the curriculum of German schools. Most notable is the 1938 work of Ernst Hiemer, *Der Giftpilz (The Poison Mushroom),* a collection of seventeen short stories for young readers and a key text making the ideology of the Third Reich widely accessible. Among its chapters is "What Christ Said About the Jews." A peasant mother, returning from working in the fields, stops with her three children near a roadside shrine of Christ:

> Children, look here! The Man who hangs on the Cross was one of the greatest enemies of the Jews of all time. He knew the Jews in all their corruption and meanness. Once he drove the Jews out with a whip, because they were carrying on their money dealings in the Church. He called the Jews killers of men from the beginning. By that he meant that the Jews in all times have been murderers. He said further to the Jews: Your father is the Devil! Do you know, children, what that means? It means the Jews descend from the Devil. And because they descend from the Devil, they live like devils. So they commit one crime after another. *Because this man knew the Jews, because He proclaimed the truth to the*

---

37. See Robert A. Krieg, "Romano Guardini's Theology of the Human Person," *Theological Studies* 59, no. 3 (1998): 457-74. Krieg notes that Guardini's book *The Lord* remains in print. Then-Cardinal Joseph Ratzinger wrote the introduction to a 1997 edition; Krieg criticizes Ratzinger's failure to call attention to the dated biblical scholarship and anti-Judaism (n. 9, p. 459).

world, He had to die. Hence, the Jews murdered him. They drove nails through his hands and feet and let him slowly bleed. In such a horrible way the Jews took their revenge. And in a similar way they have killed many others who had the courage to tell the truth about the Jews. Always remember these things, children. When you see the Cross, think of the terrible murder by the Jews on Golgotha. Remember that the Jews are children of the Devil and human murderers.[38]

Gregory Paul Wegner observes that "[n]o other society has ever devoted such a focused effort at integrating anti-Semitic thinking into curriculum intended for young children." He continues:

The language of religion expressed by various Nazi curriculum writers became another effective way in which Jews could be categorized as the negative other. The image became all the more potent through the exploitation of Golgotha. The charge of deicide against the Jews, one which survives to this day in anti-Semitic circles, carried a powerful emotional appeal for Nazi propagandists both inside and outside schools.[39]

3. The *Nostra Aetate* Trajectory on the Passion and Death of Jesus

Only with this history in mind does the significance of *NA* §4 become evident. Its most cited assertion undercuts centuries of preaching and teaching: "neither all Jews indiscriminately at that time, nor Jews today, can be charged with the crimes committed during his [Jesus'] passion."[40] But it

---

38. Cited in Gregory Paul Wegner, *Anti-Semitism and Schooling under the Third Reich* (New York and London: RoutledgeFalmer, 2002), p. 162; emphasis added.

39. Wegner, *Anti-Semitism and Schooling*, p. 181.

40. The wording of earlier drafts with regard to the issue of Jews and the death of Jesus offers a glimpse of some of the controversies behind the declaration. The earliest draft of 1961 never went to the floor of the Council. The draft of November 1963 says: "Nor should they [Jews] be regarded as a deicidal race, for the Lord by his passion and death expiates for all men's sins which were the cause of his passion and death. The death of Christ is not to be attributed to any whole people, then living, and even less to a people today. Therefore, let priests take care lest they say anything in catechetical instruction or preaching that could give rise in the hearts of hearers to hatred and contempt of Jews." A second draft of September 1964, which included the controversial statement that "it is proper to keep in mind that the union of Jewish People with the Church is part of Christian hope," has only one brief sentence about the death of Jesus: "In addition, let all take care lest there be imputed to Jews of our day what was done during the Passion of Christ." A third draft of November 1964

weakens its radicalism by beginning that sentence with: "Even though the Jewish authorities and those who followed their lead pressed for the death of Christ (cf. Jn 19:6)." Jewish complicity is alluded to in the earlier claim, "As Holy Scripture testifies, Jerusalem did not recognize God's moment when it came (cf. Lk 19:42). Jews for the most part did not accept the Gospel; on the contrary, many opposed the spreading of it (cf. Rom 11:28)."

So, while *NA* set the stage for a new relationship with the Jewish people, its depiction of Jewish authorities as responsible for the death of Jesus and assertion that Jerusalem — i.e., those Jews of the city where Jesus was crucified — failed to recognize the Son of God in their midst passes over the theological and historical complexity of the crucifixion. Further ambiguity lurks in the conflicting claims that on the one hand, "the apostle Paul maintains that the Jews remain very dear to God, for the sake of the patriarchs, since God does not take back the gifts he bestowed or the choice he made," while on the other hand, "It is true that the Church is the new people of God."

The *Guidelines* of 1974 merely repeats *NA*'s formulation: "With regard to the trial and death of Jesus, the council recalled that 'what happened in His passion cannot be blamed upon all the Jews then living, without distinction, nor upon the Jews of today.'"[41] Although the treatment of the death of Jesus in the *Notes* of 1985 is somewhat fuller, it is essentially a reiteration of *NA*:

> The delicate question of responsibility for the death of Christ must be looked at from the standpoint of the conciliar declaration *Nostra Aetate* (no. 4) and of the *Guidelines and Suggestions* (part III): "What happened in (Christ's) passion cannot be blamed upon all the Jews then living without distinction nor upon the Jews of today," especially since "authorities of the Jews and those who followed their lead pressed for the death of Christ." Again, further on: "Christ in his boundless love freely underwent his passion and death because of the sins of all men, so that

---

says: "The Jewish People is never to be represented as a reprobate race or accursed or as guilty of deicide. What was done during the passion of Christ can scarcely be blamed on the whole People living then, much less on the People of today." For texts and analysis, see James M. Somerville, "The Successive Versions of Nostra Aetate," in *Merton and Judaism*, ed. Beatrice Bruteau (Louisville: Fons Vitae, 2003), pp. 341-71.

41. Commission for Religious Relations with the Jews, *Guidelines and Suggestions for Implementing the Conciliar Declaration,* 1974; text widely available online (e.g., http://www.ccjr.us/dialogika-resources/documents-and-statements/roman-catholic/vatican-curia/277-guidelines.html). This is the only explicit mention of the passion and death of Jesus in the document; it follows the translation in an earlier edition of the documents of Vatican II.

all might attain salvation" (*Nostra Aetate,* no. 4). The *Catechism* of the Council of Trent teaches that Christian sinners are more to blame for the death of Christ than those few Jews who brought it about — they indeed "knew not what they did" (Lk 23:34) and we know it only too well. In the same way and for the same reason, "the Jews should not be presented as repudiated or cursed by God, as if such views followed from the Holy Scriptures" (*Nostra Aetate,* no. 4), even though it is true that "the Church is the new people of God" (§22).[42]

By repeating some of the negative formulations of the conciliar text, *Notes* fails to advance interpretation of the passion narratives. Perhaps some progress might have been achieved had the authors linked the discussion of the death of Jesus to a claim further on in the same document (Section IV.1.A [on the Vatican website] = §21A):

> Hence, it cannot be ruled out that some references hostile or less than favorable to the Jews have their historical context in conflicts between the nascent Church and the Jewish community. Certain controversies reflect Christian-Jewish relations long after the time of Jesus.
>
> To establish this is of capital importance if we wish to bring out the meaning of certain Gospel texts for the Christians of today.

While two documents from the Pontifical Biblical Commission, *Historical Truth of the Gospels* (1964) and *Interpretation of the Bible in the Church* (1993), have been significant in advancing biblical scholarship in the church, neither deals specifically with the question of responsibility for the death of Jesus.[43] In contrast, its more recent publication, *The Jewish People and Their Sacred Scriptures in the Christian Bible* (2001), discusses this in a number of places, taking up each Gospel in turn. What follows is a summary of that discussion.

---

42. Commission for Religious Relations with the Jews, *Notes on the Correct Way to Present the Jews and Judaism in Preaching and Catechesis in the Roman Catholic Church, 1985;* also widely available online: http://www.ccjr.us/dialogika-resources/documents-and -statements/roman-catholic/vatican-curia/234-notes.html.

43. Their importance lies principally in laying out broad methodological contours within which Catholic biblical scholars work. See Peter S. Williamson, *Catholic Principles for Interpreting Scripture: A Study of the Pontifical Biblical Commission's "The Interpretation of the Bible in the Church,"* Subsidia Biblica 22 (Roma: Editrice Pontificio Istituto Biblico, 2001).

The Pontifical Biblical Commission on the Death of Jesus (2001)

While the analysis above has centered on documents composed primarily about relationship with Jews and Judaism, *The Jewish People and Their Sacred Scriptures in the Christian Bible* differs in its exclusive focus on exegesis and in its length; it is appreciably longer than the documents discussed above, and requires a close reading.[44] Of significance is its point of departure: reference to the "abominable crimes [that] subjected the Jewish people to a terrible ordeal that threatened their very existence throughout most of Europe." In the wake of the Shoah, Christians must "reassess their relations with the Jewish people" (§1). Accordingly, the PBC inquires into what sorts of relations the Bible of Christians establishes with Jews; it is not a "straightforward relationship," but an "intimate" and "very complex" one that ranges from perfect accord on some points to one of great tension on others" (§1).

While my analysis is concerned principally with the third major section on the Jews in the New Testament, it is important to point out other key dimensions. A significant foundation is laid: in using the nomenclature "Old" Testament, the church has "no wish to suggest that the Jewish Scriptures are outdated or surpassed" (§II.A.1). Christianity's appropriation of the "Old" Testament is a rereading, a "retrospective perception" (§II.A.6) — a theological interpretation of texts we share with Jews.[45] Thus, it differs from Jewish readings, which are nonetheless "possible": "Both readings are bound up with the vision of their respective faiths, of which the readings are the result and expression. Consequently, both are irreducible" (§II.A.7).

The PBC claims that when the Gospel of Matthew was redacted, the

---

44. In booklet form, it runs to 205 pages. This document was originally promulgated in December 2001 in French and Italian; the English translation appeared on the Vatican website in April 2002.

45. "The Old Testament in itself has great value as the Word of God. To read the Old Testament as Christians then does not mean wishing to find everywhere direct reference to Jesus and to Christian realities. True, for Christians, all the Old Testament economy is in movement towards Christ; if then the Old Testament is read in the light of Christ, one can, retrospectively, perceive something of this movement. But since it is a movement, a slow and difficult progression throughout the course of history, each event and each text is situated at a particular point along the way, at a greater or lesser distance from the end. Retrospective re-readings through Christian eyes mean perceiving both the movement towards Christ and the distance from Christ, prefiguration and dissimilarity. Conversely, the New Testament cannot be fully understood except in the light of the Old Testament" (§II.A.6).

"greater part of the Jewish population had followed their leaders in their refusal to believe in Christ Jesus." Because Jewish Christians were a minority, Matthew foresaw that "Jesus' threats were about to be fulfilled" (e.g., the punishment that will befall Jerusalem [23:38] and the destruction of the Temple [24:2]). These threats, however, were not directed against the Jews as such, "but only insofar as they were in solidarity with their leaders in their lack of docility to God" (§III.B.71). The text continues:

> Matthew expresses this solidarity in the passion narrative when he reports that at the instigation of the chief priests and elders "the crowd" demands of Pilate that Jesus be crucified (Mt 27:20-23). In response to the Roman governor's denial of responsibility, "all the people" present themselves took responsibility for putting Jesus to death (27:24-25). On the people's side, adopting this position certainly showed their conviction that Jesus merited death, but to the evangelist, such conviction was unjustifiable: the blood of Jesus was "innocent blood" (27:4), as even Judas recognised. Jesus would have made his own the words of Jeremiah: "Know for certain that if you put me to death, you will be bringing innocent blood upon yourselves and upon this city and its inhabitants" (Jer 26:15). From an Old Testament perspective, the sins of the leaders inevitably bring disastrous consequences for the whole community. If the Gospel was redacted after 70 A.D., the evangelist knew that, like Jeremiah's prediction, Jesus' prediction had also been fulfilled. But he did not see this fulfilment as final, for all the Scriptures attest that after the divine sanction God always opens up a positive perspective. (§III.B.71)

In discussing Mark's passion narrative (§III.B.72), the PBC asserts that Jesus' arrest was the "work of the nation's ruling class," i.e., the Sanhedrin and the elders, chief priests, and scribes. "Inhibited only by fear of the people's reaction to their attempts to have Jesus killed," they finally succeed in inciting the crowd to choose Barabbas rather than Jesus: "The final decision of Pilate, powerless to calm the crowd, is to 'satisfy' them, which, for Jesus, means crucifixion." Yet, "this merely incidental crowd certainly cannot be confused with the Jewish people of that time, and even less with the Jews of every age. It should be said that they represent rather the sinful world (Mk 14:41) of which we are all a part."

In their reading of Mark, the PBC claims that the Sanhedrin condemned Jesus because in their perspective, Jesus had "uttered a 'blasphemy' in his affirmative and circumstantial response to the High Priest's question whether he was 'the Christ, the Son of the Blessed One' (14:61-64)." They interpret this as "the most dramatic point of rupture between the Jewish authorities and the person of Christ, a matter that continues to be the most serious point of division between Judaism and Christianity" (§III.B.72). They offer a concluding admonition, which, unfortunately they do not explicitly connect to their introductory words on the "abominable crimes" committed against the Jewish people in the Shoah:

> Any interpretation of Mark's Gospel that attempts to pin responsibility for Jesus' death on the Jewish people is erroneous. Such an interpretation, which has had disastrous consequences throughout history, does not correspond at all to the evangelist's perspective, which, as we have said, repeatedly opposes the attitude of the people or the crowd to that of the authorities hostile to Jesus. Furthermore, it is forgotten that the disciples were also part of the Jewish people. It is a question then of an improper transfer of responsibility, of the sort that is often encountered in human history.[46]

As for the Gospel of Luke and his Acts of the Apostles, the PBC sees a lessening of the polemics in Mark and Matthew. "Luke's passion narrative is not particularly severe on the Jewish authorities" (§III.B.74). The missionary or kerygmatic discourses in Acts contrast the "human cruelty which put Jesus to death and the liberating intervention of God" in raising Jesus from the dead (§III.B.75). Israel's sin was putting to death the Author of life (Acts 3:15), but this sin was "principally that of the 'leaders of the people'" (4:8-10) or the "Sanhedrin" (5:27-30). The Commission concludes that Luke does not

> hide the fact that Jesus suffered fierce opposition from the leaders of his people and that, as a result, the apostolic preaching finds itself in an analogous situation. If a sober recounting of this undeniable Jewish opposition amounts to anti-Judaism, then Luke could be accused of it. But it is obvious that this way of looking at it is to be rejected. Anti-Judaism consists rather of cursing and hating the persecutors, and their

---

46. This conclusion includes a note that reads: "This tendency continues to manifest itself: the responsibility of the Nazis has been extended to include all Germans, that of certain western lobbies to include all Europeans, that of certain illegal immigrants to include all Africans."

people as a whole. The Gospel message, on the contrary, invites Christians to bless those who curse them, to do good to those who hate them, and to pray for those who persecute them (Lk 6:27-28), following the example of Jesus (23:34) and of the first Christian martyr (Acts 7:60). This is one of the basic lessons of Luke's work. It is regrettable that in the course of the centuries following it has not been more faithfully followed.[47]

In the Gospel of John, the PBC sees that the "clear separation that existed between the Christian and Jewish communities" gave rise to the frequent use of the generalized term "the Jews" (seventy-one times, usually in the plural but three times in the singular). The Commission notes that John sometimes speaks of "the Jews" where the Synoptic authors refer to Jewish authorities. Historically, "only a minority of Jews contemporaneous with Jesus were hostile to him . . . a smaller number were responsible for handing him over to the Roman authorities . . . fewer still wanted him killed, undoubtedly for religious reasons that seemed important to them" (§III.B.77). Nevertheless, this minority "succeeded in provoking a general demonstration" in which Barabbas was freed rather than Jesus; in turn, this "permitted the evangelist to use a general expression, anticipating a later evolution" — that is, the separation of Jesus' disciples from "the Jews" evident in the "expulsion from the synagogue imposed on Jews who believed in Jesus" (§III.B.77). In conclusion, Jesus' ministry had stirred up "mounting opposition on the part of the Jewish authorities, who, finally, decided to hand Jesus over to the Roman authorities to have him put to death" (§III.B.78).

Finally, in a concluding section on "Pastoral Orientations," the PBC makes an analogy between the New Testament's "reproaches addressed to Jews" and the "accusations against Jews in the Law and the Prophets." Because, they assert, the NT's reproaches are neither as frequent nor as virulent as the OT's criticism of the Israelites, "they no longer serve as a basis for anti-Jewish sentiment." Were they to be used in such a manner, this would be contrary to the "whole tenor of the New Testament."[48] Nevertheless,

47. One might ask whether this section implies that Luke-Acts is intended as a historically accurate report of the early church.

48. See the critique by Amy-Jill Levine, "A Jewish Reading of the Document," *The Bible Today* (May-June 2003): 167-72. In that same issue, see my "A Resource for a Journey of Rethinking," pp. 141-47. See also Donald Senior, "Rome Has Spoken: A New Catholic Approach to Judaism," *Commonweal* 130, no. 2 (January 31, 2003): 20-23.

[I]t must be admitted that many of these passages are capable of providing a pretext for anti-Jewish sentiment and have in fact been used in this way. To avoid mistakes of this kind, it must be kept in mind that the New Testament polemical texts, even those expressed in general terms, have to do with concrete historical contexts and are never meant to be applied to Jews of all times and places merely because they are Jews. (§IV.B.87)

The PBC acknowledges "a profound" disagreement between Judaism and Christianity, but it is a "disagreement at the level of faith, the source of religious controversy between two human groups that take their point of departure from the same Old Testament faith basis, but are in disagreement on how to conceive the final development of that faith." Yet dialogue is indeed possible, given the common "patrimony" uniting the two traditions (§IV.B.87).

The Jewish People and Their Sacred Scriptures in the Christian Bible constitutes an important resource for grappling with the complex relation of the Testaments. It would have been an even more significant contribution had it acknowledged more frankly how the passion narratives have been used to vilify Jews and Judaism.

3. Understanding and Interpreting the Passion Narratives

How Historical Are the Passion Narratives?

Currents of contemporary biblical scholarship offer a perspective on the passion and death of Jesus that differs somewhat from that of the 2001 PBC document, *The Jewish People and Their Sacred Scriptures in the Christian Bible*. In particular, the PBC gives little attention to what many consider crucial to the interpretation of the history behind the death of Jesus: the modus operandi of Roman rule and the use of crucifixion to enforce it.[49] Nevertheless, the question of the historical basis of the passion narratives remains debated; scholars offer divergent judgments on how much reliable information the evangelists might have had, as well as on the constituency of the opposition to Jesus.

To what extent are the passion narratives to be regarded as providing reliable documentation of the historical events of the passion? Raymond E.

---

49. A brief discussion of Roman rule may be found in §III.A.3.67-69.

Brown, in his massive and meticulously detailed two-volume study, *The Death of the Messiah,* concludes that the evangelists — neither eyewitnesses nor mere reporters of eyewitness accounts — had "historical raw material" available to them. In turn, they reshaped that material, drawing upon a trove of Old Testament citations, allusions, and midrash.[50] Specifically with regard to Jewish involvement in the death of Jesus, Brown argues that (1) Jesus would have been found guilty by the "self-conscious religious majority of *any age and background*" (emphasis added); (2) Jesus lived in a time when violence often accompanied religious debates and differences; (3) those Jews who sought to put Jesus to death — and factual data about precisely who and how many they were cannot be known — might be held to be "responsible" for the death, but they were guilty only if they knew that the accused was undeserving of such punishment or had been negligent in discerning innocence; and (4) any Jews who disputed with Jesus were involved in an inner-Jewish dispute, not one between Jews and "Jesus, the Christian."[51]

John Dominic Crossan disagrees with Brown, who he says lacks "*a fair, legitimate, and valid criticism of Christianity's passion stories.*"[52] Crossan argues that the passion narratives arose from "prophecy historicized" rather than from "history remembered." That is, the disciples of Jesus, in trying to understand what had happened to Jesus, searched their Hebrew scriptures, particularly prophetic texts. Those texts gave rise to and were eventually embedded in the passion narratives. He identifies four successive stages in the growth of the passion tradition. There is the *historical passion,* that is, what actually happened. But what we know of this is the "barest minimum"; Crossan says the best summary of this is Josephus: "Pilate . . . hearing him accused by men of the highest standing amongst us . . . condemned him to be crucified." The second stage is the *prophetic passion,*

---

50. Brown, *The Death of the Messiah,* vol. 1, p. 14; see his discussion on the role of history in §1, B, pp. 13-24. See also "Appendix VII: The Old Testament Background of the Passion Narratives," vol. 2, pp. 1445-91, for a close reading of OT materials that "influenced heavily early Christian presentation of the passion, highlighting what should be recounted in order to expand the preaching outline into dramatic narratives" (p. 1444). See n. 12 above for reference to his argument with Crossan regarding the *Gospel of Peter.*

51. Brown, *The Death of the Messiah,* pp. 390-97. See also pp. 7 and 386 for explicit comments about Christian misuse of the passion accounts against Jews.

52. John Dominic Crossan, *Who Killed Jesus? Exposing the Roots of Anti-Semitism in the Gospel Story of the Death of Jesus* (San Francisco: HarperSanFrancisco, 1995), p. 35. Emphases in original.

from the more literate among Jesus' followers who searched their scriptures for texts that might enable them to understand the death-resurrection of Jesus. In turn, a third stage unfolded: the *narrative passion,* which built upon the reading of texts and turned it into a popular story. Finally, a fourth stage emerged: the *polemical passion,* the "terribly unfortunate, ethically indefensible, and eventually lethal argument that equates *the narrative passion* with the *historical passion* and claims that its detailed fulfillment of the *prophetic passion* renders Christian belief obvious and Jewish disbelief indefensible."[53] Crossan regards his disagreement with Brown as not simply an exegetical matter, but rather as an ethical one, because the passion-resurrection stories were "the matrix for Christian anti-Judaism and eventually for European anti-Semitism."[54]

Crossan's book has the tone of a manifesto. His ardent protest against the way the passion accounts have served as a foundation for hostility toward Jews and Judaism is consonant with my own claim in the initial section of this chapter that the charge of "Christ-killer" is central to the "tormented history" between the church and the Jewish people. Nevertheless, I question both his thesis and its necessity in countering anti-Judaism and antisemitism. It seems to me highly speculative to assert that in the movement from the second stage *(prophetic passion)* to the third stage *(passion narrative),* "scholarly exegetes" working in the context of "somewhat impenetrable elitism" searched the scriptures for "texts, themes, or types that show a *dialectic of persecution and vindication.*"[55] One wonders if it is not Crossan himself, the scholarly exegete, who discerns these texts, themes, and types. Moreover, in his commitment to expose the roots of anti-Judaism, Crossan has said little about the power exercised by Rome, including over the high priest.

Yet even if one were able to prove beyond a shadow of a doubt that the passion narratives are overwhelmingly literary-theological constructs with minimal historical basis, the fact is that nearly two thousand years of a largely tormented history stand between us and the early church. To claim that a text lacks solid historical basis does not alone solve the problem. One needs reading strategies to deal with troubling texts and a sense of how the text has functioned over the centuries.

Ultimately, it is doubtful that the question of historicity can be solved,

53. Crossan, *Who Killed Jesus?* pp. 219-21.
54. Crossan, *Who Killed Jesus?* p. 32.
55. Crossan, *Who Killed Jesus?* pp. 121 and 120.

as the sources do not permit us certainty. Yet it seems highly plausible, contra Crossan, that some Jewish leaders were involved. It is also the case that the Roman Empire had no compunction about crucifying a Jew like Jesus who drew crowds, particularly when Jerusalem's population was swollen with pilgrims for the Passover feast.[56]

A number of exegetes focus on the centrality of a text from Luke as offering a significant historical kernel: "Then the assembly rose as a body and brought Jesus before Pilate. They began to accuse him, saying, 'We found this man perverting our nation, forbidding us to pay taxes to the emperor, and saying that he himself is the Messiah, a king'" (Luke 23:1-2). Gerard Sloyan argues that the historical substratum may well be only this text; he sees that it offers a sort of "hard core of reminiscence" of the last day (or days) of Jesus." Sloyan offers the hypothesis that "all the remaining details in the Gospels could have been elaborations of that remembered fact." He argues that after the resurrection the disciples of Jesus reconstructed the events of that Friday "on the basis of the fact that Roman justice disposed of him, after successful priestly efforts to counter his mounting popularity by delating him on a charge of sedition."[57] Then the evangelists developed these reminiscences in "dramatic narratives" that by the second century were interpreted as history because people "had lost the Semitic skill of spotting a story crafted in the biblical style. Christians have been misreading their own holy books ever since, often making Jews pay the price of their incomprehension."[58] He concludes that it is impossible to know from the Gospels what sequence

---

56. E. P. Sanders says that the "real conflict was between Jesus and his contemporaries in Judaism." Yet it is not correct to "make a rigid distinction between 'religious' and 'political' reasons." He thinks it unlikely that even someone close to the events of the passion "knew precisely who did what" and that it is impossible the evangelists knew the "internal motives" of those involved (*Jesus and Judaism* [Philadelphia: Fortress, 1985], pp. 295, 296, and 300). Sanders sees Jesus' "attack (both by word and deed) against the temple" as an immediate cause of his death (pp. 301-4). Paula Fredriksen refutes this view, arguing that whatever symbolic action Jesus took in the Temple would have been muted by the immensity of the Temple and that his predictions of the fall of the Temple were composed after its destruction in 70. She writes: "Jewish pilgrims hailed Jesus as messiah in Jerusalem. Pilate killed him as a messianic pretender — not again because Jesus thought he was messiah . . . but because others thought and proclaimed that he was" (*Jesus of Nazareth: King of the Jews* [New York: Vintage, 2000], pp. 225-34; citation 234).

57. Gerard S. Sloyan, *The Crucifixion of Jesus: History, Myth, Faith* (Minneapolis: Fortress, 1995), pp. 27-28.

58. Sloyan, *Crucifixion*, p. 29.

of events brought Jesus to the cross. "Ambiguity is the hallmark of all four accounts."[59]

Sloyan uses the term "power class" to describe the opponents of Jesus in the passion, rather than, as does the PBC, Jewish authorities or Jewish leaders. Sloyan's nomenclature is crucial because it points to the alliance between the high priestly families and the Roman Empire, as represented by the office of the governor, Pontius Pilate. As Mary Rose D'Angelo argues, the "gospels seriously misrepresent the role of the Jews in the death of Jesus" by placing the motivation and initiative with the Jewish leaders, claiming that Pilate was forced into collaborating with them. On the contrary, "Pilate was not subject to pressure from high priests; rather the high priests held office and indeed officiated liturgically only at the sufferance of the procurator."[60]

Roman Rule and the Crucifixion as "Massive State Terrorism"

The PBC's *The Jewish People and Their Sacred Scriptures in the Christian Bible* provides little analysis of the effect of Roman rule in Palestine; some mention is made in §§66-68. Yet Rome exercised political power over Jews in the land of Israel. Since the year 6 C.E. in the province of Judea, it had ruled through governors (or prefects) appointed by the emperor. As governor, Pontius Pilate, who held the office from 26 to 36, would have had ultimate authority, including the right of capital punishment, and total legislative control of the Sanhedrin, presided over by the high priest.[61]

With relatively few troops at his command and minimal centralized bureaucracy, prefects like Pilate had to form alliances with what social scientists call the governing class: the high priestly families, Sadducees, and leading scribes; and with the retainer class typified by the Pharisees.[62] These officials were not simply religious leaders as most readers of the New Testament tend to assume, but participants in the Roman imperial system, with a

59. Sloyan, *Crucifixion*, p. 40.

60. Mary Rose D'Angelo, "Re-membering Jesus: Women, Prophecy, and Resistance in the Memory of the Early Churches," *Horizons* 19, no. 2 (1992): 199-218, citation 210.

61. See Anthony J. Saldarini, "Sanhedrin," in *ABD* 5: 975-80.

62. See Anthony J. Saldarini, *Pharisees, Scribes and Sadducees in Palestinian Society* (Wilmington, DE: Michael Glazier, 1988), p. 154. "[N]either Josephus nor the New Testament claim that all or most of the chief priests, elders and other members of the governing class were Sadducees, only that Sadducees, however few or numerous, were mostly drawn from that class." On the Pharisees as part of the retainer class, see p. 281 and *passim*.

measure of social and political power. They were, however, under Roman hegemony — and the balance of power was decidedly Pilate's.

Of particular note is the relationship between prefects and chief priests. The emperor Augustus had decreed that the prefect would exercise the same power as had Herod the Great: the appointment (and removal) of the high priest and supervision of the priestly vestments. Since Caiaphas was high priest for the entirety of Pilate's rule (in fact, from 18 to 36 C.E.), we may infer that high priest and governor formed a powerful alliance. His longevity contrasts sharply with that of the five high priests during the prefecture of Pilate's predecessor, Valerius Gratus (15-26 C.E.). By gratifying the governor, the chief priests acquired access to wealth, status, and power; they were in effect agents of Rome — and thus despised by the majority of Judeans.[63] The high priest, who supervised a guard force of several thousand to keep order in Jerusalem, especially in the precincts of the Temple, oversaw the payment of the tribute Rome exacted. That was not the sort of activity to endear him to the Jewish populace.

This chasm between the governing and retainer classes that enjoyed elite status because of their alliance with Roman officials and the vast majority of Judeans and Galileans suggests the problem in using terminology such as "Jews" or "Jewish authorities" without additional qualification. A few Jews belonged to the privileged and powerful families of the high priests or were of Herodian lineage. Under Roman rule they flourished while the overwhelming majority of Jews were overtaxed peasants. Galilean Jews lived at a distance from the Temple in Jerusalem and thus had different experiences from Judean Jews, who were more affected by the alliance between prefects and the Jerusalem elite: chief priests, Sadducees, and leading scribes and Pharisees. Many Jews lived in the Diaspora, dispersed throughout the Roman Empire and in Babylonia. Richard Horsley claims that the "people of Palestine at the time of Jesus appear as a complex society full of political conflict rather than a unitary religion (Judaism)."[64]

Not only do the various documents of the *NA* trajectory oversimplify first-century Jewish life, they completely pass over a crucial element: how Rome ruled. In the popular mind Augustus and his successors are often associated with the *Pax Romana*. This is accurate, however, only for parts of

---

63. See Warren Carter, *Pontius Pilate: Portraits of a Roman Governor,* Interfaces series, ed. Barbara Green (Collegeville, MN: Liturgical Press, 2003), p. 48.

64. Richard Horsley, *Jesus and Empire: The Kingdom of God and the New World Disorder* (Minneapolis: Fortress Press, 2003), p. 10. He speaks of "modern essentialist concepts such as 'the Jews'" (p. 11).

the empire. Conquest and victory were the watchwords, not peace. Early in his reign, Augustus engaged in what historian Susan Mattern terms "euphoric expansionism," that is, ambitious campaigns into what were perceived as the remotest corners of the world.[65]

Rome's foreign policy generally was intended to dominate and humiliate the enemy — to inspire fear and awe in those it conquered. The barbarian "must be terrified at all times."[66] It celebrated its victories by various means: collecting and publicizing lists of peoples and lands it had conquered, creating sumptuous displays of the spoils of their expeditions, humiliating leaders of enemy peoples, and engaging in triumphal processions. Some three hundred triumphal arches survive (or appear on coins or inscriptions), testifying to the glory of conquest.[67]

The empire was a pyramid in which wealthy elites, perhaps 2-3 percent of the population supported by a retainer class of bureaucrats of about 5 percent, ruled over vast lands and peoples.[68] The peasants they ruled and taxed supported Rome; the tribute from the provinces was vital to Rome's survival, enabling the emperor to placate the populace with "bread and circuses."[69] The ruling elite also extracted between 30 and 70 percent of the production of peasants and artisans.[70] After all, "to rule in aristocratic empires is, above all, to tax."[71] The empire's military enforced their privileges, and made rebellion very dangerous.

The military's chief strength was its ability to deter rebellion by terror.[72] Occupying armies were stationed to contain revolts. Campaigns were always fought on the enemy's territory, and should the enemy man-

---

65. Susan P. Mattern, *Rome and the Enemy: Imperial Strategy in the Principate* (Berkeley: University of California Press, 1999), p. 89.

66. Mattern, *Rome and the Enemy*, pp. 183 and 202. The situation with regard to Judea was somewhat more complex. It was Archelaus's (Herod's son's) incompetence that brought about the rule of Roman governors, not Rome's plans of conquest. By the time of Pilate things were different, but Tacitus (*Hist.* 5.9.2) famously stated with reference to Judea, "Sub Tiberio quies" ("Under Tiberius [14-37 c.e.] all was quiet").

67. Mattern, *Rome and the Enemy*, p. 168.

68. See K. C. Hanson and Douglas E. Oakman, *Palestine in the Time of Jesus: Social Structures and Social Conflicts* (Minneapolis: Fortress, 1998), pp. 67-68.

69. The phrase is attributed to the poet Juvenal (late 1st c. c.e.–early 2nd c.) in *Satire X*.

70. Warren Carter, *Matthew and Empire: Initial Explorations* (Harrisburg, PA: Trinity Press International, 2001), p. 18.

71. John H. Kautsky, *The Politics of Aristocratic Empires* (Chapel Hill: University of North Carolina Press, 1982), p. 150.

72. Mattern, *Rome and the Enemy*, p. 119.

age a victory, a reprisal would follow. The Romans understood the psychology of fear.[73]

What greater mechanism to inspire fear than crucifixion? Crucifixion was "highly organized, massive state terrorism, intended to intimidate the vast peasant and slave populations of the empire into passivity."[74] Or, in Paula Fredriksen's blunt description, crucifixion was a "spectacle for the edification of those watching."[75] As a public humiliation — the naked body hanging for all to see, sometimes for days — it was torture designed as the ultimate deterrent. Not even the dignity of burial was given. Remains of the crucified were piled with other corpses, left to ravens and dogs.[76] Rome reserved crucifixion only for peasants, foreigners, and slaves it deemed guilty of heinous crimes, such as fomenting rebellion, treason, and murder. Roman citizens were not subject to crucifixion.[77]

All this provides us with a closer historical reading of why Jesus was crucified. Joseph Tyson provides a succinct account:

> Jesus was put to death under the authority of the Roman governor, Pontius Pilate, for an alleged violation of Roman law. It is probable that the charge against him was political in nature, similar to the specific charges listed in Luke 23:2 and reflected in the placard on the cross. What we know about Pilate would lead us to believe that he would not have been careful to investigate thoroughly the charges against Jesus and certainly not reluctant to impose the appropriate penalty. Remember Philo's words: Under Pilate there were "executions without trial constantly repeated." Jesus' would have been one of those executions. It is also likely that some Jewish priestly leaders assisted the Romans in the apprehension and investigation of Jesus, in something like the proceedings described in Luke 22:66-71.[78]

---

73. Mattern, *Rome and the Enemy*, p. 122.

74. Stephen J. Patterson, *Beyond the Passion: Rethinking the Death and Life of Jesus* (Minneapolis: Fortress, 2004), p. 8.

75. Fredriksen, *King of the Jews*, p. 233.

76. Patterson, *Beyond the Passion*, p. 9.

77. Rome neither invented crucifixion nor was alone in employing it on a large scale. Crucifixion seems to have been a widespread form of torture in antiquity, attested at least as early as the seventh century b.c.e. Whatever the precedents, however, Rome used crucifixion to great effectiveness. Its great orator Cicero (106-43 b.c.e.) called it "a most cruel and disgusting penalty," the "extreme and ultimate penalty for a slave" (*In Verrem* 2.5.64, 66). Josephus later called it "the most pitiable of deaths" (*Jewish War* 7.6.4.203).

78. Joseph B. Tyson, "The Death of Jesus," in *Seeing Judaism Anew*, ed. Mary C. Boys

If Jesus was crucified as seditious by the power of the Roman Empire, why do the Gospels shift blame to Jews? Various hypotheses have been proffered, often involving the lowly status of the Reign of God Movement as an "illicit and illegal" religious entity in the Roman Empire. Sloyan, however, offers an alternative explanation. He notes that the evangelists would have assumed that Rome would engage in repressive behavior. The involvement of the high priest and Jerusalem council, both despised by the people as collaborators, was another matter altogether. He speculates that as the movement grew beyond the borders of Palestine, what was perceived to be the "betrayal of God's just one, Jesus, by the highest religious authority in Judea would still have rankled." Continuing debates took place between the "Jesus Jews, with their admixture of Samaritan and gentile believers, and the bulk of Jews, undoubtedly far more law-observant in their ethnic homogeneity than this new band claiming to be Israel." As a result, a polemic permeated the Gospel accounts "by means of exchanges reported as having taken place in Jesus' lifetime. For believers in Jesus, "he was the one great Jew who should have been accepted." The story of his rejection by religious authorities in Judea grew in their minds, and eventually four dramatizations were written. "In any event, this emphasis on the part played by the priests and 'the whole people' (Matt 27:25) has led to terrible consequences for Jews."[79]

Precisely because of these "terrible consequences for Jews," it is imperative that the complexity of the passion narratives become a pastoral priority for the church. We may not know precisely what happened, but we do know what misreadings of the texts have rationalized or inspired.

Interpretative Strategies for Troubling Texts

The passion narratives are not the only problematic texts in the NT's portrayal of Jews and Judaism. The depiction of the Pharisees is also at issue.[80] Moreover, the Bible as a whole has many troubling passages that appear to sanction violence, demean women, and condone slavery. Since the Bible is

---

(Lanham, MD: Rowman & Littlefield, 2005), pp. 38-45, citation 44. Recall, however, Sanders's warning that "religious" and "political" should not be separated (*Jesus and Judaism*, p. 296).

79. Sloyan, *Crucifixion*, p. 43.

80. An abundant literature has developed on the way the NT represents the Pharisees. For an accessible and creative analysis, see J. Patrick Mullen, *Dining with Pharisees*, Interfaces series, ed. Barbara Green (Collegeville, MN: Liturgical Press, 2004).

the church's book, it is incumbent upon the church to offer guidance on how such texts may be interpreted.

Recent documents offer some general counsel. For example, the 1993 instruction from the Pontifical Biblical Commission, *The Interpretation of the Bible in the Church,* advises that interpretations that go in a "direction contrary to evangelical justice and charity" (e.g., using the Bible as a justification for racial segregation, antisemitism, or sexism) must be rejected. It adds that special attention must be paid to the interpretation of "certain texts of the New Testament" that could "provoke or reinforce unfavorable attitudes to the Jewish people."[81] The passion narratives have indeed been at the root of provoking and reinforcing such attitudes.

Stating that claim in the positive — *interpretations must be consonant with evangelical justice and charity* — offers a useful principle.[82] Other reading strategies might be deduced from this same instruction, which speaks of "Sacred Scripture" as the "word of God expressed in human language."[83] That is, *situate texts in their context as artifacts of human culture; do not bypass the human reality in the search for spiritual meaning.*[84] Similarly, in the section that outlines problems with fundamentalism, the PBC says that fundamentalism "often historicizes material" that from its outset "never claimed to be historical"; furthermore, fundamentalism "unwittingly confuses the divine substance of the biblical message with what are in fact its human limitations." So a complementary principle might be formulated: *because biblical texts bear the limitations and wounds of human finitude, they must be read in a discerning manner.* Moreover, by exploring rhetorical analysis in a critical way, as the instruction mandates (see I.B.5), we may view texts that blame Jews for the death of Jesus — particularly texts such as Matthew 27:25 and John 19:15 — as "contingent polemic of late first-century churches" and thus a polemic we may reject as an artifact of the animosities of the period.[85] *The New Testament's polemic against*

81. Citations are from *Interpretation of the Bible in the Church,* IV.A.3.

82. See Clark Williamson, *A Guest in the House of Israel* (Louisville: Westminster/John Knox, 1993), p. 140, who speaks of a "normative understanding of the gospel . . . that requires us to criticize and reject its more superficial and accidental locutions."

83. *Interpretation of the Bible in the Church,* IA; see §III.D.2. Peter Williamson considers this expression the first principle of the document; see his *Catholic Principles for Interpreting Scripture,* pp. 28-30.

84. Here I draw on P. Williamson's wording in *Catholic Principles,* "No 'spiritual' bypassing of the human reality is possible," p. 30.

85. C. Williamson, *Guest,* p. 143. Williamson argues that this polemic is a religious slan-

Jews should be classified as a rhetorical strategy of the Hellenistic world that does not have authority for Christians of our time.

Still another principle might be inferred from how the PBC explains a method of interpretation known as *Wirkungsgeschichte*, or the history of the effect produced by a book or passage of Scripture: "Such an inquiry seeks to assess the development of interpretation over the course of time under the influence of the concerns readers have brought to the text. It also attempts to evaluate the importance of the role played by tradition in finding meaning in biblical texts."[86] Attentiveness to the consequences of the uses to which biblical texts have been put grounds the church in history. Thus, the principle: *in interpreting a biblical text, inquire into what the text has been used to inspire or rationalize or justify.* In the case of the passion narratives, employing this principle will make for a potent cautionary tale; hence, my decision to devote the first section of this paper to the tragic effects of the teaching that held the Jews responsible for the crucifixion.

Similarly, the section on approaches that use the human sciences (e.g., sociological, anthropological, psychological, and psychoanalytic approaches) offers a basis for another principle: *make use of disciplines that throw light on the wider context of texts.*[87] Sociological and psychological approaches invite us to consider the post-70 milieu in which the Gospels were composed and to examine the complex process of identity formation in the early church.[88]

Various other interpretational strategies might be formulated. My intention is not to draw up a full list but rather to call attention to ways we might more adequately interpret the passion narratives in light of the "tormented" history between Jews and Christians. As John Pawlikowski says in his essay, "Taking history seriously indeed forces us to reexamine our Christian identity in fundamental ways."[89]

---

der not uncommon in surrounding religious groups and not an expression of distinctive Christian witness. See also Luke Timothy Johnson, "The New Testament's Anti-Jewish Slander and the Conventions of Ancient Polemic," *Journal of Biblical Literature* 108, no. 3 (1989): 419-41.

86. *Interpretation of the Bible in the Church*, I.C.3.

87. *Interpretation of the Bible in the Church*, I.D.1-3.

88. See Barbara Bowe, "The New Testament, Religious Identity, and the Other," in *Contesting Texts: Jews and Christians in Conversation about the Bible*, ed. Melody Knowles, Esther Menn, John Pawlikowski, and Timothy J. Sandoval (Minneapolis: Fortress, 2007), p. 93.

89. See in this volume John T. Pawlikowski, "Historical Memory and Christian-Jewish Relations."

The Catholic Church must be more candid in confessing the consequences of its centuries-long accusation that the Jews were/are responsible for the death of Jesus. The important breakthroughs inaugurated by *Nostra Aetate* in 1965 must be complemented by a church speaking less ambiguously about its past and interpreting the Bible with greater respect for its ambiguities. Even as the church proclaims that all are saved in Christ Jesus, it must act in ways consonant with the God to whom he bore witness, the God of our salvation.

A Jewish Response to
John T. Pawlikowski and Mary C. Boys

Marc Saperstein

1. Introduction

Professors John T. Pawlikowski and Mary C. Boys have long-established and distinguished reputations both as academic scholars and as active participants in interfaith dialogue. Like the Hebrew prophets, they have often criticized aspects of their own tradition, especially with regard to its discourse and policy toward the Jewish people and the Jewish faith, as can readily be discerned in the essays above. For the courage and integrity of their voices I have deep gratitude and the greatest of respect. As a Jewish historian, I feel no need to add to their criticisms; indeed, if I differ slightly on specific points in the essays, or supplement them from a different perspective, it is to present a view that in some ways will be a defense of the historical record of the church against the prophetic critique. My hope is that my reactions will perhaps produce a picture with further nuance.

There are four major themes emerging from the two articles: Jews and the death of Jesus, the parting of the ways, the church's role in the history of anti-Judaism and antisemitism, and the connection between Christian anti-Jewish doctrine and the Holocaust. I shall briefly discuss each theme in turn.

2. Jews and the Death of Jesus

Professor Mary Boys (henceforth, MB) notes the great historical significance of the *Nostra Aetate* statement that "what happened in His passion cannot be charged against all the Jews, without distinction, then alive, nor against the Jews of today." Two issues arise from this formulation, which — as is indeed noted — was fraught with controversy over various proposals for the precise wording. First, it indicates that some Jews at the time of the passion and crucifixion were indeed responsible for what happened.[1] Second, "it fails to confess that for nearly two millennia the church preached and taught exactly this" — namely, that all the Jews at the time were responsible for being "Christ-killers," and that subsequent generations of Jews to the present bore that responsibility as well — "and, as a consequence, Jews suffered gravely."

To begin with the second assertion, I am reluctant to question a respected Roman Catholic scholar on the substance of church teaching throughout the centuries, but I wonder how fair and accurate it is to assert that the church preached and taught for nearly two millennia that (all) Jews were Christ-killers. This assertion seems inconsistent with the statement (from the 1985 *Notes*) cited by MB further in the same article: "The *Catechism* of the Council of Trent teaches that Christian sinners are more to blame for the death of Christ than those few Jews who brought it about."[2] This authoritative text from 1566 seems rather consistent with the *NA* formulation about the crucifixion. The complaint that *NA* "fails to confess that for nearly two millennia the church preached and taught exactly this" might perhaps more accurately be applied to the continuation of that same paragraph — "the Jews should not be presented as rejected or accursed by God, as if this followed from the Holy Scriptures" — for this is indeed what the church had taught.

What about the first issue: attributing responsibility for the crucifixion to some of the Jews in Jerusalem at the time? This does not seem to me to be either intuitively implausible or inconsistent with the historical record, insofar as we can reconstruct it from the relevant sources. It may be surprising to note that until relatively recently (perhaps the nineteenth century), Jews did not deny responsibility for the death of Jesus and tended

---

1. The statement quoted is preceded in *NA* by the assertion "True, the Jewish authorities and those who followed their lead pressed for the death of Christ."

2. Roman Catechism of the Council of Trent, 1,5,11: "This guilt [of Christian sinners] seems more enormous in us than in the Jews, since according to the testimony of the same Apostle: If they had known it, they would never have crucified the Lord of glory; while we, on the contrary, professing to know Him, yet denying Him by our actions, seem in some sort to lay violent hands on him." For a stunning application of this theme in a British Jewish sermon delivered on December 25, 1915, see Morris Joseph, "Christmas and War," in Marc Saperstein, *Jewish Preaching in Times of War* (Oxford: Littman Library, 2008), pp. 312-13.

to eliminate the role of the Romans even more thoroughly than do the Gospel accounts. More than twenty years ago, I published my translation from a manuscript of a sermon delivered following an anti-Jewish Good Friday riot at Segovia in the year 1452. Here is what the preacher said:

> And now, my brothers and friends, look and you will see how this tragedy has come upon us. You know, of course, that our hands did not shed the blood of that man in whose name our enemies in every generation have risen against us to destroy us. Rather, our righteous ancestors, basing themselves upon the Torah and justice, hanged him on a tree. A court of seventy-one came to an understanding of his case. This is the legal rule: "The false prophet is not put to death except at the order of the Great Court". . . . He is a fool who says that had it not been for that incident [the crucifixion], those murders and conflagrations and forced apostasies would never have befallen our sacred communities. Nothing prevents God from fabricating new causes and different libels to be directed against us as justification for the collection of His debt. . . . Look at the Jewish communities in Islamic lands. Murders and forced apostasies have befallen them without any libels relating to the death of that man. Instead, we should look into our behaviour, as individuals and as a community. This is why these tragedies occur.[3]

The preacher's position is dramatic and clear: (1) contemporary Jews bear no responsibility for the death of Jesus, but, (2) the proper Jewish authorities in the time of Jesus both judged him guilty of a capital crime under the law of the "false prophet" (based on Deut. 18:20) and carried out the execution; however, (3) the accusation that Jews were Christ-killers is not the true cause of contemporary Jewish suffering, it is simply an instrument exploited by God to make contemporary Christians the agents of his purpose; and (4) the true reason for Jewish suffering at the hands of Christians (and Muslims) was the transgressions of Jews against their responsibilities under the covenant (the preacher goes on to specify: "the abuse of bans of excommunication, acts of informing to the authorities, the eating of forbidden foods, and the drinking of Gentile wine"). Here we have an acceptance of the validity of the "Christ-killer" charge considerably beyond the historical reality, juxtaposed with a dismissal of its significance and relevance, by a Jewish leader facing a community that has just suffered on Good Friday.

3. Joseph ibn Shem Tov, "Sermon on Avot 3,15-16," in Marc Saperstein, *Jewish Preaching 1200-1800* (New Haven: Yale University Press, 1989), pp. 177, 179.

All this, of course, has nothing to do with the historicity of the Gospel narratives. MB provides a detailed review of the various accounts. Even a nonexpert will realize that some of the statements cannot be accepted by anyone with a nonfundamentalist approach to the texts, including the most horrifying verse of all: "And with one voice, the people cried, 'His blood be on us, and on our children'" (Matt. 27:25). Crowds of people never spontaneously call out a full sentence with one voice, unless they have been coached in advance to repeat a predetermined chant. That kind of statement is by its nature the imagination of an author (as are similar assertions in Hebrew scriptures [see, e.g., Num. 14:2-3, 1 Sam. 8:19-20] and in later chronicles).

More important than the crowd is the behavior of the Jewish authorities — the chief priests and elders. In this regard, I would suggest a structural analysis. Insofar as Jesus was claimed to be the messiah and not just a teacher and preacher, it is not surprising that the establishment leadership viewed him as a potentially dangerous troublemaker and opposed his public career. Jewish messianic claims are by their very nature a menace to the status quo. They are guaranteed to threaten established Jewish leaders, because messianic claims (like prophetic ones) trump all other claims to influence. And messianism is guaranteed to challenge the Gentile political power that supports the established leadership, since it will naturally be perceived as a movement for political independence, and therefore rebellion.

Throughout history, established Jewish leaders who accepted the messianic doctrine in principle almost invariably resisted anyone who claimed to implement it in practice; they were comfortable with a messiah only so long as he was consigned to the future, not if he appeared in the present making explicit demands.[4] That some of the leaders wanted the historical figure Jesus of Nazareth out of the way, whether because of concern for their own positions or because they genuinely believed that the Romans would respond in a manner that would harm the entire population, is not surprising. That position, of course, becomes far more problematic in retrospect with the overlay of christological doctrine, of which the contemporary leaders were totally ignorant.

---

4. The major exception to this generalization is of course the seventeenth-century movement around Sabbatai Sevi, in which Jewish leaders were divided, and many of them, including respected rabbis, for a short period supported the messianic figure, as is evident in Gershom Scholem's magisterial survey, *Sabbatai Sevi: The Mystical Messiah* (Princeton: Princeton University Press, 1973).

3. Parting of the Ways

With regard to the "parting of the ways," Professor John Pawlikowski (henceforth JP) raises a significant issue, which he applies to the church, but which has relevance to Jews as well. He notes that the consensus of modern historical study by Christian and Jewish scholars alike is that the idea of a decisive rupture between Jews and Christians, which at one moment established Christianity as a separate religion, can no longer be historically sustained. Daniel Boyarin has suggested a totally different metaphor in place of the "fork in the road" that still influences our thinking. He points out that while French is today the official language on one side of a border, whereas Italian is spoken on the other side, in the early Middle Ages, the reality would have been quite different. Then one Romance dialect would have been spoken in Paris, and another in Rome, but as a traveler from Paris moved south toward the current border, there would have been no sudden change from one to the other. Rather, more and more elements of the Roman dialect would become apparent, and the Parisian elements would gradually become rarer, until the Italian elements began to predominate. Whether this analogy fits the reality of the first centuries may be debated, but it may well have reflected the reality on the ground in the year 50 or 100 or 150 more accurately than the image of travelers parting company at a fork.[5] Certainly a considerable body of believers who were in the middle — Jewish Christians who retained elements of both teachings — remained for several centuries.

The larger issue this raises is the relationship between contemporary historical scholarship and religious doctrine. For those with a fundamentalist approach to religion, the choice is clear: if historical critical scholarship leads to conclusions that contradict authoritative religious teaching, it must be refuted, condemned, rejected, or ignored. Most of us engaged in interreligious dialogue hold a position that takes seriously the best of contemporary scholarship as a tool to help us understand our respective religious traditions. Thus, as JP points out, the historical understanding raises significant problems with the doctrine that the Catholic Church was established by Jesus during his lifetime through his selection of Peter. Yet the preponderance of evidence is that the historical Jesus had no intention of establishing a separate religious entity, but that he remained throughout

---

5. Daniel Boyarin, *Dying for God: Martyrdom and the Making of Christianity and Judaism* (Stanford: Stanford University Press, 1999), p. 9.

his life within the spectrum of contemporary Jewish diversity. Does this mean that the statement "Thou art Peter, and upon this rock I establish my church . . ." (Matt. 16:18) was attributed to Jesus at a date significantly later than his death, in order to validate and justify the Roman church? And would such a conclusion have any real significance for the authority of the Roman papacy throughout history, and today?[6]

The same question of historical study and belief is of course relevant to Jews. Modern critical scholarship of the Bible, leading to the "documentary hypothesis," posed a significant challenge to the traditional belief that the entire Pentateuch was revealed by God to Moses on Mount Sinai in a form identical word for word with the accepted text today. Historical study of the rabbinic period and of Jewish law challenges the belief that the "oral law," which supplements the written law of the Torah, was also revealed at Sinai, transmitted orally through the centuries, and has always been unchanging.

The Progressive movements within Judaism have insisted that our beliefs must not be held with obliviousness to the truths established by historical scholarship. More recently the Conservative rabbi of a large Los Angeles congregation evoked considerable controversy in a sermon delivered to a full congregation on April 8, 2001, the first morning of Pesach, when he said that historical scholarship cannot sustain the accuracy of the narrative of the Egyptian enslavement and the Exodus recounted in the second book of the Torah.[7] Does that invalidate the holiday that was being celebrated by Jews throughout the world? Does it make any difference at all? This is an issue that Jews and Christians have in common, and should be the topic of fruitful discussion.

4. The Church, Anti-Judaism, and Antisemitism

At issue here is "the church's centuries-long record of contemptuous teachings against Jews." JP affirms that a theological understanding that

---

6. I once heard Professor George MacRae, a distinguished Jesuit New Testament scholar and Stillman Professor of Catholic Studies at Harvard Divinity School, say to a group of Roman Catholic undergraduates, "It is extremely unlikely that we can know for certain *anything* that Jesus actually said." That did not seem to affect his personal faith or his standing in the church.

7. The sermon was widely covered in the local, national, and international media (including Malissa Radler, "Conservative vs Orthodox: Did Exodus Happen?" *Jerusalem Post,* April 29, 2001; Gustav Niebuhr, "Religion Journal: A Rabbi's Look at Archaeology Touches a Nerve," *New York Times,* June 2, 2001).

Jews had been expelled from their former covenantal relationship with God because of their refusal to recognize the messiah when he came and their responsibility for his death "was not confined to academic realms but had terrible practical consequences for the members of the Jewish community throughout much of European history," and that this has implications for ecclesiology, the very nature of the church. Having taught this history for some thirty years, to students at Harvard Divinity School, to American undergraduates, and to European rabbinical students, I am certainly not unaware of the horrors of the historical record. Indeed, many Jews can recite a litany of horrors that they identify with Christianity and specifically the Catholic Church: Crusades, blood libel and ritual murder accusations, the required sign of identification on Jewish clothing, burning of the Talmud, charges of desecrating the consecrated host and poisoning the wells, Inquisition, Good Friday pogroms, expulsions — the list continues. It is certainly appropriate, indeed admirable, for Christians to recognize and confront this record. Yet a full historical understanding requires not just an honest recognition of the negative, but also an attempt to engage this material with balance and perspective.

To some extent, our evaluation of this material depends on our working assumptions about how different national, ethnic, or religious groups relate to each other. If we begin with the rather optimistic post-Enlightenment assumption that the normative model, the default pattern of intergroup relations, is one of mutual acceptance and respect, then we are surprised and appalled by the prevalence of hostility and violence throughout the centuries. But if we start with a somewhat more pessimistic assumption — that the default pattern is one of competition, tension, resentment, antipathy, hostility — an assumption that appears to be validated not only by the realm of nature but by the empirical evidence of our own time, then we might marvel more at the reality of coexistence when it appears.

And for well more than 1,000 years, when Christians had the power to eliminate Jews entirely from their realm, there was extensive coexistence. The central doctrine, to be sure, was that Jews were a reprobate people who had lost their special status in God's sight because of their behavior when the awaited messiah came. But another part of the central doctrine was that, nevertheless, God wanted the Jews to remain within the Christian world, continuing to observe their own traditions, and that it was a sinful violation of God's will to kill or even to harm Jews.

This teaching, formulated by Augustine and reiterated as the *Sicut*

Judaeis tradition by popes throughout the Middle Ages, was in its context a doctrine of toleration, which contrasted dramatically with the doctrine that there would be no toleration for pagans with their idolatrous worship, and no toleration for Christian heretics. Of course, the rationale for this tolera-tion of Jews — that Jews living a life of subservience in Christian society serve as a constant reminder of the consequences of rejecting God's messiah — does not begin to pass muster by contemporary standards.[8] But my guess is that Jews historically cared far less about the rationale provided for the doctrine than for the practical conclusion, expressed, for example, in a papal bull issued by Clement VI as anti-Jewish riots swept through Europe in the wake of the Black Death: "Let no Christian dare to wound or kill the Jews."[9]

In addition, there is a need to assess carefully the nature of the church's responsibility for the acts of persecution committed by medieval Christians. A quick review suggests that each category must be evaluated separately in order to make an appropriate moral judgment. Pope Urban II proclaimed what we call the First Crusade, and this remains a source of understandable tension with the Muslim world especially in the Middle East. But there was no anti-Jewish component in this papal summons, and the Crusaders who massacred Jews in the Rhineland in 1096 — whether or not their main motivation was religious zeal — were clearly acting in a manner that the popes did not permit or approve. Medieval and early modern popes consistently repudiated accusations of ritual murder and Jewish use of Christian blood as libels without any factual basis.

The Jewish badge was mandated by the Fourth Lateran Council, but this was in a society where *every* distinctive group was supposed to be identifiable by the clothing they wore. The investigation and burning of the Talmud at Paris in 1242 was indeed instigated by the papacy following

8. I have found that many students today focus on the negative discourse and some-times miss appreciating the substantive conclusion of medieval texts. For example, reading the sentence by Pope Gregory I, "For, when any one is brought to the font of baptism not by the sweetness of preaching but by compulsion, he returns to his former superstition, and dies the worse from having been born again," they respond, "How terrible that he refers to Judaism as a 'superstition,'" rather than appreciating the importance of this papal prohibi-tion against forced conversion. Jacob Rader Marcus, *The Jew in the Medieval World* (Cincinnati: HUC Press, 1999), p. 125.

9. Edward A. Synan, *The Popes and the Jews in the Middle Ages* (New York: Macmillan, 1967), p. 133; see Marcus, *The Jew in the Medieval World*, p. 52: "the Jews were burnt all the way from the Mediterranean into Germany, but not in Avignon, for the pope protected them there." This unambiguous condemnation during a period of widespread trauma might have served as a precedent worthy of emulation for Pope Pius XII in his Christmas message of 1942.

accusations that the Talmud contained intolerable language about Jesus (which it did), but subsequent popes relented and allowed Jews to retain their (suitably edited) Talmud texts without further interference until the era of the Reformation. The Inquisition had no jurisdiction over Jews per se, only over those defined by the church as Christian. Observing a Jewish practice or professing a Jewish belief was permitted for Jews; it was heresy only for Christians. And expulsions were the decisions of kings, not of popes; the European city with the longest uninterrupted Jewish residence, without any expulsion, is Rome.

All of this is not to deny the appalling acts that human beings committed in the name of religion. It is rather to suggest that generalizations about the history of the church's teaching of contempt for and cruel oppression of the Jews often require refinement and contextualization, lest they serve as a means to foster guilt among the descendants of the community of perpetrators, and self-righteousness among the descendants of the community of victims.

5. The Church's Teaching of Contempt and the Holocaust

This is a central theme in the article by JP, and a subsidiary but not inconsequential theme in the article by MB.

There is a spectrum of positions taken on the relationship between the legacy of the church's historical policies and doctrines regarding the Jewish people and the Shoah. One end of the spectrum is the case made several years ago by Daniel Goldhagen in *A Moral Reckoning: The Role of the Catholic Church in the Holocaust and Its Unfulfilled Duty of Repair* (New York: Knopf, 2002), arguing that the church continued to engage in the worst offenses of the past during the period of Nazi mass murder. More than just sins of omission — that the church "thundered silence," which can "reasonably be construed as approval" of the mass murder — Goldhagen accuses it of deep active involvement in the annihilation of the Jews. The church was directly implicated in crime by "providing the motive [to murder Jews] for many of the criminals." It was thereby as guilty of "criminal incitement" to murder as was Julius Streicher, convicted at Nuremberg of crimes against humanity. According to Goldhagen, during the Nazi period the church "wilfully, actively, and consistently [did] harm and promote[d] suffering" against the Jews. Church officials, high and low, "contributed to and in some cases engineered aspects of the mass murder itself." This is in my judgment a diatribe that no fair-minded reader can find remotely persuasive.[10]

The other extreme is to view Nazism as a neo-pagan attack on monotheistic religion in general, including Christianity, to emphasize the novelty of the Holocaust, and to conceptualize Nazi antisemitism and Nazi policy toward the Jews as a radical break from the past. JP notes that this appears to be the position held by Pope Benedict XVI.[11] I would point out that this is the way the Nazi onslaught was generally understood, or at least presented, by Jewish leaders in the 1930s and 1940s.[12] It is possible that this was a strategic decision made by Jews at the time: during a period when Jews felt increasingly isolated and desperately sought allies in the struggle against the Nazi regime, it made more sense to argue that they were only the first victims of an ideology that was fundamentally anti-religion in general, indeed opposed to all the best values of Western civilization. In this context, it would not have helped very much to turn against Christian leaders and say, "Look where your teachings have led." But the contemporary texts give the impression that they reflected what was genuinely believed by many at the time: that believing Christians and Jews were together endangered by the values of the Nazis.

Between these are intermediate positions, which recognize the novelty of Nazi antisemitism yet nevertheless insist on some degree of continuity with a legacy from the past. In our papers, MB writes that "it seems undeniable that the teachings of Christianity about Judaism played their own nefarious role. And at the heart of Christian teaching about Judaism was the accusation that Jews had killed Jesus and thus rejected God. To claim,

---

10. See my review of this book published in *America*, December 2, 2002: http://www.americamagazine.org/content/article.cfm?article_id=2647. For more moderate and responsible (though in my judgment not unproblematic) formulations of what I call the "continuity model" by Jules Isaac, James Parkes, Raul Hilberg, Hyam Maccoby, Dagobert D. Runes, Simon Wiesenthal, and Hal Lindsey, see Marc Saperstein, "Christian Doctrine and the 'Final Solution': The State of the Question," in *Remembering for the Future: The Holocaust in an Age of Genocide*, ed. John K. Roth, 3 vols. (Hampshire, UK: Palgrave Publishers, 2001), pp. 815-20 [814-41].

11. For formulations of what I call the "discontinuity model" by Marcel Simon, Yosef Yerushalmi, Richard Rubenstein, and Steven Katz, see Marc Saperstein, "Christian Doctrine and the 'Final Solution,'" pp. 820-22.

12. For examples, see Harold I. Saperstein, *Witness from the Pulpit: Topical Sermons 1933-1980* (Lanham, MD: Lexington Press, 2000), pp. 25-26 (1933), 42 (1934), 48-49 (1936). Saperstein here was following the approach of his teacher and mentor at the Jewish Institute of Religion, Rabbi Stephen S. Wise.

as did Catholic theologian Bernhard Bartmann, that by killing Jesus the Jews had rejected God was to provide a religious buttress for Nazi race hatred." JP writes that the Holocaust provided "compelling evidence of the continuing influence of its classic antisemitic tradition." Later he asserts that "we cannot obfuscate the fact that traditional Christianity provided an indispensable seedbed for the widespread support, or at least acquiescence, on the part of large numbers of baptized Christians during the Nazi attack on the Jews. . . . Christian antisemitism definitely had a major role in undergirding Nazism in its plan for Jewish extermination. . . ."

As indicated above (note 10), I have discussed at length the issue of continuity versus discontinuity in the historiography of the Holocaust. My own conclusion is that the element of continuity asserted in both of our essays is perhaps more complicated than it appears. The formulations cited from our authors — "provided an indispensable seedbed" and "a religious buttress for Nazi race hatred" and "undergirding Nazism in its plan for Jewish extermination" — rely on metaphors, not data, for their persuasive power. Although the power of such metaphors is considerable, we should be wary of allowing them to substitute for hard historical evidence that would support the assertion that the legacy of Christian anti-Jewish doctrines and policies was "indispensable" for the Nazi program of genocide against the Jewish people to be conceived and implemented. I am not persuaded that such evidence exists. The following points seem to me to problematize the metaphors of continuity:

- Mainstream Nazi antisemitic ideology, as expressed in the discourse of Hitler, Himmler, Goebbels, and others, did not draw on classical Christian religious motifs; it was rooted in nineteenth-century pseudo-scientific racist and mystical-nationalist thought. The Jew was mythologized as the Bolshevik Enemy — the sworn antagonist of the German people, the cause of the war, the reason for every German soldier's death — and dehumanized in pseudo-scientific categories, presented as vermin, bacilli, molecular parasites, pestilence-causing germs, all alien to traditional Christian discourse.[13]

13. A stunning example: asked how he could reconcile his participation in mass murder at Auschwitz with his Hippocratic Oath, SS physician Fritz Klein replied not that the Jews deserved to be killed because they had killed Jesus and were cursed by God, but that they had to be eradicated because when an appendix becomes infected, it must be removed, and the Jews were "the gangrenous appendix of mankind" (Ella Lingens-Reiner, *Prisoners of Fear* [London: Victor Gollancz, 1948], pp. 1-2, cited in Robert J. Lifton, *The Nazi Doctors* [New

- Research into the explanations given for joining the Nazi Party at a relatively early stage do not indicate traditional Christian belief (and in many cases do not even indicate antisemitic attitudes) as a factor. There is no correlation between voting for the Nazi Party in elections of the late 1920s and early 1930s and traditional religious belief. The Catholic Center Party was certainly not a stronghold of Nazi support; indeed it was the opposite.
- I know of no responsible Christian spokesman, whether Catholic or Protestant, who justified the mass murder of the Jews as consistent with Christian teachings.[14] The classical Catholic doctrine, as noted above, was that it was a sin against God's will to kill Jews.

My own position is, in a sense, rather more pessimistic than the claim that it required a "fertile field" of anti-Jewish teachings, cultivated over centuries, for the weeds of Nazi hatred to take root. All too many examples in recent times seem to reveal the capacity of totalitarian regimes in a relatively brief period to define a segment of the population as demonic, outside the circle of toleration, unworthy of life, and to find citizens ready to perpetrate mass murder against their former neighbors. The Nazis did use traditional Christian motifs as part of their pervasive propaganda machine, including the ritual murder charge in *Der Stürmer* and the horrendous passage in *Der Giftpilz (The Poison Mushroom)* cited by MB. But, in my judgment, the claim that these were an integral and necessary component of the development and implementation of mass murder remains to be demonstrated.

Significantly weaker is the assertion by Pope Benedict XVI (as Cardinal Ratzinger) that the legacy of traditional Christian anti-Judaism explains the "insufficient resistance to this atrocity" of genocide by Christians. That is a statement about bystanders, not perpetrators, and the distinction remains critical. Yet there were certainly many other explanations as well for the failure of Christians to resist the Nazi regime in its implementation of mass murder during the war. In occupied Poland, civilians knew that the punishment for sheltering a Jew who sought refuge at

---

York: Basic Books, 1986], pp. 15-16, 232, and see 488-89). See Hitler's metaphor in his letter of September 16, 1919, his first known antisemitic writing: "In [the Jew's] effects and consequences he is like a racial tuberculosis of the nations."

14. See on this issue Marc Saperstein, *Moments of Crisis in Jewish-Christian Relations* (London: SCM Press, 1989), p. 42 and especially n. 11 on p. 75, and the fuller discussion in "Christian Doctrine and the Holocaust," pp. 833-34.

their door was summary execution, and sometimes destruction of an entire village. Do we need the legacy of negative Christian teachings to explain the reluctance of the majority to resist the occupying power? Should we not appreciate the extraordinary courage of those who did, whether because of their religious convictions or despite them?[15]

The tendency today is to emphasize continuity, even by those who in different contexts will insist on the "uniqueness" of the Holocaust and who resent comparisons with other examples from the past in which Jews were persecuted. Many Jews are convinced that Treblinka and Auschwitz were simply the last scene in the sordid drama of Christian persecution of Jews beginning with the Gospels.[16] Perhaps we need to reexamine and reclaim the position that places more emphasis on the restraints imposed by the church throughout the Middle Ages, restraints that the Nazis (as the Communists) felt no longer applied to them.

15. See Nechama Tec, *When Light Pierced the Darkness: Christian Rescue of Jews in Nazi-Occupied Poland* (Oxford: Oxford University Press, 1986), pp. 64-68 on execution of Poles who sheltered Jews and burning of their villages; and pp. 57-58 on saving behavior *despite* traditional antisemitic attitudes.

16. Thus, for example, Hyam Maccoby: "As a result of the Gospel story, the Jews were made into an outcast, accursed nation in Christendom and were persecuted in all Christian lands. The massacre of six million Jews in Nazi Europe was only the most recent and worst of these persecutions" (*New Society*, January 6, 1983).

Reading the Epistle to the Hebrews Without Presupposing Supersessionism

Jesper Svartvik

1. Introduction

The Epistle to the Hebrews has been an exceptionally significant text in Christian-Jewish relations. In particular, certain passages have been interpreted in ways that assume that Christianity supersedes Judaism.[1] Whereas biblical scholars continue to grapple with the "whence" of Hebrews (i.e., authorship, context, genre, structure, date, etc.), no one can be in doubt of its "whither."[2] This anonymous text of unknown origin, with its tremendously influential metaphors and thoughts, has been at the very center of Christian theology in at least three respects.

First, the author of Hebrews uses first-century sacrificial nomenclature when interpreting the life and death of Jesus of Nazareth: Jesus is be-

---

1. Daniel J. Harrington, *What Are They Saying About Hebrews?* (New York/Mahwah, NJ: Paulist, 2005), actually seems to state the opposite (p. 2: "Hebrews is one of the more neglected writings in the New Testament"), but he is referring to another question, i.e., to what extent the text is *explicitly* discussed. In the present chapter it is argued that Hebrews *implicitly* has set the tone and provided the discourse for Christian-Jewish relations. For a similar understanding, see Harrington, p. 4: ". . . [the author of Hebrews] is more responsible than any other New Testament writer for our expression 'Old Testament.'"

2. For introductions to Hebrews, in addition to Harrington, *What Are They Saying About Hebrews?* see, e.g., Craig R. Koester, *Hebrews* (New York: Doubleday, 2001), and, especially, Andrew Lincoln, *Hebrews: A Guide* (London: T. & T. Clark, 2006). For an anthology with numerous relevant articles, see Gabriella Gelardini, ed., *Hebrews: Contemporary Methods — New Insights* (Leiden/Boston: Brill, 2005).

Thanks are due to Johannes Börjesson, Mary Boys, Hans Hermann Henrix, Astrid Hotze, Göran Larsson, and Inger Nebel for stimulating discussions and constructive criticism.

ing compared both to the high priest who brings forth the sacrifice (e.g., 6:20 and 10:12) and to the sacrifice being brought forth (8:12-14). He is also compared to the veil that separated the Holy of Holies from the rest of the Holy (10:20) (Hebrew: *parokhet*, e.g., Exod. 26:33; Greek: *katapetasma*). Due to this metaphorical multiplicity, the various images collide. If they are taken too literally, they negate each other: in a literal sense, he cannot be the high priest, the sacrifice, and the veil at the same time.

Second, this epistle played an important role in early Christian debates on whether it was possible for Christians to return to faith after having relapsed. We ought to ask ourselves whether it is a coincidence that Hebrews, emphasizing the *one*-ness of Jesus' sacrifice, also wrestles — perhaps more than any other early Christian text — with the question of whether there is forgiveness a *second* time for sinners.[3] In other words, is there a connection between the emphasis of a sacrificial *ephapax* (Heb. 9:12, "once for all") and the once-for-all forgiveness?[4] Is there a correspondence between a daily forgiveness and a discourse of continuing sacrifice?[5] Is the Christian church primarily a society of saints or a school for sinners?[6]

Third, another area of immeasurable influence is the discourse of an "old" and a "new" covenant in a salvation history approach.[7] This has led to a default setting of much Christian theology when it comes to Christian-Jewish relations as comparative, i.e., that Christianity is "better" than Judaism. This is certainly not isolated exclusively to Christian-Jewish

3. See, e.g., Hebrews 6:4-6 and 10:26f.

4. See, e.g., 10:14, which maintains that by one offering Jesus has perfected forever those who are being sanctified. See also v. 18, which emphasizes that no sacrifice is needed if there are no sins to forgive.

5. For a similar train of thought, see Nehemia Polen, "Leviticus and Hebrews . . . and Leviticus," pp. 213-25 in *The Epistle to the Hebrews and Christian Theology*, ed. Richard Bauckham et al. (Grand Rapids/Cambridge: Eerdmans, 2009), pp. 224f.: "Hebrews argues for *perfection*, . . . Leviticus glories in the endless *repetition* . . ." (italics added).

6. It may be necessary to emphasize that this is a corollary to the key question in Hebrews, which is that the implied readers are exhorted not to apostatize. In the history of interpretation of Hebrews, however, the question of school for sinners versus society of saints has been central. In addition, we see that the author does not consider the recipients of the epistle to be flawless; see, e.g., 5:12 (they should, by now, be *didaskaloi*, but instead they themselves need someone to teach them the basics of the word of God) and 12:7-13 (the *paideia* motif).

7. Michael D. Morrison draws our attention to the fact that Hebrews, although the text comprises less than 5 percent of the NT, has more than 50 percent of all NT occurrences of the word *diathēkē* ("covenant"); see *Who Needs a New Covenant? Rhetorical Function of the Covenant Motif in the Argument of Hebrews* (Eugene, OR: Pickwick, 2008), p. xi.

relations, but it is, no doubt, accentuated in an unparalleled way in Christian-Jewish encounters. Few Christians in the pews and ministers in the pulpits would spontaneously argue that Christianity has "fulfilled" Hinduism or "terminated" Buddhism. Those Christians who are critical of other faith traditions are perhaps inclined to state that these are "at fault"; but when it comes to Judaism, it is likely that they would assert that Christianity is "better" than Judaism and that Judaism, theologically speaking, has ceased to exist after Christ.[8]

In short, it seems that few biblical texts have influenced Christians' understanding of the relation between Jews and Christians more than has Hebrews. Its impact is enormous, and a past without its *Wirkungsgeschichte* ("the effective history," i.e., the text's influence) is unimaginable.[9] Subsequent christological thinking has been nourished from Hebrews, but detrimental models of how to understand Judaism have also profited from this epistle. In the words of Jennifer L. Koosed, ". . . when the old covenant is labelled 'obsolete' (8:13) it is only a small shift to imagine the old covenant people as 'obsolete' as well."[10] Now, given this alleged supersessionist — or even anti-Jewish — theology of Hebrews, should not those interested in improved Christian-Jewish relations simply avoid, ignore, or dismiss Hebrews? Indeed, William Klassen asks whether it is the epistle *to* the Hebrews or, rather, *against* the Hebrews.[11] The student of Hebrews soon recognizes that it is, at least, often *inter-*

8. Lincoln, *Hebrews*, p. 26, points out that Hebrews begins with a comparison between God speaking in former times and in the last days. In his famous address in Mainz in 1980, Pope John Paul II described the relation between Jews and Christians with the help of covenant terminology: ". . . the meeting between the people of God of the old covenant, which has never been revoked by God . . . and the people of God of the new covenant . . . ," quoted in, e.g., Norbert Lohfink, *The Covenant Never Revoked: Biblical Reflections on Christian-Jewish Dialogue*, trans. John J. Scullion (New York/Mahwah: Paulist, 1991 [German: *Der niemals gekündigte Bund: Exegetische Gedanken zum christlich-jüdischen Gespräch*, 1989]), p. 5.

9. For a summary of the *Wirkungsgeschichte*, see, e.g., Koester, *Hebrews*, pp. 19-63. Numerous scholars distinguish reception history from effective history. Whereas the former refers to the *explicit* usage (i.e., references and quotations) of a text, the latter includes also the *unintentional* and *involuntary* impact of a text.

10. Jennifer L. Koosed, "Double Bind: Sacrifice in the Epistle to the Hebrews," in *A Shadow of Glory: Reading the New Testament after the Holocaust*, ed. Tod Linafelt (London: Routledge, 2002), pp. 95, 96.

11. William Klassen, "To the Hebrews or Against the Hebrews? Anti-Judaism and the Epistle to the Hebrews," in *Anti-Judaism in Early Christianity. Volume 2: Separation and Polemic*, ed. Stephen G. Wilson (Waterloo, ON: Wilfred Laurier University, 1986), pp. 1-16.

preted as a letter against the Hebrews. If this were the case, should those involved in interfaith relations refer to and read other biblical texts — and leave this epistle to those who wish to give vent to a supersessionist theology, which holds that Christianity has replaced Judaism?[12]

In this chapter it is argued that we should do exactly the opposite: we need to reread Hebrews and ask questions of importance to interreligious relations: Is Hebrews inevitably a stumbling block or might it be understood as a steppingstone?[13] In the following discussion I will argue that there is in this particular epistle a potential for vitalization of the current discussion.[14] Three questions will be posed. First, we must address the issue of polyphony in the biblical texts. Not only are there different emphases in different books in the Bible, but we might even detect different emphases in one and the same verse, depending on which version of the Bible we are reading. Second, what is it that the author of Hebrews is referring to when he writes about ". . . what is becoming obsolete and growing old is ready to vanish away"?[15] Is he actually talking about Judaism, about God's covenant with the Jewish people? Third, we have to ask whether interpreters of Hebrews have acknowledged sufficiently the pilgrimage motif in Hebrews. What would happen if they did?

---

12. *Nostra Aetate* refers to and quotes biblical texts that underline the continuity, e.g., Romans 9:4f. and 11:17-24.

13. For three examples of rereadings of Hebrews, see Pamela Eisenbaum, "Hebrews, Supersessionism and Jewish-Christian Relations" (http://www.hebrews.unibas.ch/documents/2005Eisenbaum.pdf); Robert P. Gordon, *Hebrews*, 2nd ed. (Sheffield: Sheffield Phoenix Press, 2008), pp. 36-53; and Richard B. Hays, "'Here We Have No Lasting City': New Covenantalism in Hebrews," in *The Epistle to the Hebrews and Christian Theology*, pp. 151-73, esp. 151f.

14. One of the many important issues to consider is the time perspective in Hebrews. A careful reading of Hebrews provokes a series of crucial questions, one of which is whether its author believed that the end was near. If yes, we need to ask whether the author was wrong. If yes, must we not read the verdict on "the old covenant" in the light of this insight? That these questions are inevitable for the student of Hebrews becomes evident when we consider that the verb *palaioun* ("to grow old") occurs twice in the text, once referring to the old covenant and once referring to the end of this *aiōn*, this age. Indeed, it is no minor insight that this world has been around for 2,000 years longer than most early Christians imagined when they wrote the texts.

15. Ruth Hoppin, *Priscilla's Letter: Finding the Author of the Epistle to the Hebrews* (San Francisco: Christian UP, 1997), argues that a woman named Priscilla or Prisca wrote the epistle, but since she has not convinced all scholars, we will refer to the author as "he," without arguing that it necessarily has to have been written by a man.

2. Comparing the Hebrew and Greek Versions of the Bible: The Complexities of a "Biblical Understanding"

A mentality that haunts and paralyzes Christian-Jewish relations is the quest for the alleged "biblical" understanding of the relation between the two religions. Nothing is said explicitly in the Bible about Hinduism, Buddhism, and Islam. Hence, those who want "biblical" advice have to find analogies, but quite a number of readers of the Bible see it as establishing the fundamental contours of Christian-Jewish relations. In addition to the fact that such an approach is downright anachronistic (there was no "Christianity" in any historical sense at the time of the composition of the Hebrew Bible, and what we today know as "Judaism" and "Christianity," respectively, were not forged in New Testament times), it also disallows a meaningful debate. The purpose of the following discussion is to highlight the deficiencies of such a presupposition, because those in quest of an alleged "biblical" understanding are faced with a tough choice between reading the Bible in the original and reading one of its translations. It is generally recognized that the author of Hebrews quotes or alludes to the Septuagint (i.e., the most influential translation of the Hebrew Bible into Greek; abbreviated "LXX"), which at times deviates from the Masoretic text (i.e., the authoritative version of the Hebrew Bible with vowels and other diacritical marks).[16] The most relevant passage to this assessment is Hebrews 8:8f., which describes the relation between two covenants:

> The days will come, says the Lord, when I will establish a new covenant with the house of Israel and with the house of Judah; not like the covenant that I made with their fathers on the day when I took them by the hand to lead them out of the land of Egypt; for they did not continue in my covenant, so *I paid no heed to them,* says the Lord. (italics added)

The last sentence is undoubtedly the cornerstone in much of Christian supersessionist theology: the people of Israel no longer find favor with the God of Israel, because God has made the Christian church a new declara-

---

16. On the ideology of LXX, see Naomi Seidman, *Faithful Renderings: Jewish-Christian Difference and the Politics of Translation* (Chicago/London: University of Chicago Press, 2006). For a study on the relation between the LXX and Hebrews, see Radu Gheorghita, *The Role of the Septuagint in Hebrews: An Investigation of Its Influence with Special Consideration to the Use of Hab 2:3-4 in Heb 10:37-38* (Tübingen: Mohr [Siebeck], 2003).

tion of love.[17] What obstructs this understanding, however, is that this passage is radically different in the Hebrew original in Jeremiah 31:31f.:

> The days are surely coming, says the Lord, when I will make a new covenant with the house of Israel and the house of Judah. It will not be like the covenant that I made with their ancestors when I took them by the hand to bring then out of the land of Egypt — a covenant that they broke, *though I was their husband*, says the Lord. (italics added)[18]

Admittedly, there are several possible ways to translate Jeremiah 31:31 (Hebrew: . . . *asher-hemah heferu et-beriti we-anokhi ba'alti vam*). The two most obvious are likely "although they broke the covenant, I remained faithful to them" or "in spite of the fact that I was their Lord, they broke the covenant." But no matter how we choose to interpret the Hebrew text, we are faced with the greater question: How are we to explain the substantial difference between Hebrews 8:9 and Jeremiah 31:32? It is, indeed, an insurmountable difference between the perspectives in the two texts, between, on the one hand, the Greek version (". . . I paid no heed to them . . .") and, on the other hand, the Hebrew text (". . . though I was their husband . . ."). The Septuagint describes a relation that has been terminated, God is seeking a divorce; the Hebrew uses traditional covenantal and matrimonial language, God wants to continue the relationship. Both the Septuagint and Hebrews use the verb *amelein*, meaning "to ignore," "not to care about," "to abandon." In the Hebrew Bible we find the verb *ba'al*, which can be translated as "to be a husband," "to be faithful," "to be the Lord."[19]

How should we explain the difference between the Hebrew phrase in the Masoretic text and the Greek text of the Septuagint, which is quoted in Hebrews? The two most plausible suggestions seem to be that the translators of the Septuagint either (a) were translating from a Hebrew manuscript that contained the almost homophone (i.e., sounding almost in the same way) and *homoscripta* (i.e., looking similar in Hebrew square writing) word *ga'al*, which means "to despise," "to abandon," or (b) misread

17. It should be noted that a sacramental understanding of Christian marriage, i.e., that marriage is for life and cannot be replaced by another relation, does not seem to have prevented Christian replacement theology.

18. Jeremiah 31:32 in the Masoretic text corresponds to 38:32 in the LXX.

19. Luke Timothy Johnson translates the LXX sentence as "'and I grew unconcerned about them'. . . . The verb *amelein* can scarcely be understood in any other way," see *Hebrews: A Commentary* (Louisville/London: Westminster/John Knox, 2006), p. 207. See also his excursus on "Old and New Covenants," pp. 210-15.

the very manuscript that they were translating, understanding the *baʿal* as *gaʿal*. If one of these suggestions is correct, then the argument of Hebrews 8 is actually based upon a reading that is fundamentally different from the Masoretic text. In turn, this means that those who use Hebrews 8:9 as a cornerstone for their theology at the same time silently confess that the Hebrew *Vorlage* ("prototype") in Jeremiah 31:31f. is without importance. In other words, it is crucial to draw attention to the fact that it is not a question of being "biblical" or "unbiblical," but rather a premeditated or unpremeditated choice between two biblical manuscript traditions. It is certainly not a matter of "to have and have not" a biblical understanding. Hence, the readers should ask themselves whether *baʿal* ("to be faithful") or *gaʿal* ("to despise") best represents how the God of Israel is described in the biblical texts *in toto*.

3. What Is It That Is "Growing Old"?

If we are in search of a single verse in Hebrews that has shaped Christian-Jewish relations, we have to turn to 8:13: "In speaking of a new covenant he treats the first as obsolete. And what is becoming obsolete and growing old is ready to vanish away" (*en to[i] legein kainēn pepalaiōken tēn prōtēn. To de palaioumenon kai gēraskon engys aphanisamou*).

Christians are so used to referring to the Jewish Bible as "the Old Testament" and to Judaism as "the old covenant" that they might not be able to see what the author here actually has in view. They might forget that this was in no way an established discourse — and "the old covenant" was certainly not a technical term for Second Temple Judaism — at the time of the composition of Hebrews. Hence, there are good reasons for avoiding the offensive term "Late Judaism," which claims that Judaism ceased to exist after the rise of Christianity.[20] For this reason we have to pose the principal

---

20. For an article on the interpretations of *diathēkē* ("covenant") in Hebrews, see Scott W. Hahn, "Covenant, Cult, and the Curse-of-Death: *Diathēkē* in Heb 9:15-22," in Gelardini, ed., *Hebrews: Contemporary Methods — New Insights*, pp. 65-88. Hahn argues that *diathēkē* consistently be understood within the cultic-covenantal framework, see p. 85. For the pejorative term "Late Judaism" (German: *Spätjudentum*), see, e.g., Gabriele Boccaccini, *Middle Judaism: Jewish Thought, 300 B.C.E. to 200 C.E.*, with a foreword by James H. Charlesworth (Minneapolis: Fortress, 1991), p. 21. (On p. 49, Boccaccini argues that this term was not coined until 1903, which seems to be incorrect, as it can be found in scholarly literature dating from the nineteenth century.)

question: Exactly what it is that is "growing old" in Hebrews 8:13? The last word in this verse *(aphanismos)* is a so-called *hapax legomenon* in the New Testament, i.e., it occurs only once in the textual corpus. It stems from the letter *a*, called *alpha privativum* ("not"), and the verb *phainein* ("to be seen"). Once again, what is it that soon *(engys)* will vanish away? Is the author actually stating that "Judaism" will soon disappear, or is this an anachronistic reading? What happens when we read Hebrews without presupposing supersessionism?

Two things need to be pointed out before we continue our investigation. First, a fact that complicates the interpretation of Hebrews is that the author is notoriously ambiguous in his usage of what is often referred to as the "horizontal" and "vertical" parameters. These two terms refer to a *temporal* understanding (the horizontal parameter: "already now, but not yet") and a *spatial* dichotomy (the vertical parameter: "earthly" and "heavenly").[21]

Second, already after a perusal of Hebrews it becomes obvious that the author seeks to convince the readers that Jesus of Nazareth supersedes everything: this world, the present *aiōn;* indeed, everything that has previously been seen and heard. This way of comparing the Christ event with everything else is inevitably part and parcel of the author's theology, mainly because the epistle gives vent to the philosophical ideas of Middle Platonism, which was in flower from roughly the mid-second century B.C.E. to the late third century C.E. One of its key elements

> . . . was a dualistic cosmology, in which this material world was viewed as transient and unstable in comparison with the invisible permanent world of ideal reality. What happened in the material world could be seen as insubstantial shadows and copies of the real world of beauty and truth. To find fulfillment and achieve their true destiny people needed, therefore, to escape from the physical world and return to their souls' true home in that other upper world.[22]

How can we interpret Hebrews 8:13 without anachronistically presupposing supersessionism? It might be good to start by analyzing the context, i.e., the intriguing metaphors in chapter 9. In what way does the author

21. See, e.g., Johnson, *Hebrews,* p. 218: "The author works with two basic axes. One is spatial, the other is temporal. Each axis, however, is itself polyvalent; and, to make matters even more confusing, Hebrews is capable of merging the two."

22. Lincoln, *Hebrews,* p. 45.

employ the two concepts "the outer [lit. 'the first'] tent" (*hē prōtē skēnē;* Heb. 9:2, 6, and 8) and "the inner [lit. 'the second'] tent" (*hē deuterē skēnē;* Heb. 9:3)? It has already been mentioned that the author of Hebrews frequently merges horizontal and vertical images, and this seems to be such an instance. Craig R. Koester points out that it is difficult to interpret this tabernacle symbolism "because the imagery is not stable."[23] What makes it difficult to understand and easy to misunderstand is that *spatial* categories are being referred to in order to enlighten an argument based on *temporal* categories. According to various commentators the tabernacle refers to the Torah, the Temple, Judaism, and the "old covenant," which have all been replaced by Christianity.[24] But the expressions "the first tent" and "the second tent" are not chronological descriptions of the first tabernacle in the desert and the temples in Jerusalem in contrast to the Christian era. To what, then, do they refer?

It is imperative to note that Hebrews 9:9 explicitly states that "the outer tent" is symbolic for *the present age (hētis parabolē eis ton kairon ton enestēkota).*[25] According to this line of thought, *prōtos* refers to the present age, to earthly life (see 9:1), and *deuteros* refers to the *coming world,* to the future, to heaven. This is not farfetched, since, as Koester points out, "The Tabernacle's two chambers were said to represent earth and heaven."[26] For Middle Platonists, such as the author of Hebrews, earthly life was less than satisfactory compared to the invisible reality. The mistake some — if not most — interpreters of the New Testament make, however, is that they take for granted that the invisible reality to which the author is referring — and longing — is "Christendom," which allegedly has replaced "Judaism," but this is an anachronistic reading.[27]

It is therefore crucial to note that in 9:8 the outer tent refers to the present age: "the way into the sanctuary is *not yet opened as long as the outer tent* [symbolic for *the present age*] *is still standing.*" Once we have detected that a *spatial* metaphor refers to that moment in *time* we have several possibilities. First, if the text predates Jerusalem's fall in 70 c.e. the rea-

23. Koester, *Hebrews,* p. 400. There are also, in addition, differences between the descriptions in the Pentateuch and in Hebrews; see pp. 402-4.

24. See, e.g., Koester, *Hebrews,* pp. 393-406.

25. See Koester, *Hebrews,* p. 398: "Most take it as the author's own time."

26. Koester, *Hebrews,* p. 401.

27. Koester, *Hebrews,* p. 405. See also Mathias Rissi, *Die Theologie des Hebräerbriefs: Ihre Verankerung in der Situation des Verfassers und seiner Leser* (Tübingen: Mohr [Siebeck], 1987), pp. 41-43.

son might be that the author longs for the destruction of the Temple and would applaud it as a victory of the invisible reality over against the visible world. But is this realistic? A second possibility is that if the text is written after the fall of the Temple, the author might be referring to the tabernacle in order to avoid mentioning the Temple.[28] A third option is that the spatial metaphor refers to chronology and eschatology, regardless of the date of Hebrews, be it a pre-70 or a post-70 c.e. document.[29] In the following discussion we will see that the third suggestion is the most plausible.

What is so important to the author — and, hence, also to the reader — is that *the outer tent is still standing.*[30] In other words, in the ninth chapter there is a contrast between the present tense and the future. The author states that he is living in the present time (9:9: *eis ton kairon ton enestēkota*), but that he longs for "the time of a better order" (9:10: *mechri kairou diorthōseōs epikeimena*). The author argues that the invisible service — impossible to see for our human eyes and impossible to hear for our ears, and impossible to grasp for our minds — is already going on, in which Jesus Christ serves as the high priest. But the time of the new covenant has not been realized, not yet. It is in this context that the statement in Hebrews 8:13 should and must be read. Hence, the verse should not be interpreted as a prediction of the fall of the Temple (or, if Hebrews is a post-70 c.e. document, as theological *Schadenfreude*), but as *an eschatological expectation,* as a longing for the future, a yearning for a fulfilled and perfected world. In the words of Peter Tomson: "The 'new covenant,' if we may thus accentuate it, is valid only in heaven, not yet upon earth. The 'good things,' of which Christ is the direct image, are yet to come."[31]

---

28. See, e.g., Morna D. Hooker, "Christ, the 'End' of the Cult," in *The Epistle to the Hebrews and Christian Theology,* p. 207: "If our author was writing after a.d. 70, then the catastrophic events in Jerusalem could have provided the spark which led our author to think of Christ as replacing the cult."

29. It should be pointed out that the tablets of the Law were kept in the *deuteros* of the tabernacle.

30. Sacrifices belong to the present age because in the world to come there is no need for sacrifices; the Law, however, awaits the people of God in the future, in the *deuteros.*

31. Peter Tomson, *"If This Be from Heaven": Jesus and the New Testament Authors in Their Relationship to Judaism* (Sheffield: Sheffield Academic Press, 2001), p. 362. See also Knut Backhaus, "Das wandernde Gottesvolk — am Scheideweg. Der Hebräerbrief und Israel," in *"Nun steht aber diese Sache im Evangelium . . ." Zur Frage nach den Anfängen des christliche Antijudaismus,* ed. Rainer Kampling (Paderborn: Schöningh, 1999), pp. 301-20, and Martin Karrer, "Der Hebräerbrief," in *Einleitung in das Neue Testament,* ed. Martin Ebner and Stefan Schreiber (Stuttgart: Kohlhammer, 2008), pp. 474-95.

Tomson is not alone when underlining that "Judaism" and "Christian-ity" are not being compared in Hebrews — as if such a comparison could be made during the first century c.e. — but "present time" and "future," earth and heaven. Clark M. Williamson and Ronald J. Allen draw a similar conclusion: "Heaven is a place of perfection, which in this sermon refers to immediate access to God. To be perfected is to be in the full, immediate presence of God. The earth is a realm of imperfection in which access to God is partial and available only through intermediaries."[32]

When the new time comes, there is no need for a temple, because on that day there will be nothing but a heavenly service. This perspective dominates also in Revelation, the most apocalyptic text in the entire New Testament: "Behold, the dwelling of God is with men. He will dwell with them, and they shall be his people, and God himself will be with them. . . . And I saw no temple in the city, for its temple is the Lord God the Al-mighty and the Lamb."[33]

As time went by, Christian theologians would regularly describe Juda-ism as "the old covenant," but that is not what the author of Hebrews is re-ferring to. In this profoundly eschatological text, what the author refers to is actually *the present age,* which he hopes will soon vanish away.[34]

In addition, we have to consider how to interpret the verb *palaioun* ("to grow old") in 8:13. The verb occurs three times in the NT: once in the Gospel of Luke and twice in the Epistle to the Hebrews. The Lukan protag-onist in 12:33 encourages his disciples to sell what they have and give alms, so that they provide themselves moneybags that *do not grow old,* a treasure in the heavens, that does not fail as do earthly goods. The Lukan usage of the verb is set in a comparison between earthly possessions (which are per-ishable) and the heavenly treasure (which never grows old). A similar us-age of the verb is found in Hebrews 1:10-12 (quoting Ps. 101:26-28): "And,

32. Clark M. Williamson and Ronald J. Allen, *Interpreting Difficult Texts* (London/Phil-adelphia: SCM/Trinity, 1989), p. 53. They are not as explicit in this respect as is Tomson. On the one hand, they argue that "in a direct and forceful way Hebrews claims that Judaism is a second-rate religion," (p. 54) but, on the other hand, they point out that "[t]he gospel itself compels us to criticize these texts so that justice may be done to the Jewish community, and so that our interpretation of the texts does not deny the promise of the love of God to each and all" (p. 55).

33. Revelation 21:3 and 22.

34. The author seems to argue that the new era to a certain extent already has com-menced; see, e.g., 9:11, which both says that Christ, on the one hand, has already appeared *(paragenomenos)* and, on the other hand, that he is a high priest for the things to come *(archiereus tōn genomenōn agathōn).*

'In the beginning, Lord, you founded the earth, and the heavens are the work of your hands; they will perish, but you remain; they will all wear out like clothing; like a cloak you will roll them up, and like clothing they will be changed. But you are the same, and your years will never end.'"

It is essential to note that it is "the heavens" that "will all wear out [*palaiōthēsontai*] like clothing." At a first glance, Luke 13:22 and Hebrews 1:11 might seem to contradict each other since they both refer to "the heavens," but, as a matter of fact, they point in the same direction. They both contrast the transience of earthly existence (including "the heavens" of *this* world) with divine reality. How, then, is *palaioun* used in the third, and last, instance in the New Testament? In Hebrews 8:13 it is often understood as referring to the fact that "Christianity" supersedes "Judaism." We have already seen that in 1:11 it refers to the fact that this world in which we are living will not last forever. One day the heavens and the earth will "grow old" — but God will remain. *It is ironical that the mainstream interpretation of Hebrews reverses these two statements: a majority of commentators would probably argue that God actually does change, since God is understood as someone who prefers newer religion to older religions, wishing that the latter soon disappear.* This understanding is the very opposite of what the author of Hebrews asserts, namely, that "But you [i.e., God] are the same" (Heb. 1:11).

4. The Pilgrimage Motif in Christianity

In 1937 Ernst Käsemann gave a sermon on Isaiah 26:13 ("O Lord our God, other lords besides you have ruled over us, but we acknowledge your name alone") and was imprisoned by the Gestapo for insubordination. It was in his prison cell that he wrote the manuscript to his book *The Wandering People of God: An Investigation of the Letter to the Hebrews,* the purpose of which was to unveil the pilgrimage motif in Hebrews: *"the form of existence in time appropriate to the recipient of the revelation can only be that of wandering."*[35] He argued that this pilgrimage motif was due to Gnostic influence, but it is far more plausible to understand it as an expression of an eschatological frame of reference. Nevertheless, his unveil-

---

35. Ernst Käsemann, *The Wandering People of God: An Investigation of the Letter to the Hebrews,* trans. Roy A. Harrisville and Irving L. Sandberg (Minneapolis: Augsburg, 1984 [German: *Das wandernde Gottesvolk: Eine Untersuchung zum Hebräerbrief,* 1957]), p. 19 (italics as in the original).

ing of the wandering people theme in Hebrews is a lasting contribution to the scholarly discussion.

In an illuminating article William G. Johnsson, too, has explored the pilgrimage motif in Hebrews. He argues that both the terminology ("rest," "alienation," "homeland," etc.) and the structure of the epistle support this thesis.[36] It seems reasonable to assume that there is a pilgrimage motif in Hebrews, which is most palpable in passages toward the end of the epistle, such as 11:15f. ("But as it is, they desire a better country, that is, a heavenly one. . . . God . . . has prepared a city for them") and 13:14 ("For here we have no lasting city, but we are looking for the city that is to come"). A holistic interpretation of Hebrews must take this motif into consideration. In a similar way, Richard B. Hays states that Hebrews has "a remarkably open-ended eschatology."[37]

However, the traditional and polemical reading of Hebrews tends to conceal this important motif. In Hebrews 12:18-29, the author compares the Jewish master story, i.e., the revelation at Mount Sinai, to his own understanding of his readers' coming to "Mount Zion and to the city of the living God, the heavenly Jerusalem" (Heb. 12:22). Now, is it important to recognize not only the difference (Sinai vis-à-vis Zion) but also the similarity, i.e., that the implicit readers of Hebrews are standing at the foot of a holy mountain. They are in front of Mount Zion, they are standing before the gates of Jerusalem, *but they have not yet entered the city.* In other words, *the "not yet" element is manifest even in arguably the most "realized eschatology" paragraph in the entire epistle.* This observation leads to the conclusion that the pilgrimage motif in Hebrews is even stronger than the realization of the promises. It is even more of "not yet" than "already now" in the entire epistle, also in these passages.[38] *Nothing suggests that the readers of the epistle are any less a wan-*

36. William G. Johnsson, "The Pilgrimage Motif in the Book of Hebrews," *Journal of Biblical Literature* 97, no. 2 (1978): 239-51. In his Ph.D. dissertation ("The Muslim Pilgrimage: Journey to the Center," University of Chicago, 1967), using a phenomenological model, H. B. Partin wants to identify the religious structure of pilgrimage. He argues that there are *four* essential elements. Johnsson presents these four criteria and seeks to find parallels in Hebrews: (a) he argues that the motif of *separation* is strong in Hebrews; (b) there is certainly a motif of *journeying to a sacred place;* (c) the *fixed purpose* of this journey is a dissatisfaction with what is "home" to others; and (d) being on the way involves various kinds of *hardship.*

37. Hays, "'Here We Have No Lasting City,'" p. 166.

38. It is often recognized that there is a tension between "already now" and "not yet" in Hebrews. One of the most palpable examples is 4:9-11 and 12:18-24. One wonders whether the addressees are supposed to look upon themselves as being on their way ("not yet") or already at the goal ("already now"). If they are already in the heavenly Jerusalem, why should

dering people than is Israel. As a matter of fact, it is the pilgrimage motif which is the very basis for the typological reading. If the readers of Hebrews were not wanderers, the type would not fit the *antitype*. In this light the profoundly eschatological framework of Hebrews comes into sight.

It seems that Hebrews is often quoted in two contexts: chapters 8 and 9 are referred to in *polemical* milieux, first and foremost in various anti-Jewish diatribes. Other texts are cited in *parenetical* (i.e., exhortatory) situations, e.g., 13:13f.: "Let us then go to him outside the camp and bear the abuse he endured. For here we have no lasting city, but we are looking for the city that is to come." It is intriguing to note that readers detect the eschatological perspective in the parenetical passages, but that somehow they tend not to see it in the polemical paragraphs. A holistic reading of the epistle would suggest that the author is no less eschatological in chapters 8 and 9 than in chapter 13.

An important aspect of the mainstream interpretation of Hebrews is that all the prophecies in the Hebrew Bible are being fulfilled in and with Jesus of Nazareth. The words of the prophet Isaiah about the suffering servant are fulfilled in Jesus, the words of the prophet Jeremiah about a new covenant are fulfilled in Jesus, and the vision of the prophet Ezekiel about a time when human hearts of stone will be replaced are being fulfilled in and with the Christian church. But is this true? Have all hearts of stone disappeared? Is it true that Christians need not teach each other? Do all Christians know the Lord — from the smallest to the greatest?

Does the answer to these questions suggest that a church that understands itself to be on its way should be an *ecclesia docens* ("a teaching church") as well as an *ecclesia discens* ("a learning church")? Once again, the implied readers of Hebrews are no less a wandering people than is Israel. In the words of Hays: "A strong dialectical eschatology tends to temper triumphalist supersessionism, for those who know that they have no lasting city are likely to recognize that they themselves stand under impending judgment. Perhaps they are also more likely to recognize the provisional character of their own understanding and to acknowledge that God's ultimate redemptive grace may yet hold surprises."[39]

---

they continue their pilgrimage? In addition, it is also intriguing that the author argues that the physical Mount Sinai is "so fearful" *(outō phoberon)* and the eschatological Mount Zion — the Heavenly Jerusalem, the city of the living God who, surrounded by thousands of angels, will judge all — would be *less* terrifying.

39. Hays, "'Here We Have No Lasting City,'" pp. 166f.

5. Conclusion: Reading Hebrews
Without Presupposing Supersessionism

Many interpreters read the New Testament through the lens of a limited number of programmatically understood verses. One of these paradigmatic statements is Hebrews 8:13, which, according to most interpreters, declares that with the advent of Christianity God has terminated the old covenant with the Jewish people. There is, however, no ground for such sweeping statements, as this chapter has demonstrated: it is both possible and plausible that what the author of Hebrews actually compares and contrasts in this passage are the earthly world and the heavenly reality. To a Middle Platonist such as the author of Hebrews, heaven always trumps earth. Generally speaking, the metaphorical discourse of Hebrews is directed toward the future, not toward the past. In short, what is being compared are not Christianity and Judaism, but rather the future and the present, heaven and earth. These circumstances should be taken into consideration by those who refer to Hebrews in order to find arguments in favor of a supersessionist understanding of Christianity. Replacement theology is far too blunt an instrument to do justice to early Christian texts — and, to an ever-higher degree, to the history and spirituality of the Jewish people, whether in the past or present.

The interpretation of Hebrews suggested here may or may not convince the present readers. Some may be fascinated by the possibilities that this perspective offers; other readers, for different reasons, may prefer the supersessionist interpretation, arguing that Hebrews should be understood as an early example of the triumphalistic theology that would evolve and increase during the subsequent centuries, and also cause so much harm for two millennia. All readers, however, will agree that the interpretation that has been presented here provides theological space for the Jewish people after Christ, which is the meta-question of this anthology: How might Christians reaffirm their faith in Jesus Christ even as they affirm Israel's covenantal life with God?[40] When reading the epistle without presupposing supersessionism, Hebrews will be acknowledged as one of those subject matters which, in the words of *Nostra Aetate*, "human beings have in common and which tend to bring them together" *(... quae hominibus sunt communia et ad mutuum consortium ducunt).*[41]

---

40. A related yet different task is to explore how the author of Hebrews understands Israel *before* Christ.

41. *Nostra Aetate* §1.

The Gradual Emergence of the Church and the Parting of the Ways

Daniel J. Harrington, S.J.

1. Introduction

The "parting of the ways" between Judaism and Christianity has been a topic of great interest among scholars in recent years.[1] The term refers to the point at which Christianity ceased to be a sect within Judaism, and became a separate religion and began defining itself over against Judaism. On being asked when the parting took place, I generally use the now-familiar formula that it happened "at different times in different places." While historically accurate, that answer ignores some even more difficult questions. The word "ways" can suggest greater uniformity and coherence in both Judaism and early Christianity than ever really existed. The term "parting" can indicate a situation in which the two religions were sealed off from all contact between them.

While an attractive and even romantic term, its looseness means that the parting of the ways can be traced either to a point very early in Christian history (Paul's letters), or to one well into the patristic era (John Chrysostom's homilies), or somewhere in between. One recent survey of scholarship on the matter concluded that the thrust of recent studies can even be interpreted as indicating that the ways never parted at all![2]

In this essay I want to explore three key moments in the parting of the ways in the New Testament: Christianity within Israel (Paul, with special

---

1. James D. G. Dunn, *The Parting of the Ways between Christianity and Judaism and Their Significance for the Character of Christianity*, 2nd ed. (London: SCM, 2006).

2. S. C. Mimouni, "Les origines du christianisme: Nouveaux paradigmes ou paradigmes paradoxaux? Bibliographie selectionnée et raisonnée," *Revue Biblique* 115 (2008): 360-82.

attention to his letters to the Galatians and Romans), rivalry among Jewish groups (the Gospels of Matthew and John), and transcending historic Israel (the letters to the Colossians and the Ephesians). I am not suggesting that a definitive parting of the ways occurred in New Testament times. Rather, my contention is that within these New Testament writings it is possible to discern different elements that led eventually to what has come to be known as the parting of the ways. My focus will be what these different moments meant for the development of christology and ecclesiology. I want to show how much these moments have done to shape the relationship between the church and the Jewish people through the centuries, with regard to both the ways taken and the ways not taken.

2. Paul Within Israel: Galatians and Romans

The seven undisputed Pauline letters — 1 Thessalonians, Galatians, 1 and 2 Corinthians, Philippians, Philemon, and Romans (in rough chronological order) — are the earliest complete documents (from the 50s of the first century c.e.) in the New Testament.[3] They were extensions of Paul's pastoral ministry as he responded to problems and questions that arose in his absence from communities that he had founded (except for Romans). In them Paul boasts of his having "advanced in Judaism beyond many of my people" (Gal. 1:14), and lists his impressive credentials as a Jew including "as to righteousness under the Law, blameless" (Phil. 3:5-6). Nevertheless, Paul's experience of the risen Jesus on the road to Damascus (see Acts 9, 22, and 26) changed everything, to the point that he came to regard his prior achievements in Judaism as "loss" and even "rubbish" (Phil. 3:8).

It is tempting to locate the parting of the ways in Paul's own ministry. He interpreted his "conversion" to be also a call to bring the gospel (the "good news" about the saving significance of Jesus' death and resurrection) to non-Jews, and insisted that Gentiles did not have to become fully Jewish (undertaking circumcision, Sabbath observance, and purity rules) in order to become part of the "the Israel of God" (Gal. 6:16). Moreover, Paul seems to say some harsh things about "the Jews" who killed Jesus and the prophets (1 Thess. 2:14-15), and claims that Jews read their own scriptures with "a veil over their minds" (2 Cor. 3:15). Also, Paul was hounded by

3. For a concise guide to Paul and his writings, see my *Meeting St. Paul Today* (Chicago: Loyola Press, 2008).

other Jewish Christian missionaries who questioned the validity of his ministry to Gentile Christians and urged their complete conversion to Judaism; see Galatians, 2 Corinthians, and Philippians.

However, as the "new perspective on Paul" has shown, it appears more likely that Paul, far from disavowing Judaism, regarded Jesus as the fulfillment of God's promises to Israel, the Christian movement as a group within Judaism, and himself as part of the loyal remnant of Israel.[4] Here I want to focus on two texts — Galatians 3 and Romans 11 — that reflect moments in which Paul the Jewish Christian sought to understand God's plan within the context of Israel as God's own people.

Paul wrote to the Galatians (in central Asia Minor, present-day Turkey) in the mid-50s of the first century C.E.[5] They were Gentiles whom Paul had brought to Christian faith before moving on to found communities in other places. Meanwhile, some rival Jewish Christian missionaries came along and tried to convince the Galatians to convert fully to Judaism. When Paul heard about this development, he was astonished that the Galatians were in danger of going over to "a different gospel" (1:6). He was convinced that the Galatians had already received the Holy Spirit by believing what they heard (his gospel) rather than by doing "the works of the Law." Thus Paul's defense of his gospel is passionate, angry, and emotional.

Paul's quarrel was not with Judaism per se, but rather with the rival Jewish Christian missionaries and the Gentile Christians in Galatia. In Galatians 3:6-29, Paul offers a complex biblical argument to defend his gospel, that through Christ Gentiles could become part of God's people without becoming fully Jewish. He argued that membership in God's people is dependent on faith rather than on circumcision and other "works of the Law." Since Paul wanted to show that he knew Israel's scriptures better than his rivals did, he constructed his argument in Galatians 3 by referring to biblical texts at almost every point.

The starting point of Paul's argument in Galatians 3:6-29 is the statement in Genesis 15:6 that Abraham "believed God, and it was reckoned to him as righteousness." That declaration flowed from Abraham's trust in God's promise that Abraham would have as many descendants as the stars

4. See Krister Stendahl, *Paul among Jews and Gentiles, and Other Essays* (Philadelphia: Fortress, 1976); E. P. Sanders, *Paul and Palestinian Judaism: A Comparison of Patterns of Religion* (Philadelphia: Fortress, 1977); James D. G. Dunn, *The New Perspective on Paul,* rev. ed. (Tübingen: Mohr Siebeck, 2005); and N. T. Wright, *Justification: God's Plan and Paul's Vision* (Downers Grove, IL: InterVarsity Press, 2009).

5. Frank J. Matera, *Galatians,* rev. ed. (Collegeville, MN: Liturgical Press, 2007).

in the skies. Because Abraham trusted in God's word, God judged him to be "righteous," that is, in right relationship with God. Paul then used Genesis 15:6 to show that faith (in its basic sense of trust in and fidelity to God's word) is what distinguishes the true children of Abraham.

In the course of his argument, Paul insisted that the true "seed" or "offspring" of Abraham was Christ, and that it was through Christ that God's promise was being fulfilled in the community of Jews (like himself) and Gentiles (like the Galatian Christians). He also insisted that since Abraham was declared "righteous" (justification) before and apart from the giving of the Torah to Moses, doing the "works of the Law" cannot be the fundamental principle of right relationship with God. Those "works" can be interpreted either comprehensively as the 613 precepts of the Torah or restrictively as the identity markers that made Jews distinctive in the Greco-Roman world (circumcision, Sabbath observance, and purity rules).[6] Paul describes the purpose of the Law variously as preparation for Christ, a stimulus to sin, and a temporary disciplinarian *(paidagogos)*. The argument leads to the conclusion that the true children of Abraham (and thus members of God's people) are those who have been "baptized into Christ" as the "seed" of Abraham (3:27). In this people of God, there is "no longer Jew or Greek," since all are "one in Christ Jesus" (3:28-29).

In the Bible, salvation history begins with Abraham. For Paul, Jesus is the pivotal figure in salvation history and the true "seed" of Abraham. The thread running through salvation history is faith understood as trust in God's promises and fidelity to God's covenant. It is this kind of faith that makes it possible for Gentiles to be part of God's people. It is through "the faith of Jesus Christ" (Gal. 2:16), that is, the trust and fidelity displayed by Jesus (subjective genitive) in his death and resurrection, that all this has become possible.[7]

Romans 9–11 represents Paul's mature reflection on God's plan in salvation history and the place of Jesus and the church within it. While passionate and emotional in expression, it also represents Paul's *eureka* moment in trying to understand the workings of God.[8]

In Romans 9:1-5 Paul protests that he would be willing to be cut off

6. Dunn, *The New Perspective on Paul*.

7. Richard B. Hays, *The Faith of Jesus Christ: The Narrative Substratum of Galatians 3:1–4:11*, rev. ed. (Grand Rapids: Eerdmans, 2002).

8. Daniel J. Harrington, *Paul and the Mystery of Israel* (Collegeville, MN: Liturgical Press, 1992). In this book (pp. 21-39) I also deal with the more problematic (potentially anti-Jewish) Pauline texts such as 1 Thessalonians 2:14-15 and 2 Corinthians 3 mentioned above.

from Christ (now the most important thing in his life!) if only more of his fellow Jews would accept the gospel. Then he rehearses the privileges or prerogatives of Israel in salvation history: "the adoption, the glory, the covenants, the giving of the Law. . . ." Near the end of his argument Paul affirms that "the gifts and the calling of God are irrevocable" (11:29).

Between his affirmations of Israel's preeminence in salvation history, Paul uses many biblical texts to show how Jewish Christians like himself constitute the remnant of Israel, and how through the mercy of God Gentiles who had been "not my [God's] people" and "not beloved" have become "my people" and "my beloved" through the power of Jesus' death and resurrection. Paul attributes the failure of many of his fellow Jews to accept the gospel to their misplaced zeal for the Law as the principle of right relationship with God and to their failure to recognize that Christ is the *telos* of the Law, that is, the goal or end toward which it was pointing all the time.

Paul's *eureka* moment came with his thought that the success of the Gentile mission would make his fellow Jews jealous, and that they would then eventually embrace the gospel. In Romans 11:17-24 Paul uses the analogy of the olive tree to express his discovery. The root of the olive tree is constituted by Jewish Christians like himself. Gentile Christians are branches from a wild olive tree that have been successfully grafted on to the cultivated olive tree. And non-Christian Jews are branches that have been temporarily broken off. Paul reasons that if God could graft the Gentiles on to the olive tree, how much easier will it be for God to graft the natural branches back on to it!

In Romans 11:25-26 Paul summarizes his insight in this way: "a hardening has come upon part of Israel, until the full number of Gentiles has come in. And so all Israel will be saved." Here Paul uses the biblical notion of "hardening" (see Isaiah 6) and the apocalyptic notion of a quota to explain Israel's unbelief and the admission of Gentiles into God's people. Unfortunately Paul does not tell us the precise identity of "all Israel" (each individual Jew, Israel as a collectivity, or the church?), how all Israel will be saved (by missionary activity, in a separate way, or through a dramatic intervention like's Paul's own experience?), and when it will be saved (at some point in history, or at the end of human history?).

Throughout his missionary career, Paul regarded himself as a Jew, and indeed as a member of the holy remnant that was preserving the heritage of Israel. He acknowledged Israel's preeminence in salvation history and viewed Christ as the *telos* toward which Israel's scriptures pointed. He situated Christ in the wider context of God's promise to Abraham, God's covenantal relationship with Israel, and the proper response to it (faith). He looked on Jesus' death and resurrection as the pivotal moment in God's plan, one that opened up membership in God's people to all persons of faith after the pattern of Abraham and Jesus. Although Paul's christology and ecclesiology may have paved the way for the definitive separation between Jews and Christians, that is not what Paul himself seemed to have had in mind.

3. Rivalry with Other Jewish Groups: Matthew and John

In recent New Testament scholarship it has become common to interpret the Gospels of Matthew and John against the background of the crisis facing all Jews after the Roman destruction of Jerusalem and its Temple in 70 C.E. The three great pillars of Second Temple Judaism had been the Temple, the land, and the Law. After the Roman defeat of the First Jewish Revolt, the Temple was no more and the land was even more fully under Roman military and political control. Thus there arose among various Jewish groups a fierce competition as to who best preserved and carried on the spiritual heritage of Israel.

The Jewish apocalyptists represented by *4 Ezra* and *2 Baruch* hoped for a spectacular divine intervention that would fulfill God's promises to Israel. In the meantime careful adherence to the Torah was demanded. The spirit of military rebellion that issued in the First Jewish Revolt and the destruction of Jerusalem and its Temple in 70 C.E. did not die out totally. The result was the equally disastrous Bar Kokhba Revolt of 132-35 C.E. The early rabbinic movement (also known as formative Judaism) gathered traditions from various strands of pre-70 Judaism (Pharisaic, priestly, scribal, etc.) and focused on solidifying Israel's identity as God's holy people through faithful observance of the Torah.[9] In this context the Gospels of Matthew and John appear as Jewish Christian responses to the crisis. Despite their literary and theological differences, these two Gospels insist that the heritage of Israel after 70 C.E. is best preserved and carried on by the movement gathered around Jesus of Nazareth as its definitive teacher and interpreter.

9. Jacob Neusner, *From Politics to Piety: The Emergence of Pharisaic Judaism* (Englewood Cliffs, NJ: Prentice-Hall, 1973).

Matthew's Gospel is generally viewed as a revised and expanded version of Mark. One of the evangelist's major concerns seems to have been to root Jesus even more firmly within Judaism than his predecessor had done.[10] The Gospel was composed in Greek, and presupposes a location with a large Jewish population such as Antioch in Syria. It is generally dated to 85 or 90 C.E., sometime after the destruction of Jerusalem and its Temple. While accepting the geographical outline of Jesus' public ministry (Galilee, journey, Jerusalem), Matthew expanded greatly the teaching material by shaping sayings taken from Mark, the Sayings Source Q, and some unique traditions (M) into the five great speeches of Jesus in chapters 5–7, 10, 13, 18, and 24–25.

By placing the genealogy of Jesus (1:1-17) at the very beginning of his Gospel, Matthew established Jesus' identity as the descendant of Abraham and David, while preparing for his unusual birth by mentioning four very unusual biblical women (Tamar, Rahab, Ruth, and Bathsheba). In explaining how Jesus the Messiah came to be born of the Virgin Mary (1:18-25) Matthew quotes Isaiah 7:14 ("the virgin shall conceive . . ."). This is the first of the many explicit "formula" or "fulfillment" quotations ("to fulfill what had been written . . .") that are especially prominent in the infancy narrative but are also present throughout the Gospel. In using the already common christological titles (Messiah, Son of David, Son of Man, Son of God, etc.), Matthew places them in contexts that evoke more fully than Mark did their biblical and early Jewish backgrounds.

The Matthean Jesus is first and foremost a teacher. In his five great speeches Jesus emerges as the Jewish wisdom teacher and prophet of God's kingdom par excellence. The way in which Matthew tells about Jesus' conflicts with his opponents indicates that he is familiar with matters debated among Jewish teachers of his time. In the midst of much popular resistance and rejection, Jesus in 11:25-30 identifies himself as the recipient of divine wisdom and invites those who seek genuine wisdom to come to his school. In his rebuke of the scribes and Pharisees in chapter 23, the Matthean Jesus reminds his followers that "you have one instructor, the Messiah" (23:10). Throughout the passion narrative Matthew suggests by means of many biblical quotations and allusions that all these events are proceeding according to God's will expressed in the Jewish scriptures. Fea-

---

10. Daniel J. Harrington, *The Gospel of Matthew*, rev. ed. (Collegeville, MN: Liturgical Press, 2007).

tures such as these have won for Matthew the title of "the most Jewish Gospel."[11]

However, in some circles Matthew is also regarded as "the most anti-Jewish Gospel."[12] Like the other Gospels, Matthew has to be read on two levels — that of Jesus' public ministry around 30 C.E., and that of the evangelist and his community around 85 or 90 C.E. In the latter context the emotionally charged encounters between Jesus and his opponents (especially the scribes and Pharisees) seem to reflect the competition between the Matthean Jewish Christians and other Jewish movements to carry on the heritage of Israel.

In that context Matthew's somewhat sneering reflections on "their synagogues" (as opposed to Jesus' *ekklēsia*) make sense, at least historically. Likewise, the scathing indictments of the scribes and Pharisees in chapter 23 as false leaders and hypocrites need to be interpreted in the same late first-century setting. Furthermore, the people's self-curse at Jesus' trial before Pilate ("His blood be on us and on our children," 27:25) is best understood as Matthew's way of blaming the destruction of Jerusalem and its Temple on both the opponents of Jesus in his own time ("on us") and the next generation in 70 C.E. ("on our children"). The anti-Jewish potential of Matthew's Gospel can (and has) become actual when it has been taken out of its historical context in the rivalry between Jewish groups in the late first century and applied to Jews in very different historical contexts.

John's Gospel presupposes a setting similar to that of Matthew's Gospel: conflict over which Jewish group best carries on the heritage of Israel after 70 C.E. While the final edition of John's Gospel has traditionally been linked to Ephesus in Asia Minor, the bulk of the Gospel tradition reflects the activity of a Johannine circle or school in the eastern Mediterranean world and a connection with a figure known as the Beloved Disciple.[13] On several historical matters John is very likely more correct than the Synoptic Gospels: Jesus' three-year public ministry, his several visits to Jerusalem,

11. J. Andrew Overman, *Matthew's Gospel and Formative Judaism: The Social World of the Matthean Community* (Minneapolis: Fortress, 1990).

12. Michael J. Cook, "Interpreting 'Pro-Jewish' Passages in Matthew," *Hebrew Union College Annual* 54 (1983): 135-46.

13. Raymond E. Brown, *The Community of the Beloved Disciple* (New York: Paulist, 1979). Brown was strongly influenced by J. Louis Martyn's 1968 work, *History and Theology in the Fourth Gospel.* The most recent (expanded) edition of Martyn's work was published in 2003 by Westminster/John Knox. For a recent critique of his approach, see Adele Reinhartz, "Judaism in the Gospel of John," *Interpretation* 63 (2009): 382-93.

and the celebration of the Last Supper before the official Passover celebration began. The geographical references are generally correct and presuppose a firsthand knowledge of the Holy Land.

The prologue to John's Gospel (1:1-18) identifies Jesus as "the Word of God" who became flesh and dwelt among us. The most obvious background for these affirmations is the personification of Wisdom in Proverbs 8, Sirach 24, and Wisdom 7. In his public ministry in John 2–12, Jesus frequents the Jerusalem Temple and uses the Jewish calendar of festivals (Passover, Sabbath, Tabernacles/Booths, and Dedication/Hanukkah) as occasions for solemn declarations about his identity and his work. The basic insight of John's Gospel is that Jesus is both the revealer and the revelation of God. How Jesus fulfilled the Jewish scriptures is a major theme. Everything suggests that the Johannine Christians viewed themselves as practicing a more perfect form of Judaism than their ancestors or their rivals did.

The chief rivals of the Johannine Christians are generally designated in the Gospel as *hoi Ioudaioi* ("the Jews").[14] Their interaction with Jesus reaches a low point when Jesus describes them as children of the devil (8:44), and they accuse Jesus of being a Samaritan and possessed by a demon (8:48). The negative portrayal of "the Jews" is best explained by reference to the two levels — Jesus around 30 C.E. and the Johannine community around 85-90 C.E. — at which the Gospel must be read. Johannine Christianity faced a severe crisis when its adherents were being expelled (or at least threatened with expulsion) from the synagogue (*aposynagogoi;* see 9:22; 12:42; and 16:2).

Matthew and John (and their followers) most likely viewed themselves not as apostates from Judaism but rather as authentic representatives of the Jewish tradition by continuing the Jewish heritage with reference to Jesus as the divinely authorized interpreter of the Torah (Matthew) and as the revealer and revelation of God (John). At the same time, their intense focus on Jesus as "the one instructor" (Matthew) and as "the Word of God" (John) probably looked to other Jews as going beyond the boundaries of Judaism. Both Gospels in their portraits of Jesus provided some of the seeds that led to the later definitive parting of the ways.

Despite their similarities, however, the Jewish Christianities represented by these two Gospels eventually went in different directions. Of

14. R. Bieringer, D. Pollefeyt, and F. Vandecasteele-Vanneuville, eds., *Anti-Judaism and the Fourth Gospel: Papers of the Leuven Colloquium 2000* (Assen: Van Gorcum, 2001).

course, the core of these two Gospels became part of the Christian canon of Sacred Scripture and the basis for mainline or orthodox Christianity, with the Matthean Jesus providing much doctrinal and ethical content and the Johannine Jesus becoming the measure of christology. However, the Matthean ideal of keeping all the commandments in the Torah (5:17-19) and observing the Sabbath at all costs (24:20) led to a strict Jewish Christianity that eventually withered away. Likewise, the internal controversies in the Johannine movement about the incarnation (see 1 John 2:19-22; 4:2-3; 2 John 7) drove at least part of that community into Gnosticism.

4. Transcending Historic Israel: Colossians and Ephesians

Two of the so-called Deuteropauline letters — Colossians and Ephesians — seek to remain faithful to the Pauline tradition while going beyond it with regard to Christianity's relationship to Judaism. Though seldom quoting the Jewish scriptures directly, they both use "biblical" language because that was the theological language of the Pauline school. However, they are more interested in the cosmic Christ than in the Jewish Jesus and in the church as the worldwide body of Christ than in the local community or its place in Judaism. Rather than situating the Christian movement within Judaism (as Paul did) or in conflict with other Jewish groups (as Matthew and John did), they each moved beyond historic Israel and prepared for the emergence of an overwhelmingly Gentile church beyond Judaism.

The Letter to the Colossians appears to have been written to deal with a real crisis facing a church in western Asia Minor.[15] While a case can be made for its direct Pauline authorship, most scholars today view it as written around 80 C.E. by an admirer of Paul. The crisis seems to have involved an invitation by the local Jewish community (not Jewish Christians!) to Gentile Christians to embrace Judaism (of a somewhat esoteric kind) in its fullness.[16] The author insists that Gentile Christians already have everything they need in Christ, and that their baptismal dignity lived out properly is absolutely sufficient with regard to right relationship with God.

---

15. Margaret MacDonald, *Colossians and Ephesians* (Collegeville, MN: Liturgical Press, 2000).

16. Daniel J. Harrington, "Christians and Jews in Colossians," in J. A. Overman and R. MacLennan, eds., *Diaspora Jews and Judaism: Essays in Honor of, and in Dialogue with, A. Thomas Kraabel* (Atlanta: Scholars Press, 1992), pp. 153-61.

The key text in Colossians is the early Christian hymn preserved in 1:15-20 that celebrates Christ as the Wisdom of God, first in the order of creation, and then in the order of redemption. The language of the first part echoes terms and concepts found in various Jewish texts that personify Wisdom (see the discussion of John 1:1-18 above). It first portrays the risen Christ as ruling over the cosmos and as the head of the church (which is his "body"). Then it interprets Jesus' death and resurrection as bringing about reconciliation on a cosmic scale. The hymn provides the basis for the rest of the letter (and for Ephesians also), which argues that the one in whom the fullness of God pleased to dwell (Christ) far transcends the beliefs and practices that the local Jewish community had to offer.

As Colossians 2:8-23 shows, what they had to offer included circumcision, food laws, festivals, asceticism or self-abasement, a kind of mysticism ("worship of angels"), and various rules and regulations. Compared with participation in the life of the cosmic Christ and in the body of Christ, those practices fade into insignificance. At best they were only "a shadow of what is to come," while "the substance belongs to Christ" (2:17). Though rooted in Pauline thought and Judaism, the theology of Colossians transcends Judaism and moves Christianity in the direction of becoming a world religion apart from Judaism.

The Letter to the Ephesians is generally regarded as a revised and expanded version of Colossians. Underlying its theology are the hymn's themes of the cosmic Christ and the church as the body of Christ. It is more a theological essay than a response to a specific situation or crisis. It is both a profound synthesis of Pauline theology and an extension of it in a time (after 80 C.E.) when the church's connections to historic Israel were fading.

One of the author's major themes is how Jesus through his death and resurrection has brought together Jews and Gentiles so as to form a new entity ("one new humanity in place of the two," 2:15). Through Jesus' death and resurrection God has broken down the wall that previously divided Jews and Gentiles, abolished the Law "with its commandments and ordinances" (2:15), and given both groups equal access to God. Now instead of Paul's great discovery in Romans 11:25-26 about the salvation of all Israel, the "mystery" is how "the Gentiles have become fellow heirs, members of the same body, and sharers in the promise in Christ Jesus through the gospel" (3:4). Historic Israel's pivotal role in salvation history has been taken over by the church as "the one new humanity" in Christ.

5. Conclusion

We began with the familiar formula that the parting of the ways between Judaism and Christianity occurred "at different times in different places." We have seen that Paul regarded himself as extending what he considered a more perfect form of Judaism to non-Jews, and felt the need to relate his gospel to the biblical tradition and to situate it within God's covenantal relationship with historic Israel. Likewise, it appears that both Matthew and John were convinced that God's promises to his people were being fulfilled in the movement gathered around Jesus, and that this movement represented the fullness of Judaism over against the claims of other contemporary Jewish movements. The Deuteropauline letters to the Colossians and Ephesians do seem to move beyond the confines of historic Israel with their emphasis on the cosmic Christ and the church as the worldwide body of Christ. But even in them the risen Christ is portrayed in terms of the biblical/Jewish figure of personified Wisdom. In none of these cases is there a definitive rejection of the biblical tradition or of Judaism as a separate or "foreign" religion. Indeed, in every case the starting point is the biblical/Jewish tradition. The ways had not yet fully parted.

Nevertheless, as we have seen, these New Testament writings carried within them the seeds or roots of what turned into the parting of the ways between Christianity and Judaism: Jesus as the "Lord Jesus Christ" whose death was the perfect sacrifice for sins and the principle of justification or right relationship with God (Paul), as "the one instructor" (Matthew) and the Word of God (John), and as the Wisdom of God (Colossians and Ephesians). Likewise, these texts show the development of the church from local communities spread over the Mediterranean world (Paul), through largely Jewish Christian conventicles defining themselves over against other Jewish groups (Matthew and John), to the worldwide body of Christ (Colossians and Ephesians). Whenever and wherever the parting of the ways took place, christological and ecclesiological insights like these had prepared the way and provided doctrinal foundations.[17]

Where did these developments leave the relationship between Christians and other Jews? Paul, of course, was intensely concerned with those Jews who had not embraced the gospel (Rom. 9:1-5) and was convinced that God still had a place for them in his plan of salvation history (Rom.

---

17. Daniel J. Harrington, *God's People in Christ: New Testament Perspectives on the Church and Judaism* (Philadelphia: Fortress, 1980).

11:17-26). The bitterness of the conflicts between the Matthean and Johannine Christians and their Jewish rivals after 70 C.E. left little room for mutual understanding and concern once the dust settled. And the universalistic thrusts of Colossians and Ephesians tended to leave Judaism behind as a historical curiosity while concentrating on the new entity ("the one new humanity") created by the body of Christ. For its part, early rabbinic (or formative) Judaism paid little attention to the Christian movement, whether out of lack of interest or an exercise in *damnatio memoriae.*

When and where the ways between Christianity and Judaism parted definitively, I cannot say. But it does seem that the seeds planted in the New Testament contributed to this eventual development. Yet history need not be destiny. While we cannot repair the breach, we can understand it and try to formulate a new and more appropriate relationship for the twenty-first century and beyond.

How might we Christians in our time understand our faith claim that Jesus Christ is the savior of all humanity, even as we affirm the Jewish people's covenantal life with God? What the delegates at Vatican II did in crafting *Nostra Aetate* §4 may provide a good example and an effective starting point. In trying to articulate the shape of a new relationship between the Catholic Church and the Jewish people in the present and the future, they went back to the earliest documents in the Christian canon of Scripture — Paul's letters, and Romans 9–11 in particular. There they found a way of envisioning the relationship "organically" by returning to the very early history of the relationship and Paul's image of the olive tree. Without denying the universal saving significance of Jesus Christ, they at least found (as Paul had done) a place for the Jewish people in God's unfolding plan. There they also discovered an opening to a way forward, by which Christians and Jews might be partners in an effort at mutual understanding and respect as they move together "shoulder to shoulder" (Zeph. 3:9) and as they await the Day of the Lord and the fullness of God's kingdom.

Revisiting Our Pasts and Our Paths: A Jewish Response to Jesper Svartvik and Daniel Harrington

Tamara Cohn Eskenazi

The statement commented upon exceeds what it originally wants to say; that what it is capable of saying goes beyond what it wants to say; that it contains more than it contains; that perhaps an inexhaustible surplus of meaning remains locked in the syntactic structure of the sentence, in its word-groups, its actual words, phonemes and letters. . . . Exegesis would come to free, in these signs, a bewitched significance that smolders beneath the characters or coils up in all this literature of letters.

EMMANUEL LEVINAS[1]

1. Introduction

It is a privilege and a pleasure to participate in the "Christ Jesus and the Jewish People Today" project. The persistent commitment of Christians to reexamine traditions sensitively and rigorously, with a concern for their impact on Jews and Judaism, is itself inspiring. The resulting, impressive essays in this volume establish the work undertaken as a landmark in Jewish-Christian dialogue. I thank the organizers for including me in the conversation.[2]

---

1. Emmanuel Levinas, "On Jewish Reading of Scriptures," in *Beyond the Verse: Talmudic Readings and Lectures* (Bloomington: Indiana University Press, 1994; orig. French 1982), p. 109.

2. In writing this response I wish to acknowledge the crucial role played by Rabbi, Professor Michael A. Signer, Z'L, not only in the grander project of Jewish-Christian relations, but in my own relation to the work. His spirit and memory continue to guide as a blessing.

In focusing on two of the essays, I respond as a Jew and a biblical scholar who believes that it is essential to continue to rethink our interpretations of scriptures and their lived ramifications. As Levinas observes, the significance that smolders or is coiled in sacred texts awaits discovery. Each generation is charged with the task of releasing meanings so that they can illumine our paths. The essays of Jesper Svartvik and Daniel Harrington exemplify analyses that indeed shed fresh light on Christian texts and on their messages regarding Judaism.

Both Jesper Svartvik and Daniel Harrington show that the foundational Christian texts, when placed in their historical contexts, do not have to be interpreted as destructive to contemporary Jews and Judaism. According to Svartvik, the Letter to the Hebrews can be understood less as an obstacle to congenial Jewish-Christian relations and more as a stepping-stone. According to Harrington, the key New Testament texts contain seeds that led to a parting of the ways between Judaism and Christianity; but these texts in the New Testament do not in themselves demand such a parting of the ways. These helpful and clarifying assessments of Christian sources set the stage for more constructive dialogue between the two traditions. Together, these essays indicate that certain types of anti-Judaism that characterized a dominant thread of Christian relation to Judaism, and Christian antagonisms toward Jews, are neither integral to these sources nor the necessary development stemming from these sources.

From a Jewish perspective, such analyses are naturally welcome and are good news for Jewish-Christian relations. These essays raise the hope that authentic forms of Christianity can be freed from a legacy of conflict with Judaism (and vice-versa); they open the way to a new partnership between sister religions. At the same time, such reflections on what the New Testament does and does not say also raise more forcefully certain questions about the history of Jewish-Christian relations. First, one must ask, if the developed animosity against Jews is not to be fully credited to the founding texts of Christianity, then how does one account for the pervasive tendency throughout history to use Scripture as a weapon against Jews? Second, one asks, how can we possibly correct the use made of these texts in later Christian circles?

Answering the first question is beyond the scope of this paper. As for the second question, it is directly and indirectly the subject of this volume as a whole. In what follows I review the key contributions of the two excellent essays by Svartvik and Harrington as a prelude to reflecting on the roles of hermeneutics in scriptural traditions.

2. Jesper Svartvik's "Reading the Epistle to the Hebrews Without Presupposing Supersessionism"

In his cogent analysis of Hebrews, Svartvik accomplishes a number of important things. First, Svartvik challenges the use of the Hebrew Bible to claim that God rejects the "old" covenant and the people Israel. This claim is implicit in how Hebrews 8:8-9 has been interpreted on the basis of its reference to Jeremiah 31:31. But as Svartvik observes, the Jeremiah version that Hebrews 8:8-9 uses is more negative than the one preserved in the Hebrew version of Jeremiah (and transmitted in both Jewish and Christian translations of the book of Jeremiah). Svartvik's point here is twofold: (A) At most, readers can claim that the Jeremiah tradition is polyphonic, and therefore they are invited to decide which one of the two versions of biblical Jeremiah more accurately reflects God's will; and (B) the mention of the "old" covenant in Jeremiah and in Hebrews does not refer (as it often does in subsequent Christian interpretations) to Judaism or Jews. In other words, Hebrews here does not claim that God rejected Judaism or the Jews.

Second, Svartvik challenges the interpretation of 8:13 as a reference to the "old" covenant or Judaism as that which has been rendered obsolete and replaced by "Christianity." Rather, Svartvik argues, when Hebrews is read in its context, it can be recognized as making a temporal claim with an eye to eschatology: everything worldly (including the world the readers still inhabit) will grow old and vanish, except for the reality of God (pp. 85-88). Consequently, it is a misreading to argue that Hebrews' goal is to render Jews and Judaism obsolete.

Third, Svartvik highlights the pilgrimage motif that Hebrews applies to its readers. Far from having arrived at their destination, Hebrews' readers, ancient and modern, are still on the way. The expectations have not been fulfilled. "The implied readers of Hebrews are no less a wandering people than is Israel" (pp. 89-90). Attributing triumphalist supersessionism to Hebrews, Svartvik concludes, is a misreading of Hebrews.

As Svartvik acknowledges, reading Hebrews without presupposing supersessionism may not be everyone's choice. But recognizing such an interpretation as a possible and legitimate reading would open up space for a Christian theology that does not negate the ongoing worth of Jews and Judaism in God's plan. Such a reading would be consistent with the goals of *Nostra Aetate* and also with Pope John Paul II's comments on Judaism and Christianity in his 1980 address in Mainz (n. 8).

Svartvik's effective analysis of Hebrews brings to the fore the role and influence of exegesis in scriptural religions like Judaism and Christianity (as well as Islam). If texts can generate more than one interpretation, what can be said about the authority of Scripture? This is why reflecting together as Jews and Christians about the nature of hermeneutics is an essential part of the conversation.

It is therefore all the more heartening to see several hermeneutical approaches at work in Svartvik's compelling analysis of Hebrews. This document, after all, has been typically read as a letter *against* the Hebrews, rather than merely *to* them, and as a foundational text for supersessionism. Shorn of such presuppositions, Svartvik shows, Hebrews articulates some messages that have been ignored by early interpreters but that are as vital now as they originally were. Seen from a Jewish perspective, Svartvik's understanding of Hebrews removes the sting from Hebrews' complex messages. In addition, this interpretation equips Christians with theological tools with which to understand new potential roles in today's world, even as it opens up space for a more constructive Jewish-Christian dialogue.

3. Daniel J. Harrington's "The Gradual Emergence of the Church and the Parting of the Ways"

In his illuminating essay Harrington traces textual evidence for the perception of the relationship between the emerging movement later labeled "Christianity" and other Jewish groups. Harrington notes that the parting of the ways is not reflected in the key New Testament texts. Rather, as Harrington amply demonstrates, the New Testament basically reflects a debate among competing Jewish groups about their legitimacy as heirs of the biblical (i.e., Jewish Bible) traditions. His analysis highlights some of the seeds that later germinate and shape the parting of the ways.

First, Harrington examines the undisputed Pauline letters and shows that Paul never disavows Judaism. In Galatians 5:6 and Romans 11 Paul expands the lineage of Abraham to include Gentiles, but not to displace Jews. "Although Paul's christology and ecclesiology may have paved the way for the definite separation between Jews and Christians, that is not what Paul himself seemed to have had in mind" (p. 97).

Second, Harrington examines the Gospels of Mathew and John (considered the most anti-Jewish among the Gospels) in their contexts as responses to the Jewish crisis in the first century, namely, the destruction of the Temple. As Harrington shows, Matthew places Jesus more firmly within Judaism than does its source, Mark: Jesus' genealogy and speeches in Matthew are examples of such a move. Like Svartvik, Harrington offers an understanding of biblical messages in their own context and in relation to the religious and historical reality to which they respond.

Harrington focuses on a passage in Matthew that "has been taken out of its historical context" (p. 99) and had become throughout history a key in anti-Jewish polemic, namely, Matthew 27:25. According to Harrington, this verse is best understood "as Matthew's way of blaming the destruction of Jerusalem and its Temple on both the opponents of Jesus in his own time ('on us') and the next generation in 70 C.E. ('on our children')" (p. 99). It is not intended to justify an ongoing persecution of Jews, even though it has been used in this manner.

As for John's Gospel, Harrington suggests that the work reflects a particular struggle for the position of the legitimate heir of Israel's traditions. The circle to which John's teachings most likely belong claims to be practicing a more perfect form of Judaism than its rivals (or ancestors). Neither Matthew nor John advocates a parting of the ways.

Third, Harrington examines the so-called Deuteropauline letters, Colossians and Ephesians. Colossians, while rooted in Pauline thought, develops a response that expands Christian theology into a more global and cosmic religion and thereby transcends Judaism. Similarly, Ephesians, which offers a synthesis of certain Pauline teachings, expands the role of the church beyond that of historic Israel.

According to Harrington, none of these texts rejects the biblical traditions of Judaism as a "foreign" religion. What one can see in them are seeds or roots that later encourage separation.

Historical circumstances account for how the seeds have developed, "Yet history need not be destiny" (p. 104). Going back to these foundational sources, Harrington indicates, has already enabled the church to redefine its relationship to Judaism in a more affirming way. *Nostra Aetate* §4 is an example and an "effective starting point" (p. 104) in that the participants in Vatican II found a way of envisioning a different and better relationship between the church and the Jewish people.

As Harrington shows, the parting of the ways is not the only course of development mandated by the New Testament. Perhaps more important, a parting of the ways need not have been and surely does not have to be hostile. The New Testament, after all, also contains other seeds that like the proverbial seeds in Jesus' parable seem to have landed on rocky ground and failed to sprout — at least until now.

Harrington's review of the parting of the ways, like Svartvik's rereading of Hebrews without presuming supersessionism, underscores the malleable nature of scriptural traditions and opens new possibilities for moving a Jewish-Christian dialogue forward in a more positive — yet authentic — mode. Although certain New Testament seeds developed in a particular manner, this development was not inevitable, and such New Testament seeds were not the only sources of supersessionism. We know that biblical traditions, including the New Testament, include many seeds that lie dormant awaiting discovery when circumstances are amenable. The parable of Jesus is a colorful example indeed of such a potential. From a Jewish perspective, the famous midrash on Jeremiah 23:29 exemplifies a related perspective (see below).

4. Reflecting on Hermeneutical Challenges

When Phyllis Trible, in 1973, published her trailblazing article, "Depatriarchalizing in Biblical Interpretation,"[3] she argued that sexist interpretation of the Hebrew Bible was the work of interpreters and their bias, not the intent of the biblical authors. Her subsequent major work, *Texts of Terror*,[4] indicates, however, that the picture is more complex. As a result, several different approaches to scriptures have since been identified by feminists as ways to address a legacy of misogynist interpretation. Alice Ogden Bellis surveys the explicit or implicit hermeneutics that those for whom the Bible is authoritative have cultivated in order to deal with texts that challenge contemporary perspectives.[5]

I mention this because a number of these approaches also characterize Jewish and Christian interpretation over the centuries when different generations attempted to make Scripture responsive to changing circumstances and values. It is therefore helpful to review briefly Bellis's list of strategies that contemporary feminist scholars use to address and redress the influence of the Bible on one group of people.

3. *Journal of the American Academy of Religion* 41 (1973): 35-42.
4. Phyllis Trible, *Texts of Terror: Literary-Feminist Readings of Biblical Women* (Philadelphia: Fortress Press, 1984).
5. Alice Ogden Bellis, *Helpmates, Harlots, and Heroes: Women's Stories in the Hebrew Bible*, 2nd ed. (Louisville/London: Westminster/John Knox, 2007), pp. 20-25.

According to Bellis, interpretive strategies include identifying a hierarchy among texts when they contradict each other on the relevant issues. Such hierarchy or priority can be determined on the basis of major and minor themes in the Bible. For example: Ephesians 5 should be understood in accordance with Galatians 3:28 for the New Testament; or, the Exodus message of liberation should override oppressive teachings in the Hebrew Bible. Hierarchy or priority can also be defended by differentiating timeless messages from those that are specific to time and place but need not be universalized.[6]

Contextualizing biblical texts and their messages in their early historical setting is another way to rethink the tradition. At times, this enables interpreters to counteract an appropriation of meaning that may no longer do justice to original intent. It also enables interpreters to see how what was meant for a particular time and place can be more authentically applied to a contemporary situation.

An additional approach acknowledges that there may also be a need at times to counteract original intent and canonize readers' experience, instead, in light of the impact of texts on actual lives and historical development.[7]

In some important sense, all traditions engage in relying on a "canon within a canon." Indeed, the interpretation of scriptures in Judaism and Christianity exemplifies every one of the strategies that Bellis notes — and others as well. After all, Jewish and Christian scriptures include a large number of challenging texts. Each tradition therefore has cultivated specific hermeneutical strategies in response to challenging texts and to changed understanding.

What has become distinctive of current hermeneutical thinking is the more widespread acknowledgment that texts are susceptible to multiple legitimate interpretations. Consequently, one must become more self-conscious of the processes, more honest about the lenses one uses, and more responsible for our choices of tools and of interpretations.

This is one of the many reasons that the essays by Svartvik and Harrington are so exciting. In an important sense, both these essays present a fresh response to Christian thought and empower Christian scholarship and theology to reflect on its sources in a more inclusive way. From a Jewish perspective, such steps are important first, because they alter how we

---

6. Bellis, *Helpmates, Harlots, and Heroes*, pp. 21-22.

7. See, for example, the approaches proposed by Elisabeth Schüssler-Fiorenza in *But She Said: Feminist Practices of Biblical Interpretation* (Boston: Beacon Press, 1992), pp. 146-49.

may understand the New Testament, and second, because of what they disclose about current Christian approaches to Judaism. The readiness in these essays to redirect a legacy of supersessionism and to develop an affirmative theological stance toward Judaism is an enormously significant step. This in itself, even apart from the significant exegetical results, is a most welcome event. It is even more impressive and promising when the rationale for change includes an awareness, as these essays imply, that such rethinking of the sources might also restore to Christianity an authentic part of its tradition that had been lost.

These steps are especially important, because many Jews are not familiar with Christian texts. The impact of Christianity on Jews and the attitude of most Jews toward Christianity are typically not shaped by direct engagement with Christian theology but by the use that Christians make of their traditions. It is a given, in Jewish circles, that texts hold a variety of possible interpretations. It seems to me that often the problem for Jews is less the fact that Christians might have anti-Jewish texts and more the selective use made of such sources. After all, Judaism also has some texts that cause modern and postmodern Jews to wince. The crux of the matter is determined by the choices a community makes. This is why hermeneutics is so important and why interpreters must take responsibility for the interpretation they "bestow" upon a text.

In Jewish circles this awareness of the plurality of possible meanings has generated a voluminous body of teachings. In this enterprise, Jeremiah's statement that God's Word is comparable to a hammer shattering a rock (Jer. 23:29) provided a rationale for searching and embracing multiple, even contradictory meanings. The rabbinic sages thus taught: "Just like a hammer splits a rock into many splinters, so does one verse have several meanings."[8] The goal of students of scriptures is to gather as many of these meanings as possible in order to grasp the fullness of God's messages.

Levinas's reflection on texts in the Jewish tradition sums up one of the ways that rabbinic exposition of the Bible has been understood. In emphasizing the inexhaustible nature of Scripture and its capacity to generate new meanings and insights, Levinas writes that

the totality of truth is made out of the contributions of a multiplicity of people: the uniqueness of each act of listening carries the secret of the text; the voice of Revelation, in precisely the inflection lent by each per-

8. B. Sanhedrin, 34a.

son's ear, is necessary for the truth of the Whole. The fact that God's living word can be heard in a variety of ways does not only mean that the Revelation adopts the measure of the people listening to it; rather, that measure becomes, itself, the measure of Revelation. The multiplicity of people, each one of them indispensable, is necessary to produce all the dimensions of meaning.[9]

Levinas articulates a contemporary Jewish approach to such unfolding of meaning through time. But one can also point to the Apostle Paul, it seems to me, for a New Testament expression of a related notion. I have in mind Paul's statement that, "For now we see in a mirror, dimly, but then we will see face to face. Now I know only in part; then I will know fully, even as I have been fully known" (1 Cor. 13:12).

If Christians and Jews are on a pilgrimage from a certain reality still partially under a veil to one that grows closer to a fuller manifestation of God's presence in our midst, then the unfolding of texts' meanings in light of changing circumstances can be acknowledged with integrity, and without annulling earlier understandings or denigrating them.

Svartvik's work on Hebrews makes possible a different and fresh understanding of Hebrews, and Harrington's review makes possible rethinking the direction of Christianity's historical relationship to Judaism. Together, these essays and the larger project encompassed by this volume place Jews and Christians on a very important path as we explore together our shared yet distinctive journeys.

9. Emmanuel Levinas, "Revelation in the Jewish Tradition," in Sean Hand, ed., *The Levinas Reader* (Oxford: Blackwell, 1989), p. 195.

The Son of God Became Human as a Jew: Implications of the Jewishness of Jesus for Christology

Hans Hermann Henrix

1. Introduction

The relationship between theology and the church's teaching authority is sometimes understood as a relationship between progress and the status quo. But in reflecting on the church's and theology's relationship with Judaism, this understanding does not fully hold. Two decades ago, the Protestant systematic theologian Friedrich-Wilhelm Marquardt noted:

> We come up against an astonishing and rare reversal in the relationship between theological scholarship and the church as it has been throughout the history of the church and of theology. Although normally theology with its open discussions is "farther along" than the church with its formulated doctrinal decisions, in the case of the Christian-Jewish relationship today this is . . . clearly the other way around. While the majority of theological scholars still try to block the renewal of theology with regard to the relationship to Judaism, churches have already committed themselves to it in a surprisingly rapid and ever more energetic way.[1]

The thesis that the church's teaching authority is ahead of theology as such is not intended to deny that doctrinal statements with regard to theological views of Israel take up and reinforce theological developments. Moreover, today Marquardt's thesis requires refinement. Actions during the papacy of Benedict XVI, such as his Good Friday prayer for the Tridentine Rite and the decree lifting the excommunication of the four bishops from

1. Friedrich-Wilhelm Marquardt, *Von Elend und Heimsuchung der Theologie. Prolegomena zur Dogmatik* (München: Gütersloher Verlagshaus, 1988), p. 396.

the Priestly Society of St. Pius X, raise questions about whether the "advance" has slowed, or even stopped. We have also witnessed in the past two decades considerable progress on the theological front.

Nevertheless, theology has not caught up with aspects of doctrinal statements and ecclesial documents on the relationship of the church with Jews and Judaism. Theology has indeed picked up the emphasis on the Jewishness of Jesus in numerous ecclesial documents of the 1970s and 1980s.[2] Yet, it is questionable whether the Jewishness of Jesus has been regarded with sufficient seriousness by theologians writing in the area of christology. Marquardt offers one reason for this:

> The concept of the "human being" is higher than that of the "Jew," because it is more general. Above all, the concept of the "human being" is higher . . . because it seems to fit conceptually to "God"; only the fact of being human as such, all human beings, can serve and correspond with the "greatness" of God. The relationship between "God" and "human being" is so general that individual historical determinations certainly do not need to be denied, but they do lose significance. . . . The Jewishness of Jesus did not speak to [this christology], did not have any content for proclamation, and that is why it just wasn't "worth mentioning."[3]

In this essay, I argue that the Jewishness of Jesus deserves a central place in christology. I unfold this argument in four stages: (1) examining how the Vatican's *Notes on the Correct Way to Present Jews and Judaism in Preaching and Catechesis in the Catholic Church* and Pope John Paul II have presented the Jewishness of Jesus; (2) examining how Pope Benedict XVI deals with Jesus the Jew in his book *Jesus of Nazareth;* (3) interpreting incarnational christology through the lens of the Jewishness of Jesus;[4] and (4) analyzing individual elements in incarnation christology.

---

2. As an example of this, see the indications in the index for the key words "Jesus der Jude/Jesu jüdische Identität," in the two volumes of documentation, *Die Kirchen und das Judentum,* Volume I: *Dokumente von 1945 bis 1985,* ed. Rolf Rendtorff and Hans Hermann Henrix (Paderborn/Gütersloh: Bonifatius/Gütersloher Verlagshaus, 2001); and *Die Kirchen und das Judentum,* Volume II: *Dokumente von 1986 bis 2000,* ed. Hans Hermann Henrix and Wolfgang Kraus (Paderborn/Gütersloh: Bonifatius/Gütersloher Verlagshaus, 2001). Quotations from these two volumes will be indicated as *KuJ I* or *KuJ II.*

3. Thus Friedrich-Wilhelm Marquardt, *Das Christliche Bekenntnis zu Jesus, dem Juden. Eine Christologie,* 2 vols. (München: Chr. Kaiser, 1990 and 1991), vol. 1, pp. 138f.

4. It is the particular purpose of this third stage to link the universal significance of Jesus Christ with Israel's theological dignity — this book's meta-question — in the context of incarnational theology.

2. Taking the Jewishness of Jesus Seriously:
Doctrinal Contributions to Theology

In the 1985 *Notes on the Correct Way to Present Jews and Judaism in Preaching and Catechesis in the Catholic Church*, the fact that Jesus was a Jew seemed not only worth mentioning, but even worth praising. The notes introduced reflections on the Jewish roots of Christianity with the following sentences:

> Jesus was and always remained a Jew; his ministry was deliberately limited "to the lost sheep of the house of Israel" (Mt 15:24). Jesus is fully a man of his time and of his environment — the Jewish Palestinian one of the first century, the anxieties and hopes of which he shared. This cannot but underline both the reality of the Incarnation and the very meaning of the history of salvation, as it has been revealed in the Bible (cf. Rom 1:3-4; Gal 4:4-5). . . . Thus the Son of God is incarnate in a people and a human family (cf. Gal 4:4; Rom 9:5). This takes away nothing, quite the contrary, from the fact that he was born for all men [and women] (Jewish shepherds and pagan wise men are found at his crib: Lk 2:8-20; Mt 2:1-12) and that he died for all men [and women] (at the foot of the cross there are Jews, among them Mary and John: Jn 19:25-27, and pagans like the centurion: Mk 15:39 and parallels).[5]

Here the church's teaching authority is instructing its members to consider the reality of the incarnation in very concrete terms. If one does this, one automatically comes up against the Jewish milieu in Roman-ruled Palestine, and the family and people of Jesus of Nazareth become present.

Pope John Paul II took up this line of thought in his statements on the correct understanding of the incarnation of the Son of God. For example, in an address to the members of the Pontifical Biblical Commission on April 11, 1997, he spoke of the New Testament's inseparable bond with the Old Testament. In emphasizing that the Old Testament is necessary for understanding the incarnation, the pope spoke of the human identity of Jesus. He offered this short formula for it:

> Jesus' human identity is determined on the basis of his bond with the people of Israel, with the dynasty of David and his descent from Abra-

---

5. *KuJ I*, pp. 92-103, 98. See www.vatican.va/roman_curia/pontifical_councils/chrstuni/relations-jews-docs/rc_pc_chrstuni_doc_19820306_jews-judaism_en.html. Citations from §12 and §15.

ham. And this does not mean only a physical belonging. By taking part in the synagogue celebrations where the Old Testament texts were read and commented on, Jesus also came humanly to know these texts; he nourished his mind and heart with them, using them then in prayer and as an inspiration for his actions. Thus he became an authentic son of Israel, deeply rooted in his own people's long history. . . . To deprive Christ of his relationship with the Old Testament is therefore to detach him from his roots and to empty his mystery of all meaning. Indeed, to be meaningful, the Incarnation had to be rooted in centuries of preparation. Christ would otherwise have been like a meteor that falls by chance to the earth and is devoid of any connection with human history. From her origins, the Church has well understood that the Incarnation is rooted in history and, consequently, she has fully accepted Christ's insertion into the history of the People of Israel.[6]

The pope considered the concreteness of Jesus' Jewish identity significant. He took up this idea again in preparing for the Great Jubilee Year 2000 when he explicitly asked the historical-theological commission preparing the celebration of the millennium to address the roots of anti-semitism in Christianity. As he spoke of the church's relationship with the Jewish people during the Vatican consultation on October 31, 1997, Pope John Paul II reaffirmed his understanding of the ongoing election of Israel and of the Jewish people as "people of the covenant." He continued:

> The Scriptures cannot be separated from the people and its history, which leads to Christ, the promised and awaited Messiah, the Son of God made man. . . . That is why those who regard the fact that Jesus was a Jew and that his milieu was the Jewish world as mere cultural accidents, for which one could substitute another religious tradition from which the Lord's person could be separated without losing its identity, not only ignore the meaning of salvation history, but more radically challenge the very truth of the Incarnation and make a genuine concept of inculturation impossible.[7]

---

6. *KuJ II*, pp. 102-5, 103f. See: http://www.vatican.va/holy_father/john_paul_ii/speeches/1997/april/documents/hf_jp-ii_spe_19970411_pont-com-biblica_en.html.

7. *KuJ II*, pp. 107-9, 108f. Cited from: http://www.vatican.va/holy_father/john_paul_ii/speeches/1997/october/documents/hf_jp-ii_spe_19971031_com-teologica_en.html. A text by the European churches of the Reformation shows that a consensus among churches is also possible with regard to emphasis on the incarnation. The study of June 24, 2001, "Church and Israel: A Contribution from the Reformation Churches in Europe to the Relationship

John Paul II emphatically underlined that the incarnation of the Son of God has its specific place in the history of Israel. This specific place is part of the "mystery" of the incarnation. The pope took up the fundamental theological category of "mystery" in order to give weight to his emphasis. In Jesus Christ, the incarnation does not immediately and directly go to the human in general. Rather, Jesus Christ is a "true son of Israel," the Son of God become a human being. He is rooted in the history of Israel. That has to do not only with the prehistory of the incarnation, but with the life and work of Jesus himself.

Separation from the incarnation's real rootedness means losing the meaning of its mystery. The bond with the people of Israel determines the human identity of Jesus over and beyond physical belonging. The reality that is determined in such a concrete way is a fundamental component of his identity, without which "the mystery of Christ cannot be fully expressed." The pope castigates the neglect of this concreteness of salvation history. He views this neglect as an attack on "the truth of the incarnation itself." This statement implicitly affirms the importance of taking the Jewish identity of Jesus seriously. With this plea, the pope corrected the tendency of a long theological tradition that thinks of the incarnation of the Son of God in general human terms and neglects the concrete historical place of the incarnation. One can see this neglect most vividly in the absurd attempts of the Nazis to deny that Jesus was a Jew. The pope's stress on the necessity of taking seriously the Jewish identity of Jesus impels us to understand the Son of God's becoming human as his becoming a Jew.

Even such an important theologian as Karl Rahner did not see the

---

between Christians and Jews," reflects on the revelation of the God of Israel in Jesus Christ as follows: "The confession 'God was in Christ reconciling the world with himself' comprises the confession of the person of Jesus as the 'Christ' and the 'Son of God' and as the incarnation of God's creative word (John 1:14). This content of the faith in Jesus Christ is expressed in the confession that Jesus is 'truly God and truly man' *(vere Deus — vere homo)*. This confession maintains the content of faith in the incarnation only when 'became truly man' immediately and inseparably includes 'truly a Jew.' It was not just any man but precisely this man — a Jew by birth, a member of the people of Israel, descended from the family of David — who was revealed at Easter as the Christ, the Son of God. When God reveals Jesus the Jew as the true witness to the coming of God's reign, that testifies that this bond with Israel is final. The incarnation of the pre-existent Son of God in a member of the people of Israel expresses God's bond with Israel. Therefore the Christian faith cannot view it as a mere historical coincidence. Indeed, the history which leads to God's self-revelation in Christ is the history of God with Israel and with no other people" (§2.1.4-5); see http://www.jcrelations .net/en/?item=1009.

connection of Jesus' Jewishness to the incarnation. He reflected on the incarnation of the Word and Son of God at a depth that only few theologians reached, but he did so in traditional theological terms.[8] Rahner said that theology "contemplates the Incarnation and the hypostatic union and is actually little interested in the concreteness of Jesus."[9] Thus he also spoke of the incarnation in a relatively abstract and general way — or in a way that was obligated to ontology or that corresponded with the fact that its starting point was in transcendental theology. When Pinchas Lapide, a Jewish conversation partner, asked him whether in reflecting on the incarnation one could ignore the Jewishness of Jesus, he had difficulty in understanding Lapide. Rahner replied,

> If they say, for instance, that Jesus was just, that Jesus regarded men and women equally, then if I am a Christian I can naturally say that these attitudes, which he in fact ultimately got from his Jewish tradition, are obviously binding for Christians too. However at least many such attitudes of Jesus, which were for him actually Jewish and which are binding even for me, are nevertheless basically general human self-understandings. Perhaps they were preached in a grand manner in the Judaism of the period before Jesus and were naturally also realized by Jesus himself, but the Jewish origin in Jesus is of no interest for Christians today.
> . . . As a Jew you cannot deny, in spite of all the chosenness of the Jews, that you and I are two people who simply on the basis of our common humanity have reciprocal obligations.[10]

Here, the fact that Jesus was rooted in the history and reality of Israel is considered to be an arbitrary coincidence without any theological value, a quasi-docetism.

Against this erasure of the Jewish identity of Jesus of Nazareth in Karl Rahner's understanding, it must be said that the Son of God, God's Word in Jesus of Nazareth, is "not a human being in the abstract, nor a general or neutral human being. Rather, he became Jewish flesh, a Jew, the son of a Jewish mother and as *such* a concrete human being. Becoming human happened in becoming a Jew. That is anything but 'an incidental and acci-

---

8. Karl Rahner, *Schriften zur Theologie* (Zürich/Einsiedeln/Köln: Benziger, 1954-60). See vol. 1 (1954), pp. 169-222; vol. 2 (1955), pp. 7-94; vol. 4 (1960), pp. 137-55 and others.

9. Karl Rahner and Pinchas Lapide, *Encountering Jesus — Encountering Judaism: A Dialogue*, trans. Davis Perkins (New York: Crossroad, 1987), p. 48.

10. Rahner and Lapide, *Encountering Jesus*, pp. 51-52, 54.

dental identification.'"[11] The incarnation of the Son of God happened in the "authentic son of Israel," Jesus of Nazareth. His concreteness as a Jew is a fundamental fact of Christian theology. It is a fundamental fact that at the same time has universal significance, since the authentic son of Israel represents the whole of humanity for its benefit, and Israel's messiah is the savior of the world.[12] By his words, Pope John Paul II encouraged and even impressed upon us theology's obligation to take seriously the concrete reality of the incarnation in Jesus Christ as a son of Israel.

3. Taking the Jewishness of Jesus Seriously: A Further Doctrinal Contribution

Pope Benedict XVI has reaffirmed his desire to continue the steps taken by his predecessor in ameliorating relations with the Jewish people.[13] When examining Pope Benedict XVI's addresses to Jewish delegations or in synagogues, however, he does not seem to recognize adequately the theological horizon of the church's unique relationship that John Paul II had drawn. Although his speeches are all based on the fundamental conviction that Jews and Christians must encounter one another from the depths of faith, they tend to be more exhortative and less theological.

However, Pope Benedict XVI does engage in more detailed theological

11. Thus Hans Hermann Henrix, "Ökumene aus Juden und Christen: Ein theologischer Versuch," in Hans Hermann Henrix and Martin Stöhr, eds., *Exodus und Kreuz im ökumenischen Dialog zwischen Juden und Christen,* Aachener Beiträge zu Pastoral-und Bildungsfragen 8 (Aachen: Einhard-Verlag, 1978), pp. 188-236, 194, referring to Karl Barth's statement that God's Son did "not become 'flesh,' a human being . . . in some general way, but Jewish flesh. The whole ecclesial teaching on incarnation and reconciliation became abstract, cheap, and meaningless to the extent to which one began to consider this to be a passing and incidental determination" (Karl Barth, *Kirchliche Dogmatik,* vol. 4 [Zollikon: Evangelischer Verlag, 1953], pp. 181f.).

12. Thus with Jochen Denker, *Das Wort wurde messianischer Mensch. Die Theologie Karl Barths und die Theologie des Johannesprologs* (Neukirchen/Vluyn: Neukirchener Verlag, 2002), pp. 149f.

13. Pope Benedict XVI, Address to a delegation of the International Jewish Committee for Interreligious Consultations on June 9, 2005, in *L'Osservatore Romano. Weekly edition in German.* Vatican City, no. 24 of June 17, 2005, 9; also: http://www.vatican.va/holy_father/benedict_xvi/speeches/2005/june/documents/hf_ben-xvi_spe_20050609_jewish-committee_ge.html; cf. his address during his visit to the Cologne synagogue on August 19, 2005, in: http://www.vatican.va/holy_father/benedict_xvi/speeches/2005/august/documents/hf_ben-xvi_spe_20050819_cologne-synagogue_ge.html.

exploration about the Jewishness of Jesus in his book *Jesus of Nazareth*. This is particularly evident in his dialogue with Rabbi Jacob Neusner on the subject of the Sermon on the Mount.[14] For the pope, the heart of the Sermon on the Mount is found in Matthew 5:17–7:27; after "a programmatic introduction in the form of the Beatitudes," the Sermon reveals the "Torah of the Messiah" (p. 100). He continues: "At the very beginning there stands, as a sort of epigraph and interpretive key, a statement that never ceases to surprise us. It makes God's fidelity to himself and Jesus' fidelity to the faith of Israel unmistakably clear: 'Think not that I have come to abolish the Law and the Prophets; I have come not to abolish them but to fulfill them' [Matt. 5:17]" (p. 101).

In the first part of his conversation with Neusner on the matter of disputes about observing the Sabbath, the pope explains what the expression "Torah of the Messiah" means. First, he corrects a "conventional interpretation" of the saying attributed to Jesus by Mark (2:27) — "The sabbath was made for humankind, and not humankind for the Sabbath." Many interpret this, the pope says, to mean that Jesus "broke open a narrow-minded legalistic practice, and replaced it with a more generous, more liberal view" (p. 106); they then use the text as a basis for the "image of the liberal Jesus." In the conflict around the Sabbath, however, Benedict XVI claims that "we are dealing not with some kind of moralism, but with a highly theological text, or to put it more precisely, a Christological one" (p. 110). Neusner's sharp objection to seeing Jesus taking the "place of the Torah" seems to have led Benedict XVI to claim: "The issue that is really at the heart of the debate is thus finally laid bare. Jesus understands himself as the Torah — as the word of God in person" (p. 110). Drawing upon Matthew's words (12:26: "I tell you, something greater than the temple is here" [p. 108]), and in response to Neusner, Pope Benedict XVI speaks of Jesus' claim "to be Temple and Torah in person" (p. 111). He takes up other expressions concerning Jesus as Torah from his dialogue with Neusner and seems to be in the process of developing an unusual key category or even a new title for Christ: "Jesus who is himself God's living Torah" (p. 169). When Benedict XVI says that "Jesus understands himself as Torah," and adds "as the word of God in person," he links this understanding to the "tremendous prologue of John's

14. Joseph Ratzinger/Pope Benedict XVI, *Jesus of Nazareth: From the Baptism in the Jordan to the Transfiguration,* trans. Adrian J. Walker (New York: Doubleday, 2007); the book includes the pope's discussion with Jacob Neusner and his book, *A Rabbi Talks with Jesus* (Montreal: McGill-Queen's University Press, 2000). In my discussion of Benedict's *Jesus of Nazareth,* the page numbers of the quotations appear in parentheses.

Gospel" (p. 110). Thereby, "a new light [is shed] on the person of Jesus."[15] This new light leads to a deepening of the meaning of the christological Logos title. Jesus Christ's title as Torah in person announces an abiding reference to Israel, to whom its God entrusted the Torah. By calling Jesus Christ "God's living Torah," we might also speak of the Torah incarnate. Benedict XVI has traced a path that should be continued in theological discussion. It stimulates reflection on incarnational christology and leads to one aspect of the Son of God's becoming a human being as a Jew.

4. The Son of God's Becoming a Jew as a Way of Interpreting Incarnational Christology

The concreteness of the Son of God's becoming a human being as a Jew is one way of expressing the fact that theology takes the Jewishness of Jesus seriously. It is an exhortative or paranetic metaphor.[16] Speaking of Jesus' becoming a Jew is a way of interpreting incarnational christology. It does not, of course, say everything that might be said about the dogma of the incarnation, but it highlights one aspect insufficiently heeded throughout the history of theology and builds upon the suggestions of John Paul II and Benedict XVI.

The following reflections aim first of all to demonstrate that taking Jesus' Jewishness seriously is not impeded by classical christological formulations. The individual elements in incarnational christology will then serve as examples of how to link with the concrete Jewish identity of Jesus Christ. These not only concern the birth of Jesus of Nazareth but rather the entirety of Jesus' life from his birth to his resurrection. Thus, they reflect not only on the "Christmas" mystery of the Son of God's becoming a human being, but also on that of "Easter."

15. Wolfgang Löser, "Jesus — der neue Mose. Zwölf Annäherungen an das Jesusbuch von Papst Benedikt XVI," *Theologie und Philosophie* 82 (2007): 382-91, 382.

16. In this respect I can agree with Barbara Meyer's point in *Christologie im Schatten der Shoah — im Lichte Israels. Studien zu Paul van Buren und Friedrich-Wilhelm Marquardt* (Zürich: TVZ Theologischer Verlag, 2004), p. 100, that the expression I used more than thirty years ago concerning "becoming a Jew" "can fulfill a paraenetic or at least a memorializing task, but [it] does not yet represent the acquisition of a critical reflection on Incarnation Christology." See also Hans Hermann Henrix, *Gottes Ja zu Israel. Ökumenische Studien christlicher Theologie* (Berlin/Aachen: Institut Kirche und Judentum, 2005), pp. 103-20. The ideas developed in this chapter now aim at responding to Barbara Meyer's call to go beyond giving a key word by developing a critical reflection on incarnational christology.

a. God's Son "Becomes" a Jewish Human Being: New Testament Foundations

The New Testament and the church testify repeatedly and in ever new ways to the "becoming human" of God's Word and God's Son in Jesus Christ as the central content of Christian faith. Saying that the Word of God "becomes" means, in philosophical language, a change in the way of God's being. It is not a transformation that would lead to God's dressing up and making a mask out of the human person Jesus as the place of God's presence. God's "becoming human" does not change God into a creature, nor does it change a creature into God.[17] Both would be a game of hide and seek. God's Son "becoming a human person" does not revoke God's being God and the human person's being human; instead of concealing something, it is a revelation of God. In God's "becoming" as a change in God's way of being lies an indication of direction from above to below: God's Son takes on humanity and "becomes" a human being. This sentence is not reversible in the sense of a human being becoming God's Son by his or her own power. Rather, God's Son becomes a human being. In this process, there is neither a disempowerment of the divine into the human nor a raising up of the human into the divine. Moreover, becoming a human person happens concretely. It is not a general divinity that becomes human, but God's Son; he does not become humankind but one human being, specifically, a Jewish human being. The reason and precondition for this is not a general ability of the human being to become a god or divine, but God's initiative in binding God's self in the covenant with Israel. Israel's covenant-God makes Israel the place of God's presence and God's dwelling, which finally happens in Jesus Christ through "becoming a human person," revealing God's self and becoming incarnate as a person.

The prologue of John inspires this christological reflection, in particular the link between John 1:1 and 1:14. It interprets the central statement in John 1:14a, "And the Word became flesh and dwelt among us," in the sense that the Word, the Logos, became "Jewish flesh" and dwelt in the midst of

---

17. Walter Kasper, in *Jesus der Christus*, Gesammelte Schriften, vol. 3 (Freiburg: Herder, 2007), p. 350, maintains "that God and the human person do not form a natural symbiosis; in becoming a human person, God does not become a principle within the world; he neither becomes spatial nor something bound to time. God's transcendence is maintained just as the independence and freedom of the human person is maintained." ET: *Jesus the Christ* (New York/Mahwah, NJ: Paulist, 1976).

Israel.[18] Understandably, exegesis has paid particular attention to "became" (Greek, *egeneto*):

> *Egeneto* expresses a change in the way of being of the Logos; before, he
> was with his Father in glory (cf. 17:5.24); now, he takes on the lowliness
> of earthly-human existence; before, he was "with God" (1:1b); now, he
> pitches his tent among human beings and in human form, in the full re-
> ality of the *sarx* [flesh], in order to attain again the glory of the heavenly
> way of being after his return to his Father (17:5). That is a contemplation
> of the history of salvation. . . . Thus the "becoming flesh" of the Logos
> indicates a turning point in the history of salvation; a series of events in
> salvation history [is being described].[19]

Or, in the words of Michael Theobald, "*Egeneto* has the nature of an event."[20] Karl Barth drew attention to the fact that in speaking of "becoming," every Platonic way of thinking is shattered: "Concreteness, contingency, individual historical existence is attributed to the Logos."[21] The *sarx* concept, the word concerning the "flesh," has many meanings. It can mean the infirm being who is moving toward death, but it also has the meaning of a blood relationship, so that the Logos of God becomes "the relative of the people of Israel, a Jew," and embodies "Jesus' membership of the concrete human people Israel."[22] Exegesis in general recognizes that John's prologue alludes to Jewish speculation on wisdom as well as to the revelation at Sinai and to the tent of meeting.[23] Yet John differs from the way

---

18. Thus with Denker, *Das Wort,* pp. 3, 52, 98, 108, 115f., 118, 134-37, 142, 167, 209, 260, 301, 303, 315. Paul van Buren emphasized the aspect of covenantal theology: "The covenantal Word of the God of the covenant became flesh and dwelt among, being one of, the covenanted people." *A Theology of the Jewish-Christian Reality: Part III: Christ in Context* (San Francisco: Harper & Row, 1988), p. 222.

19. Rudolf Schnackenburg, *Das Johannesevangelium. I. Teil. Einleitung und Kommentar zu Kap. 1–4,* Herders Theologischer Kommentar zum Neuen Testament IV, 1 (Freiburg: Herder, 1979), p. 242.

20. Michael Theobald, *Das Evangelium nach Johannes. Kapitel 1–12* (Regensburg: Friedrich Pustet, 2009), p. 127.

21. Quoted according to Denker, *Das Wort,* p. 22.

22. Denker, *Das Wort,* pp. 250f. and 80. This dimension of meaning here aims particularly at reflecting on the concreteness of becoming human as becoming a Jew.

23. See the many references to this in Klaus Wengst, *Das Johannesevangelium. 1. Teilband: Chapters 1–10,* Theologischer Kommentar zum Neuen Testament 4, no. 1 (Stuttgart: Kohlhammer, 2000), pp. 35-75 and the literature cited there, as well as Theobald, *Das Evangelium,* pp. 117f., 126f. 134, 137, 140f.

these texts speak about wisdom or the Torah. An idea that can perhaps be encountered in Jewish literature as a marginal statement lies at the center of John's prologue. Karl-Heinz Menke claims that "John says about the Logos: He is God. In saying this, the author of the gospel is not attributing a genre concept to God. For he distinguishes between the Father as *ho theos* [the god] and the Logos as *theos* [god]. So the Logos is God in a singular way."[24] Within the divine, a differentiation is made, without this leading to something like a "faith in two gods."[25] John's Gospel with its prologue (1:1-18) and with the statements of the Johannine Jesus about himself (e.g., 8:42, 10:30, or 14:9) is the primary biblical basis for the dogmatic development in the christological councils from the years 325 to 787, along with the hymns in Philippians 2:6-11 and Colossians 1:15-20, as well as Hebrews 1:1-14. People have generally regarded the developments in these councils, especially the Council of Chalcedon in 451, as a manifestation of Hellenization and thus as a movement away from Israel. If, however, one understands the development in the christological councils less as a departure from biblical, Jewish thinking and more as a transformation of Hellenistic ways of thought into Jewish-New Testament contents and categories, then one can begin to look for the traces of such a transformation.

b. Traces of "Becoming Human" as "Becoming a Jew" in the Chalcedonian Text

The famous Decree of the Council of Chalcedon (from the year 451) states:

> Following the saintly Fathers, we all with one voice teach the confession of one and the same Son, our Lord Jesus Christ: the same perfect in divinity and perfect in humanity, the same truly God and truly man, of a rational soul and a body; consubstantial with the Father as regards his divinity and the same consubstantial with us as regards his humanity; like us in all respects except for sin; begotten before the ages from the Father as regards his divinity, and in the last days the same for us and for our salvation from Mary, the virgin God-bearer as regards his humanity; one and the same Christ, Son, Lord, only-begotten, acknowledged in two natures which undergo no confusion, no change, no division, no

24. Karl-Heinz Menke, *Jesus ist Gott der Sohn. Denkformen und Brennpunkte der Christologie* (Regensburg: Friedrich Pustet, 2008), p. 199.
25. See Theobald, *Das Evangelium*, pp. 110f.

separation; at no point was the difference between the natures taken away by their union, but rather the property of both natures is preserved and comes together into a single person and a single subsistent being.[26]

In the Decree of Chalcedon, one can see these traces of Jewish worldviews from the New Testament:

1. The formal and doctrinal form of expression in the so-called "definitions" of Chalcedon could sound so ontological as to obscure the nature of the text as a profession of faith and to lose its historical characteristics. But it is in fact a text that professes faith, and those who are the subject of the text are the "we" of the council fathers, who are mentioned repeatedly. The confessionally invoked name of Jesus Christ is at the beginning and the end of the text, and at its center the name of Mary is mentioned.

2. The text speaks of a twofold birth of Jesus Christ: as God's Son, "begotten before the ages from the Father as regards his divinity, and in the last days the same for us and for our salvation from Mary, the virgin God-bearer." The emphasis on the twofold birth contradicts the idea of a *physis* (nature) with Hellenistic characteristics that would have come about through the unification of the divine Logos with the human reality of Jesus, so that the human reality would have dissolved like a drop of honey in the ocean. Mary's giving birth to Jesus marks him unmistakably as the son of a Jewish mother, from whom he takes on "flesh." The presence of Mary's name stands for the birth of a Jewish human being and recalls the concreteness of becoming human as a Jew. The text indirectly echoes this concreteness when, at the end, it places Jesus within the prophetic tradition. By speaking of the Son's second birth from Mary, the text shows that Israel is the latent context of Chalcedon's christology. Thus, it forms a counterbalance to the exclusive understanding of the cosmos as the context of this Council's christology.

3. The concreteness of becoming human as a Jew may be seen when the text uses its own language in its description of the relationship between the divine and the human natures. This specificity is evident as

---

26. Quoted according to *Decrees of the Ecumenical Councils*, ed. Norman P. Tanner, at http://www.piar.hu/councils/ecumo4.htm#Definition%20of%20the%20faith.

well in its paradoxical talk about both entities with the vocabulary of negative theology. Chalcedon insists on the independence of both natures as being without confusion or separation, and it speaks of their unification in one person. In Jesus, the divine and the human do not melt together, nor are both elements separated. In a paradoxical difference and unity (not identity), the text thinks what cannot be thought, what cannot be grasped logically: "The more radically being human is thought of, the less it may be identified with the divine, and the more radically the divine nature of Jesus is expressed, the less it may be equated with the human. And at the same time, both must be in relationship with one another in such a way that the one face of Jesus is maintained."[27] This formulation does not seem to contribute to a close relationship with Judaism. Yet I agree with Josef Wohlmuth, when he notes "that the 'without confusion' of Chalcedon has remained the Jewish thorn for Christology."[28] Chalcedon's insight into faith implicitly takes up something — over and beyond every profound difference — that is to be encountered in a Jewish objection that emerged from a misunderstanding of classical christology.

In actual fact, Christian theology aided and abetted Jewish misunderstanding of classical christology by thinking of the togetherness of God and Jesus Christ as such condescension of God in the flesh that the divine was robbed of its power by being made human, and by seeing the way of being in the flesh as a divinization. Thus, seen from the outside, Jesus Christ could appear to be a divine-human hybrid. Against a one-dimensional and nondialectical collapsing of the two natures into one, as in Monophysitism, and which can frequently be reflected in Jewish descriptions, it must be said that: "The Council of Chalcedon emphasized not only the unity of divinity and humanity in Jesus, but insisted yet more resolutely on their difference and separateness."[29]

27. Josef Wohlmuth, "Herausgeforderte Christologie," in *Emmanuel Levinas — eine Herausforderung für die christliche Theologie,* ed. Josef Wohlmuth (Paderborn: Schöningh, 1998), pp. 215-29, 218.

28. Josef Wohlmuth, *Die Tora spricht die Sprache der Menschen. Theologische Aufsätze und Meditationen zur Beziehung von Judentum und Christentum* (Paderborn: Schöningh, 2002), p. 182.

29. Wohlmuth, *Die Tora spricht die Sprache der Menschen,* p. 246. Cf. also Jean-Bertrand Madragule Badi, *Inkarnation in der Perspektive des jüdisch-christlichen Dialogs. Mit einem Vorwort von Michael Wyschogrod* (Paderborn: Schöningh, 2006), p. 256.

Ever since the Middle Ages, the concept of *shittuf* (a connection, a communion, an association)[30] has expressed the Jewish uneasiness with Christian incarnational christology. This concept of *shittuf* expresses Jewish criticism of the Christian worship of Jesus Christ as the Son of God equal in being to the Father; in Jewish perspectives, this adds an element of confusion to God's self. Michael Wyschogrod expressed Jewish concern when he said:

> There is good reason for sharpness in the Jewish rejection of the incarnation. No matter how close God comes to the human being in the Hebrew Bible, no matter how much God takes part in human hopes and fears — God still remains the eternal Judge of the human person, whose nature is in fact in the image of God (cf. Gen 1:26f.), but who may not be confused with God. . . . In this light, the statement that a human being was God can only give rise to the most profound concern in the Jewish soul.[31]

Christian theology will not be able to silence or pacify this Jewish criticism and concern. But it must develop sensitivity toward it by taking care not to interpret the relationship between the human and the divine natures in Jesus Christ in terms of confusion, or a melting together and symbiosis. The text of Chalcedon contains that sensitivity, which certainly does not do away with the Jewish concern, but it does signal a clear intention: the text does not mean some in-between being that comes about through the confusion of the divine and the human, but rather the one and same Christ "in two natures that are without confusion." Since Chalcedon, "Christian theology may no longer cover up the line of separation between God and the world."[32] And ever since the Jewish-Christian dialogue of our day, the "without confusion" of Chalcedon can be seen, in Josef Wohlmuth's phrase, as the Jewish thorn in christology (which needs to be interpreted or translated): "That which Chalcedon calls the humanity of Jesus 'without confusion' is the real human being Jesus of Nazareth. . . . The humanity without confusion is to be taken seriously in such a way that the unseparated divine

---

30. Edward Kessler, s.v. "Shittuf," in *A Dictionary of Jewish-Christian Relations*, ed. Edward Kessler and Neil Welborn (Cambridge: Cambridge University Press, 2005), p. 404.

31. Michael Wyschogrod, "Ein neues Stadium im jüdisch-christlichen Dialog," *Freiburger Rundbrief* 34 (1982): 22-26, 26; see also by Wyschogrod, "Christologie ohne Antijudaismus?" *Kirche und Israel* 7 (1992): 6-9.

32. Wohlmuth, "Herausgeforderte Christologie," p. 224.

nature can no longer allow the human being of Jesus to retreat into the background or to be suppressed."[33] The "without confusion" of Chalcedon is fidelity to Israel's profession of the one and only God insofar as it keeps far away from the one and only God a confusion with what is not divine and excludes an apotheosis of the human being.

When Chalcedon is understood first of all as an expression of faith that is in the process of leaving Israel, the biblical content and the traces of Jewish-New Testament categories in its text are insufficiently recognized. This Council did not simply abandon itself to unbiblical Hellenistic thinking; rather, it used this thinking and transformed the categories into biblical categories. Thus its "without confusion" can be seen as "the Jewish thorn in Christology." Chalcedon's incarnational christology does not close itself off hermetically from the concreteness of the Son of God's becoming human in becoming a Jew, but rather it contains indications of its own expression of this concreteness.

5. Individual Elements in Incarnational Christology and the Jewish Identity of Jesus Christ

The attempt to look more deeply into the biblical content and the traces of Jewish New Testament categories in Chalcedon's incarnational christology has an affinity with the voices in current christological discussion which emphasize that in the incarnation and in becoming human, God's Son "not only took on a human nature, but a human history, and that only in this way he initiated the fulfillment of history."[34] The incarnation does not exclusively concentrate on the birth of Jesus. It does not stand only for the "Christmas" mystery. Over and beyond the beginning of Jesus' life, it means the whole of his life, work, and destiny. "The statement concerning the incarnation is not to be understood exclusively in relation to the beginning of Jesus' path, nor does it mean only a later event, but rather the whole of his path and of the person of Jesus as both appear in the light of the resurrection."[35] Incarnation means the concrete historical existence of the Son throughout his life. "Incarnation of the Son in the person of Jesus

33. Wilhelm Thüsing, *Die neutestamentlichen Theologien und Jesus Christus. Grundlegung einer Theologie des Neuen Testaments. III. Einzigkeit Gottes und Jesus-Christus-Ereignis* (Münster: Aschendorff, 1999), p. 315; cf. also pp. 299, 319, 419.

34. Kasper, *Jesus der Christus*, pp. 72f.

35. Wolfhart Pannenberg, *Grundzüge der Christologie* (Gütersloh: Mohn, 1966), p. 317.

means that this human being in person is the Son of God and that he is that to the whole extent of his path."[36] So if incarnation means "that the Jesus Christ who was crucified and raised up is the event of God's self-expression and promise of self,"[37] and if incarnation is understood to embrace the whole of the path and destiny of Jesus, then we must conclude that the reality that the Son of God became a Jewish human being is paradigmatic and is an interpretive key to comprehending the Christ event. What is the importance of this realization for some of the contents and categories of christology?

a. Jesus Christ, an "Authentic Son of Israel," Is God's Son

By emphasizing that in becoming human the Son of God took up a specific place in the people of Israel, Pope John Paul II alluded in outline to the way Jesus lived and learned[38] and observed: "Thus he became an authentic son of Israel, deeply rooted in his own people's long history." That is a remarkable summary of the Jewish identity of Jesus, which does not overlook the christological resolutions of Chalcedon and the other councils.

In the theology of the fathers, an opposition had developed between a christology of unification and a christology of separation. The former was created in the region around Alexandria and emphasized the subjective unity of Christ, thus assuring the salvific presence of God in the earthly reality of the human being Jesus. The second was at home in Antioch and described the unity of the divine Logos with the human being Jesus as a unity of two. The people of Antioch reproached those of Alexandria with interfusing God and humanity, whereas the people of Alexandria feared a separation of Jesus Christ into two sons, one son of the Father within the divinity and one an adopted human son of God.[39] This theological debate resounded in the christological councils before being largely resolved at

36. Wolfhart Pannenberg, *Systematische Theologie*, vol. 2 (Göttingen: Vandenhoeck & Ruprecht, 1991), p. 360. ET: *Systematic Theology*, trans. Geoffrey W. Bromiley (Grand Rapids: Eerdmans, 1994).

37. Peter Hünermann, "Inkarnation," in *Lexikon für Theologie und Kirche*, vol. 5 (Freiburg: Herder, 1996), pp. 498-500, 500.

38. Wilhelm Bruners, *Wie Jesus glauben lernte* (Freiburg: Herder, 2006).

39. On Karl-Heinz Menke's quotations and remarkable reconstruction of the history of the theology and the councils from the second to the fifth and the fourth to the eighth centuries, see his *Jesus ist Gott der Sohn*, pp. 204-81, 220, and 233.

the Council of Chalcedon. Chalcedon insisted on its "without confusion" phrase in order to emphasize the unabridged and true humanity in Christ along with his unabridged and true divinity.

This was also Pope John Paul II's intention when he stressed in practical terms the rootedness of Jesus Christ in the history of Israel and the determination of his identity through his inclusion among the people of Israel by speaking of him as an "authentic son of Israel." The pope's expression and its theological consequences are thus not a revival of the early church's debate, in which there was talk of two sons whose unity of subject was controversial. John Paul II's expression does not aim at a duality of sonship, but is rather a commentary on the concreteness of Jesus' humanity, to which the Logos or the Son of God was united. In this concreteness as an "authentic son of Israel," he is an "authentic human person." The Jewish identity of Jesus belongs to the mystery of the Son of God becoming a human being and has its place within that mystery.

b. Jesus Christ as the "Torah in Person" or the Torah Incarnate[40]

The second papal suggestion, which characterizes Jesus Christ as "living Torah," and as the "Torah in person," was expressed by Pope Benedict XVI and manifests an abiding reverence for Israel. For the Torah is Israel's Torah, which the God of Israel entrusted and gave to his chosen people Israel as his covenantal partner. The Torah is the epitome of the covenant and the whole of God's teaching that is to be inscribed in the life and the everyday reality of the covenanted human person. How can the idea of Jesus Christ as Torah incarnate be utilized theologically? What would be its limits?

In his christology, Karl-Heinz Menke discusses the thesis that "ultimately Jesus Christ is nothing other than the Torah become a person." He identifies the concept of Torah with that of the Logos and uses the thesis to translate John's prologue: "In the beginning was the Torah, and the Torah was with God, and the Torah was God. In the beginning it was with God. Everything came into being through the Torah, and without the Torah, nothing that came into being was. In it was life, and the life was the light of men. . . . And the Torah became flesh and lived among us" (John 1:1–

---

40. As regards this phrase, see also the comments on the "Torah incarnate" in the contribution by Elizabeth Groppe to this volume, "The Tri-Unity of God and the Fractures of Human History."

4:14).[41] Menke criticizes the concept expressed in such a translation; namely, that Jesus Christ is the Torah become a person. He counters that this thesis overlooks important facts. One such fact is "that no Jew can say: 'And the Torah was God.'" However, this fact is not as certain as Menke thinks. For there are some Jewish texts and passages that speak of God as Torah, so that precisely in the theme of the Torah, Jewish authors perceive an analogy with the Christian idea of the incarnation and can speak of a Jewish theology of incarnation.[42] A second argument from John 1:17 is more important to Menke: "For the law was given through Moses; grace and truth came through Jesus Christ." Even if this does not signify a devaluation of the law, the fourth evangelist nevertheless considers

the pre-existent . . . Word that became flesh in Jesus Christ not as a concretization, personification or repetition of Israel's Torah, but on the contrary, as its basis, what makes it possible, its criterion and measuring

41. Menke, *Jesus ist Gott der Sohn*, p. 33.

42. For example Elliott R. Wolfson, "Judaism and Incarnation: The Imaginal Body of God," in Tikva Frymer-Kensky, David Novak, Peter Ochs, David Fox Sandmel, and Michael A. Signer, eds., *Christianity in Jewish Terms* (Boulder, CO: Westview, 2000), pp. 239-54. See the section "God as Torah," pp. 246-51. There are numerous references both in Jewish discussions of incarnation and in Christian exegesis and theology to the close relationship between Torah and Wisdom. Alon Goshen-Gottstein moves to the actual issue of incarnation, using preexistence as his yardstick, and notes that the "pre-existence of the Torah is commonplace within rabbinic literature. Following Proverbs 8, the Torah is identified with wisdom and is taken to be pre-existent. The Torah is a heavenly being. Its coming into physical form can legitimately be viewed as an instance of incarnation. . . . [t]his is one of the most significant senses, if not the most significant sense, of incarnation" (Alon Goshen-Gottstein, "Judaisms and Incarnational Theologies: Mapping Out the Parameters of Dialogue," *Journal of Ecumenical Studies* 39 [2002]: 219-47, 229f.). Discovering a similarity between the Jewish and Christian concepts of divine presence, Edward Kessler makes "comparisons with the Jewish understanding of Torah. Mainstream rabbinic Judaism taught that Moses received the Torah from Sinai but there was also a tradition that the Torah was in existence before the creation of the world (e.g., Ben Sira 1:1-5), or even before the creation of the Throne of Glory (Genesis Rabbah 1:4). Torah was equated with Wisdom (Proverbs 8:22) and Philo wrote about the pre-existence and role in creation of the word of God *(logos)*, which he identified with the Torah" (Edward Kessler, in Hans Hermann Henrix and Edward Kessler, *God's Presence in Israel and Incarnation: A Christian-Jewish Dialogue*, http://www.jcrelations.net/en/?item=2990). Moreover, Christian exegesis in general recognizes that John's prologue alludes to Jewish speculation on wisdom as well as to the revelation at Sinai and to the tent of meeting (see the corresponding references in footnote 26 and further allusions to the nearness between Torah and Wisdom in the essay of Groppe, "The Tri-Unity of God").

rod. . . . The Torah is the interpretation of the eternal Logos and not the other way around, the Logos become flesh is the mere illustration of the Torah. Obedience to the Torah brings the Israelite into communion with YHWH and is therefore the mediation of the same salvation that Jesus also proclaimed. But contrary to Jesus Christ, the Torah as such *is* not communion with YHWH (eternal life).[43]

Menke's claim that John 1:17 does not devalue the law can be reaffirmed in a more positive way. For John 1:17a and 17b are not to be read antithetically.[44] The law given through Moses definitely participates in grace and truth, and the grace that came through Jesus Christ is not without any reference to the law. How else could it be the same salvation — as Menke rightly says — that is transmitted through obedience to the Torah and that Jesus proclaimed? In addition, Menke's position attributes a markedly christological finality to the Torah by calling Jesus Christ the reason for the Torah and the reality that makes the Torah possible. If one accepts this position, it becomes theologically possible to emphasize the relationship between Torah and Jesus Christ and to understand Jesus Christ as the illustration of the Torah, as the Torah becomes a living person. Only at first glance, this characterization would seem to have a parallel, for example, when Rabbi Eliezer ben Hyrkanos is called a living Torah scroll or an embodiment of the Torah.[45] For in Jewish self-understanding, Hyrkanos remains *one* teacher of the Torah and he belongs to a chain of teachers, alongside of or in opposition to many other teachers of the Torah. Years ago already, Franz Mussner[46] drew attention to a distinguishing feature between Judaism and Christianity: whereas on the Jewish side reference to a

---

43. Menke, *Jesus ist Gott der Sohn,* p. 33; see also p. 200.

44. Schnackenburg, *Das Johannesevangelium,* p. 252, and the extensive discussion in Denker, *Das Wort wurde messianischer Mensch,* pp. 292-310, and Theobald, *Das Evangelium nach Johannes,* pp. 133-35.

45. Jacobus Schoneveld, "Die Thora in Person. Eine Lektüre des Prologs des Johannesevangeliums als Beitrag zu einer Christologie ohne Antisemitismus," *Kirche und Israel* 6 (1991): 40-53, 46. See also Theobald, *Das Evangelium nach Johannes,* p. 137. But cf. also Peter von der Osten-Sacken, "Logos als Tora? Anfragen an eine neue Auslegung des Johannesprologs," *Kirche und Israel* 9 (1994): 138-49.

46. Thus the reference already in Franz Mussner, "Die Beschränkung auf einen einzigen Lehrer. Zu einer wenig beachteten differentia specifica zwischen Judentum und Christentum," in Gotthold Müller, ed., *Israel hat dennoch Gott zum Trost. FS Sch. Ben-Chorin* (Trier: Paulinus-Verlag, 1978), pp. 33-43. See also Franz Mussner, *Traktat über die Juden* (Göttingen: Vandenhoeck & Ruprecht, 1979), pp. 363-70.

chain of teachers is essential in interpreting the Torah, on the Christian side the one teacher of the Torah, Jesus, is essential: "You have one teacher" (Matt. 23:10).

When Pope Benedict XVI speaks of the "living Torah" or the "Torah become a person," he does not mean that in Jesus Christ "only" or "nothing other than" the repetition of Israel's Torah is to be seen. Rather, what he says is in response to Jacob Neusner's fear, when in his Jewish understanding of Jesus, he sees Jesus in the place of the Torah and at the height of God. What shocks Neusner is Benedict's point of reference in the affirmation: Jesus has the authority of the Torah and of the giver of the Torah. His Torah is the "Torah of the Messiah," which the pope compares with the Torah of Moses. The fulfillment of the Torah of the Messiah "demands more, not less righteousness" (p. 133). Benedict does not want to speak in favor of abolishing the Torah of Moses through Jesus.[47] His emphasis, however, on the radically new interpretation of the Torah through Jesus obliges him to seek correspondences between the new interpretation by Jesus and the "inner structure of the Torah itself" (p. 159). He sees within the Torah itself an "opposition between changeable, casuistic law . . . and the essential principles of God's law" that the prophets themselves impressed upon their listeners. Jesus takes this up and "corresponds with the inner structure of the Torah itself." Thus he is before us "as the prophetic interpreter of the Torah. He does not abolish it, but he fulfills it, and he does so precisely by assigning reason its sphere of responsibility for acting in history" (pp. 159f.). Of this prophetic interpreter we are told "a statement that never ceases to surprise us. It makes God's fidelity to God's self and Jesus' fidelity to the faith of Israel unmistakably clear: 'Do not think that I have come to abolish the Law and the Prophets; I have come not to abolish but to fulfill . . .' (Mt 5:17-19)" (p. 133).

The characterization of Jesus as the personified Torah, which has the nature of a title, means positively that Jesus fulfills the Torah, that he was a son of the people of Israel who faithfully adhered to the Torah, and that the Torah became incarnate in him. Over and beyond this central positive content, however, the title of Jesus Christ as incarnate Torah also has considerable critical significance.[48] It shows the problematic nature of a tradi-

47. On the fact that this danger is not entirely absent, see Hans Hermann Henrix, "'Die lebendige Tora Gottes': Zum Dialog von Papst Benedikt XVI mit Rabbiner Jacob Neusner in seinem Jesus-Buch," *Theologie und Philosophie* 83 (2008): 209-24, 222-24.

48. The following thoughts were stimulated indirectly by the reflections on the "grammar of difference" and "theologia negativa" by Gregor Maria Hoff in his essay elsewhere in this volume.

tion in theology and the church that was and is in danger of saying a persistent or fundamental "no" to Israel's Torah. This is not only the danger confronting the church of the Reformation with its slogan "freedom from the law" and its proclamation of a Torah-free gospel. It is also the danger caused by a relative lack of relationship that separates Jesus and the Torah by saying: the Torah belongs to the Jews, Jesus to the Christians. Thomas Aquinas could acknowledge: *"lex vetus manifestabat praecepta legis naturae,"* that is, "the old law contains natural law," but therefore "the old law" is only valid insofar as it belongs to natural law. Aquinas argued that the additions to the "old law" that go beyond natural law and are not imposed upon the other nations are only binding on the Jewish people and aim at preparing them for the coming of Christ. With the coming of Christ, these "additions" are dead, and for Christians they even bring death (cf. *Summa Theologica* 1/II q. 98,5; q. 103,4; 104,3).[49] A long tradition in theology and the church follows Aquinas's position, which acknowledged the Torah as God's teaching only insofar as it was of a universal nature. In such a tradition, the Decalogue was not judged to be God's teaching because it was given at Sinai to Moses and his people, but rather because it was in accord with natural law. This logic, however, forfeited not only the divine origins of the Sinai covenant and the Decalogue's relationship to revelation, but also the reality of Jesus as a follower of the Torah and of the Decalogue. The theological understanding of Jesus Christ as the personified Torah claims precisely this relationship between Jesus and the Torah.

Thus, understanding Jesus as the personified Torah stands critically against a tradition of separation between Jesus and the Torah. It also challenges the contemporary Christian-Jewish encounter to clarify how the Torah is to be understood, something that above all requires critical reflection on different Jewish and Christian experiences. Jewish exegetes who work with the New Testament emphasize that Jesus was Torah-observant, and see him within the normal Jewish debate over the proper ways of living a Torah-based life.[50] This exegetical acknowledgment makes possible the further Jewish perception that for Christians as well as for Jews, faith embodies a way of acting that is pleasing to God and in accordance with

49. For a discussion of this position, see not only Klaus Müller, *Tora für die Völker. Die noachidischen Gebote und Ansätze zu ihrer Rezeption im Christentum* (Berlin: Institut Kirche und Judentum, 1994), pp. 210-13, but also Michael Wyschogrod, *Abraham's Promise. Judaism and Jewish-Christian Relations* (Grand Rapids: Eerdmans, 2004), p. 208.

50. See the sketch in Meyer, *Christologie im Schatten der Shoah*, pp. 104-7, and Osten-Sacken's comments, "Logos als Thora?" pp. 140-42.

his teaching. Although some Jewish voices insist that the Torah is God's gift only for Israel and that it thus distinguishes Israel from all the nations of the world, other Jewish scholars grant that Christian ethics go beyond the concept of the seven Noahide laws and are similar to Torah ethics.[51]

Nevertheless, Jews pose this critical question: Why does the Christian "observance" of the Torah include only parts of the Torah and proceed selectively?[52] This query is not silenced simply by understanding Jesus Christ as the personified Torah. The question is not directed toward the Jesus who lived the Torah, but toward Christians who in their understanding of the Decalogue or the interpretation of the Torah by Jesus in the Sermon on the Mount (Matthew 5–7) seem to respect the Torah only partially and selectively.[53] A theology that takes seriously the characterization of Jesus as the embodied Torah is thus questioned critically. The Torah is impressed upon and transmitted to the church by its Lord in accordance with Matthew 5:17f. and through his lived obedience to the Torah, which led him even to his death. In her contribution to this volume, Elizabeth Groppe hints at a pneumatological point in this: "At Pentecost, the Spirit of Christ who was Torah incarnate was poured out on people of all nations of the earth."[54] Analogous to the Jewish understanding, one could say: just as the written Torah is transmitted to the Jewish people through the oral Torah of the Talmud, the Torah is transmitted to the church through Jesus (or the Spirit who raised Jesus from death). Paul van Buren concluded: "We could say that the story of Jesus is the church's Talmud that takes us to Torah. That is why the church can recite the Shema, for Jesus teaches the church to love the Lord our God with all its heart and strength, and to love the neighbor as oneself."[55]

In order to take Jesus seriously as the Torah incarnate, Paul van Buren's ecclesiological thoughts should also be considered:

51. Thus, for example, the fourth thesis in "Dabru Emet": "Jews and Christians accept the moral principles of Torah," in Frymer-Kensky et al., eds., *Christianity in Jewish Terms*, p. xvi.

52. Examples of the critical discussion around the Torah can be found in the contributions by David Novak, Elliott N. Dorff, and Stanley Hauerwas, in *Christianity in Jewish Terms*, pp. 115-40.

53. That can occur very directly and in a very personal way, as happened to the author when Michael Wyschogrod spontaneously asked me during a walk: "Hans Hermann, why do you eat pork?" The question caught me defenseless and its challenge remains.

54. Groppe, "The Tri-Unity of God," p. 176.

55. Paul van Buren, "Torah, Israel, Jesus, Church — Today," http://www.jcrelations.net/en/?item=791.

The connection between the Torah and the church is and should be fundamental, because Christians can never relate to the real, the living Jesus without the Torah. A Jesus apart from Torah is not the real Jesus, not the Jew of Nazareth, not the living Jesus who died and rose for us according to the Scripture, but a figment of pious imagination. Set the church adrift from Torah and you set the church adrift, not merely from its foundations in Israel, but adrift from its foundation in Jesus Christ. The future for the church, if it is to have a future as the church of the God and Father of Jesus Christ, lies in its discovering, precisely as Gentiles and not Israel, the priority of the Torah and so of its Old Testament in its liturgy and for life, and so of its learning to re-read its New Testament always in the light of the Old Testament.[56]

Jesus' christological title as the personified Torah thus teaches us to take Israel's Torah seriously in a new way. It puts the right of and the talk about a Torah-free gospel to the test and counters such tradition by asking more precisely about the "Torah contours" of Christian identity and existence.[57] Thus, in the midst of the difference between Judaism and Christianity, Jesus' title of Torah incarnate maintains a critical awareness of the abiding relationship of faith in Christ to the Torah.

Over and beyond this, a soteriological consequence of this title can also be perceived.[58] If Christians trust in God's blessing upon Jewish walking in accord with Israel's Torah and if this halakhic "walking" can be considered salvific only when related to the fundamental Christian belief that every salvation is the salvation of Jesus Christ, then saying that Jesus Christ is the living Torah can be understood as denoting such mediation. Then that which for Jews is salvific — life according to the Torah, trust in God's Word, faith in God's promise — would be in contact with Jesus Christ and would be taken up in him in a way that confirms, reaffirms, or reinforces, since Jesus Christ is obedient to the Torah and fulfills it. He is the "Yes" of it (see 2 Cor. 1:19); he does not abolish it, but rather does it, reinforces and

---

56. Van Buren, "Torah, Israel, Jesus, Church — Today."

57. Thus the question arises, how being in conformity with Christ through a Christian life is to be interpreted as conformity with the Torah, as Philip A. Cunningham and Didier Pollefeyt discuss in their contribution. A more visible "conformity with the Torah" of Christian existence might then be the precondition for articulating in dialogue Jewish living according to Israel's Torah being in conformity with Christ.

58. Regarding soteriological reflection, see Christian M. Rutishauser, "'The Old Unrevoked Covenant' and 'Salvation for All Nations in Christ' — Catholic Doctrines in Contradiction?" elsewhere in this volume.

fulfills it, as Benedict XVI says in emphatic reference to Matthew 5:17 (see pp. 100 and 133). Jesus Christ learns the Torah[59] and his journey and life are lived Torah. Jesus is the Torah become a living person; he is the Torah incarnate. Whoever obeys the Torah as a Jew and strives toward the goal "to be an incarnation of the Torah,"[60] walks on his or her way in a manner that, because of Jesus Christ's link with the Torah, Christians believe to be salvific communion with Christ as the Torah incarnate. Klaus Hemmerle once expressed this as follows: "Jesus' communion with the faith and the history of Israel . . . indicates the point at which the specific and exclusive Christian way to salvation, Jesus Christ himself, takes into himself and comes into inner contact with that which has salvific significance for Jews: life according to the Torah, concrete faith in God's promise as it is . . . expressed by Jews, acceptance from God's hand of the destiny of suffering."[61] Here we find expressed theologically what Yves Congar noted decades ago in his interpretation of the French bishops' document, "The Attitude of Christians towards Judaism" of April 16, 1973: Jews "are saved by the observance of their religion and by putting their religion into practice."[62]

59. Thus in his address of April 11, 1997, John Paul II pointed out that "Jesus also came humanly to know these texts; he nourished his mind and heart with them . . ." *KuJ II*, pp. 103f.

60. Thus the astonishing phrase by Abraham Joshua Heschel, *God in Search of Man: A Philosophy of Judaism* (New York: Farrar, Straus & Cudahy, 1995), p. 311: "The Torah has no glory if man remains apart. The goal is for man to be an incarnation of the Torah." Jacob Neusner uses the term "incarnation" in a very particular sense and gives its connection with the Torah another formulation, when naming the sage a "Torah incarnate"; similarly Goshen-Gottstein, "Judaisms and Incarnational Theologies: Mapping Out the Parameters of Dialogue," pp. 230-32. On Heschel's understanding of the Torah, cf. also Groppe's notes in "The Tri-Unity of God."

61. Klaus Hemmerle, *Freiburger Leitlinien zum Lernprozess Christen Juden. Theologische und didaktische Grundlegung,* ed. Günter Biemer (Düsseldorf: Patmos, 1981), pp. 145-50, 149; see also Menke, *Jesus ist Gott der Sohn,* pp. 471, 521: the Torah is "similar to Christianity's seven sacraments that are an effective symbol of communion with God and cannot be separated from Christ. . . . [w]hoever understands them like Jesus as the Father's grace, is brought into conformity with Christ through their incarnation in his or her own life — also when he or she does not confess Jesus as the Christ. For Christ did not abolish the Torah, but through his life and death, he determined it to continue as a sacrament of communion with the Father."

62. Yves Congar, "Das bischöfliche Dokument über die Juden. Ein Schritt zu einem besseren Verständnis," *Freiburger Rundbrief* 25 (1973): 37f. The French bishops' document can be found in: *KuJ I,* pp. 149-56. On a soteriological thesis in a broader sense that is based on the Pontifical Biblical Commission and its 2001 document's statement concerning the "great value [of the Old Testament] as the Word of God" and that attempts trust in the salvation of Israel without explicit christological mediation, see Hans Hermann Henrix,

c. Participation of Jewish Identity in the "Eternal Significance of the Humanity of Jesus" (Karl Rahner)

The challenge to take seriously the Jewishness of Jesus as christologically relevant means looking at the Jewish identity of the incarnation as the whole of the life, work, and destiny of Jesus. This challenge extends as well to his death as a Jewish death,[63] and to his resurrection in its relationship to Israel. First attempts have been made. Thus, for example, Friedrich-Wilhelm Marquardt did not shy away from interpreting the resurrection as "a Jewish faith experience" and from calling Easter "a story to be understood in the sense of the Old Testament."[64] And Paul van Buren understood Easter as a confirmation of the covenant with Israel, and saw Easter as a sign "that God's affair with Israel is continuing."[65] To conclude this essay, we shall now consider a different subject that has to do with a very specific tradition of Christian piety that Karl Rahner discussed in a contribution to his christology.

Karl Rahner was impressive as a theologian not least because he moved beyond the usual confines of theological thinking and looked again and again at the existential side of the faith that was being reflected upon theologically. Conversely, he uncovered the theological implications of existential piety. He did not want the piety in the thinker and the thoughtfulness of the pious to be separated from one another. Therefore, he also worked theologically on devotion to the Sacred Heart, a specifically Christian expression of piety. To Jewish piety, it seems worlds away, but perhaps this devotion is after all not hermetically closed to Jewish understanding.[66] Rahner asked whether the Christian's pious devotion really reaches "what we call the heart of Jesus" (p. 35).[67] "This heart — if it is not turned into

---

Judentum und Christentum — Gemeinschaft wider Willen (Regensburg: Friedrich Pustet, 2008), pp. 110-33.

63. Such a characterization of the death of Jesus is relevant to the theme of the church's teaching on this death that is discussed by Mary Boys, "Facing History: The Church and Its Teaching on the Death of Jesus," elsewhere in this collection.

64. Marquardt, *Das Christliche Bekenntnis zu Jesus, dem Juden*, vol. 2, pp. 293ff.

65. Paul van Buren, "Eine Antwort an Wolfgang Schweitzer," in Wolfgang Schweitzer, ed., *Der Jude Jesus und die Völker der Welt. Ein Gespräch mit Paul M. Buren* (Berlin: Verlag Institut Kirche und Judentum, 1993), pp. 173-88, 184.

66. Thus to my astonishment, Zalman Schachter admitted to me with disarming openness during an encounter in Aachen in May 1980: "I love the devotion to the Sacred Heart because it reminds me of the open heart of God."

67. Karl Rahner, "The Eternal Significance of the Humanity of Jesus for our Relation-

just another, more colorful word for God and for the incomprehensibility of his unbounded love — is a *human* heart." This human heart must not be merely "the object of a backward-looking adoration which refers to the historical Lord during his life on earth." Rather, "this heart, which exists now, which no longer belongs to the world around us . . . is to be honored, adored and loved" (p. 39). If the heart of Jesus, the eternal now, is honored and adored, it is "the mediating object of the one act of *latria* [adoration] which has God for its goal" (p. 45). In answer to the question whether the human heart and the humanity of Christ can now be reached by the believer's worship, Rahner speaks of the relationship between the Creator-God and the creature. In his christology, Rahner thinks of the relationship between the Creator and the creature as parallel to the relationship between God and Jesus Christ; in the latter is the foundation and the goal of the Creator-creature relationship. "The true God is not the one who kills so that he himself can live. He is not 'the truly real' which like a vampire draws to himself and so to speak sucks out the proper reality of things different from himself. . . . The nearer one comes to him, the more real one becomes; . . . the more independent one becomes oneself." The creature is certainly that which is conditional, but as such, it "is loved unconditionally by the Unconditioned." Hence the creature has "a validity which makes it more than something merely provisional"; it does not dissolve before God (pp. 40-41). God has a "truly serious and unconditional love of created reality." That is why we may and even must also love that which God creates and loves "as something valid in the sight of God, as something eternally justified and hence as something divinely and religiously significant before God" (p. 41).

The mystic is not free of the temptation to let everything disappear in the face of God in mystical immersion in God's love and to think that he or she does not need to deal "with the humanity of Christ." Rahner emphasized the need to take seriously in the religious act the reality created and loved by God — this religious act as the lived relationship with God is *dulia*, an act of honoring the other, as a reality created and loved by God, and as an act of veneration. And he considered finding the creature *in* God, "the small in the great, the circumscribed in the boundless, the creature (the very creature itself) in the Creator," as the "highest phase of our relationship to God" (p. 43). In saying this, Rahner praised the "positive nature of creation,"

---

ship with God" (1953), in *Theological Investigations*, vol. 3, *The Theology of the Spiritual Life* (London: Cambridge University Press, 1967), pp. 35-46.

which reaches "its qualitatively unique climax . . . in Christ. For, according to the testimony of the faith, this created human nature is the indispensable and permanent gateway through which everything created must pass if it is to find the perfection of its eternal validity before God" (p. 43). Jesus of Nazareth is the "finite concrete being, this contingent being, who remains in all eternity."[68] His remaining eternally is relevant for our salvation:

> Jesus, the Man, not merely *was* at one time of decisive importance for our salvation, i.e. for the real finding of the absolute God, by his historical and now past acts of the Cross, etc., but — as the one who became man and has remained a creature — he is *now* and for all eternity the *permanent openness* of our finite being to the living God of infinite, eternal life; he is, therefore, even in his humanity the created reality for us which stands in the act of our religion in such a way that, without this act towards his humanity and through it . . . the basic religious act towards God could never reach its goal. (p. 44)

That is why Rahner wanted to draw upon his piety to ask whether, along with the beatific vision, the believer "might still be able to derive an 'accidental' joy from the humanity of Christ in heaven" (p. 44) as a way of corresponding with "the incarnational structure of the religious act." As a subjective parallel, the religious act thus structured corresponds with "the basic objective condition: viz. that in the Incarnate Word, God has communicated himself to the world, so that this Word remains eternally the Christ" (p. 45). For Rahner, the heart of Jesus meant "the original center of the human reality of the Son of God." The believing Christian's religious act "is mediated by and goes through this center to God" so that "the Heart" "really means the human heart." This heart has a love that "distinguished [it] — though inseparably — from the mystery of divine love," which "has incarnated itself in the heart of Jesus, in the flesh of our flesh" (p. 46). The center of the human existence of Jesus of Nazareth, his heart, is for the Christian the abiding "center of mediation, without which there can be no approach to God" (p. 46).

---

68. This position is not to be confused with the thesis of the Alexandrian church father Julian, bishop of Halikarnassos, according to which "the human nature of the redeemer after the hypostatic unification of the two natures was just as immortal as the nature of the Logos," thus according to Menke, *Jesus ist Gott der Sohn,* p. 264. In Rahner's question regarding the eternal significance of the humanity of Jesus, the reality of Jesus' death from which the resurrection liberates is not denied but rather presupposed.

In his thinking about the eternal significance of the humanity of Jesus for the relationship of the Christian to God, Rahner took seriously that which is created, human, and conditional, and yet it did not occur to him to honor the Jewish identity of the humanity of Jesus. Even nearly three decades later, as he conversed with Jewish scholar Pinchas Lapide, he still did not consider it of interest. In spite of all his reflection on the ontologically concrete — the human person of Jesus and his heart — he was not able to see the historically concrete, the Jew Jesus and his Jewish heart. And yet it is possible to inscribe that which is historically concrete into his thinking about the eternal significance of the humanity of Jesus. The heart of Jesus, which Rahner repeatedly emphasized, was a human heart — was, in fact, a Jewish heart. As John Paul II pointed out, Jesus nourished his heart with the texts of Israel's Bible, which were read and commented on during the gatherings in the synagogue. Jesus used them in his prayers and in his conduct; he was entirely penetrated by them and thus showed that he was an "authentic son of Israel." If the humanity of Jesus is of eternal significance, the defining element of Jewish identity also is eternally significant. It is an aspect that should also be included when the heart of Jesus is meant, venerated, and loved. Then love for the heart of Jesus also acquires the component of a love for Israel. And the love of Jesus is lived as love of Israel. In this faith act of the Christian, in his or her love for Jesus as love for Israel, this one concrete, individual "son of Israel" Jesus Christ is meant, venerated, and loved. But this act also contains a preliminary decision for respect, affection, and love as part of the fundamental Christian attitude toward the people whose son Jesus of Nazareth was. This would be a movement that belongs to the Christian relationship with God and does not simply indicate a private preference. For the God who is the object of devotion to the Sacred Heart showed his love for the whole of creation and humanity in his love for the people of Israel, and this God lives his love for the whole of humanity without forgetting his fidelity to Israel as the people that was first chosen.

5. Conclusion

The reflections in this essay have attempted to take the Jewishness of Jesus seriously for christology. They invoked relevant doctrinal or papal suggestions and then turned to incarnational christology. In sum, they affirmed that the Son of God became a Jew, understood not only as an instructional metaphor and an admonitory note of remembrance, but rather as a key for interpretation. Fundamental perspectives from theology and dogmatic history explored this interpretative key more deeply. Its significance was then pursued with regard to the characterization of Jesus Christ as son of Israel and incarnate Torah. In taking his Jewish identity seriously in connection with the eternal significance of the humanity of Jesus for humanity's relationship with God, as Karl Rahner did, new insights about the incarnation arise. The incarnation is not only a "Christmas" mystery having to do only with the birth of Jesus, but also embraces the whole of the life, work, suffering, and resurrection of Jesus, the son of Israel. Thus incarnational christology is linked to the concrete Jewish identity of Jesus Christ. Thereby, a bridge has been drawn between the incarnation and the Jewishness of Jesus.

The Dogmatic Significance of Christ Being Jewish

Barbara U. Meyer

1. His Story and His Memory

There is no traditional theological category for the Jewishness of Jesus and no developed discourse of its theological meaning. This is a chance to openly explore the matter by involving and also transcending disciplines such as christology, soteriology, and ecclesiology. Beyond the frameworks of traditional Christian teachings, the Jewishness of Jesus entails inseparably intertwined historical and theological dimensions. This link is not unusual in biblical thought and logic, and is already within the Bible referred to as memory.[1] But what exactly makes the Jewishness of Jesus christologically important? In what way is his being Jewish significant for the covenant, salvation, and reconciliation?

No serious theologian has denied the fact that Jesus was Jewish. Even New Testament scholars who were not sure about the historicity of Jesus as such did not deny his having been Jewish![2] Still, in New Testament scholarship the fact of Jesus' Jewishness is not stated often. Here, the debate re-

---

1. The most prominent example for the inseparable historical-theological link is the Exodus, which is referred to as a key memory for the relationship between God and the people Israel.

2. An exception is the Nazi "theologian" Walter Grundmann, who came to the conclusion that Jesus was not a Jew; his research, however, can hardly be designated as serious scholarly work. His Nazi-ideological attempt to "de-judaize" the New Testament eventually led to a "de-christianized" text, as had Marcion. Cf. Walter Grundmann, *Jesus der Galiläer und das Judentum* (Leipzig: Georg Wigand, 1940), p. 200. For analysis of Grundmann and his Nazi "Institute for the 'de-judaization' ('Entjudaisierung') of the New Testament," see Susannah Heschel, *The Aryan Jesus: Christian Theologians and the Bible* (Princeton: Princeton University Press, 2008).

volves around which of the Second Temple groups Jesus was closest to and whether he actually belonged to a specific group.[3]

Jesus' Jewishness is not explicitly stated in any of the founding ecumenical church creeds of the first centuries. His being Jewish is unanimously known from scripture, but it is not especially expressed in these early dogmatic writings. Maybe it had not been forgotten yet, and so no one saw a need to remind future generations of this matter. Apparently, it was not a question and thus no dogmatic discourse developed out of this specific attribute. However, this does not mean that the Jewishness of Jesus is not present in the creeds of the ecumenical councils. We will later see how Jesus' humanity and even his divinity are indeed qualified by Jewishness.

It is in contemporary church documents on the Jewish-Christian relation[4] where the Jewishness of Jesus is declared in explicit statements: they clearly function as theological sentences and are not supposed to be historical information.[5] The addressees are Christians, but also Jews whom the church approaches in an atmosphere of recognition and reconciliation. Jews need the information of Jesus being Jewish even less than Christians; in the nineteenth and the beginning of the twentieth centuries we meet a wave of Jewish literature embracing Jesus the Jew.[6]

Seen against Nazism and the Shoah, the memory of Jesus as being Jewish expresses resistance and criticism. Thus, Dietrich Bonhoeffer famously said that the expulsion of the Jews from Europe would lead to the expulsion of Jesus Christ: "for Jesus Christ was a Jew."[7]

---

3. Most enlightening is the comparative research of Shmuel Safrai, who could show remarkable closeness between Jesus and Second Temple Hasidism; see "Shmuel Safrai, Jesus and the Hasidic Movement" (Hebr.), in *The Jews in the Hellenistic Roman World*, ed. Isaiah Gafni et al. (Jerusalem, 1996). ET: Shmuel Safrai, "Jesus and the Hasidim," *Jerusalem Perspective* 42, 43, and 44 (1994): 3-22.

4. For a representative overview, see the website of the International Council of Christians and Jews: http://www.jcrelations.net/en/?area=Statements.

5. For a broad analysis of the matter, cf. Barbara U. Meyer, *Christologie im Schatten der Shoah, im Lichte Israels. Studien zu Paul van Buren und Friedrich-Wilhelm Marquardt* (Zürich: Theologischer Verlag, 2004), pp. 91-111.

6. Embracing the Jewish Jesus can imply criticism of Christian interpretations as well as criticism of traditional Jewish distance from Jesus. Cf. Aaron Abraham Kabak, *The Narrow Path: The Man from Nazareth* (Tel Aviv: Hebrew Literature Press, 1968; Hebr. 1937); Sholem Asch, *The Nazarene: A Novel Based on the Life of Christ* (New York: G. P. Putnam's Sons, 1939).

7. Dietrich Bonhoeffer, *Ethics* (New York: Touchstone, 1995), p. 91. Bonhoeffer wrote this in 1940.

In church statements of the second half of the twentieth century, we see the notion of Jewishness elaborated and "increased": that Jesus was born a Jew is highly consensual. Only in later documents we read that he also died as a Jew. But apparently the most difficult thing for Christian theologians is to say that he *lived* as a Jew. Jewish life leads back to a life of Torah, and viewing Jesus as an observant Jew can disturb a Christian identification with Jesus and striving to live in *imitatio Christi*.[8]

Even the simplest mentioning of Jesus being Jewish is pregnant with meaning.

But what precisely is the theological significance of this historical matter? The phenomenon of interwoven theological-historical dimensions fits the category of memory: the Jewishness of Jesus is deeply rooted in collective memory, at times suppressed, at other times recalled. Yosef Haim Yerushalmi distinguishes between "memory *(mneme)* and recollection *(anamnesis)*"; he characterizes memory as "essentially unbroken, continuous," and *anamnesis* as "recollection of that which has been forgotten."[9] Remembering Jesus the Jew seems to be both continuous and in recurring need of recollection. Never has this memory been eradicated in church history. Still, there has always been the need to remind Christians of it. According to accounts in both Paul's letters and in the Gospels, Jesus used the word *anamnesis* to inaugurate the memory of him in wine and bread. That which has become the Christian sacrament par excellence was for Jesus the Jewish blessing *(Kiddush)*. Thus the commandment to unite in memory of Christ, "do this to my anamnesis" (1 Cor. 11:24-25), is born out of the Jewish liturgy of Jesus.

Memory is not at all a vague occurrence and can even be more precise than historical testimonies. Its enfolding character makes it different from testimony. The memory of the Jewish Jesus invites us to imagine him within his Jewish community, as a member of a Jewish family who observed the *mitzvot* and was involved in halakhic discussions.

The Synoptic Gospels hardly use the attribute "Jewish" for anybody; when everybody is Jewish, there is no need to state the Jewishness of Jesus' followers and friends, let alone his own. But when Jesus and the disciples encounter non-Jews, this is mentioned. Only the Gospel of John names Jews, which has led to Christian violence in history and ongoing confu-

---

8. See David Flusser, *Jesus* (Jerusalem: Magnes Press, 1998).

9. Yosef Hayim Yerushalmi, *Zakhor: Jewish History and Jewish Memory* (New York: Schocken Books, 1989), p. 107.

sion, because "the Jews" are explicitly mentioned as the people persecuting Jesus. This is usually seen as the problem of a potentially anti-Jewish Gospel. But one could also say that the distortion primarily lies in not mentioning the disciples, friends, family, and Jesus himself as Jewish. In that case, in an overall Jewish context, opponents can also be Jewish — but not more Jewish than the disciples and Jesus himself.[10]

2. Paranetic Spirituality of Difference

In Paul's Letter to the Romans, his last and theologically most reflective letter, he emphasizes that Jesus is from Israel according to the flesh (Rom. 9:5). This fact is increasingly important for a growing majority of non-Jews in the Jesus movement and corresponds to the metaphor of the olive tree in Romans 11. Here the readers of Paul's appeal — not to forget the roots and not to boast over them — are explicitly without Jewish background. Thus, reminding the Jesus-followers of their non-Jewish background has a parenetic and preaching character already in scripture: the *parenesis,* the teaching of a certain state of mind as the spiritually appropriate behavior, comes to bear precisely in the difference of identity. Paul foresees the dangers of oblivious identification and undisturbed identity. Those who were far and are now close, those who were foreigners and are now are citizens (Eph. 2:19), need to remember the difference of their past. The unity in Christ is based on acknowledgment of difference. Realizing one's own otherness thus entails a spiritual exercise that precedes union in belief. True discipleship does not dissolve this otherness. And while it is historically not the first way of discipleship, it has become the main Christian experience. Christian belief and discipleship do not simply evolve out of identification. The primary spiritual exercise is remembering one's own otherness as well as indebtedness to the Other. Being one in Christ (Gal. 3:28) builds on this grateful memory and does not cross it out.

10. The explicit statement in *Nostra Aetate* that Jews are not to blame for the death of Jesus might seem superfluous in an enlightened world, but has in fact helped to reduce antisemitism more than any other saying of the church.

3. Identity Trouble

In a 1947 lecture Karl Barth emphasized the theological significance of the Jewishness of Jesus with remarkable rhetoric:

> When the Christian Church confesses Jesus Christ as the savior and servant of God for us, for all human beings, so also for the vast majority of those who have no direct connection with the people Israel, it does not make this confession of faith in Jesus Christ in spite of the fact that he was a Jew (as if this Jewishness of Jesus were a *pudendum* that one could and should ignore!). We can also not think that we believe in Jesus Christ who just happened to be an Israelite, but who could just as well have come from another people. No, here we must think very firmly: Jesus Christ, in whom we believe, whom we Christians from the Gentiles call our savior and praise as the one who fulfills God's work, was of necessity a Jew.[11]

What does it mean that Jesus Christ was "necessarily" Jewish? How does this attribute relate to his other qualities and properties? Are the other aspects of his identity interchangeable? And is his being Jewish connected to further features and characteristics, or does it stand in contrast to them?

African American liberation theologians have sometimes affirmed that Jesus was black. The question whether the color of Jesus' skin has an effect on his sending, changes his message, or has repercussions for salvation and reconciliation is not as simple as it might sound at first. Identification is an important aspect here: Would black people be more in Jesus' realm and reach if he is black? Will Jesus Christ reconcile whites and blacks if he is black? Nothing is said in the scriptures about Jesus being white. He is also not referred to as black. His skin might have been of color, but the texts do not care to mention it. Regarding reconciliation, it is certainly christologically wrong to say that Jesus Christ is white. This, however, does not lead to the conclusion that Jesus was black. But if descendants of former slaves remember the blackness of Jesus, it should be taken seriously like other

---

11. Karl Barth, *Dogmatik im Grundriß* (Zollikon/Zurich: Evangelischer Verlag, 1947), pp. 88ff. This text was part of the first lecture series that Barth gave to German theology students in the summer of 1946, shortly after World War II. The theme of the semester was the Apostolic Credo, and the quoted text is part of the explanation of the name Jesus and the title Christ and thus belongs to the basics of Christian belief.

strong memories.[12] The memory of the Exodus is also generally more intense for black than for white Christians, which underlines that remembering is connected to certain contexts promoting revelation or religious understanding.[13] James Cone has remarkably connected Jesus' being black to his being Jewish: "the blackness of Jesus brings out the soteriological meaning of his Jewishness. . . ."[14] But in what way blackness exactly serves to further qualify Jewishness is still to be explored. Cone sees a connection of both identities in their being oppressed. But both the Jewish and the black identity have lately been presented and experienced as free, proud, even powerful. Would then black success make Jesus more white? If it did, then the crucial attribute would not be black, but oppressed or disadvantaged. In a more recent revision of Cone's *God of the Oppressed,* he seems to qualify blackness with Jewishness: "He *is* black because he *was* a Jew."[15] Here Jewishness is not part of Christ present while blackness is. As Cone is remarkably sensitive to the soteriological significance of Jesus' Jewishness, this formulation is somewhat disappointing. His christological argumentation for the ongoing blackness of Christ would be even better supported by referring also to his Jewishness in the present.

Similarly, would Jewish sovereignty "Christianize" Jesus? May that never happen, Paul would say. The contemporary secular talk about Palestinians as the Jews of today regards Jewishness in a similar way. The statement that Jesus was Palestinian is often used politically to contrast with his Jewishness. But when the attribute "Palestinian" is combined with "Jew," an old-new horizon of truth opens: to describe Jesus as a Palestinian Jew is historically and geographically correct and can be helpful and inspiring to develop a hermeneutics of the many local metaphors in the Apostolic writings. In contemporary christology, to formulate Palestinian identity by reconciling idiomatically with Jesus the Jew expresses the spirit of Christ's mission to bring peace to Israel and the peoples.

Is there any meaning in the fact that Jesus was born a man? Neither the Gospels nor Paul is interested in Jesus' sex or gender. His being a man is not made a theme on its own account, though his being a Jewish man does

12. See Jacquelyn Grant, *White Women's Christ and Black Women's Jesus* (Atlanta: Scholars Press, 1989).

13. This corresponds to Dietrich Ritschl's understanding of revelation as "occasions" that "lead to 'rediscovery' of elements of tradition which were in the memory of the church." Dietrich Ritschl, *The Logic of Theology* (Philadelphia: Fortress Press, 1987), pp. 75-77.

14. James Cone, *God of the Oppressed* (Maryknoll, NY: Orbis, 1997), 124.

15. Cone, *God of the Oppressed,* p. 123.

carry theological relevance: circumcision is the sign of belonging to the covenant. In the Hebrew Jewish tradition, this connection is apparent as the Hebrew word for circumcision is *brit mila* (covenant of circumcision). Besides that, his being a man is not reported as being significant. Jewish women were and are members of the covenant just as men. Jewish feminists have discussed the question of an equivalent sign for women, but have not inaugurated one. As Hans Hermann Henrix points out, Jesus' Jewishness is due to his mother Mary,[16] so it can probably be said that it is not relevant for salvation that Jesus was a man.

To qualify Jesus' being Jewish as necessary means that the story of Jesus would have been a different story had he not been Jewish. And indeed, the story of Jesus Christ is unthinkable apart from the context of Israel. It would not make sense if oblivious to the memories and hopes of the Jewish people. Being Jewish is not a variable identity category like being a man and being black for understanding Jesus, though both of these features can have significance when connected to his Jewishness. The early Christians saw that they could not understand Jesus Christ disconnected from the history of Israel and uprooted from his Jewish surroundings. They opposed Marcion and regarded the idea of an "uprooted" Jesus Christ as a heresy: just as the God who sent Jesus is not an unknown God, Jesus is not of unknown belonging. On the contrary, Jesus knows his sacred text, his prayer, his law. He knows this God's word when he becomes God's Word. The story that the God of Sarah and Abraham is telling with the sending of Jesus cannot be told with a non-Jewish Jesus. The God of Israel could not have spoken the Word differently. Thus it can be said in the idiom of the church fathers, that there was no time when the Son was not Jewish.

4. Covenanted Belonging

Precisely as a Jew, Jesus does belong to the covenant. He is circumcised, he reads from the written Torah (Luke 4:17), he observes and discusses the oral Torah (Mark 12:18-27), and says *"Sh'ma Israel"* (Mark 12:29). Salvation, redemption, and reconciliation are all matters of the covenantal history, embedded and rooted in the relation between God and Israel. Whatever wounds Jesus heals, the healing occurs in God's covenanted reality. As Paul van Buren puts it, there was no time when God was not cove-

16. See his comments on pp. 125-27.

nanted.[17] God was not a God of creation first and became more specific later on. Rather, as Karl Barth underlines, creation is for the sake of the covenant.[18] Given the covenantal context, it becomes clear that Jesus' Jewishness is not only his central attribute but the heart of God's revelation. Had Jesus not been Jewish, he could not have led the peoples to the God of Abraham and Sarah, Moses and Miriam. The opening of the covenant for all peoples is sealed in Jesus' being Jewish.

5. True *Mensch,* True Jew

Although early dogmatic discourse engages primarily in the question of the Son's divinity, a denial of his full humanity has likewise been regarded as heresy. Docetism, the claim that Jesus Christ had not fully lived the human experience, was ruled out as a possibility to perceive the life of Jesus. The true suffering of Jesus was the key argument against Docetism. The mention of Jesus as Jewish emphasizes his concrete humanness against an abstract understanding of a principle of humanity. Thus using an idiom from Torah discourse, the memory of Jesus' Jewishness functions like a "fence" against Docetism, protecting the dogma of full humanness. Precisely as a Jew, Jesus Christ is truly and fully human and capable of suffering.

In theological attempts to emphasize the connection between Judaism and Christianity owing to the Jew Jesus, Jewishness has mainly been referred to as qualifying the human nature of the Son. Talking about the divinity of Jesus Christ seemed to reinforce the distance between Judaism and Christianity, which was seen as undesirable by many Christians involved in Jewish-Christian dialogue. Only recently Christian theologians have begun to develop a new appreciation of difference. The question used to be whether a christological statement was acceptable to Jews. In a new approach, the objective of nonmissionary christology is not to be harmful to Jews, and a christology that emphasizes Jesus' Jewishness might still be lacking the recognition of the remaining Jewish difference. A classical historical example is Luther's early writing "That Jesus Christ was born a Jew," known for its positive, but clearly missionary, attitude to Jews.

17. See Paul van Buren, *Christ in Context,* Part 3, *A Theology of the Jewish-Christian Reality* (San Francisco: Harper & Row, 1988), p. 227.

18. This is one of the structuring theological assumptions in Karl Barth's major opus, *The Church Dogmatics;* see Karl Barth, *Kirchliche Dogmatik* III/1 (Zürich: Evangelischer Verlag Zollikon, 1947), p. 261.

Especially in the early years of Christian-Jewish dialogue, Christian theologians who emphasized the Jewishness of Jesus tended to minimize talking about the divinity of Christ.[19] Here, the Anglican theologian Paul van Buren stands out in his deliberate discussion of Christ in the context of Israel.[20] He often mentions Jesus' Jewishness but elaborates throughout his christology how this Jewish belonging is relevant for the Jewish-Christian reality today. By not avoiding the title "Christ," van Buren succeeds in highlighting the present as the first tense of christology,[21] and thus fosters the Christian commitment to present-day Jewry.

In what way then can we say that the attribute of Jewishness qualifies the Son's divinity? Secular Israelis sometimes talk about "the Jewish God" in comparison with what they view as "the Christian God." But Christians believe that Jesus Christ called them to the God of Abraham and Sarah, to the God of Israel. While God has no religion, the God of Israel is determined by the partners in covenant. Just as it was not the principle of humanity that was present in Jesus Christ, it is not the principle of abstract transcendence that shines in him. Jesus Christ is truly *Mensch*,[22] and his being Jewish qualifies and thus underscores his humanness. When the church fathers said that Jesus Christ is Godly, they were thinking of the God of the Bible, the God of Israel, the God of the Jewish people. If any God is present in Jesus Christ, it is the God of the Jews.

Going back to Chalcedon, both the humanness and the godliness of the Son are qualified by Jesus' Jewishness, his membership in the covenant of Israel.

Jesus Christ draws the peoples to the God of Israel. His Jewishness is not just a matter of his own Jewish life and his human solidarity with his fellow Jews of yesterday and tomorrow. Precisely in the spirit of Paul's *paranesis*, his Jewishness reminds the believing peoples of their past and leads them into the gratitude of those who have found grace alongside Is-

---

19. Friedrich-Wilhelm Marquardt argues his decision to write of "Jesus from Nazareth" instead of "Jesus Christ" with his intention to hereby emphasize Jesus as Jew; Friedrich-Wilhem Marquardt, *Das christliche Bekenntnis zu Jesus, dem Juden. Eine Christologie*, vol. 2 (München: Kaiser, 1991), p. 47. Interestingly, Marquardt does not reduce the divinity of the Son, see pp. 420-38.

20. See van Buren, *Christ in Context*.

21. Van Buren, *Christ in Context*, p. 12.

22. I like to use the German inclusive term here instead of the English "man." The echo of the Yiddish is a conscious choice. Here "Mensch" stands for a particularly warm and caring person.

rael, which has lived and will live in the grace of the covenant. In Paul's logic, the Jewishness of Jesus is meaningful and salvation-relevant precisely for the non-Jewish believers.

6. The Jew and the *Muselmann*

For many Christian theologians engaged in Jewish-Christian dialogue, it became difficult to talk about the divinity of Jesus the Jew. But the rethinking of humanity is no less of a true challenge after the Shoah. Back in 1982 the Jewish philosopher Emil Fackenheim turned to Christian theologians with painful christological questions. His first question was, "Where would Jesus of Nazareth have been in Nazi-occupied Europe?"[23] Paul van Buren answered: "As a Jew, he would in all likelihood have been with his fellow Jews, in or on his way to the death camps." And van Buren adds: "only a few of his disciples were there where he surely would have been."[24] Appropriate to the tenor of the question, van Buren answers with Christian self-criticism. Many Christians today would support this response that shows the memory of Jesus' Jewishness as evoking Christian theological repentance and responsibility. Another question of Fackenheim remains extremely difficult to answer: "Could Jesus of Nazareth have been made into a *Muselmann*?"[25]

The term *Muselmann* was used in the concentration camps and subsequently in testimonial literature of survivors; it is an old German word for Muslim. Giorgio Agamben has recently extensively written on the term, whose origin is not quite clear.[26] Primo Levi describes the *Muselmann* as "non-men who march and labor in silence, the divine spark dead within them, already too empty to really suffer. One hesitates to call them living: one hesitates to call their death death, in the face of which they have no fear, as they are too tired to understand."[27]

Does full humanity mean that Christians need to believe that Jesus

23. Emil Fackenheim, *To Mend the World: Foundations of Post-Holocaust Thought* (New York: Schocken Books, 1989), p. 280.

24. Van Buren, *Christ in Context*, p. 71.

25. Fackenheim, *To Mend the World*, p. 286.

26. See Giorgio Agamben, *Remnants of Auschwitz: The Witness and the Archive* (Brooklyn: Zone Books, 2000).

27. Primo Levi, *Se questo è un uomo* (Turin: Einaudi, 1976 [1958]), p. 113; ET: *If This Is a Man/The Truce*, trans. Stuart Woolf, with an introduction by Paul Bailey and an afterword by the author (London: Abacus, 1987), p. 96.

could have been turned into a *Muselmann?* Agamben argues that not only life, but also death has been denied its dignity. This is a troubling thought for any christological thinking about the cross. But also christologies that focus on the resurrection are challenged here. Does "truly human" include the possibility of losing the "divine spark"? If we are compelled to view Jesus as someone who could have become "too empty to suffer" and that his death could not be called death, then we need to see Docetism as an option. This would, according to Athanasius, question salvation.

The painful memory of the *Muselmann,* who does not feel pain anymore, calls for a renewed commitment to humanity. In a world that has seen the destruction of humanity and looked away, witnessing Jesus Christ the Jew means first and foremost commitment to the divine in human beings. Gil Anidjar has recently drawn attention to the striking paradox of the suffering Jew who is turned — in language — into a Muslim. However, the etymology of the death-camp term will not be a good starting point for Christian-Jewish-Muslim relations and should not be overinterpreted. But in accordance with the paranetical function of memory, Christians might be reminded that humiliating Jews can hurt also Muslims.

In terms of an ethics of responsibility for the Other as articulated by Emmanuel Levinas, a commitment to the Jewish people is a Christian priority: an *a priori,* a given responsibility and a calling, rather than a transient preference of dialogue.[28] But like "the third" in Levinasian philosophy, who disturbs and balances unlimited responsibility for the one specific Other, there are further responsibilities to face. Repairing a wounded Jewish-Christian relationship cannot be durable at the expense of Muslims.[29]

7. Otherness and Identification

The Jewish identity of Jesus encourages a continuing conversation between scripture and dogma. Perceiving the Jewishness of Jesus not only as a historical fact but as a memory leads to a critical theological reflection that opens further discourses of identity and belonging. The critical function of Jesus' Jewishness evolves from the identity gap between Jesus and

28. Emmanuel Levinas, *Otherwise Than Being or Beyond Essence* (Pittsburgh: Duquesne University Press, 1998), p. 10.

29. See Barbara Meyer, "Der Andere des Anderen ist ein Anderer," in *Von Gott reden im Land der Täter. Theologische Stimmen der dritten Generation seit der Shoah* (Darmstadt: Wissenschaftliche Buchgesellschaft, 2001), pp. 110-22.

his followers and believers, the overwhelming majority of whom today are not Jewish. (For Jesus-believing Jews, his Jewishness does not have this critical function, which does not mean that it is less meaningful.) This is different from all other identities of Jesus, which are often emphasized in order to empower disadvantaged groups of believers through direct identification. But shall Christians recognize Jesus' Jewishness at the expense of their closeness to him? Identifying with Jesus the *Mensch* is encouraged not only in pious Christian groups, but already in the early church. The church fathers made an explicit connection between identifying with Christ's humanity and being saved in him. Marginalized groups of believers may find the focus of the weakness attributed to them empowered by a black, feminist, womanist, or Palestinian Jesus. This would be in line with Chalcedon's affirming message "like us in all respects." An idealization of the oppressed can be avoided while remembering the whole phrase: "like us in all respects except for sin."

Does "like us in all respects" disregard Jesus' Jewish otherness for the majority of non-Jewish Christians? Only Paul continually formulates the truth of Christ differently for believers with or without Jewish heritage (especially in his Letter to the Romans). The ecumenical councils of the early church pronounced the same creed for all Christian men and women, and there are no acculturations for diverse futures prepared here.

The Jewishness of Jesus does not instantaneously empower Christians without Jewish family ties. But it also does not stand for an unbridgeable difference between the believers and Christ, like being without sin. In his being Jewish Jesus shares something with Jews that he does not share with Christians. The alternatives of pure identification versus pure difference will be too narrow here. In an anti-missionary encounter between Jews and Christians, Jews have new opportunities to relate freely to Jesus today, especially in Israel, where Christianity does not present any contemporary threat. Jewish Israelis often sense an intuition for Jesus, which they usually perceive in contrast to Christianity. In literature and poetry this is expressed as reinforcement of Jesus' humanity.[30] It is even among very learned Israeli academics widely overlooked that Jesus' full humanity is not heresy but dogma for all Christians. Still, the Jewish defense of Jesus against Christian traditional and official interpretations reminds us of a

---

30. See the latest Jesus-poetry by a professor for Mikra (Bible) at the Hebrew University of Jerusalem, Yair Zakovitch, *Jesus Reads the Gospels* (Hebr.) (Tel Aviv: Am Oved Publishers, 2007).

bond older than Christianity. After all those years, and after considerable changes within Judaism,[31] even secular Jewish Israelis today recognize Jesus as a Jew — like themselves in this respect.

Jews are not closer to Jesus than Christians are and don't aspire to be. But Jesus might be closer to them. Christians need not feel any competition here. In a post-Shoah world, the Jewish recognition of Jesus as a Jew is more than Christians could have hoped for. It is the deepest recognition imaginable, even, and maybe especially, in a context of Jews criticizing Christianity.

The postmodern identity discourse has brought up unprecedented choices. Ontological limitations have been replaced by cultural flexibilities and the prospect of choosing one's belonging rather than being born into it. The freedom of self-representation and performance has dominated the gender-discourse. But how would this new choice of self-perception translate into christology?

Whether Jewish identity should be regarded as a fact or a choice remains a highly complex question between religious and cultural understandings. The theological category of chosenness transcends both. Jesus is chosen by God, and the human expression and answer to this God's choice is Jewishness. But Jewish life and identity change with time and place. The Jewishness of the living Christ is not limited to expressions of Jewish heritage in the Second Temple period. Rather, the continuity of Jewish identity lies in the Jewish people, in true persons. This is the reason why the thoughts and feelings and belongings of today's Jews are relevant for contemporary christology.

Thus, the truth of "like us in all respects" is not lessened by Jesus' Jewish otherness. It is deepened by the witness of the Other who is and will be first (Rom. 1:16).

Among the various identities of Jesus Christ, it is his Jewishness that binds Christians to the living God of the living covenant. The memory of Jesus' being Jewish brings with it a re-membering of this Jew to his fellow Jews. Their recognition of Jesus as a Jew is a meaningful acknowledgment and a sign of Christian belonging to the same God. Thus without conversion or confusion, Christians are inseparably and indivisibly responsible to the Jewishness of the one Jew and the other Jews.

---

31. See Daniel Boyarin, *Border Lines: The Partition of Judaeo-Christianity* (Philadelphia: University of Pennsylvania Press, 2004).

A Jewish Response to Hans Hermann Henrix and Barbara Meyer

Edward Kessler

Barbara Meyer and Hans Herman Henrix offer two profound papers on the theological significance of the Jewishness of Jesus. Although Christians increasingly take for granted that Jesus was born, lived, and died a Jew and that the first Christians were Jews, both scholars admit that the theological implications are rarely considered. In the twenty years I have been engaged in teaching and writing on Jewish-Christian relations, I have often wondered to what extent Christian awareness of Jesus' Jewish belief and practice remained mere background for Christian self-understanding and formation of identity. As Henrix tentatively acknowledges, "it is questionable whether the Jewishness of Jesus has been regarded with sufficient seriousness by theologians writing in the area of christology" (p. 115). I welcome their endeavor to tackle challenging theological questions, which is part of a quest by all the contributors of this book, to regain the momentum in the Jewish-Christian encounter which has been slowing considerably in the last ten years or so.

In any such study we should first of all recognize the achievements in Jewish-Christian relations since 1965, the year of the promulgation of *Nostra Aetate*. Jewish-Christian relations have reached a point where, to a great extent, the church now asserts its debt to its Jewish heritage and respect for Judaism, while repudiating triumphalism. Although anti-Jewish Christian sentiment still exists, less and less do we come across the old and prejudiced attitudes that had for so many centuries pervaded the pews of the churches, the halls of the seminaries, and the citadels of the religious authorities. Applying this transformation to the topic under consideration, we note that Christian memory no longer ignores that Jesus and his entire family were observant Jews, and both Henrix and Meyer rightly point out that the Jewishness of Jesus has been (and remains) the subject of numerous official (and unofficial) church statements. No serious Christian theologian or New Testament teacher today can ignore this fundamental change, which as John Pawlikowski has reminded us, represents the most radical development in the ordinary magisterium of the Catholic Church to emerge from the Second Vatican Council (p. 16).

Yet, Christian memory faces multiple distortions if the theological significance of the Jewishness of Jesus remains unconsidered. What makes these two papers original and potentially significant is that in their exploration of the Jewishness of Jesus they avoid the temptation to consider Jesus Jewish in an ethnic sense only, in other words, simply as part of the Jewish people. Rather, they explore what it means that Jesus was Jewish in a religious sense also. Jesus' faith in God was shaped by the covenant at Sinai, nourished by Jewish narratives about God's saving deeds in history, and expressed by the prayers, rituals, and practices of Judaism as well as by observance of Torah. According to Meyer, "the memory of the Jewish Jesus invites us to imagine him within his Jewish community . . . involved in halakhic discussions" (p. 146). Both scholars reflect on the significance of the religious identity of Jesus the Jew in terms of either incarnational theology (Henrix) or covenantal membership (Meyer).

One of the challenges faced by Henrix (and to a lesser extent, Meyer) is the means of reexamining the varied and complex doctrinal discussions in the early church councils in the context of the Jewish-Christian encounter. First-century Judaism was just as varied and diverse, but unfortunately unremarked upon by either contributor. Of course, it is difficult to do justice to the complexity of early (not "late"!) Judaism, but both papers might have benefited from more reflection on this in their discussion of the theological significance of the Jewishness of Jesus. (And, to be fair, space limitations may have prevented the authors from considering the implications of Jewish diversity in the early centuries.)

For example, although Jesus' major dealings were with Pharisees and Sadducees, they were two among many "Judaisms" in the first century C.E., including significantly (as I shall mention below), Philo and the Greek-speaking Jews. Although the Sadducees were a powerful faction in Judean politics, unlike the Pharisees they did not survive the destruction of Jerusalem in 70 C.E.

The Pharisees are prominent as the main rivals of Jesus in the Gospel accounts of his ministry, yet they had more in common with Jesus than other contemporary Jewish groups. They shared many beliefs such as belief in the coming of the messiah, in life after death and the resurrection of the dead, immortality, and a Day of Judgment. Indeed, the level of overlap and coherence between the teachings of Jesus and the Pharisees probably outweighs the areas of difference of opinion. (The harsh criticism of the Pharisees in the Gospels has as much to do with rivalry between the communities in which the texts were written — especially the Matthean community — as with anything that happened during the lifetime of Jesus.)

Balancing the need to take seriously first-century Jewish diversity, it is also important to acknowledge that a combination of belief and practice continued to identify Jews, even when they were widely scattered and/or diverged in practice. For all the differences within the divergent interpretations of Judaism of that time, there was much more in common, and two convictions especially, that bound all Jews together. The first, which may be helpful for Henrix's exploration of incarnational christology, is a belief in the one and only God, who accepted no rivals. God made behavioral demands of his people (for Jews, this may be described as ethical monotheism). The second, which sheds light on Meyer's analysis of covenantal christology, is that God has entered into a special covenantal relationship with the Jewish people. In the call of Abraham, the Exodus from Egypt, and the giving of the Torah on Sinai, God had elected and chosen his own people.

For Meyer, "there was no time the Son was not Jewish" (p. 150). Her theological reflection is based on a covenantal christology because Jesus' humanity *and* his godliness are "qualified by Jesus' Jewishness, his membership in the covenant of Israel" (p. 152). It is therefore important for Christians to ponder the fact that Jesus was Jewish in a religious sense. Meyer refers to the significance of the religion of Jesus the Jew by quoting Karl Barth, who stated that "Jesus Christ, in whom we believe . . . was of necessity a Jew" (p. 148).

My understanding of her paper is that she implies that both Jews and Christians can justly claim to be chosen by God. She does not assert this as a new doctrine, for it is surely a reexpression of an old doctrine expressed by Paul in his Letter to the Romans (especially chapters 9–11). If the church, as the New Israel, replaced the Old Israel as the inheritor of God's promises, does this mean that God reneges on his word? If God has done so with regard to Jews, what guarantee is there for the churches that he won't do so again, this time to Christians?

One might argue against Paul by saying that, if the Jews have not kept faith with God, then God has a perfect right to cast them off. It is interesting that Christians who argue this way have not often drawn the same de-

duction about Christian faithfulness, which has not been a notable characteristic of the last two millennia. Actually, as Meyer implies, God seems to
have had a remarkable ability to keep faith with both Christians and Jews
(even when they have not kept faith with him, a point of which Paul is profoundly aware). For Meyer, like Paul, it is impossible for God to elect the
Jewish people and later displace them. The church's election derives from
that of Israel, and the Jewishness of Jesus implies, theologically, that God's
covenant with Israel remains unbroken — irrevocably.

Yet there remains a theological problem, illustrated by the following
quotations from *Nostra Aetate*. On the one hand, "the church is the new
people of God," while on the other, "the Jews remain most dear to God because of their fathers, for He does not repent of the gifts He makes nor of
the calls He issues (cf. Rom. 11:28-29)." In a mysterious way, it seems, the
Jewish people are in some way still elect even though the Christians are the
New Israel. Consequently, the church discovers the bond of identity between Jews and Christians when it searches into the meaning of its own existence. It has a relationship with Judaism unlike any other religion because
of an "intrinsic" link through Christ. According to the *Notes on the Correct
Way to Present Jews and Judaism in Preaching and Catechesis in the Roman
Catholic Church* (1985), §25, "The permanence of Israel (while so many ancient peoples have disappeared without trace) is a historic fact and a sign to
be interpreted within God's design. . . . It remains a chosen people, 'the pure
olive on which were grafted the branches of the wild olive which are the
gentiles' (John Paul II, March 6, 1982 [alluding to Rom. 11:17-24])."

The Hebrew Bible identifies three key features of the people of God,
each of which resonates with Meyer's reflection. First, the people enter into
a relationship with God through God's election, e.g., Deuteronomy 14:1-2,
which implies that although all peoples belong to the Lord, Israel is God's
special possession and becomes known as a holy people. Second, God's
choice of Israel is associated with the land of Israel, which becomes a constitutive element of being a people of God, e.g., Genesis 17:8: "I will give to
you and to your descendants after you the land of your sojournings, all the
land of Canaan for an everlasting possession; and I will be their God."
Third, the people of God receive a mission, which is often described in
terms of "being a light to the nations" (Isa. 42:6). Israel is not chosen as the
people of God out of arbitrary preference for a particular people but in order that God's name be blessed (Gen. 12:2-3). God does not force the people that he chooses and calls *ami* (my people); rather, something is sought
in return, and as a result God and the people of God are described as part-

ners in a relationship. All three features are acknowledged, albeit implicitly, in Meyer's discussion of the covenantal christology.

From the Jewish perspective, of course, no change took place in the Jewish people's covenantal relationship with God after the "Christ event," but there is no reason — please excuse the double negative — why God should not establish a covenant with another faith community, i.e., Christians.

As far as Christianity is concerned, however, a radical break has occurred: Christianity introduces a radical transformation of the old covenant, but this does not annul the previous covenant. The relationship between God and his people is mediated decisively through his son Jesus Christ but, in opposition to the *adversus Judaeos* tradition, the appearance of Christianity does not signify an end for the role of the Jewish people because, as Meyer makes clear, "if any God is present in Jesus Christ, it is the God of the Jews" (p. 152). Jesus' Jewishness is of vital enduring theological significance. Thus, "Christians are inseparably and indivisibly responsible to the Jewishness of the one Jew and the other Jews" (p. 156). Abrogation of the covenantal relationship between God and the Jewish people is not an option for Christian theology.

For Henrix, the focus is on incarnational christology, a subject that he has explored over many years. He explains that the Jewishness of Jesus is essential because "separation from the incarnation's real rootedness means losing the meaning of its mystery" (p. 118). After offering a summary of the views of Popes John Paul II and Benedict XVI, Henrix discusses the importance of God's son not being a generic human being, but "specifically, a Jewish human being" (p. 123).

Unlike Meyer's covenantal christology, I wonder whether incarnational christology exceeds the limits of Judaism, even though it develops central Jewish themes. Yet while there is this divide, it does not mean the topic should be put to one side. For Jews, one way to approach the Christian understanding of incarnational christology is to view this alongside the Jewish insistence on God being with his people. The term *Shekinah* is the closest Jewish analogue to incarnation: "when they [Israel] went into Egypt, the Shekinah went with them; in Babylon the Shekinah was with them" (Babylonian Talmud, *Megillah* 29a). An important image of the *Shekinah* is the continuity of the divine presence even when in exile, seen in the cloud and fire leading the people in the Exodus account, and later taken to be present after the fall of the Temple in 70 C.E. The prologue to John's Gospel might have been developing similar concepts, especially with the allusion there to the "tabernacling" of the Word. Drawing upon a pun in Greek where the word for "tent" is similar to the Hebrew for "to dwell" (1:14), Jesus, the Word of God, is depicted as encamping with the people of the world — "and the word became flesh and dwelt [lit. tabernacled] among us."

Yet, like Meyer's paper, there remains an intrinsic problem that is illustrated by the Jewish belief in the one and only God, who accepts no rivals. Henrix acknowledges this Jewish "no" to Jesus with reference to the Jewish concept of *shittuf,* a halakhic term that means "partnership" or "association" of an additional power with God. In rabbinic Judaism, this was understood as a false "mixing" *(sh'taf)* of the Name of God with an alien cult. A pragmatic position eventually emerged in the Middle Ages: while *shittuf* compromised monotheism and was thus prohibited to Jews, it was not incompatible with the Noahide laws and thus Christians were not actual idolaters. Henrix acknowledges the Jewish concern that incarnation can be a "confusion" and refers to the writings of Michael Wyschogrod. Henrix admits that Christian theology will not be able to "silence or pacify this Jewish criticism and concern" (p. 128), but he calls for sensitivity to the concern in reflecting on the theological significance of the fact that the Son of God became a Jewish human being.

Henrix moves on to a second theme of his paper — Jesus as Torah — which also has interesting Jewish analogies although again it seems to exceed the limits of Jewish theological reflection. Mainstream rabbinic Judaism taught that Moses received the Torah from Sinai, but there was also a tradition that the Torah was in existence before the creation of the world (e.g., Ben Sira 1:1-5), or even before the creation of the Throne of Glory (Genesis Rabbah 1:4). Torah was equated with Wisdom (Prov. 8:22), and Philo wrote about the preexistence and role in creation of the word of God *(logos),* which he identified with the Torah. The description of Christ who "bears the very stamp of God's nature" (Heb. 1:3) is not dissimilar.

Although Philo and the Greek-speaking Jews did not have the same understanding of the incarnate *logos* that is found in the prologue to John's Gospel, it is striking that a Jew who lived at the same time as the authors of the New Testament, and who probably never even heard of Jesus, spoke of the fatherhood of God and of the *logos* as his image: "Even if we are not yet suitable to be called the sons and daughters of God, still we may be called the children of his eternal image, of his most sacred word *(logos)*" (*On the Confusion of Tongues,* 147). Later, of course, Christianity understood *logos* as the "Word of God," which referred to Jesus as God incarnate.

Rabbinic Judaism also personified Torah, describing how God discussed the creation of the world with the Torah, and the Torah is also depicted on many occasions as Israel's bride. Another feature of the Torah according to the rabbis is that it was eternal. Jesus' statement in Matthew 5:17 that he has come not to destroy but to fulfill the Torah is reminiscent of the rabbinic teaching of its non-abrogability. The rabbis taught that the Torah would exist in the world to come, but interestingly it was also argued that changes to the Torah would take place in the messianic age (*Genesis Rabbah* 98:9), although this was later rejected by Maimonides. It is worth pointing out, however, that the divine origin of Torah is never viewed as the self-manifestation of God.

The rabbinic understanding of Torah, like the concept of *Shekinah,* may help Jews understand better incarnational christology and the theological significance of the Jewishness of Jesus. Although I do not find much common ground in Henrix's paper, there is a convergence of thinking; as Wyschogrod stated, Jews are not entitled to dismiss the Christian claim about God's incarnation in Jesus out of hand. To reject the incarnation on *a priori* grounds would be to impose external constraints on God's freedom, a notion fundamentally foreign to Judaism. According to Wyschogrod, there is only one condition under which Israel would be entitled to reject the church's claims about Jesus out of hand, and that is if these claims were to imply that God had repudiated God's promises to Israel. For that is something that Israel can safely trust that God will never do, not because God is unable, but because God honors God's promises.

The key question, then, from a Jewish perspective is whether incarnational or covenantal christology implies the abrogation of God's promises to Israel. For Meyer and Henrix, such an abrogation (leading to supersessionism) is not an option for Christian theology. Their papers represent a desire to ask their Jewish partners to consider challenging theological doctrines in their goal to establish a *chevruta,* a partnership, in which we seek not only to build respect but also to further understanding. I thank them.

Separately and together, we must work to bring healing to our world. In this enterprise, we are, as Christians and Jews, guided by the vision of the prophets of Israel:

> It shall come to pass in the end of days that the mountain of the Lord's house shall be established at the top of the mountains and be exalted above the hills, and the nations shall flow unto it . . . and many peoples shall go and say, "Come ye and let us go up to the mountain of the Lord to the house of the God of Jacob and He will teach us of His ways and we will walk in his paths." (Isa. 2:2-3)

163

The Tri-Unity of God and the Fractures of Human History

Elizabeth Groppe

1. Introduction

The Feast of Trinity Sunday is celebrated in the Catholic Church on the first Sunday after Pentecost. In my experience, priests presiding at liturgy on this day often make no mention of the feast day, perhaps because they are daunted by the prospect of offering a homily tailored to the occasion. Many Catholics have been raised to approach the doctrine of the Trinity as an incomprehensible teaching about three persons who somehow exist as one. Sometimes even those with advanced graduate education are of the impression that this is a doctrine that belies common sense but that nonetheless must be accepted in faith. It is said that when the great Jesuit theologian Bernard Lonergan learned as a seminary student that "God is five notions, four relations, three persons, two processions, and one nature" he made his own addition to this mnemonic formula: "and zero comprehension!"[1] If even Lonergan shook his head at some formulations of trinitarian theology, it is no wonder that many Catholics (and surely also many Jews) feel perplexed when the Trinity is invoked.

In the past decades, there has been a significant renewal of the Christian trinitarian tradition. This renaissance has emphasized that the doctrine of the Trinity is not an abstract formula but a doctrine grounded in the Christian experience of salvation through Jesus Christ and the Holy

---

1. Catherine Mowry LaCugna, "The Trinitarian Mystery of God," in *Systematic Theology: Roman Catholic Perspectives*, ed. Francis Schüssler Fiorenza and John P. Galvin (Minneapolis: Fortress, 1991), vol. 1, p. 153. For a brief explanation of the scholastic distinctions of notion, relation, person, and procession, see p. 153, n. 5.

Spirit. In this essay, I will briefly introduce this trinitarian renewal and then discuss its implications for Christian-Jewish dialogue. Today's revitalized trinitarian theologies can contribute to the construction of a theology that can affirm both the place of Jesus Christ as universal savior and the eternal character of God's covenant with the people Israel. At the same time, the unprecedented developments in Christian-Jewish dialogue that have taken place since *Nostra Aetate* can stimulate new approaches to trinitarian reflection.

2. The Renewal of Christian Trinitarian Theology

Karl Rahner's 1967 monograph *The Trinity* is a major landmark in the renewal of trinitarian theology within Roman Catholicism.[2] In this short but dense volume, the German Jesuit observed that the doctrine of the Trinity had become marginalized from the lived practice of the Catholic faith. Catholics readily professed their faith in a triune God, yet this affirmation had so little bearing on the discipline of theology and the actual lived practice of the faith that "should the doctrine of the Trinity have to be dropped as false, the major part of religious literature could well remain virtually unchanged."[3] God's tri-unity was approached primarily as a verbal and conceptual datum made known through metaphysical reflection on revelation. As such, it had little bearing on Catholic spirituality or ethics.

Yet in truth, Rahner believed, the doctrine of the Trinity concerns the mystery of God's very self-communication in Word and Spirit to our searching and questioning hearts. Rather than an abstract teaching, it is a doctrine with fundamental existential and spiritual significance. "The Trinity," he emphasized, "is a mystery of *salvation*."[4] How had this been obscured? Rahner's analysis of the problem focused on the neo-scholastic theological manuals that were at this time standard seminary fare. These textbooks were neatly divided into discrete sections on different theological topics, including the treatise "On the One God" *(De Deo Uno)* and the treatise "On the Triune God" *(De Deo Trino)*. Key theological issues such as

2. Karl Rahner, "Der dreifaltige Gott als transzendenter Urgrund des Heilsgeschichte," in *Die Heilsgeschichte vor Christus*, vol. 2 of *Mysterium Salutis, Grundriss heilsgeschichtlicher Dogmatik* (Einsiedeln: Benziger, 1967). ET: *The Trinity*, trans. Joseph Donceel (New York: Herder & Herder, 1970; New York: Crossroad, 1997).

3. Rahner, "Der dreifaltige Gott," pp. 10-11.

4. Rahner, "Der dreifaltige Gott," p. 21.

God's existence and attributes were typically treated in the treatise "On the One God," with no explicit consideration of the trinitarian character of God known through Christ and the Spirit. *De Deo Uno* became an account of the necessary metaphysical properties of God that did not treat of "God as experienced in salvation history in his free relations to his creatures."[5] The treatise on the triune God *(De Deo Trino)*, in turn, was typically a metaphysical account of divine notions, relations, persons, and processions with little sustained reflection on God's acts of creation and redemption.[6] With this abstraction from the economy of salvation (the *oikonomia* of Eph. 1:9-10) came the decline of a tradition that had identified vestiges of the Trinity *(vestigia Trinitas)* in the Old Testament and the history of religions.[7]

Rahner's alternative to the neo-scholastic methodology was to reframe the entire theological enterprise firmly within an account of the history of creation and redemption in which God is known as triune. Theology, he emphasized, must do justice to the biblical testimony of God's acts of creation and redemption, and it must take seriously the ongoing divine economy in which God continues to communicate God's very self to us as Logos and Spirit. We live, know, hope, and love within the mystery of the incarnation of the very Logos of God and the gift of God's Holy Spirit. Rahner summarized his position with the axiom: "The 'economic' Trinity is the 'immanent' Trinity and the 'immanent' Trinity is the 'economic' Trinity."[8] In other words, the God known to us through the incarnation of the Logos and the gift of the Holy Spirit (the "economic Trinity") *is* God as God truly is (the "immanent Trinity"), and the eternal God truly communicates God's very self to us in the economy of creation and redemption. Trinitarian theology, then, is not a mere verbal or conceptual construct, but a reflection on God's activity among us in the course of human history. It includes an account of God's proximity to us in prophetic word and covenant; reflection on the way in which the human creature composed of spirit and matter finds its eschatological end in the God-man Jesus Christ; and a theology of the Holy Spirit, the uncreated grace of God communicated to us in love and forgiveness.[9]

Rahner's 1967 *The Trinity* marked the beginning of a major renewal of Catholic trinitarian theology. Some theologians modified his axiomatic

5. Rahner, "Der dreifaltige Gott," p. 18.
6. Rahner, "Der dreifaltige Gott," pp. 20-21.
7. Rahner, "Der dreifaltige Gott," p. 22.
8. Rahner, "Der dreifaltige Gott," p. 22.
9. Rahner, "Der dreifaltige Gott," pp. 41, 67.

principle that "The 'economic' Trinity is the 'immanent' Trinity and the 'immanent' Trinity is the 'economic' Trinity." Piet Schoonenberg, for example, affirmed the epistemological principle that the encounter with God in history is primary to our knowledge of God as triune, but he stressed that there can be no strict ontological identity of the immanent and economic Trinity, given the freedom of both the divine self-expression and the human response.[10] The triune God need not have created and redeemed the world, but did so freely.

Walter Kasper cautioned against dissolving the immanent Trinity in the economic Trinity and modified Rahner's axiom to emphasize that the economic Trinity is the free, gracious, kenotic, and nondeducible presence of the immanent Trinity within history: "[I]n the economic self-communication the intra-trinitarian self-communication is present in the world in a new way, namely under the veil of historical words, signs and actions, and ultimately in the figure of the man Jesus of Nazareth."[11] Catherine Mowry LaCugna, whose work will shape the later part of this essay, noted the limitations of the very terminology of "economic Trinity" and "immanent Trinity" and proposed an alternative paradigm for trinitarian reflection employing the biblical and patristic Greek terms *oikonomia* (economy) and *theologia* (theology).[12] The mystery of God *(theologia)*, she emphasized, is inseparable from the mystery of the creation and redemption of the cosmos through Jesus Christ and the Holy Spirit *(oikonomia)*.[13]

Whatever a particular theologian's differences from Rahner, there has nonetheless been widespread agreement with his position that trinitarian theology must reflect God's activity in history. The doctrine of the Trinity should not be approached only as a complicated metaphysics of a divine nature with distinct manners of subsisting,[14] but also as a reflection on

10. Piet Schoonenberg, "Trinity — The Consummated Covenant: Theses on the Doctrine of the Trinitarian God," *Studies in Religion* 5 (1975-76): 111-16.

11. Walter Kasper, *The God of Jesus Christ*, trans. Matthew J. O'Connell (New York: Crossroad, 1984), p. 276.

12. The term *oikonomia* is used in the letter to the Ephesians in reference to God's plan of salvation: "With all wisdom and insight God has made known to us the mystery of his will, according to his good pleasure that he set forth in Christ, as a plan [*oikonomia*] for the fullness of time, to gather up all things in Christ, things in heaven and things on earth" (Eph. 1:9-10).

13. Catherine Mowry LaCugna, *God for Us: The Trinity and Christian Life* (San Francisco: HarperCollins, 1991). See also Elizabeth T. Groppe, "Catherine Mowry LaCugna's Contribution to Trinitarian Theology," *Theological Studies* 63 (2002): 730-63.

14. Common trinitarian formulations speak of "one God in three persons," but insofar as the word "person" has come to connote an individual or Cartesian center of conscious-

God's presence in human history through the Word and the Spirit. As such, it should not be an isolated teaching reduced to abstract formulae, but rather a reflection deeply rooted in spirituality, liturgy, and the lived practice of the Christian faith.

3. Trinitarian Renewal and the Transformation of Christian-Jewish Relations

Concurrent with the renaissance of trinitarian theology[15] is the dramatic transformation of Christian-Jewish relations that has taken place over the past fifty years. For the most part, however, these two theological developments have been like ships passing one another in the night. Both are mighty vessels whose wake is redrawing the theological horizon, but until

---

ness, it is an imprecise translation of the Greek word *hypostasis* with which the doctrine of the Trinity was originally formulated. Rahner proposed that we speak of Father, Son, and Spirit not as three persons but as distinct divine modes of subsisting *(Subsistenzweisen).* Rahner, *The Trinity,* pp. 42-45, 51-57, 73-76. On this point, see also LaCugna, "The Trinitarian Mystery of God," pp. 178-80; *God for Us,* pp. 243-317.

15. In addition to the works already cited, contributions to this renaissance include Boris Bobrinskoy, *Le Mystère de la Trinité* (Paris: Cerf, 1986); Leonardo Boff, *La Trinidad, La Sociedad y La Liberacion* (Madrid: Ediciones Paulinas, 1987); Joseph Bracken, *The One in the Many: A Contemporary Reconstruction of the God-World Relationship* (Grand Rapids: Eerdmans, 2001); David Coffey, *Deus Trinitas: The Doctrine of the Triune God* (New York: Oxford University Press, 1999); Yves Congar, *The Word and the Spirit* (New York: Harper & Row, 1987) and *I Believe in the Holy Spirit,* 3 vols. (New York: Seabury, 1983); David S. Cunningham, *These Three Are One: The Practice of Trinitarian Theology* (Malden, MA: Blackwell, 1998); *The Trinity,* ed. Stephen T. Davis, Daniel Kendall, and Gerald O'Collins (New York: Oxford University Press, 1999); Michael Downey, *Altogether Gift: A Trinitarian Theology* (Maryknoll, NY: Orbis, 2000); Colin Gunton, *The Triune Creator: A Historical and Systematic Study* (Grand Rapids: Eerdmans, 1998); William Hill, *The Three-Personed God* (Washington, DC: University Press of America, 1983); Robert Jenson, *The Triune Identity* (Philadelphia: Fortress Press, 1982); Elizabeth Johnson, *She Who Is: The Mystery of God in Feminist Theological Discourse* (New York: Crossroad, 1996); Eberhard Jüngel, *God as the Mystery of the World* (Grand Rapids: Eerdmans, 1983); James Mackey, *The Christian Experience of God as Trinity* (London: SCM, 1983); Jürgen Moltmann, *The Trinity and the Kingdom* (New York: Harper & Row, 1981); Gerald O'Collins, *The Tripersonal God: Understanding and Interpreting the Trinity* (New York: Paulist, 1999); Kathryn Tanner, *Jesus, Humanity, and the Trinity: A Brief Systematic Theology* (Minneapolis: Fortress, 2001); Miroslav Volf, *After Our Likeness: The Church as the Image of the Trinity* (Grand Rapids: Eerdmans, 1998); Hans Urs von Balthasar, *Theo-Drama,* 5 vols. (San Francisco: Ignatius Press, 1988); John Zizioulas, *Being as Communion: Studies in Personhood and the Church,* 2nd ed. (London: Darton, Longman & Todd, 2004).

recently there has been little exchange between the two sea craft. It is not surprising that Rahner's *The Trinity* (1967) made only passing mention of God's covenant with the people Israel in its account of God's economic self-communication.[16] The theological dictionary that Rahner edited with Herbert Vorgrimler describes this covenant as something that has come to an end.[17] Yet even some trinitarian works published amidst the Catholic-Jewish dialogue initiated in the decades after *Nostra Aetate* (1965) did not directly engage the implications of this dialogue for trinitarian theology. Yves Congar's *I Believe in the Holy Spirit* (French ed. 1979-80) and *The Word and the Spirit* (French ed. 1984) are cases in point.[18]

That this engagement was not immediately forthcoming is due in part to the character of the standard narratives of the economy of redemption that have been reinvigorated by the trinitarian renewal. R. Kendall Soulen observes that the basic "plot" of the Christian theological canon is creation, fall, redemption in Jesus Christ, and final consummation.[19] God's covenant with the people Israel is merely implicit in the plot line as the necessary preparation for redemption in Jesus Christ, and the rabbinic Judaism of the Mishnah and Talmud that developed after Rome's destruction of the Temple in Jerusalem is entirely absent from the storyline. "The [now] rejected theology of supersessionism," Soulen comments, "is deeply, perhaps inextricably, ingrained in the classical conception of the economy of salvation."[20]

The Christian tradition is broad and diverse, and it is too simplistic to paint all Christian theologians with the same supersessionist brush.[21]

16. Rahner, *The Trinity*, p. 41. See also the pertinent discussion in Hans Hermann Henrix's essay elsewhere in this collection.

17. The entry "Old Testament, Old Covenant" in the *Kleines Theologisches Wörterbuch* reads: "Jesus brings to completion the law and, in his blood, he determines the end of the old covenant." *Kleines Theologisches Wörterbuch*, ed. Karl Rahner and Herbert Vorgrimler (Freiburg: Herder, 1976), p. 15. Cited in Erich Zenger, "The Covenant That Was Never Revoked: The Foundations of a Christian Theology of Judaism," in *The Catholic Church and the Jewish People*, ed. Philip A. Cunningham, Norbert Hofmann, S.D.B., and Joseph Sievers (New York: Fordham University Press, 2007), p. 97. Some years after the publication of this dictionary, Rahner did engage in a significant dialogue with the Orthodox Jewish New Testament scholar Pinchas Lapide. See Karl Rahner and Pinchas Lapide, *Encountering Jesus — Encountering Judaism: A Dialogue* (New York: Crossroad, 1987).

18. Yves Congar, *Je crois en l'Esprit Saint*, 3 vols. (Paris: Cerf, 1979-80); *La Parole et le Souffle* (Paris: Desclée, 1984).

19. R. Kendall Soulen, "YHWH the Triune God," *Modern Theology* 15 (1999): 27.

20. Soulen, "YHWH the Triune God," p. 29.

21. For a survey of different Christian approaches to God's covenant with Israel, see Steven J. McMichael, "The Covenant in Patristic and Medieval Christian Theology," in *Two*

There are very significant differences between the theology of St. Paul, who affirmed that the Jews remain God's beloved covenant people (Romans 11), and the *Epistle of Barnabas* (ca. 130 C.E.), which maintained that the covenant has been taken from the Jews who "were not worthy to receive it because of their sins."[22] Augustine (354-430) articulated a fourfold scheme of salvation history, distinguishing the periods prior to the Law *(ante legem)*, under the Law *(sub lege)*, under grace *(sub gratia)*, and in peace *(in pace)*, and he maintained that the Jews failed to see in Christ the fulfillment of the Law that they had rightfully observed. Nonetheless, Augustine granted Jews scattered in the Diaspora an important and enduring role in the economy of redemption in the period *sub gratia:* they carry ancient scrolls that testify to pagans of the authenticity of the prophecies that Christ has fulfilled, and thereby serve the mission of the church.[23] John Chrysostom (347-407), in contrast, excoriated Christians who visited synagogues that held the scrolls of the Law and the Prophets. The Jews bore no needed witness; they had transgressed the Law at the time that it was to be observed, and then obstinately clung to it in the time it ceased to bind. Their synagogues had become Godforsaken dwellings of demons.[24]

Today, some four decades after *Nostra Aetate,* there are within the Catholic Church a diversity of attitudes toward Jews and Judaism. Yet in many years of work on Christian-Jewish relations with people from parishes all across the United States, Mary Boys has found that most Catholics share a common story of Jewish and Christian origins. According to this pervasive narrative, God called the Jews to be a covenant people, but they failed to be faithful. God nonetheless sent the Messiah foretold by the prophets, who offered a gospel of love that transcended the old religion of the law. The Jews, however, rejected Christ's message and crucified him. His resurrection gave rise to a new religion that flourished in the Roman

---

Faiths, One Covenant? Jewish and Christian Identity in the Presence of the Other, ed. Eugene B. Korn and John T. Pawlikowski (Lanham, MD: Rowman & Littlefield, 2005), pp. 45-64.

22. "Epistle of Barnabas," in *The Apostolic Fathers* II, Loeb Classical Library 25, ed. and trans. Bart Ehrman (Cambridge, MA: Harvard University Press, 2003), 14.1. According to Bart Ehrman, this letter was widely read in churches in the second and third centuries. Bart Ehrman, *After the New Testament: A Reader in Early Christianity* (New York: Oxford University Press, 1999), p. 98.

23. Augustine, *City of God,* 4:34, 18:46. See also Paula Fredriksen, *Augustine and the Jews: A Christian Defense of Jews and Judaism* (New York: Doubleday, 2008).

24. John Chrysostom, *Discourses Against Judaizing Christians,* I.II.3; I.III.1; and I.V.2-4. See also Robert L. Wilken, *John Chrysostom and the Jews: Rhetoric and Reality in the Late 4th Century* (Berkeley: University of California Press, 1983).

Empire, while the Jews denied Christ's divinity and Judaism diminished in importance.[25] Given this popular storyline as well as the opprobrious place of Jews in most theologies of the Christian tradition, Boys finds the emphasis on salvation history that has been so foundational to the renewal of trinitarian theology to be "a problematic category" in today's work of building bridges between Christians and Jews.[26]

Indeed, our master narratives of the economy of redemption do need to be reconceived. Augustine, unlike Chrysostom, gave Jews an enduring place in the period of salvation history *sub gratia,* but only as a witness to the pagans, not as the "dearly beloved brothers [and sisters]" to Christians of whom Pope John Paul II spoke in our own day.[27] In Gregory of Nazianzus's division of history into the era of idols, the era of the Law, and the era of the Gospel, Jews have a wholly legitimate place as a Torah-observing community only within the era of the Law.[28] Thomas Aquinas (1224-74) distinguished three stages of salvation history: the time of the Old Law, the time of the New Law, and the state of glory; whether or not Aquinas believed that God's covenant with the Jewish people endured after its fulfillment in the New Law is debated.[29] Yet today, as Philip Cunningham and Didier Pollefeyt discuss in their contribution to this volume, Catholic teaching affirms that God's covenant with the Jewish people endures after the Christ event as a source of ongoing spiritual vitality. "We must remind ourselves," the Pontifical Commission for Religious Relations with the Jews stated in 1985, "how the permanence of Israel is accompanied by a continuous spiritual fecundity, in the rabbinical period, in the Middle Ages and in modern times."[30] Similarly, the Pontifical Biblical Commis-

---

25. Mary Boys, *Has God Only One Blessing? Judaism as a Source of Christian Self-Understanding* (Mahwah, NJ: Paulist, 2000), p. 77.

26. Boys, *Has God Only One Blessing?* p. 212.

27. Pope John Paul II, *Spiritual Pilgrimage: Texts on Jews and Judaism 1979-1995,* ed. Eugene J. Fisher and Leon Klenicki (New York: Crossroad, 1995), p. 63.

28. Gregory of Nazianzus, *Orat* V:24-25.

29. For a variety of perspectives on this question, see Steven Boguslawski, *Thomas Aquinas on the Jews: Insights into His Commentary on Romans 9–11* (Mahwah, NJ: Paulist, 2008); Jeremy Cohen, *Living Letters of the Law: Ideas of the Jew in Medieval Christianity* (Berkeley: University of California Press, 1999); Matthew Levering, *Christ's Fulfillment of Torah and Temple: Salvation According to Thomas Aquinas* (Notre Dame: University of Notre Dame Press, 2002); McMichael, "The Covenant in Patristic and Medieval Theology."

30. Pontifical Commission for Religious Relations with the Jews, *Notes on the Correct Way to Present Jews and Judaism in Preaching and Teaching in the Roman Catholic Church* (1985), VI.1.

sion affirmed in a 2001 statement that there is a validity to the Rabbinical exegetical traditions developed in the post-biblical period: "*The Jewish reading of the Bible is a possible one,* in continuity with the Jewish Sacred Scriptures from the Second Temple period, a reading analogous to the Christian reading which developed in parallel fashion."[31]

The dominant master narratives of salvation history presume a clear and sharp break between the time of the Law and the time of the Gospel, and this too must be reconsidered in light of recent biblical and historical scholarship. John Pawlikowski's essay in this volume highlights the work of John Meier, Robin Scroggs, and Anthony Saldarini, who describe Jesus as the leader of a special community or reform movement *within* Judaism — not the leader of a new religion with a non-Jewish identity. Paul, in turn, was the leader of a *Jewish* mission to the Gentiles. Moreover, when Christianity and rabbinic Judaism did begin to emerge as two distinct religious bodies sometime in the second century C.E., this division was not a swift and clean break. In *The Ways That Never Parted,* Annette Yoshiko Reed and Adam H. Becker explain that the literary and archeological data testify to an array of complex, messy, ambiguous relationships between people we have now come to know as "Jew" and "Christian." Their own religious self-understanding and their relationships to one another had a broad range of regional and cultural variation, and in some cases boundaries between them were blurred for centuries.[32] According to James Dunn, the separation of "Jew" and "Christian" that our Christian master narratives presume may or may not have been inevitable in 70-135 C.E. — and may or may not have appeared inevitable to those who lived through this period.[33]

3. Sketching New Narratives of Salvation History

Although the separation of one community of Jews from another community of Christians may not have been inevitable in the first century, it has

---

31. The Pontifical Biblical Commission, *The Jewish People and Their Sacred Scriptures in the Christian Bible* (Vatican City: Libreria Editrice Vaticana, 2002), no. 22. Emphasis added.

32. Annette Yoshiko Reed and Adam H. Becker, "Introduction: Traditional Models and New Directions," in *The Ways That Never Parted: Jews and Christians in Late Antiquity and the Early Middle Ages,* ed. Adam H. Becker and Annette Yoshiko Reed (Tübingen: J. C. B. Mohr, 2003), pp. 1-33.

33. James Dunn, ed., *Jews and Christians: The Parting of the Ways,* A.D. 70 to 135 (Tübingen: Mohr, 1992; paperback Grand Rapids: Eerdmans, 1999), p. 368.

been our reality for hundreds of years. It is therefore now quite complicated to attempt to construct a cohesive narrative of God's activity in human history that includes not only Christian but also Jewish experience. Although the boundaries that have separated Christian and Jew may never have been as impermeable as we have sometimes presumed, each religious community developed its own distinctive modes of liturgy, biblical exegesis, and theological discourse. The meaning of language, as Wittgenstein has elucidated, is so thoroughly usage- and context-dependent that we cannot assume that when the Jewish sage Abraham Joshua Heschel speaks of the "supernal Torah" he means precisely the same thing as what Thomas Aquinas means by the eternal Logos. Nor can we assume that Rabbi Akiva means by the *Shekinah* exactly the same thing that Gregory Nazianzus intends when he speaks of the Holy Spirit.[34] Interreligious dialogue, as John Dunne testifies, is a "passing over" into a different realm of spiritual meaning through a sympathetic understanding and a "coming back" into one's own spiritual world.[35] This crossing-over can never be perfectly realized in this life, nor can the insights garnered in the journey ever be perfectly translated into the terminology of one's own religious community. This is not cause to abandon the interreligious enterprise, but rather an indication of the imperative of ongoing dialogue, refinement, and reformulation of interreligious theologies.

With that in mind, how might Christians begin to reformulate our master narratives of the economy of salvation in dialogue with Judaism, and with awareness of historical scholarship on the complicated character of Christian origins? This is a task, of course, that cannot be done properly within the confines of this essay.[36] Below I will simply sketch out one at-

---

34. For a synopsis on Wittgenstein's reflections on meaning and language, see Gerd Brand, *The Central Texts of Ludwig Wittgenstein*, trans. Robert Innis (Oxford: Basil Blackwell, 1979), pp. 105-24. For a Christian theology of *Shekinah*/Spirit constructed in dialogue with Judaism from the perspective of process theology, see Michael E. Lodahl, *Shekinah/Spirit: Divine Presence in Jewish and Christian Religion* (New York: Stimulus, 1992).

35. John Dunne, *The Way of All the Earth: Experiments in Truth and Religion* (New York: Macmillan, 1972).

36. For a more sustained and developed endeavor, see Robert Jenson, *Systematic Theology*, vol. 1: *The Triune God* (New York: Oxford University Press, 1997). Jenson writes of three *dramatis dei personae*, or "characters in the drama of God" — God who identifies himself with Israel, the *Shekinah* who shares Israel's lot and the Lord's being, and the Word of God who comes to Israel, God's son. See also his "Toward a Christian Doctrine of Israel," at http://www.ctinquiry.org/publications/reflections_volume_3/jenson1.htm. For a Jewish response, see Peter Ochs, "A Jewish Reading of *Trinity, Time, and the Church*: A Response to the Theology of Robert W. Jenson," *Modern Theology* 19 (2003): 419-27.

tempt at a trinitarian narrative shaped by engagement with the writings of Jewish scholar Abraham Joshua Heschel and Christian trinitarian theologian Catherine Mowry LaCugna. Like the standard master narratives of the Christian theological tradition, this storyline emphasizes the giving of the Law and the incarnation of the Word of God in Jesus Christ as major turning points in the economy of salvation. Unlike the standard master narratives, however, it describes these events as moments not only of revelation and progress toward the eschatological end of communion with God, but also as events of divine concealment and exile within the fractures of our human history. The narrative is my own construction, although it paraphrases extensively from Heschel and LaCugna:

The origins of creation are shrouded in mystery. In a manner unfathomable to us, the cosmos was brought into being through the supernal Torah (Logos)[37] and the Spirit of God *(Shekinah)* in an act of free and ecstatic love. The cosmos exists in both likeness and distinction from God and is sustained in every moment and in every last detail by God's ongoing faithfulness.[38]

Unique within the cosmos is the human creature, capable of spurning God's free love or responding in kind. Recognizing our capacity for both good and evil, God countered our evil inclination by extending to us a participation in the holy.[39] In Eden, Adam and Eve were given a share of God's Torah. This included one *mitzvah* — a commandment, or a prayer that takes the form of deed.[40] When Adam and Eve ate of the forbidden fruit they stripped themselves of the one *mitzvah* they had been given, and they knew that they were naked (Gen. 3:7).[41]

Exile ensued. Lost was the garden to Adam and Eve, and exiled also was God's Torah, which cannot exist outside of Eden in its pure spiritual

---

37. Heschel follows others in his tradition in using the word "Torah" in two senses: the supernal Torah and the Torah revealed at Sinai. The supernal Torah existed before the creation of the world and is equated with Wisdom (Prov. 8:22). The Greek-speaking Jew Philo referred to this Torah as "Logos." According to the rabbis, Moses received Torah at Sinai — but not all of the Torah. See Abraham Joshua Heschel, *God in Search of Man: A Philosophy of Judaism* (New York: Farrar, Straus & Giroux, 1955), pp. 262 and 276, n. 7; *Heavenly Torah as Refracted Through the Generations* (New York: Continuum, 2005), p. 327.

38. On this point, see Heschel, *God in Search of Man*, p. 93; LaCugna, *God for Us*, p. 304.

39. Abraham Joshua Heschel, *Between God and Man: An Interpretation of Judaism from the Writings of Abraham J. Heschel*, ed. Fritz A. Rothschild (New York: Free Press, 1959), p. 195.

40. Heschel, *Between God and Man*, p. 194.

41. Heschel, *Between God and Man*, p. 187. Reference is to *Genesis Rabba*, 19:17.

form. God "is a stranger on earth" (Ps. 119:19), and the *Shekinah,* the presence of God, cannot be found in the company of sinners. When we can truly say once again, "I am my beloved's," then the *Shekinah* will return.[42]

God's desire is for all the nations — the children of Cain and the children of Abel and all of their descendants. But it was only a small group of the sons and daughters of the family of Abraham and Sarah who accepted God's invitation to ascend the mountain of Sinai.[43] After fleeing slavery in Egypt, they were bound to God through Torah in a unique way that changed forever the identity of both covenant partners. Sinai's overwhelming awe gave rise to deeds of worship, and Israel became God's unique witness among the nations, sharing God's name and commanded to walk in God's ways of righteousness and justice (Gen. 18:19).[44] God, in turn, was bound to Israel, and shared in Israel's sufferings with divine *pathos.*[45]

Yet on this side of Eden, even the Torah to which Israel bears witness is in some sense a Torah in exile. In order to dwell in this world ridden with imperfections, the supernal Torah had to adjust itself to the condition of humanity and assume a garb lacking in beauty and comeliness. This garb includes such words as those of Deuteronomy 2:23 and Genesis 36.[46] The Torah is both revealed and concealed, wedded to Israel and exiled from earth, given at Sinai and hidden in shells until that messianic time when all violence will cease (Isa. 11:1-10), all flesh will worship together on the mountain of God (Isa. 2:1-4), and the purifying Holy Spirit will be poured out from on high.

At a time when the people Israel lived under the brutality of the Roman Empire, Mary of Nazareth gave her free assent to God's Spirit, and she bore a son *Yeshua* in whom the supernal Torah of God took flesh. The communion of divinity and humanity that God so desired was consummated, but in a veiled garb adjusted to our human condition. The child *Yeshua* was laid in a manger and carried in flight to Egypt, threatened with death (Luke 2:12; Matt. 2:13).[47] As an adult, he hungered,

---

42. Heschel, *God in Search of Man,* pp. 156 and 147.

43. On the refusal of other nations to accept the Torah, see, for example, *Sifre: A Tannaitic Commentary on the Book of Deuteronomy,* Yale Judaica Series XXIV, trans. Reuven Hammer (New Haven: Yale University Press, 1986), piska 343, pp. 352-53.

44. Heschel, *God in Search of Man,* pp. 140, 167, and 288.

45. Heschel, *Between God and Man,* pp. 116-24.

46. Heschel, *Between God and Man,* p. 263.

47. On the question of the historicity of the birth narratives in Matthew and Luke, which agree in few details and are even discrepant with each other on some points, see Ray-

thirsted, and grew weary. Yet he proclaimed with passion that God's messianic reign had come (Mark 1:14-15) and that the Torah was not to be abolished but perfected (Matt. 5:17). A fiercely tender presence, he was the hand of God's love, mercy, and forgiveness outstretched to sinners, lepers, and outcasts.[48] He spoke and acted with authority (*exousia*), but he claimed nothing for himself and referred all his actions back to God (Luke 18:19).[49]

Throngs of people came to him, arousing the concern of the imperial authorities who conspired with the chief priests of the Temple to arrest *Yeshua*. The Roman prefect then authorized his crucifixion. *Yeshua* cried out on the cross in lament to God, and spoke words of forgiveness for his tormentors. When he gave his last breath, the veil of the Temple was rent (Mark 15:38), a sign of God's mourning and grief beyond consolation.[50]

Yeshua was buried according to the Jewish custom, and on the third day the women who had come to the tomb bore witness to his resurrection in the power of the Holy Spirit. His disciples proclaimed his death and resurrection and anticipated the final consummation of God's messianic promises. At Pentecost, the Spirit of Christ who was Torah incarnate was poured out on people of all nations of the earth (Acts 2:1-13). The apostles went forth to baptize them in the name of God the Father, the Son, and the Holy Spirit (Matt. 28:19).

Some among the nations received the Spirit. Others murdered the apostles Stephen, Peter, and Paul. The Roman legions razed the Temple of God to the ground (70 C.E.), and barred the people of the covenant from Jerusalem (136 C.E.). Those baptized into Christ were persecuted under the reigns of the Emperors Nero, Domitian, Trajan, Marcus Aurelius, and Decius. The Torah and the *Shekinah* of God once again were sent into exile. The Logos that had become flesh in *Yeshua* was both revealed in Christ and concealed in the violent fractures of human history.

In this context, members of the people of Israel exiled from Jerusalem reconstructed a life of worship without the Temple. They welcomed the compassionate accompaniment of the *Shekinah* and prayerfully

---

mond E. Brown, *The Birth of the Messiah: A Commentary on the Infancy Narratives in Matthew and Luke* (Garden City, NY: Doubleday & Company, 1977), pp. 25-38.

48. This portion of the narrative comes from LaCugna, *God for Us*, p. 294.

49. LaCugna, *God for Us*, p. 294.

50. See Rosann M. Catalano, "A Matter of Perspective: An Alternative Reading of Mark 15:38," in *Seeing Judaism Anew: Christianity's Sacred Obligation,* ed. Mary C. Boys (Lanham, MD: Rowman & Littlefield, 2005), pp. 187-99.

studied the written and oral Torah they had carried from Sinai,[51] but they could not proclaim a messiah in a world still groaning for redemption. Some members of the people Israel and a growing number of Gentiles did recognize the inbreaking of the messianic era in the love *(agape)* of Christian fellowship and the bread and wine of the Eucharistic table. But in the written and oral Torah of the Rabbis, they perceived only the exterior shells and the garb without comeliness.[52] Like the crucified messiah, the Torah revealed at Sinai still bore the marks of God's exile. Those who saw through this garb to the divine glory hidden beneath were dismayed to see Gentiles taking up the scriptures without observing the Law, and they recommitted themselves to that Torah which bound them to God.

Over time, those bound in covenant to the Torah revealed at Sinai became known as Jews, and those who followed the way of the Torah incarnate in Christ became known as Christians.[53] In a fractured world in which God's presence is both revealed and concealed, most members of each community were unable to perceive in the other the dwelling of the Spirit. But each community continued in its own way to witness to the fragmented redemption with which it had been entrusted. On that day when every tear is wiped away (Rev. 21:4), the divine glory will shed its veil of exile, and then the Torah as known by Jews and the Torah as known by Christians will be one, and God will be all in all (1 Cor. 15:28).

5. Eternal Covenant and Universal Savior

The earliest trinitarian formulations in what eventually become the Christian tradition were liturgical and narrative in character: Gospel accounts of the life, death, and resurrection of Jesus Christ; baptisms administered in the name of Father, Son, and Spirit; and Eucharistic prayers offered to God through Christ. In liturgical prayer and narration, the followers of a Jewish messianic movement recounted and enacted the drama of salvation

---

51. Heschel, *Heavenly Torah*, pp. 104-10.

52. Heschel, *God in Search of Man*, p. 263.

53. In the first century, according to Daniel Boyarin, the term *Ioudaios* meant primarily "Judean." "There was no *Ioudaismos*, as the name of the Jewish religion, before there was *Christianismos*. Although the term *Ioudaismos*, of course, existed before the Christian Era, it meant something else than what we call Judaism." Boyarin, "Semantic Differences; or, 'Judaism'/'Christianity,'" in *The Ways That Never Parted*, p. 67.

from sin and death into which they had been baptized. The texts that eventually became the canonical Gospels did not elaborate on the precise character of the relationships between God the Father, Jesus Christ, and the Holy Spirit, and were open to a variety of interpretations. In the fourth century, for example, the priest Arius maintained that Jesus Christ was a creature, and based his case on scriptural passages such as "Jesus grew in wisdom" (Luke 2:52) and "My God, my God, why have you forsaken me?" (Matt. 27:46). Bishop Alexander of Alexandria countered with a theology of Christ's divinity that appealed to texts such as John 1:1-3 and John 1:14 for support ("In the beginning was the Logos and the Logos was with God and the Logos was God. . . . And the Logos became flesh and dwelt among us").[54] Engaging a debate that was dividing communities, the church found it necessary to go beyond biblical narratives and introduce ontological categories in order to clarify the relations of God the Father, Christ, and Spirit. Bishops in attendance at the Council of Nicea were reluctant to employ any nonbiblical terms in their theological formulations, but ultimately the Council agreed to the statement that Jesus Christ is *homoousios* (of the same being, nature, or substance) as God the Father.

Likewise, the narrative of salvation history that I have briefly sketched above does not directly address the overarching question of the Christ Jesus and the Jewish People Today Project: How might we Christians in our time affirm both the people Israel's covenantal life with God and our faith claim that Jesus Christ is the Savior of all humanity? The narrative does emphasize Israel's ongoing covenantal life, and it describes Jesus Christ as the Messiah and the supernal Torah (or Logos) incarnate. But a complete response to the question at hand requires not only a narrative of the economy of redemption but also an attendant ontological reflection.

The revitalization of Christian trinitarian theology has produced some fresh approaches to trinitarian ontology grounded in the renewed emphasis on the economy of redemption. Catherine Mowry LaCugna, for example, has articulated a relational trinitarian ontology in which "person, not substance, is the ultimate ontological category" and God's to-be is to-be-in-communion.[55] The term "person" can only be predicated of God in an analogous sense; God is not "person" in the manner of you or me. But the perfections we associate with personhood — love, freedom, knowledge, wisdom — are proper to the God revealed to us through

---

54. Athanasius, *Orations Against the Arians*, III:26-29.
55. LaCugna, *God for Us*, pp. 14, 246, 334.

Christ and the Spirit in a manner more eminent than our own limited understanding and experience of these qualities. "God alone," LaCugna writes in a reflection on God as immutably personal, "exists at every moment in perfect communion. God alone is both unoriginated and the origin of everything; God alone is incorruptible love; God alone cannot perish; God alone can thoroughly empty Godself *(kenosis)* without ceasing to be God; God alone never succumbs to isolation and withdrawal; God alone exists in right relationship; God alone is infinitely related to every last creature, past, present, and future."[56]

LaCugna's relational ontology in which "person" is ultimate provides a constructive framework for reflection on our affirmation of both God's enduring covenant with the people Israel and God's incarnation in Jesus Christ. In some ways, the questions raised by these affirmations are similar to the questions raised by serious dialogue with people of all other faiths — questions that have been addressed by *Nostra Aetate* and a wide variety of theological works. Yet, in other ways, the questions generated by our relationship to Jews and Judaism are unparalleled. As Pope John Paul II emphasized, we have a unique spiritual bond with the Jewish people.[57] We share with them a book of scriptures, and the origins of our faith are found in the life, death, and resurrection of a devoted Jew. This gives us a special kinship with the Jewish people that we have with no other religious community. At the same time, it also generates a unique set of complicated problems. Our separation from Judaism occurred only with a great deal of sibling rivalry and polemic, and the history of our relationship to the Jewish community includes social ostracism, scapegoating, and even pogroms and persecution. Today, as other contributors to this volume have noted, there have been multiple expressions of remorse for this history.

Yet in most of our extant theological and liturgical frameworks, it is still difficult to affirm both our own faith in Jesus Christ and God's covenant with the people Israel without some degree of condescension. Yes, God's troth may be eternal, but is not the Jewish people's lived practice of this covenant of a lesser quality than our own, since they do not recognize God's incarnation in Christ and the post-resurrection outpouring of the Holy Spirit? Is it not true that "Jerusalem did not recognize God's moment

---

56. LaCugna, *God for Us*, p. 301.

57. Pope John Paul II, *Spiritual Pilgrimage: Texts on Jews and Judaism 1979-1995*, ed. Eugene J. Fisher and Leon Klenicki (New York: Crossroad, 1995). See esp. his address on April 13, 1986, at the Great Synagogue of Rome, §4 on p. 63.

when it came"?[58] Should it not have been the Jews — far more so than the Gentiles — who saw in Christ the fulfillment of the promises they themselves had carried? Is not their lack of faith in Christ culpable in a way that the disbelief of the Hindu or Muslim or Buddhist is not?

Our dominant theologies encourage us to approach Jews with presuppositions of the inadequacy of Jewish covenantal life. But these assumptions can be challenged by direct personal encounter with Jews who have a deep spiritual life and practice.[59] The faith I find in the writings of Abraham Joshua Heschel, for example, or in the life of my late teacher Rabbi Michael Signer, is certainly a faith different than my own, but not lesser. The world would be spiritually poorer, not richer, were all Jews to stop hallowing the Sabbath, to cease grappling with the meaning of Torah, and to abandon their commitment toward *tikkun olam* (the repairing of the world) in anticipation of the inauguration of the messianic era. Indeed, the Pontifical Biblical Commission has stated that "Jewish messianic expectation is not in vain. It can become for us Christians a powerful stimulant to keep alive the eschatological dimension of our faith."[60]

LaCugna's trinitarian ontology of a profoundly personal and relational God can help us articulate a theology that incorporates the Catholic Church's new recognition of the ongoing spiritual vitality of God's covenant with the Jewish people. If we think of God primarily as an unchanging divine substance, we may well be inclined to think of God's providence as an immutable divine plan foreordained from all eternity. In this case, a Christian who professes that Jesus Christ is the unique and universal savior of all humanity readily comes to the conclusion that the Jewish understanding of covenantal history is inferior to our own. *But if God is immutably personal, and if salvation history is not the unfolding of a preordained plan that existed eternally* in se *but rather a living relationship between God and creature, then the particular historical form this relationship takes will be determined in part by the way in which humanity receives or spurns God's overtures.*

As the incarnation of the supernal Torah or Logos of God, Jesus Christ is "infinitely related to every last creature, past, present, and future."[61] In this

---

58. *Nostra Aetate*, §4.

59. For multiple accounts of this experience, see John Merkle, ed., *Faith Transformed: Christian Encounters with Jews and Judaism* (Collegeville, MN: Liturgical Press, 2003).

60. The Pontifical Biblical Commission, *The Jewish People and Their Sacred Scriptures*, §21.

61. LaCugna, *God for Us*, p. 301.

sense, Christ is truly the unique and universal savior of all humanity, both Jew and Gentile. In this sense, too, the covenantal bond between God's Torah and the people Israel is also of unique and universal soteriological significance. Our deliverance from sin and death into the eternal communion with God for which our hearts long would not be possible without the giving of Torah at Sinai and the incarnation of the supernal Torah in Jesus Christ.

But humanity's response to these events was not commensurate with God's desires. Israel alone ascended the mountain of Sinai, although the Torah had been extended to all nations. And the Law that Israel did carry from Sinai was, as Heschel writes, an exiled Torah garbed in a manner commensurate with the imperfect state of the human condition. The incarnation of the supernal Torah in Christ was intended to inaugurate the messianic reign of perfect righteousness and *shalom* — but humanity responded by crucifying the messiah and destroying God's Temple. Most of those persons who did accept baptism into Christ's name did so only in forgoing much of the Law that Christ had come not to abolish but perfect.

Amidst these failings and fractures of human history, God's personal providence allowed for the emergence of two distinct religious communities: Jew and Christian. As the Vatican Commission for Religious Relations with the Jews affirms, "The permanence of Israel (while so many ancient peoples have disappeared without trace) is a historic fact and a sign to be interpreted within God's design."[62] The supernal Torah and the *Shekinah* of God dwell within each community in distinct ways. God can also be exiled by each community. Nonetheless, we can know the trinitarian God more truly and more fully by approaching God not only through our limited understanding of the Christ who is the supernal Torah incarnate, but also through encounter with those who carry knowledge of the Law that is Torah in covenant.

6. Conclusion

"Nothing in Jewish life," Heschel writes, "is more hallowed than the saying of the *Shema:* 'Hear, O Israel, the Lord is our God, the Lord is One.'"[63] These words are recited with affection twice each day, and have required at times the act of martyrdom. Why, Heschel ponders, are these words worth

62. Vatican Commission for Religious Relations with the Jews, "Notes on the Correct Way to Present Jews and Judaism," VI:1.
63. Heschel, *Between God and Man,* p. 104.

that price? Most Jews commonly assume that the affirmation that God is "One" means simply that God is "not many" — but since God is not in time or space, the term "one" understood in a numerical or quantitative sense is just as inapplicable to God as the term "many." The *Shema* is not a prayer about divine mathematics but a prayer affirming that God is incomparably and ineffably unique, one and the same both here and beyond, in nature and history, in justice and in mercy. "One," Heschel continues, also means "unity," but "the world is *not* one with God, and this is why His power does not surge unhampered throughout all stages of being. Creature is detached from the Creator, and the universe is in a state of spiritual disorder. Yet God has not withdrawn entirely from this world. The spirit of this unity hovers over the face of all plurality. . . . The goal of all efforts is to bring about the restitution of the unity of God and the world."[64]

It may appear that Jewish monotheism and Christian trinitarianism are radically at odds. Historically, indeed, the doctrine of the Trinity has been a source of division between Christians and Jews.[65] Yet there is a striking similarity between Heschel's exegesis of the *Shema* and Catherine Mowry LaCugna's position that the doctrine of the Trinity concerns our vocation to "be united with the God of Jesus Christ by means of communion with one another."[66] Both Heschel's commentary on the unity of God and LaCugna's theology of God's tri-unity are a summons to a fractured creation to respond to God's desire for communion. "The restoration of that unity," Heschel writes, "is a constant process and its accomplishment will be the essence of Messianic redemption."[67] Until this redemption, which Christ inaugurated, is complete, both the Jew who daily recites the *Shema* and the Christian who has never prayed these words so important to Jesus of Nazareth (Mark 12:29) each hold a distinct shard of the fractured light of the glory of God.

64. Heschel, *Between God and Man*, p. 103.

65. Christian trinitarian theology was formulated by way of contrast to Jewish belief. Athanasius, for example, wrote of Arius's theology: "this sort of madness is a Jewish thing, and Jewish in the way that Judas the traitor was Jewish" (*Orations Against the Arians*, III:28). Once developed, the doctrine of the Trinity became a subject of Jewish critique. Hasdai Crescas, for example, noted that the Christian "says God, may He be blessed, has three separate attributes, which he calls Persons, and the Jew denies this." Crescas, *The Refutation of the Christian Principles*, trans., with introduction and notes, Daniel J. Lasker (Albany: State University of New York Press, 1992), p. 25.

66. LaCugna, *God for Us*, p. 1.

67. Heschel, *Between God and Man*, p. 103.

The Triune One, the Incarnate Logos, and Israel's Covenantal Life

Philip A. Cunningham and Didier Pollefeyt

1. Introduction: Incompatible Beliefs?

The essays in this volume explore the relationship between two apparently incompatible Catholic convictions. The first is that "Jesus Christ is the mediator and the universal redeemer."[1]

Such doctrinal statements can sometimes be distorted or even abused.[2] The conviction that Jesus Christ is the Savior of all humanity has occasionally led to the self-serving view that non-Christians, or even non–Roman Catholics, stand outside the power of God's saving love, with certain biblical texts adduced to support this restrictive, self-serving view.

The second religious conviction seems in tension with the first. It is the renewed appreciation — in the aftermath of the Shoah — that the Jewish people have never ceased to be in covenant with God. As the late John Paul II frequently expressed it, Jews are "the people of God of the Old Covenant, never revoked by God,"[3] "the present-day people of the covenant

---

1. Congregation for the Doctrine of the Faith, *Dominus Iesus* (2000), §11. Cf. its more expanded statements: "Jesus Christ has a significance and a value for the human race and its history, which are unique and singular, proper to him alone, exclusive, universal, and absolute" (§15); and at the center of the saving plan "willed by the One and Triune God . . . is the mystery of the incarnation of the Word, mediator of divine grace on the level of creation and redemption" (§11).

2. N.B.: "[T]he meaning of the pronouncements of faith depends partly on the expressive power of the language used at a certain point in time and in particular circumstances" (Congregation for the Doctrine of the Faith, *Mysterium Ecclesiae* [1973], §5). See also the essay by Gregor Maria Hoff in this volume on the limits of religious speech.

3. John Paul II, "Address to the Central Council of Jews in Germany and the Rabbinical Conference in Mainz, West Germany," November 17, 1980.

concluded with Moses."[4] Benedict XVI has also described Jews as "the people of the Covenant" and "the people of the Covenant of Moses."[5] The two popes' repeated statements about the permanence of Jewish covenantal life contrast vividly with numerous Christian pronouncements over the centuries that Jews were cast off from God, supposedly accursed because of their alleged collective rejection and crucifixion of Jesus.[6] This view of Judaism complemented an exclusivist view of salvation: if Jews rejected and killed Jesus, they obviously would lie outside the salvation granted only to the baptized.[7] However, if today it is understood that Jews remain covenanted with God, then it seems logically necessary that Jews also remain the constant beneficiaries of God's saving grace.

The Catholic Church's reawaking to Jewish covenantal life that followed in the wake of the Shoah and the Second Vatican Council has led to the composition of numerous important magisterial teachings. These include that Christians "must strive to learn by what essential traits Jews define them-

4. John Paul II, "Address to the Central Council of Jews in Germany."

5. Benedict XVI, "Address at the Great Synagogue of Rome," January 17, 2010, §§2, 3.

6. E.g., *Peri Pascha* 93, usually attributed to Melito of Sardis: "Therefore, the feast of unleavened bread has become bitter to you [ungrateful Israel] just as it was written: 'You will eat unleavened bread with bitter herbs.' Bitter to you are the nails which you made pointed. Bitter to you is the tongue which you sharpened. Bitter to you are the false witnesses whom you brought forward. Bitter to you are the fetters which you prepared. Bitter to you are the scourges which you wove. Bitter to you is Judas whom you furnished with pay. . . . Bitter to you is the gall which you made ready. Bitter to you is the vinegar which you produced. Bitter to you are the thorns which you plucked. Bitter to you are your hands which you bloodied, when you killed your Lord in the midst of Jerusalem." See the collection of texts at http://www.ccjr .us/dialogika-resources/primary-texts-from-the-history-of-the-relationship.html. See also the essay by Mary C. Boys on the interpretation of the Gospel passion narratives elsewhere in this volume.

7. Although it stresses the centrality of Jesus as Savior, the Catholic Church does not today endorse the restricted view of salvation expressed, for example, by Pope Eugene IV in his papal bull, *Cantate Domino,* of 1441: "The most Holy Roman Church firmly believes, professes and preaches that none of those existing outside the Catholic Church, not only pagans, but also Jews and heretics and schismatics, can have a share in life eternal; but that they will go into the 'eternal fire which was prepared for the devil and his angels' (Matt. 25:41), unless before death they are joined with Her. . . ." In contrast, the Second Vatican Council declared: "Those who, through no fault of their own, do not know the Gospel of Christ or his Church, but who nevertheless seek God with a sincere heart, and, moved by grace, try in their actions to do his will as they know it through the dictates of their conscience — those too may attain eternal salvation" (*Lumen Gentium,* The Dogmatic Constitution on the Church [1964], §16). This Catholic perception that Christ's grace is operative outside of the church's borders has special implications for relations with the Jewish community.

selves in the light of their own religious experience";[8] and that "the permanence of Israel [was] accompanied by a continuous spiritual fecundity, in the rabbinical period, in the Middle Ages and in modern times . . . so much so that 'the faith and religious life of the Jewish people as they are professed and practiced still today, can greatly help [Catholics] to understand better certain aspects of the life of the Church' (John Paul II, 6 March 1982)."[9]

Such quotations express what can be called a "robust" understanding of the Jewish people's covenantal life with a saving God. It sees the Jewish people's uninterrupted relationship with the God of Israel as continuing to be dynamic and developing within its own frames of reference. While not denying that he is involved with Israel's life in covenant, this robust perspective clearly has implications for how Christians have conventionally understood the core conviction that all humanity is saved by Jesus Christ. Presumably for this reason, the Pontifical Commission for Religious Relations with the Jews in 1985 rejected theological models that posited two unrelated Jewish and Christian covenants in which both communities find salvation independently: "The Church and Judaism cannot, then, be seen as two parallel ways of salvation and the Church must witness to Christ as the Redeemer for all. . . ."[10]

In preferring so-called "single-covenant" approaches over "two-covenant" paradigms in which the covenants are totally unrelated,[11] the

---

8. Pontifical Commission for Religious Relations with the Jews, "Guidelines and Suggestions for Implementing the Conciliar Declaration," *Nostra Aetate* 4 (1974), prologue.

9. Commission for Religious Relations with the Jews, *Notes on the Correct Way to Present Jews and Judaism in Preaching and Teaching in the Roman Catholic Church* (1986), VI, 25.

10. *Notes on the Correct Way,* I, 7.

11. Walter Cardinal Kasper has provided a concise contrast between one- and two-covenant models: "The One Covenant Theory correctly maintains the unity of God's plan of salvation, but it presumes a unified canonical biblical covenant concept which does not exist. . . . It stands in danger of either claiming Judaism for Christianity or making Christianity into a sort of reformed Judaism, thus obscuring either the particularity of Judaism or the uniqueness and universality of Christ Jesus. The Two Covenant Theory avoids these dangers. Its strength is that it can maintain the relative autonomy of Judaism and Christianity. Even if it wishes to maintain the interconnectedness of Judaism and Christianity, this is not totally successful; it runs the risk of considering the two as totally independent entities. It must therefore on the one hand play down the Jewish roots of the church while on the other hand failing to do justice to the universal Christological claim. The relationship of Judaism and Christianity is thus so complex both historically and theologically that it cannot be reduced to one of the two theories or to a formula which is valid for all time" ("The Relationship of the Old and the New Covenant as One of the Central Issues in Jewish-Christian Dialogue," paper delivered at the Centre for the Study of Jewish-Christian Relations, Cambridge, De-

Catholic magisterium ran the risk of imposing Christian categories on the Jewish experience of covenant, particularly if the Vatican's admonition to learn from Jewish self-understanding went unheeded. Catholic theologies that fail to engage with the integrity of the ongoing Jewish tradition on its own terms tend to reduce Judaism to being the bearer of fulfilled "promises" and fail to recognize the dynamism of Jewish interaction with God today (see the discussion below on Cardinals Dulles and Vanhoye).

An important effort to assert both the church's faith in Jesus Christ as universal savior and its recognition of the vitality of Judaism's covenantal life was offered by Walter Cardinal Kasper in 2001. In commenting on the questions for Catholic-Jewish relations raised by a document that had recently been issued by the Congregation for the Doctrine of the Faith, the incoming president of the Commission for Religious Relations with the Jews stated:

> One of these questions is how to relate the covenant with the Jewish people, which according to St. Paul is unbroken and not revoked but still in vigor, with what we Christians call the New Covenant. As you know, the old theory of substitution is gone since the Second Vatican Council. For us Christians today the covenant with the Jewish people is a living heritage, a living reality. There cannot be a mere coexistence between the two covenants. Jews and Christians, by their respective specific identities, are intimately related to each other. It is impossible now to enter the complex problem of how this intimate relatedness should or could be defined. Such a question touches the mystery of Jewish and Christian existence as well, and should be discussed in our further dialogue.
>
> The only thing I wish to say is that the document *Dominus Iesus* does not state that everybody needs to become a Catholic in order to be saved by God. On the contrary, it declares that God's grace, which is the grace of Jesus Christ according to our faith, is available to all. Therefore, the Church believes that Judaism, i.e. the faithful response of the Jewish people to God's irrevocable covenant, is salvific for them, because God is faithful to his promises.[12]

Here multiple ideas are held together: (1) God's grace comes through Jesus Christ; (2) Jews and Christians, despite having specific identities, are inti-

---

cember 6, 2004). Available at http://www.ccjr.us/dialogika-resources/themes-in-todays -dialogue/conversion/524-kasper04dec6.

12. Walter Cardinal Kasper, *"Dominus Iesus,"* paper delivered at the 17th meeting of the International Catholic-Jewish Liaison Committee, May 1, 2001, p. 3.

mately related; and (3) Jewish covenantal life, seen on its own terms as "the faithful response of the Jewish people," possesses salvific qualities because of God's unfailing faithfulness.[13]

As Kasper himself observed, it was impossible in his brief 2001 paper "to enter the complex problem of how this intimate relatedness should or could be defined." In particular, the question of how God's Christ-mediated grace was active in Judaism's salvific covenantal life was not addressed, which this volume attempts to do, albeit with awareness that this question cannot be easily resolved. It is no exaggeration to state that this question could never have been raised in those centuries when Christians presumed that Jews were cursed by God, their covenant with God either terminated or withered.

It is perhaps a legacy of earlier, negative portrayals of Judaism that some Catholic thinkers today are uncomfortable with such robust descriptions of Jewish life-in-covenant. For them it seems that the confession of Christ as universal savior must be inversely proportional to the vitality of Jewish life. To assert a full and robust Jewish covenantal existence is tantamount, in this perspective, to denying the salvific centrality of Christ. Conversely, for them a full and intense assertion of Christ as the savior of all demands the minimization of Jewish covenanting.

Thus, in critiquing a dialogue document that had argued on the basis of a robust understanding of covenant that Catholics should not mount campaigns to convert Jews, Avery Cardinal Dulles wrote that "The most formal statement on the status of the Sinai covenant under Christianity appears in the Letter to the Hebrews, which points out that in view of the new covenant promised by God through the prophet Jeremiah, the first covenant is 'obsolete' and 'ready to vanish away' (Heb. 8:13). The priesthood and the law have changed (Heb. 7:12). Christ, we are told, 'abolishes the first [covenant] in order to establish the second' (Heb. 10:9)."[14] In a

---

13. It should be noted that Jews and Christians have somewhat different understandings of "salvation." In very broad brushstrokes, Jews tend to think of being "delivered" by God in more historical and communal terms, while Christians tend to think of "being saved" in terms of the individual and the afterlife. See the helpful discussion of "Salvation" by S. Daniel Breslauer and Celia Deutsch in Leon Klenicki and Geoffrey Wigoder, eds., *A Dictionary of the Jewish-Christian Dialogue* (New York/Ramsey: Paulist Press/Stimulus Books, 1984), pp. 179-85. For the diversity of Christian views, see Clark Williamson, "What Does It Mean to Be Saved?" in Philip A. Cunningham, ed., *Pondering the Passion: What's at Stake for Christians and Jews?* (Lanham, MD: Rowman & Littlefield, 2004), pp. 119-28.

14. Avery Dulles, "Covenant and Mission," *America* 187, no. 12 (October 21, 2002): 10.

later article, he opined that *Nostra Aetate* "left open the question whether the Old Covenant remains in force today."[15] Besides being exegetically unsound, these efforts to characterize Jewish adherence to the Torah as outmoded run counter to the trajectory of post–*Nostra Aetate* Catholic teaching, such as John Paul II's praise of Jews as "the present-day people of the covenant concluded with Moses."[16] In this regard, it is also notable that Dulles never cited any of the magisterial documents of the Commission for Religious Relations with the Jews.

A similar idea was more recently expressed by Albert Cardinal Vanhoye at the 2008 Synod of Bishops. In commenting on a study of the Pontifical Biblical Commission, *The Jewish People and Their Sacred Scriptures in the Christian Bible,* he also turned to the Letter to the Hebrews:

> The polemic text of the Letter to the Hebrews is, generally speaking, consciously or unconsciously, ignored in the soothing declarations on the permanent validity of the first Covenant. The Document does not quote this text, but takes it into account, because it refrains from asserting the permanent validity of the Sinai Covenant. It mentions the permanent validity of the "covenant-promise of God," which is not a bilateral pact such as the Sinai Covenant, often broken by the Israelites. It is "all merciful" and "cannot be annulled" (No. 41). It "is definitive and cannot be abolished." In this sense, according to the New Testament, "Israel continues to be in a covenant relationship with God" (No. 42).[17]

Here, Vanhoye portrays ongoing Jewish spiritual life as a "covenant-promise," with the emphasis on the "promise" of Christ, thereby casting doubt on "the permanent validity of the Sinai covenant." There is no regard for Jewish self-understanding. By observing that the Sinai covenant was "often broken by the Israelites" without considering how often Christians may have "broken" their covenantal life in Christ, Vanhoye recalls the polemics of patristic-era anti-Jewish literature.[18]

---

15. Avery Cardinal Dulles, "The Covenant with Israel," *First Things* (November 2005). http://www.firstthings.com/article.php3?id_article=256.

16. "Address to the Jewish Community in Mainz, West Germany," November 17, 1980.

17. Zenit.org, "Cardinal Vanhoye on Jews and Scripture," October 7, 2008. http://www.zenit.org/article-23841?l=english. See the essay on Hebrews by Jesper Svartvik elsewhere in this volume.

18. E.g., Tertullian, *Adversus Judaeos,* 1:6-7: "[A]ccording to the records of the divine Scriptures, the Jewish people — that is, the more ancient — were devoted to idols, as they had deserted God, and were addicted to images, as they had abandoned the divinity. The

We believe that efforts to diminish the covenantal vitality of Judaism today serve to avoid grappling with the profound question to which this book is dedicated. They are biblically untenable[19] and effectively put the church back on the slippery slope of pre–*Nostra Aetate* supersessionism. If their aim is to safeguard the key Christian confession of Christ as universal Savior, they are also theologically unnecessary. It is not an either/or question. We believe that Catholics and other Christians can — by reclaiming the Christian trinitarian tradition often overlooked in Western Christianity — simultaneously assert *both* the universal saving significance of Christ *and* the perpetual and saving dynamism of Jewish covenantal life with God. This conviction is the driving force of our essay.

2. Covenantal Life and Salvation

At this point it would be helpful to expand upon our use of the adjective "robust" when describing Israel's covenantal life. For Jews and Christians

---

people were saying to Aaron, 'Make us gods who may go before us.' When the gold from the women's necklaces and from the men's rings had been melted in the fire by these people and an ox head had come forth for them, as they had abandoned God, all Israel delivered honor to this figure saying, 'These are the gods who brought us out from the land of Egypt.' For thus, in later times, when kings ruled them, they, together with Jeroboam, were cultivating in worship golden calves and sacred groves and sold themselves to Baal. From this, by means of the divine Scriptures, there is proof that they were marked out indelibly as answerable for the crime of idolatry. In fact, our [Christian] people — that is, the later — having forsaken the idols to which previously we used to be devoted, were converted to the same God from whom Israel had departed, as we mentioned above" (Geoffrey D. Dunn, *Tertullian* [London: Routledge, 2004], pp. 69-70).

19. It goes beyond the scope of this essay to explore the biblical issues here. Suffice it to say that we consider the diminution of Jewish covenantal life on the basis of biblical texts to be untenable for two general reasons. First, such arguments tend to invoke "Old Testament" passages in a selective manner and exclusively through "New Testament" lenses without regard for their meaning *within* the traditions of Israel both past and present. The latter is a form of circular logic that concludes that Israel's covenantal life is inferior on the basis of an interpretative methodology that has already excluded Jewish understandings of its own covenantal experience. Second, New Testament passages are often interpreted out of context by assuming that they are discussing the relationship between a separate and distinct "Judaism" and "Christianity." However, this was not the situation in the New Testament era. Such anachronism, often seen with regard to the Letter to the Hebrews, is sometimes also linked to a failure to appreciate the different eschatological perspectives between the biblical authors and modern interpreters.

to be in covenant with God is to be in a permanent relationship that brings mutual responsibilities to all parties. Human beings in covenant with the One God experience that relationship both as members of their respective communities and as individual Jews and Christians. Since the ever-faithful God is one of the participants, this relationship is permanent until the end of historic time, even though the human partners retain their freedom to sin. To put it another way, Jews and Christians in covenant with God can and do "break" the covenant, but because God is ever-faithful the covenantal relationship itself endures to be reiterated and reexpressed over and over again. God's covenantal faithfulness encourages human repentance and recommitment.

Thus, the Jewish scriptures, the *Tanakh,* and the two Testaments of the Christian scriptures, both contain various articulations of covenantal life with God. As perceived by their human authors at various moments in time, some focus on individuals, some are community-centered. Some are phrased conditionally, others unconditionally. Because God is the divine partner, all covenants have a permanent character. Even those with conditions should be understood as "covenants with conditions" rather than "conditional covenants."[20]

Many iterations look forward to an eschatological culmination at the end of historic time as we experience it. Thus, for example, Jeremiah speaks of "coming days" in a which a new covenant will be written on the hearts of the people of Israel, and "they all shall know me, from the least of them to the greatest" (Jer. 31:31-34), while in the Synoptic tradition Jesus at the Last Supper says, "This is my blood of the covenant, which will be shed for many. . . . I shall not drink again the fruit of the vine until the day when I drink it new in the kingdom of God" (Mark 14:24-25). The various biblical expressions of covenantal life, in sum, link such relationship with God to God's plan of salvation for the world, God's intended destiny for all existence.

It is axiomatic in the Christian tradition that salvation is both "already" and "not yet."[21] There are indeed many ways in which Christians define salvation,[22] but almost all of them would agree with this observation about Catholic preaching:

20. This phrasing was voiced by Eugene J. Fisher in remarks given at Georgetown University on May 28, 2009.

21. See the essay by Gregor Maria Hoff in this volume, pp. 215-16.

22. See, for example, Clark Williamson, "What Does It Mean to Be Saved?" in Cunningham, ed., *Pondering the Passion,* pp. 119-28.

Christians believe that Jesus is the promised Messiah who has come (see Luke 4:22), but also know that his messianic kingdom is not yet fully realized. . . . Since this dimension can be misunderstood or even missed altogether, the homilist needs to raise clearly the hope found in the prophets and heightened in the proclamation of Christ. This hope includes trust in what is promised but not yet seen. While the biblical prophecies of an age of universal shalom are "fulfilled" (i.e., irreversibly inaugurated) in Christ's coming, that fulfillment is not yet completely worked out in each person's life or perfected in the world at large.[23]

Thus, God's invitation to the communities of Israel and the church to share in divine covenant is linked to the already/not yet nature of salvation. By living covenantal lives, God's human partners are contributing to the unfolding of God's saving intentions for the world. In a sense, they prematurely experience in historic time God's ultimate salvation that will climax eschatologically.

3. The Distinctive Experiences of Covenant of the Jewish and Christian Peoples

For us, this robust understanding of covenant must apply to both Israel's and the church's covenantal lives or else God's faithfulness is thrown into doubt. As the two communities have walked with God down through the centuries, their evolving understandings of covenantal life manifest distinctive features, even though they are organically related because of their common divine partner and their common origins in ancient Israel.

Thus, the Jewish people seek to enact God's will by "grappling with God" (the meaning of "Israel") through the words of the Torah. We are understanding "Torah" here in the broadest sense, referring both to the *Tanakh* (the entire Hebrew Bible: the Teaching of Moses, the Prophets, and the Writings) and to the rabbinic and post-rabbinic commentary, elaboration, and debate upon it. This living tradition of engaging God's Word has dynamically adapted to new situations and challenges over the centuries right up to the present.

A particularly significant period of Jewish renewal unfolded after the

23. Bishops' Committee on the Liturgy, National [United States] Conference of Catholic Bishops, *God's Mercy Endures Forever: Guidelines on the Presentation of Jews and Judaism in Catholic Preaching* (Washington, DC: U.S.C.C., 1988), §11.

destruction of the Jerusalem Temple in 70 C.E. Jewish covenantal life gradually shifted from a Temple-centered to a Torah-centered way of walking with God. In a process that spanned centuries, study, prayer, and good works replaced sacrifices, and the Jewish home replaced the Temple court as the locus of worship. The *Tanakh* was reread and reinterpreted through the lenses of rabbinic discourse, and new meanings were constructed to live covenantally in a changing world.

Analogously, the Christian people seek to do God's will by walking in the way of Jesus Christ. As will be further discussed below, the church understands the Jew Jesus to be "Christ," the one who incarnates God's divine Word or Logos. Through his life, death, and resurrection to glorified life, Jesus brought the church into being as a community covenanting with God until the end of time. Through the church, the glorified Jesus continues his earthly mission of heralding and inaugurating God's Reign in human history.

Importantly, the church's early self-understandings were also shaped by the demise of the Jerusalem Temple. Jesus' death on the cross was seen as replacing the sacrifices offered in the Temple, the Eucharistic meal replaced the meal offerings of the Temple, and the New Testament was understood as the climax of the Old Testament. We would argue that for social and historical reasons, and not for any theological inevitability, the possibility of two covenantal modalities was an option that was not pursued.[24] A "zero sum" approach prevailed in which for one tradition to be correct, the other had to be incorrect. Social forces prevented serious exploration of the possibility that God might desire to walk through history in covenant with two distinct but interrelated communities.

Thus, Jewish covenantal life is Torah-shaped and Christian covenantal life is Christ-shaped. Both Israel and the church experience God's saving works in the past, the present, and in hope of the eschatological future. They both seek to do God's will, and, although both regularly sin, God's covenantal faithfulness endures, enabling Jews and Christians to ask forgiveness and to reform. In different ways, both Jews and Christians understand that their covenantal lives are meant to prepare for the Age to Come, God's eschatological Reign over all creation.

We note only in passing here that this understanding of Judaism and

---

24. Note this interesting prohibition in the nonbiblical late first-century Epistle of Barnabas: "Do not be like certain persons who pile up sin upon sin, saying that our covenant remains to them also" (4:6).

Christianity logically leads to the conclusion that God intends Jews and Christians to collaborate with each other and with God in bringing salvation to its eschatological climax. Pope John Paul II expressed this idea in these now famous words: "As Christians and Jews, following the example of the faith of Abraham, we are called to be a blessing for the world [cf. Gen. 12:2ff.]. This is the common task awaiting us. It is therefore necessary for us, Christians and Jews, to be first a blessing to one another."[25] The fact that until only very recently Christians delegitimized Judaism, too often marginalizing and demeaning Jews in Christian lands, can therefore only be viewed as a great tragedy and as inarguable evidence of the sinfulness that is possible even for people in covenant with God.

Today, however, it has become more possible for Jews and Christians to perceive each other's traditions as manifestations of covenantal life. This insight is possible because of the depth of dialogue and relationship that have provided opportunities for us to resonate with each other's distinctive experiences of covenant with God. For Christians, this includes a recognition that God's Word animates Jewish covenantal life today.

But it also raises the challenge with which we began this essay: How does God's Word expressed in the Torah relate to God's Word whom Christians experience as incarnated as Christ? Answers to this question for Christian theology and self-understanding are found in the Christian understanding of God as triune and in the Christian understanding of revelation.

4. Covenanting with the Triune One: A Christian Affirmation of Judaism's Covenantal Life

It is not possible for either Christians or Jews to survey reality, including each other's reality, completely removed from their own religious and historical horizons. There is no "helicopter perspective" from which we can regard the Jewish or Christian other with majestic neutrality. We are all participants in the interreligious encounter, not simply observers. Since we cannot access some transcendent viewpoint next to or above these living and lived particular Christian and Jewish perspectives, it is necessary that the effort to understand the other in one's own terms be accompanied by a simultaneous, complementary effort to hear and understand the other

25. "Address on the Fiftieth Anniversary of the Warsaw Ghetto Uprising," April 6, 1993.

within the other's frames of reference. This dialectical dynamic militates against the imposition of Christian categories on Judaism (or vice-versa).

During interreligious dialogue, then, there is an exchange of these diverse internal and external points of view, seeking to uncover how, on the negative side, contrasting perspectives can become sources of exclusion and even violence, and on the positive side, how they can enrich each other. Interreligious dialogue is therefore an important touchstone for every theological enterprise that considers religious others.

It is a defining characteristic of Christianity's perspective that through their covenantal life with God in Christ, Christians have come to experience God as triune: as a unity of three ways of interrelated divine being. Christians have traditionally referred to the Trinity as the Father, the Son or Word, and the Holy Spirit. The relevance of trinitarian thinking for Christian understandings of Jewish covenantal life was noted in the annual 1999 Joseph Cardinal Bernardin lecture by the late Anthony J. Saldarini:

> The triune Christian God is one reality with inner relations among three subsistents, the begetter, the begotten and the spirated one. . . . In all else, in all activity, in all relationships with humans, God is, acts, loves and saves as one, indivisibly. To say that God saves humans means that the Father saves as do the Son and the Spirit. To say that Jesus the Son of God saves is to say that God saves. When God saves Israel, in the Christian understanding of God, the Spirit of God and the Son of God as well as God the Father save Israel. God has acted and acts today in and for Israel and the church.[26]

For the purposes of this essay, it may be helpful to understand that the Father is experienced by Christians as creating and sustaining all things, that the Word or Logos is experienced by Christians as God's invitation to covenantal relationship with God, and that the Spirit is experienced by Christians as enabling the acceptance and pursuit of that covenantal life.[27]

Despite the limitations of our perceptions, life "in Christ" (as the Apostle Paul put it) has gradually enabled Christians to glimpse that a life of loving relationships characterizes the very being of God. The power of this — for lack of a better word — "inner" or "immanent" relationality of

26. "Christian Anti-Judaism: The First Century Speaks to the Twenty-first Century," April 14, 1999.

27. Space does not allow an adequate treatment of "pneumatology," or the work of the Holy Spirit in human life. But see Elizabeth Groppe's related essay.

God is so great that it generates and sustains the existence of all creation, to which God reaches out with constant appeals and enablements to "exterior" or "economic" (meaning in linear history) relationships between the divine and created realms.

Christians believe that life in relationship with God allows human beings to share to some extent in the network of God's "internal" loving relationality. Christians believe that they taste "eternal life." To use the imagery of the Gospel of John, the Father, Son, and Spirit "abide in" one another. And the church enters into that abiding. In the words of the Johannine Jesus: "If someone loves me he will keep my word ['to love one another'] and the Father will love him, and we will come to him and make our home with him" (John 14:23). In Johannine terms eternal life is a sharing in the love-relationship between the Father and the Son in the Spirit. It is a love-life that transcends human death.

Thus one can say that the Logos, God's constant outreach for relationship, together with the Spirit that empowers the human acceptance of that outreach, brings into human history the very covenanting life of the Trinity. The immanent Trinity, the essential relationality of God within Godself, is the template for the life of love that should unite all who have joined into covenantal life with God, and it drives the work of the Trinity in the world (the "economic Trinity").[28]

The profundity of the trinitarian tradition is too often underappreciated in the Christian West. For various reasons over the course of history, Eastern Christianity stressed the tri-unity of God in its religious life, but in the West attention became focused on the work of the Word incarnated in Christ. In extreme cases, this emphasis could become christomonism, a myopic concern with Christ only that forgets the Father's and the Spirit's participation in every divine act.[29] Ironically, the Christian West has

---

28. Many have observed that the enormity of the Shoah calls into question neat formulas about the actions of God in the world. Although beyond the limits of this essay, we suspect that only the recognition of this coherence between the "internal life" of the Triune One and the triune work of God in human history makes it credible to speak meaningfully about the Trinity in the wake of the Shoah. Sarah Pinnock mentions Jürgen Moltmann in this regard: "The significance of the cross in view of horrendous suffering [in the Shoah] is that 'the great abyss of the world's godforsakenness is thus taken within the Trinitarian love between the Father and the Son'" (*Beyond Theodicy: Jewish and Christian Continental Thinkers Respond to the Holocaust* [Albany: State University of New York, 2002], p. 77, citing Jürgen Moltmann, *The Crucified God: The Cross of Christ as the Foundation and Criticism of Christian Theology* [London: T. & T. Clark, 1995], pp. 190-93).

29. Fred Craddock, for example, is concerned that many Christians "who sit before

tended to forget the full richness of trinitarian thought that it needs to grapple with the question of the Jewish people's covenantal life with God, while the East, which has preserved trinitarianism more fully in its daily life of faith, has yet to deal significantly with how it relates to Judaism.

With this brief presentation of Christian glimpses of the inherent relationality of God, we turn now to consider Israel's covenantal life through trinitarian lenses. With the Triune One in mind, Christians can understand God's calling the people of Israel into being as a covenantal community as an experience of God's creative power, as an invitation to enter into a permanent relationship, and as an empowerment to become a unique people. The Logos and the Spirit have been involved in Israel's covenantal life since its inception. Christians, for example, understand that the Torah is an expression of the Word of God,[30] and the Nicene Creed confesses that the Holy Spirit "has spoken through the prophets."

A distinctive aspect of Israel's life-in-covenant must be noted. Orthodox Jewish thinker Michael Wyschogrod has stressed the physicality of God's covenantal relationship with the Jewish people. He emphasizes the corporeal nature of God's choice or election of Israel:

> Israel, whatever else it may also be, and it is many other things, is first and foremost a community of family, of kinship, of descent from Abraham, of blood communion. . . . There is therefore no idea that encompasses Israel because Israel is, at it were, an idea incarnated in the flesh of a people. . . . [Circumcision] is a cutting into the flesh, the organ of generation, leaving a permanent mark in the flesh of a people that thereby embraces the covenant with its flesh.[31]

---

pulpits have been given a steady diet of Jesus Christ without a context in theology. A listener might get the impression that faith in Christ had replaced faith in God or that faith in Christ had been added to faith in God as though an increase in the number of items in one's faith meant an increase in salvific effect" ("The Gospel of God," in Thomas G. Long and Edward Farley, eds., *Preaching as a Theological Task: World, Gospel, Scripture* [Louisville: Westminster/John Knox, 1996], p. 74).

30. Thus, the post–Vatican II Good Friday intercession prays for "the Jewish people, the first to hear the Word of God."

31. Michael Wyschogrod, *Abraham's Promise: Judaism and Christian-Jewish Relations* (Grand Rapids and Cambridge: Eerdmans, 2004), p. 129. In this light, it is unfortunate that after Vatican II the observance of January 1 as the Feast of the Circumcision ceased. The restoration of this celebration of the Jewishness of Jesus would be especially meaningful in a post–*Nostra Aetate* church.

For Wyschogrod, this corporeal nature of Israel's life with God explains why Israel knows "a God who enters the human world and into relationship with humanity by means of speech and command"[32] and who is quite different from the noncorporeal and immutable deity of Greek philosophy and its heirs.[33]

Significantly, Wyschogrod from his Jewish perspective concludes that "the Christian teaching of the incarnation of God in Jesus is the intensification of the teaching of the indwelling of God in Israel by concentrating that indwelling in one Jew rather than leaving it diffused in the people of Jesus as a whole."[34] Thus, the presence of God in Jewish flesh, symbolized in the religious ritual of male circumcision, can be seen by Christians as intensified and focused in the person of the Jew Jesus, who incarnates the divine Logos.

To relate Wyschogrod's observation to trinitarian thought, we recall again that the Catholic Church now teaches that Jewish covenantal life was "never revoked by God."[35] From a Christian viewpoint this must mean that even after the time of Christ, the people of Israel have been interacting covenantally with the Triune One. The rise of rabbinic Judaism and Jewish religious life up to today must therefore be seen as expressions of the divine Logos and Spirit living in the midst of the covenanting and divinely sustained[36] community of the people Israel. Moreover, since God is the ever-faithful and saving One, that divine relationship with and within the Jewish people is certain to be vital until the eschaton, even if the inner dynamics of Israel's relationship with God are not experienced by Christians.

For Christians, Christ incarnates the divine Logos. On this point, *Dominus Iesus* is instructive. Even if this document was not written explicitly for Jewish-Christian dialogue (but rather oriented toward the broader

32. Wyschogrod, *Abraham's Promise*, p. 42.

33. Wyschogrod, *Abraham's Promise*, pp. 32-35.

34. Wyschogrod, *Abraham's Promise*, p. 178. This relates to Barbara Meyer's statements in this volume that "the story of Jesus Christ is unthinkable apart from the context of Israel" (p. 150); and "Jesus' Jewishness is . . . the heart of God's revelation. Had Jesus not been Jewish, he could not have led the peoples to the God of Abraham and Sarah, Moses and Miriam. The opening of the covenant for all peoples is sealed in Jesus' being Jewish" (p. 151). See also Hans Hermann Henrix's discussion of Wyschogrod's thought on pp. 128f.

35. John Paul II, "Address to the Jewish Community in Mainz, West Germany," November 17, 1980.

36. N.B. the 1985 Vatican Notes: "The permanence of Israel (while so many ancient peoples have disappeared without trace) is a historic fact and a sign to be interpreted within God's design. . . . We must remind ourselves how the permanence of Israel is accompanied by a continuous spiritual fecundity . . ." [VI, 25].

theology of non-Christian religions), its comments on the relation between Christ and the divine Logos have implications for our discussion:

> It is . . . contrary to the Catholic faith to introduce a separation between the salvific action of the Word as such and that of the Word made man. With the Incarnation, all the salvific actions of the Word of God are always done in unity with the human nature that he has assumed for the salvation of all people. The one subject which operates in the two natures, human and divine, is the single person of the Word. Therefore, [a] theory which would attribute, after the Incarnation as well, a salvific activity to the Logos as such in his divinity, exercised "in addition to" or "beyond" the humanity of Christ, is not compatible with the Catholic faith. (II, 10)[37]

In other words, all the saving activity of the divine Logos in the world today, most notably for this essay within the ongoing covenantal life of Jewish humanity, is done in unity with the glorified humanity of the Jew Jesus. The same first-century Jew, whom Christians are convinced incarnated the Logos, lives today in divine glory, continuing to share in the constant work of the Logos in the world.

Indeed, from a Christian point of view it might be said that God's covenantal sharing-in-life, dwelling within the flesh of the people of Israel, became even more focused, more intimate with the incarnation of the Logos in Jesus, the "authentic son of Israel."[38] From a Christian perspective, then, the glorified Christ covenantally abides both within the church and within the community of Israel because the triune God abides with both peoples. "Jesus Christ has a significance and a value for the human

37. It might be noted here that *Dominus Iesus'* formulation of this point is more nuanced than that found in the Congregation for the Doctrine of Faith's "Notification on the Book *Toward a Christian Theology of Religious Pluralism* by Father Jacques Dupuis, S.J.," January 24, 2001, I, 2: "It is therefore contrary to the Catholic faith not only to posit a separation between the Word and Jesus, or between the Word's salvific activity and that of Jesus, but also to maintain that there is a salvific activity of the Word as such in his divinity, independent of the humanity of the Incarnate Word." This briefer text does not consider the matter from within the perspective of historic time. Therefore, before the incarnation of the *logos* in Jesus of Nazareth, the divine Word was obviously salvifically active, especially within the community of Israel. *Dominus Iesus* rightly insists that after the incarnation the Logos' salvific activity is united with the Jewish humanity of Jesus. However, we argue that a distinction must be maintained between the revelation of the incarnation to Christians and the continuing salvific activity of the *logos* in the divine covenant with Israel, to whom the mystery of the incarnation has not been revealed.

38. John Paul II, "Address to the Pontifical Biblical Commission," April 11, 1997, §3.

race and its history, which are unique and singular, proper to him alone, exclusive, universal, and absolute"[39] because the incarnation of the Logos and the life, death, and glorification of the Jew Jesus were absolutely necessary for history's eventual culmination in the eschatological Reign of God. Christians cannot claim to understand fully God's designs in this matter because they will only be entirely revealed at the eschaton. Until then, "We know that the whole of creation has been groaning in labor pains until now; and not only the creation, but we ourselves, who have the first fruits of the Spirit, groan inwardly while we wait for adoption, the redemption of our bodies. For in hope we were saved" (Rom. 8:22-24a).

Jews and Christians are both correct to expect their distinctive and kindred relationships with God to achieve their ultimate destiny in the Age to Come. Or as the Pontifical Biblical Commission has put it:

Jewish messianic expectation is not in vain. It can become for us Christians a powerful stimulus to keep alive the eschatological dimension of our faith. Like them, we too live in expectation. The difference is that for us the One who is to come will have the traits of the Jesus who has already come and is already present and active among us.[40]

This leads to the conclusion that on both historical and theological grounds Jews do not need to share in the Christian experience of the Logos incarnated as Jesus to be participants in covenant with a saving God, since they continue to experience the indwelling of God within their community and people. From a Christian perspective, this indwelling necessarily involves the Logos, notwithstanding that the Word's incarnation in Jesus has not been revealed to Israel as a whole.[41] This does not make Jews "unwitting

---

39. Congregation for the Doctrine of the Faith, *Dominus Iesus* (2000), §15.

40. "The Jewish People and Their Sacred Scriptures in the Christian Bible" (2001), II, A, 5 — §21. Note, too, these comments by Bishop Jules Daem of Antwerp during the Second Vatican Council, "The Christian must bear in mind that, in accordance with the divine decree, Jews and Christians are moving toward the same fulfillment — the revelation of God's mercy in a common bond. We must follow this divine decree, not by means of unseemly proselytism, but in plain dealing and complete humility" (John M. Oesterreicher, *The New Encounter between Christians and Jews* [New York: Philosophical Library, 1986], p. 209). Bishop Daem's sentiments, expressed by other Council fathers as well, lie behind these words of *Nostra Aetate*, 4: ". . . the Church awaits the day, known to God alone, when all people will call upon the Lord with a single voice and 'serve him with one accord' (Zeph 3:9)."

41. Conversely, the ongoing self-disclosure of God to Jews through the experience of Torah-life happens in ways mysterious to Christians.

Christians," because their distinctive way of walking with God is as such "the faithful response of the Jewish people to God's irrevocable covenant."[42]

The different Christian and Jewish interrelated modes of covenanting with God will ultimately reach fulfillment at the eschaton. "[I]n what ways will their fullness be revealed?" asked Giacomo Cardinal Lercaro of Bologna during the Second Vatican Council. "Certainly, in ways that are religious and mysterious, whose mysteriousness we must respect. Those ways are hidden in the wisdom and knowledge of God."[43] Our limitations as beings immersed in linear time restrict our vision of the Age to Come. Meanwhile, our recognition of ongoing Jewish covenantal life makes it clear that Judaism is included in the divine plan of salvation until the end of historic time.

Many Christians have wondered why Jews don't enter into covenant with God through the Logos incarnated in the glorified Jesus for the salvation of all humanity. But today we must seriously wrestle with the implications of the possibility that the mysterious providential plan includes the Jewish and Christian communities living in covenant with God throughout historic time according to two organically connected modalities. If we take seriously the Apostle Paul's intuition that God was responsible for a general Jewish lack of receptivity to his preaching of the Good News (Rom. 11:7-8, 25-26), then the existence of two distinct communities in covenant with God is not the result of some sort of mistake. Rather, it was God's will.

If the continuing existence of two communities walking in covenant was the will of God, then their interrelationship must be viewed as having a positive meaning. Gregor Maria Hoff suggests one intriguing way of conceiving of the relationship between the Jewish and Christian covenanting communities. It is analogous to the Council of Chalcedon's formula to describe the relationship of the human and divine natures in Christ: Jews and Christians live covenantal lives that are "united but unmixed."[44] Meanwhile, both traditions share the duty of preparing the world for the coming of God's Reign.

The journey of Jews and Christians to God's intended end has proven to be far longer in duration than the New Testament writers ever imagined. To varying degrees, they all expected that the climax of human history

---

42. Walter Cardinal Kasper, *"Dominus Iesus,"* paper delivered at the 17th meeting of the International Catholic-Jewish Liaison Committee, May 1, 2001, §3.

43. Cited in Oesterreicher, *New Encounter,* pp. 204-5.

44. See the essay by Hoff in this volume, pp. 218-19.

would happen fairly soon. It should not be surprising, therefore, that God's plan for creation's redemption is vaster than even we who live two millennia later can imagine. A growing number of Christians are now coming to realize that God's providence includes Jewish covenantal companions on the journey to the Age to Come, covenanting with God in their distinctive Torah-shaped interactions with the inviting and revealing Logos and the empowering and inspiring Spirit.

A Realm of Differences: The Meaning of Jewish Monotheism for Christology and Trinitarian Theology

Gregor Maria Hoff

1. Revelation in the Theology of Religions: *Nostra Aetate* and the Process of Salvation amid Religious Differences

John XXIII convened the Second Vatican Council against a background of clearly defined problems that were readily discernible and that the Catholic Church could no longer evade. A clear stand had to be taken both within the church and outside the church in the face of an entirely new situation: the political, cultural and, above all, the religious pluralism of the postwar world. For the church, this problem was played out on various stages.

The question of the salvation of nonbelievers and dissenters was the driving theological question, which was ultimately linked to a challenge in the theology of revelation. How should Christians speak about God's revelation when confronted by the plurality of the world religions?[1] This dogmatic problem had to be approached from an altered theological foundation. Its starting point was the variety of grammars employed by the world's religions in conceiving of and talking about God. This variety required a clearly definable place *in* the salvific economy or plan of God — and not merely *beyond* it or *outside* it. This led, however, to the question of whether the world's religions might be the products of some type of divine revelation.

The first major achievement of the "Declaration on the Relationship of the Church to Non-Christian Religions" *(Nostra Aetate)* is the explicit

---

1. For a historical and systematic overview of this question, see Gavin D'Costa, "Revelation and World Religions," in Paul Avis, ed., *Divine Revelation* (London: Darton, Longman & Todd, 1997), pp. 112-39.

naming of the differences in religious grammar.[2] In Section 1, the Council addresses the relationship between pluralism and unity: the diversity of the world's various peoples and religions and all of humankind's striving for unity. It is under these circumstances that people struggle to talk about God. This is no accident. The situation in which people try to speak about God today is set out in the Declaration's first paragraph, and, on this basis, the second paragraph then turns to humanity's common origin in God. Thus a second distinct achievement of *Nostra Aetate* is evident. The Declaration addresses the *soteriological* problem of religious pluralism (can other religions "save"?) as a *linguistic* problem (God is beyond all human articulation). This enables us to develop a religious or theological perspective from which to take a fresh look at the problem of revelation.

The third paragraph of Section 1 deals with the "ultimate inexpressible mystery that encompasses our existence." This mystery has a place *in* this act of speech, yet at the same it bursts through it. This is of vital significance — after all the church herself is speaking. At the very outset of the Declaration, at the point of transition from the introduction to thematic development, the *inexpressible* becomes the *departure point for the definition of the relation of Christianity toward other religions*. From this starting point, Section 2 goes on to offer a linguistic atlas of the world's religious traditions. There we find "a certain perception of that hidden power which hovers over the course of things and over the events of human history." One expression is of particular consequence: the "hidden power" in which we encounter God. Unlike the subsequent designation of belief in a "Supreme Being," this phrase has a comprehensive meaning. It cannot, on purely syntactical grounds, be included among the various grammars about to be presented as preliminary religious stages prior to Christianity. These grammars or language systems that are named afterward define the point of the argumentation of the Declaration, which is ultimately directed toward Christian monotheism as the greatest and most explicit instance of divine revelation, the highest revelatory explicitness. The linguistic logic of this passage seems permanently valid: the "hidden power" is the basis of all things. Thus what is hidden can be expressed as *hiddenness*, but is, at the same time, important for our talking about the revealed God.

2. On *Nostra Aetate*, see the theological commentary by Roman Siebenrock in *Herders theologischer Kommentar zum Zweiten Vatikanischen Konzil*, vol. 3 (Freiburg: Herder, 2005), pp. 591-693. See also Josef Sinkovits and Ulrich Winkler, eds., *Weltkirche und Weltreligionen. Die Brisanz des Zweiten Vatikanischen Konzils 40 Jahre nach Nostra aetate* (Salzburger Theologische Studien 28 — interkulturell 3; Innsbruck: Tyrolia, 2007).

This becomes clear in a further linguistic-logical precondition that shapes how the text functions. The third paragraph of Section 1 addresses the problem of religious pluralism in terms of certain signs and conditions. Humankind expects "from the various religions answers to the unsolved riddles of the human condition." The corresponding questions are posed — and left unanswered. Two things happen because of this way of speaking. First, these riddles are and *remain* unsolved. The architecture of the text does not result in Christianity offering unsubstantiated solutions of its own. And, second, Christianity — the Catholic Church to be more precise — is engaging in the same process of developing a workable grammar as the other religions when facing these universal problems.

A decisive inversion facilitates this. The Council no longer works exclusively from — thereby *excluding* — the inner logic of the church's revelation, but instead confronts religious pluralism with the exterior perspective of the world as it really is. An anthropological perspective sheds light on the religious-theological problem. The respect for the diversity of religious concepts that gives the text its extraordinary power is made possible by this turn to an exterior perspective. *Soteriologically,* the text is premised by concern for humanity and rendered possible by a *theological* form of speech that recognizes the permanent mystery in each of us, i.e., in our own personal ways of conceiving of God as well. Moreover, because all human beings must struggle with inadequate human capacities to grasp ultimate mystery and must use limited grammatical structures to express their inadequate concepts, who God is can never be fully articulated even in the mode of a revealed theology.

On the basis of differences in the grammars of religious thought, an eminently powerful connecting link between the religions is thereby produced: it is the difference in all speaking about God. God can only be spoken about through the indirect mediation of signs, in diverse metaphors that are connected to a variety of situations and locations. The numerous languages for talking about God even within our own Christian tradition are connected to the differences among other religious languages. John Paul II develops these thoughts further in the encyclical *Redemptoris Missio, the Mission of the Redeemer:* "Since salvation is offered to all, it must be made concretely available to all."[3] This means that, depending on the respective religious tradition, various languages for talking about God can exist, possess a revelatory significance, and have salvific relevance re-

---

3. John Paul II, *Redemptoris Missio,* §10.

gardless of their number. The Declaration exerts a powerful appeal when it suggests that, by seeking to express the inexpressible, every religion refers to God. Christianity *must* claim for itself that in Jesus Christ this particular reference to God was uttered and was incarnated as God's own Word. Yet even this authentic speech of God is comprehensible only in the paradoxical formulaic grammar of the Council of Chalcedon that speaks of the humanity and divinity of the Word enfleshed as inseparably united yet retaining unmixed their distinctive characteristics, *indivisible* and *distinct.* This, too, is language for the inexpressible. Once such limitations are recognized in our own speech, we Christians can learn from other grammars for talking about God.

The second paragraph of Section 2 is among the most frequently quoted texts of the Council in this regard. The turn to human perspectives, the Declaration's anthropological inversion, draws our attention to the sentences: "a ray of Truth . . . which enlightens all men" and "The Catholic Church rejects nothing that is true and holy in these religions."

The (conditional) capacity for truth in other religious languages is thus recognized, thereby facilitating new relations with the other religions. By this recognition, the Council has by no means relinquished its view that the church must proclaim Christ as the definitive way to salvation because in him as God's Word, God has expressed God's very self: *Jesus Christ is the grammar of God's plan of salvation.* From now on, however, this economy of salvation *in*-cludes and no longer *ex*-cludes other languages for talking about God. The Declaration concludes with a corresponding theologically based recognition of human dignity, human rights, and religious freedom. This recognition implicitly prohibits religious discrimination as stated in the conciliar declaration *Dignitatis Humanae.*

The Council came to the conclusion that religious pluralism has a place *in* the economy of salvation because it recognized the limits of all religious speech about God. All religions speak about the Transcendent as a mystery. Even though Christians feel enabled to talk about God more precisely because of Jesus Christ, they still are made aware of the limitations of all God-language. Thus, when a real truth about God appears in other religious traditions, it is expressed in a particular, non-Christian way of talking about God; yet it is, nevertheless, a truth. We Christians are confronted by a language for talking about God that is neither known nor found nor foreseen in our own theological framework. We stand before the unexpected God.

The church has always known that God can appear unexpectedly —

the Gospels contain numerous stories in this vein.[4] The unexpected God is a subject of theological epistemology (the processes of knowing God) — particularly in the *loci alieni*, or "external sources," as foreseen in Melchior Cano's theological epistemology.[5] Foreign and unknown places exist to which theology must refer in order to be able to speak about the authority of the Gospels. The non-Christian religions are just such modern *loci alieni*. Yet the Council can only tentatively describe the revelatory value of the unexpected sources of knowledge of God from a religiously theoretical standpoint. The meaning of the unexpected truth of God in other religions remains general. This has consequences. There is a tension that could be resolved in two opposite ways: an openness to valuing religious pluralism or a preference for revelatory exclusivity. The Council opted to maintain the tension, to leave it unresolved, asserting both that truth can be reflected in other traditions and that Jesus Christ is the supreme revelation of truth.

An approach to salvation that incorporates the different grammars of a religiously plural world must also consider the revelatory significance of Israel. God revealed God's own self in and to Israel — and not just a part of Godself. Jesus did not abolish the Torah nor did he replace it. The full meaning of the Torah was retained. Thus from a Christian viewpoint with regard to Judaism, a joint participation in the fullness of divine revelation exists. Israel therefore also possesses a permanent revelatory character. God's self-disclosure in the covenant with Israel presupposes the possibility of salvation for Israel *without confessing Christ* by virtue of an intimate and living relationship based on — from a Christian point of view — indisputably authentic divine revelation. In contrast to other religions, the unresolved difference of theological perspectives between Judaism and Christianity originates from an indestructible common revelatory basis. Therefore, this particular religious difference acquires a special significance for theologies of revelation.[6]

---

4. Such as Luke 1:26-38; 4:21ff.; 24:13-35; Mark 6:45-52; John 7:53-8:11; 11:39-44; 13:6-9 etc.

5. See Elmar Klinger, *Ekklesiologie der Neuzeit. Grundlegung bei Melchior Cano und Entwicklung bis zum zweiten Vatikanischen Konzil* (Freiburg: Herder, 1978); Hans-Joachim Sander, "Das Außen des Glaubens — eine Autorität der Theologie," in *Das Volk Gottes. Ein Ort der Befreiung*, ed. Hans-Joachim Sander and Hildegund Keul (Würzburg: Echter, 1998), pp. 204-58; on Melchior Cano, see Bernhard Körner, *Melchior Cano — De locis theologicis. Ein Beitrag zur theologischen Erkenntnislehre* (Graz: Styria Medienservice, 1994).

6. On the theology of Israel in the context of *Nostra Aetate*, see Hans Hermann Henrix, ed., *Nostra Aetate — Ein zukunfstweisender Konzilstext. Die Haltung der Kirche zum Judentum 40 Jahre danach* (Aachen: Einhard, 2006).

In developing the Council's teachings, Karl Rahner made a contribution of his own with the concept of "anonymous Christians." God can appear anonymously. The phrase immediately makes clear that we must be aware of the anonymous presence of God. God's anonymity is the unexpected mode of God's salvific presence. This is an unexpected insight, with a revelatory character of its own. The Emmaus story supplies the classical theological model: God can reveal Godself as an *anonymous companion*.

This insight is healing in itself since it enables Christianity to have a new relationship with other religions. Although the Council only hinted at this, leaving theologians with the challenge of elaborating the details, *Nostra Aetate* provided a conceptual framework that must guide all further theological development.

2. Christological Exposition: On the Limitations of Christological Claims to Singularity

The plurality of grammars of religious revelation raises epistemological questions for Christian theologies of revelation: If the Ultimate Mystery can be known in different ways, what are the implications for the Christian "way-of-knowing" God? It is, therefore, not by chance that the ecumenical movement that seeks to overcome the church's fragmentation arose precisely because the encounter with multiple traditions that were rightly called "Christian" demanded new understandings of the meaning of "church."[7] "Christianity" could no longer be restricted only to one tradition such as the Roman Catholic community. It resulted, moreover, in changes to existing theologies of revelation in that they were gradually forced to grapple with other understandings of ecclesiology.

The Second Vatican Council contributed a further impetus to developing multiple approaches to theologies of revelation: the faith must be articulated in line with the signs of the times. However, this requires a precise awareness of the various peoples who are generating their own language of faith. Logically, then, the grammar of revelation demands particular attention. From the point of view of the Catholic Church, the

7. A similar point is made in Congregation for the Doctrine of the Faith, "Responses to Some Questions Regarding Certain Aspects of the Doctrine on the Church" (June 29, 2007), about the conciliar phrase: "the Church of Christ subsists in the Catholic Church." Available at http://www.vatican.va/roman_curia/congregations/cfaith/documents/rc_con_cfaith_doc _20070629_responsa-quaestiones_en.html.

Council's Dogmatic Constitution on Divine Revelation, *Dei Verbum,* permitted this. In stressing the Word of God as a historical event, attention is strongly placed on *the diverse grammars for God as part of the plan of salvation.* This raises the question of the significance of the *one* incarnation of God in Jesus Christ, in which the Christian revelation is concentrated.[8] Jesus Christ, as God's Logos, is God's language for us — but is christology the Word's only authentic expression?

In this context it is necessary to differentiate between revelation and the language(s) of revelation. In the light of this differentiation, the early church's fixation on a singular incarnation of God is the theological grammar of every subsequent Christian discussion of revelation. This happens because, "Long ago God spoke to our ancestors in many and various ways by the prophets, but in these last days He has spoken to us by a Son" (Heb. 1:1-2). The incarnated Logos, as mediator in the creation of the cosmos, expounded in Hebrews 1:2ff., determines from the start the Christian language of God — uttered in a consistent system of speech and signs — as a keynote.

The consciously selected metaphorical space comprising the *language* of words and music encompasses the paradoxical linking of utterability with unutterabilty. In the context of a theology of revelation, this paradox is bound up with the tension of God's revelation in concealment, of God's presence in absence. However, the one incarnation thus allows numerous grammars of revelation in which the reality of God is not only announced in referents derived from the speakers' specific contexts and traditions, but also undergirds them. God's sacramental presence in the Holy Spirit not only provides the necessary referents for differing ecclesiological realizations, it also points to the unutterable, undiscovered, and anonymous presences of God — the concealed character of divine revelation.

This concealed revelation cannot always be communicated in ways that are readily recognizable by the Christian tradition as coming from the Holy Spirit. In the sense of christological "deep grammar," the semantics of God's revelation through God's present absence can be expressed so as not to violate the other's "grammatical" rules. Even so this does not imply the possibility of adequately translating the shape of one language of revelation unchanged into another. The revelatory axiom of Chalcedon's

---

8. See Eberhard Jüngel, *Gott als Geheimnis der Welt. Zur Begründung der Theologie des Gekreuzigten im Streit zwischen Theismus und Atheismus* (Tübingen: Mohr Siebeck, 2001), pp. 478ff.

A Realm of Differences

christologia negativa (negatively phrased christology) prevails here. The divinity and humanity of Jesus exist "without confusion, without change, without division, without separation." Chalcedonian grammar forbids "understanding God's Incarnation in his Son in the sense of an absorption of the transcendent God and it is far truer to say that by attempting to express the inexpressible, the dual-nature dogma of 'negative theology' preserves God's infiniteness and transcendence."[9]

Once again this brings us back to Vatican II. In accordance with the "signs of the times" (*Gaudium et Spes* §4), the undiscovered semantics of God's presence must be newly determined for each different cultural realm. A pragmatic approach toward the particularities of God's revelation today must be developed in the context of *orthopraxy* (correct practice). On the other hand, this is only feasible *in the mode of a presence of the Holy Spirit*, which demands the "discernment of the spirit," thus referring again to the question of the criteria of a theology of revelation. This question is also forcefully addressed by "Pluralistic Theologies of Religions."[10] Here logostheology indicates a path that has been, above all, followed by Jacques Dupuis. The decisive point is "that there is not only neither contradiction nor contrast between the effective presence of God [in the world's religions] and the unique salvific significance of the historical event, Jesus Christ: they are instead interdependent and complementary. In God's plan of salvation both aspects combine and are adjusted to each other."[11]

This points to a trinitarian christology that permits the acts of the Logos, in the sense of a particular event in history, to be understood in their singularity as having a universal meaning, because the divine dynamic of the Logos is "not 'exhausted' or 'reduced' by being expressed through human nature."[12] When in Jesus the divine Word became united with human flesh — both indivisible and distinct, it was necessarily delim-

9. Helmut Hoping, *Einführung in die Christologie* (Darmstadt: Wissenschaftliche Buchgesellschaft, 2004), p. 154.

10. See Perry Schmidt-Leukel, *Gott ohne Grenzen. Eine christliche und pluralistische Theologie der Religionen* (Gütersloh: Gütersloher Verlagshaus, 2005), pp. 43-53. Cf. Reinhold Bernhardt and Perry Schmidt-Leukel, eds., *Kriterien interreligiöser Urteilsbildung*, Beiträge zu einer Theologie der Religionen 1 (Zürich: Theologischer Verlag, 2005).

11. Jacques Dupuis, "Die Universalität des Wortes und die Partikularität Jesu Christi," in Ulrich Winkler, ed., *Ein Testament katholischer Religionstheologie. Jacques Dupuis: Gesammelte Aufsätze aus den letzten Lebensjahren, Salzburger Theologische Zeitschrift* 10 (2006): 89.

12. Dupuis, "Die Universalität des Wortes," p. 94.

209

ited by space and time without being exhausted or reduced. Therefore, an emphasis on the incarnation of the Word in history does not exhaust or restrict God's saving activity in the world. This logic discourages the temptation to an exclusivist, singular theology of religion, but rather challenges the theology of revelation to provide for a pluralism that is inclusive. In this context, the early church's understanding of the close revelatory connection between creation and incarnation can be cited once more. It is rooted in the mediation by the Logos in the creation of the cosmos, thereby opening up the potential for universal communication. At the same time this relates to the pastoral grammar of revelation found in *Gaudium et Spes,* "For by His Incarnation the Son of God has united Himself in some fashion with every person." In this context the Council's reference to Jesus Christ as "the image of the invisible God" (Col. 1:15) acquires a particular significance (*Gaudium et Spes* §22), since the image of the invisible conveys the permanent difference between signifier and signified. It expresses something iconographically unimaginable by acquiescing to a theologically regulated iconoclasm. Following Dupuis's trinitarian logos-christology this means: there is something utterable (Jesus), which expresses itself in the mode of the Unutterable (the Logos as the Second Person of the Trinity).[13] From the point of view of a theology of communication and sign theory applied to revelation, we can draw the following conclusion: "The Christ-event, however inclusively present, does not exhaust the power of the Word of God, who became flesh in Jesus Christ."[14]

Knowledge of God is only possible in the Logos, namely, with regard to a singular event, which — qualified theologically as the incarnation — can be articulated only when its non-derivability and immeasurability are retained. For this reason in particular early Christian apologists employed the Logos in theologizing about revelation as a principle of communication. Thus revelation becomes at the same time a fundamental worldly

13. See Michael Roth, "Trinitätslehre als Rahmentheorie? Überlegungen zur Einheit Gottes in der Vielfalt seines Wirkens," *KuD* 49 (2003): 52-66; Christoph Schwöbel, "Trinitätslehre als Rahmentheorie des christlichen Glaubens. Vier Thesen zur Bedeutung der Trinität in der christlichen Dogmatik," in Christoph Schwöbel, *Gott in Beziehung. Studien zur Dogmatik* (Tübingen: Mohr Siebeck, 2002), pp. 25-51; Michael Hüttenhoff, "Die Trinitätslehre als Rahmentheorie der Religionstheologie? Kritische Überlegungen," in *Wahrheitsansprüche der Weltreligionen. Konturen gegenwärtiger Religionstheologie,* ed. Christian Danz and Friedrich Hermanni (Neukirchen/Vluyn: Neukirchener Verlag, 2006), pp. 67-92.

14. Jacques Dupuis, *Toward a Christian Theology of Religious Pluralism* (Maryknoll, NY: Orbis, 2005), p. 319.

power, and the world becomes the place for finding traces of God's revealed and revealing Logos:

> ... people could be "enlightened" by the Logos, who is the one source of divine light. Here too, however, the worldly and social character of the human being must be kept in mind. Not only could individual persons — Socrates, the Buddha and so on — receive divine truth from the Logos; but human undertakings also — Greek philosophy and wisdom, as well as Asian wisdom — were the channels through which divine light reached to persons.[15]

Two perspectives — decisive for logos-theology — are suggested: (1) in a Christian context we must be prepared for the unknown and indeterminate and, ultimately, even for indeterminable languages of God's revelation. (2) The traditional Christian language of God's revelation for us, localized in Jesus Christ,[16] remains not only somehow unutterable (the *mysterium stricte dictum* of the incarnation of God), but also as unfinished. The Judgment still awaits us. Thus every theology of revelation retains a messianic quality — something awaited.[17] The messianic hope is the coming reality of God. The God who comes judges all of our human languages of God. The language of this divine Judgment is God's last word, God's final revelation, God's own language at the end of time.[18]

God's revelation confronts us with an inexpressible magnitude, with the truth of the Judgment of our life's meaning and our relation to God. What cannot be said because it must first be imparted to us as truth marks a holy difference in every grammar for God's revelation, which is still unfinished. Every language of revelation is located in this realm of the inex-

---

15. Dupuis, *Toward a Christian Theology of Religious Pluralism*, p. 320.

16. Traditional language is meant in Karl Rahner's sense as a fundamental grammar of the encounter of God and humankind, in which the Finite and the Infinite insurmountably confront each other in the realm of formal logic — and in the real, historical world.

17. See Gabriel Fackre, *The Doctrine of Revelation: A Narrative Interpretation*, Edinburgh Studies in Constructive Theology (Grand Rapids: Eerdmans, 1997), pp. 213-24; Christoph Schwöbel, "God: Action and Revelation," vol. 3 of *Studies in Philosophical Theology* (Kampen: Kok Pharos, 1992); Richard Bauckham, "Jesus the Revelation of God," in Paul Avis, ed., *Divine Revelation* (London: Darton, Longman & Todd, 1997), pp. 174-200.

18. This corresponds to the epistemic view of a messianic hope found in the *Coming of God*. See Eberhard Jüngel, *Gott als Geheimnis der Welt. Zur Begründung der Theologie des Gekreuzigten im Streit zwischen Theismus und Atheismus* (Tübingen: Mohr Siebeck, 2001), p. 531.

pressible. These languages refract on the messianic presence of Christ.[19] As Christians we can say this presence has come to us in Jesus Christ and yet will only effectively transform us at the end of time. God's infinite absence in his presence is the realm of God's freedom and God's will. In the words of Dietrich Bonhoeffer, we are forced to believe and to live "before God with and without Him" *(etsi deus non daretur)* — and to understand precisely this as a revelatory moment.[20] This "without God" is a constitutive aspect of the history of divine revelation and typifies the problem of expressing God in some language, at once given and yet not received.

The Christian claim to have received God's authentic self-revelation is tied to the language of God. The Torah formulated this as God's command. At the same time, God's revelation is expressed in the language of creation. It reveals itself in the Torah as the language of God and gives the order of creation its significance. In its ethical prescription,[21] in its irreducible claim to maintain the other person in his or her otherness, not to *destroy* him or her, God reveals Godself in the form of an inexorable "affliction," as a "passing over," i.e., as the transcendent nature of his presence: "The revealed God of our Judeo-Christian spirituality upholds complete infiniteness of his absence, which is in the personal order itself. He only reveals himself in signs, as in Exodus, Chapter 33. To go to him does not mean to follow these, which have no indicative value, but to seek out others who follow his signs."[22]

Several points arise from this foundation, which has been developed as a grammar of theology and precisely shaped by the plurality of religious difference:

- The christological problem of language must be seen against the background of a theology of religions and *as such* become the point of departure for theological reflection;

19. See Franz Mußner, *Traktat über die Juden* (München: Kösel, 1979; rev. ed. Göttingen: Vandenhoeck & Ruprecht, 2009), pp. 124-31. ET: *Tractate on the Jews: The Significance of Judaism for Christian Faith* (Philadelphia: Augsburg Fortress, 1984); Hans Hermann Henrix, *Judentum und Christentum. Gemeinschaft wider Willen* (Regensburg: Pustet, 2004), pp. 134-56.

20. See Dietrich Bonhoeffer "Werke," in Christian Gremmels, Eberhard and Renate Bethge, eds., *Widerstand und Ergebung. Briefe und Aufzeichnungen aus der Haft* (Gütersloh: Kaiser, Gütersloher Verlagshaus, 1998), vol. 8, pp. 533f.

21. See Frank Crüsemann, *Maßstab: Tora. Israels Weisung für christliche Ethik* (Gütersloh: Kaiser, Gütersloher Verlagshaus, 2003).

22. Emmanuel Levinas, "Die Spur des Anderen," in *Die Spur des Anderen. Untersuchungen zur Phänomenologie und Sozialphilosophie* (Freiburg and München: Alber, 1987), pp. 209-35; 235.

- It operates in the realm of the unutterable, which in the mode of negative theology assumes a specific form;
- Thus the related problem of differing languages for the historically communicated experience of God, revealed in the creation, in the covenant, and — for Christians — in God's love for humankind when he became flesh, also defines the theological consideration of the relationship between Judaism and Christianity.

And so we arrive at the theological language problem of how to relate Christian talk of a triune God with Jewish monotheism. In this context we must also deal with the implications for a theology of revelation of Israel's incredulity toward the trinitarian explication of Christian monotheism, which is based on the church's christological convictions. The locus of the historical reality of this monotheism, its theologically reflected breakthrough, its consistent preservation, is ultimately Israel. Thus Israel's historical reproach that its fundamental monotheism has been relinquished by the church gives rise to a difference that is either of soteriological significance or leads to a new history of the soteriological exclusion of either Israel or the church. Or are other alternatives possible?

3. A Realm of Tensive Language

This essay has reflected upon the kinds of conceptual grammar that emerge when different peoples and cultures try to articulate their experiences or thoughts about the Ultimate Mystery. The language that results is unavoidably "tensive," meaning that it embraces paradox, contradiction, and not fully compatible concepts. Our efforts to express the inexpressible force us to define the reality of God in the course of *our* experience of God's historical reality — that is, in the context of its relevance for our salvation.

From the beginning, tensions arose in the early church over the development of christology and its attendant trinitarian elaboration. Theologically, the conflicts in the christological councils are both defining moments for the church and evidence of a process of the development of dogmatic definitions. Ongoing differences between theological schools of thought (seen today in the effort to develop trinitarian theology in accordance with Israel's monotheistic claim and in no sense to turn it *against* Israel)[23] determine the

23. See Erwin Dirscherl and Magnus Striet, *Monotheismus Israels und christlicher Trinitätsglaube* (QD 210; Freiburg: Herder, 2004).

course — as a continuous process — of God's revelation-in-history, a process that unfolds precisely because of an endless series of tensions in history. And this history is, in turn, shaped by the trinitarian concept of God. I am not speaking of a misconceived Hegelianism in which the life of the Trinity is transferred to the course of history, possibly in some teleological sense as an ultimate goal of existence. Instead, I am speaking of a tensive understanding of reality that originates and unfolds amid differences and conflicts. From a Christian point of view, reality cannot be evaluated independently of that trinitarian grammar which is seen as the decisive expression of God's creative love. This tensive character is once again confirmed in the inevitable use of theological speech that also remains conditional.

What is the significance of this approach for the problem currently under discussion? We indicated at the start that the Jewish-Christian dialogue as such, i.e., with a view to the conditions that make it possible, must be called into question with regard to the definition of the relationship between the trinitarian monotheism of Christianity and the exclusive monotheism of Israel. At the same time, it was emphasized that this very difference has a theological value, since it reflects the soteriological question of Israel's and the church's distinctive ways of approaching God. Discussing this difference brings us back to the question of the inevitable and fundamental differences that support our speaking, thinking, and experiencing.

In its turn, trinitarian theology from an Augustinian perspective is able to offer a way of interpreting this difference as a grammar of our reality. Here, too, contrasting Christian trinitarian theologies disclose the limits of language. Ongoing work on refining trinitarian conceptions illustrates the effort needed to develop human linguistic expressions vis-à-vis the ultimate silence. Furthermore, from a Christian perspective the most extreme concretization of the experience of God, the incarnation, must remain linked to its lack of credibility to Jews, without the possibility of eradicating this tension by means of a dialogical relationship. And we must also discuss with Jews the ultimate silence that befalls all of our efforts to circumscribe linguistically our experiences of God, an experience that powerfully links Judaism and Christianity.[24]

This problem of language is constitutive. It covers the impossibility of being able to say everything, and forces us to appreciate that the various trinitarian theological formulae remain problematic as expressions but il-

---

24. See Josef Wohlmuth, *Im Geheimnis einander nahe. Theologische Aufsätze zum Verhältnis von Judentum und Christentum* (Paderborn: Schöningh, 1996), p. 64.

lustrate the inescapable tensions in the realm of theological language. If this appears so even within a Christian point of view, the continuing difference between Israel and the church with respect to their underlying trinitarian-monotheism disagreement needs to be defined in ways that go beyond the soteriological model of exclusion.

The tensive approach has already introduced an eschatological perspective into our theologizing. If christology and trinitarian theology are understood as a grammar for the salvific activity of God both in the divine Logos and in the remaining presence of this Logos in the Spirit, then the nature of this grammar must be defined in its actual withdrawal, in what is missing. In other words, trinitarian theology, which is christologically inspired, must adjust itself to the *messianic* and eschatological dimensions of its differences with its Jewish sister in faith.

In the Fourth Song of the Suffering Servant, Isaiah, by committing his hope to the man of suffering, introduces a criterion equally binding on both Jews and Christians: ". . . yet he bore the sin of many, and made intercession for the transgressors" (Isa. 53:12). Crucial associations are evoked here: "The proxy suffering of God's servant is not only to the advantage of sinners belonging to God's people, Israel, but also to the [other] peoples."[25] Absence of boundaries is the mark of God's love. God's servant is not yet identified in history by Israel, but is instead preserved in the mode of hope.

Christians see that hope realized in the life, death, and resurrection of Jesus Christ.[26] The resulting difference in interpretation between Jews and Christians nevertheless unites memory and future in a drama of eschatological hope shared by Jews and Christians: God is present and awaited. God can be addressed on a human level and yet can never be defined in history in such a way as to permit us to believe that God is at our disposal. From a Christian perspective, God's self-bestowal in Jesus Christ is linked to an experience and to an understanding of the experience of withdrawal. God's self-disclosure continues to reside in the tensive speech of negative theology. We must therefore address the differing ways that Jews and Christians identify themselves in relation to their historical identification of God, i.e., God's presence as a separating and a uniting factor. The dynamics of the

---

25. Thomas Söding, "Für das Volk. Die Sendung Jesu und die Hoffnung Israels," in *Streitfall Christologie. Vergewisserungen nach der Shoah,* ed. Helmut Hoping and Jan-Heiner Tück (QD 214; Freiburg: Herder, 2005), pp. 73-124; 75.

26. Söding, "Für das Volk," p. 75.

hope of what is yet to pass unites; the messianic association, the eschatological claims are held in common. What separates Jews and Christians originates in the Christian experience of God's real and unique incursion into history, in the belief that the breach in time has already occurred.

In specifying this decisive interpretive divergence, we are forced to pose further theological questions. The Christian partner in the discussion might inquire whether, from a Jewish perspective, the Christian experience and interpretation must be rejected outright. In a nutshell: In placing our hope in the messiah, shouldn't we also hope that he can be recognized? That the historical significance of his coming for humanity — and in humanity — will really become apparent to all? What signs support this?

The eschatological associations, above all in the trinitarian speech about God, also link these signs with the hopeful expectation that the self-revelation of God which has been given will also come about fully at the end of time. According to the Christian interpretation of history this hope must also be understood in the context of the Last Judgment. Otherwise the church would already be the kingdom of God.

Trinitarian theology sees itself both as the authentic expression of God's eschatological self-communication in humankind and as understanding God's love as a relationship: God is love. God is a relationship making relationships possible where humankind is by default without love and relationships. Where God facilitates relationships, God opens the way for human beings to life and to his reality as love. In being absorbed into God's love human beings find salvation, thus redeeming them from their harmful egotism.

The essence of the trinitarian explication of God is highlighted in this brief formula. Its significance lies in the fact that the human being who denies himself and others access to love is nonetheless encompassed by God's love. The reality of the all-embracing and thus all-embracingly possible love for humankind originates in the creation. Its normative realization is in the Torah, which understands God's will in relation to humankind as instruction and law. From a Christian point of view this love is experienced in Jesus of Nazareth, the Jewish human being as the irrevocable union of God and humankind. In the sense of divine self-revelation all three moments of the reality of Jesus remain bound together. Thus Jesus confirms the validity of the Torah; as God's "mediator" (1 Tim. 2:5) he guarantees it in his life, in his death, and in his resurrection.

For Paul the Torah is still God's revelation (e.g., Rom. 7:12), even where he binds the fulfillment of the law as righteousness to the messiah, Jesus

(Gal. 2:21). This is not, however, a *theological* statement about the validity and significance of the law. It denotes an *anthropological* reality. The Torah is not in principle impossible to observe; otherwise God would be a malign deity *(deus malignus),* and the Torah a cynical concoction whose demands cannot be fulfilled. Instead it is human beings who have ignored God's law and, where they have taken it into their own hands, have completely misinterpreted it; wherever the law has been transformed to justify some human order, or where it is used to exclude people from the salvific reality of God. Internally, this understanding of the Torah concerns those who fail to comply with every stipulation contained in the 613 laws interpreted in the Torah. Externally, it refers to the heathens living in ignorance of the Torah as divine revelation. On the other hand, Paul insists on the sense of the Torah as a covenant made by God with Abraham (Gal. 3:6-14). The covenant should embrace all humanity, since it embraces life itself: a life that makes us free; a life that gives God's promises space; a life in abundance.

The distorted interpretation of the law by human beings, in Paul's understanding, demands the initiative of God in penetrating a human notion of justice, which is ultimately self-dependent. Ultimately, the inclusion of the whole of humankind in the life-realm of God can only be realized by God, in the humanity of Jesus. And precisely this is a messianic process, manifesting its power in the resurrection of the crucified Christ and dynamized in the *awakening* of Paul. Faith as trust in God grants access to this divine love which has assumed a human form, penetrating humanity's reliance on itself. For this, God creates what appears impossible: love on the cross, life in death beyond death itself.

This love continues to be the meaning of the creation described in the tales of paradise. God's covenant with his people is its manifestation. It remains the goal of the law. Thus a soteriological consequence for Jewish theology results: whoever complies with the law and so fulfills its meaning gives it a salvific sense. He or she lives the love of God, which bestows liberty (Gal. 5:13), and will "inherit the kingdom of God" (Gal. 5:21). It is the "one and only God" (Gal. 3:20): the God of the creation stories, of the history of the covenant and the revelation of the law. For Paul it is the same God who from the beginning imparted the messianic reality of the world in its full dynamic potential, setting it free in the Jewish man, Jesus of Nazareth; "For in him every one of God's promises is a 'Yes'" (2 Cor. 1:20). As God's *Son* (2 Cor. 1:19) he is God's presence for us.

Additional questions regarding the messianic reality of the crucified and risen Christ must now be asked. They must be posed in the Pauline sense, i.e., on the basis of the recognition of the single reality of the one undivided God. Jesus prayed to the Father as his *abba*. Jesus obviously thought of himself as distinct from the Father.[27] However, as the risen Christ, ". . . declared to be the Son of God with power . . ." (Rom. 1:3), he is inseparable from the Father. The approach to the Father, to the *"only"* Holy One (see Mark 10:18), takes place through him (Rom. 16:27).

During the centuries after Paul this approach was invoked to preserve God's indivisibility and to ensure that God's saving self-disclosure in history was not separated from God by thinking of it as something external, as mere communication of an intention, of a thought, an idea. The messianic breakthrough in history was understood from the start as having realized the possibilities inherent in creation and its orientation. The messiah subsequently shares in the reality of God, as a constitutive part of the origin without origin, which is God. Were this not so, then the salvific love in God would not have existed from and, therefore, before, any beginning. It would have been a later addition, a moment of God's own gradual self-realization. From a Christian perspective we could say that the renunciation of a trinitarian explication as a language for the expression of God's creative power of love and life might be offensive to strict monotheism: the moment of messianic salvation would prove to be an additional moment of God's reality. *Thus the meaning of Christian trinitarian theology lies in the consistent preservation of Israel's monotheism, whose value lies in the inclusion of all humankind in God's love.*

4. Consequence: Trinitarian Theology as the Basis of Jewish-Christian Dialogue After the "Mission to the Jews"?

This logic alters the classification of Jewish and Christian monotheism yet again. Both grammars for the reality of God must insist on their right to be considered authentically revelatory. From a Christian point of view Judaism and Christianity are both interdependent — and as expressed in the language of the Council of Chalcedon — *inseparable and distinct,* linked together. God's self-revelation in history desires the salvation of all humanity. This disallows any notion that Israel is to be excluded from salvation for failing to recognize Jesus of Nazareth as the messiah. Were this not

---

27. See Georg Essen, *Die Freiheit Jesu. Der neuchalkedonische Enhypostasiebegriff im Horizont neuzeitlicher Subjekt- und Personenphilosophie* (Regensburg: Pustet, 2001).

so then the history of the covenant with Israel would be annulled; the meaning of the Torah as the bond between God and the people of Israel would be dissolved.

Conversely, when confessing Christ, Christians must be alert to confess only what should be confessed. Confessing Christ includes an eschatological aspect. Fulfillment of the law and the desire to confess Christ as the Son of God are subsumed within that tension already articulated in the formative phase of Christianity as text.[28] The New Testament crystallizes this tensive tradition. The Christ-tradition developed from the outset a highly suspenseful plurality of christological perspectives (the Synoptics as compared with John, e.g.), titles, and thus religious "grammar." As text and with regard to what is written, every confession remains an instance of impure presence, a partial correspondence to the reality of the confessed. The singular revelation-event of messianic time determines our own time. We must seek to be adequate to it by always using the twofold mode of every presence as also something given and withdrawn. Thus, the confession of Christ implies the messianic character of that hope shared by Jews and Christians in its specific difference, and this must not be allowed to divide us, since both Jews and Christians have awaited the final fulfillment of this hope from the very beginning and continue to wait today. This waiting together becomes the mode of a confession that Jews and Christians *share*. Separating-uniting, as Giorgio Agamben in the shadow of Auschwitz formulated his reading of St. Paul in the context of the ancient story of Apelles: the cut is too fine for the exact point of separation to be identified.[29]

Yet, however fine, this incision cannot be passed over in silence; it must be *communicated*. In the context of this ongoing problem, already exacerbated by the burdensome concept of the mission to the Jews, we must consider the possibility of a new understanding of mission in the framework of a reciprocally critical dialogue. I am referring to the joint theological discussions of our concepts of God. These concepts are separate and will remain different. I am also referring to the open dialogue recognizing God's self-revelation bestowed on Israel and her history, based on the presupposition that Israel need not be converted to the one God; in the belief that Israel's way to salvation, to which the irrevocable covenant of the Old

---

28. See Florian Bruckmann, *Die Schrift als Zeuge analoger Gottrede. Studien zu Lyotard, Derrida und Augustinus* (Freiburg: Herder, 2008).

29. See Giorgio Agamben, *Il tempo che resta. Un commento alla "Lettera ai romani"* (Turin: Bollati Boringhieri, 2000); ET: *The Time That Remains: A Commentary on the Letter to the Romans* (Stanford: Stanford University Press, 2005).

Testament bears witness, will remain unhindered for all time because of God's unalterable faithfulness. This implies a joint Jewish-Christian mission in the sense of an ongoing theological identification of a difference that we must name and verbalize together. The aim of this dialogue is to articulate this difference as the binding confession of a separation in a shared faith in the God of Israel.

A Jewish Response to Elizabeth Groppe,
Philip A. Cunningham and Didier Pollefeyt,
and Gregor Maria Hoff

Adam Gregerman

Over the last half a century, Catholics have made a stunning break with centuries of anti-Judaism. For a religion that values continuity and faithfulness to past traditions, this has required profound reassessment of fundamental theological beliefs. In seeking to challenge hostile attitudes toward Jews and members of other religions, scholars painstakingly and sometimes painfully have had to reconsider traditional topics such as God, christology, and covenant, to name only a few.

The authors of these three chapters tackle one of the most complex of these topics, trinitarianism. They do so with a full acceptance of the remarkable new spirit in the relationship between Jews and Catholics, as they consider how to affirm an ongoing Jewish covenant with God alongside the claim that Christ is savior of all humanity. Like other authors in this book, they reject the view, held for nearly all of Christian history, that the Jewish covenant with God had been abrogated. As summarized by Cunningham and Pollefeyt, in the past "Christians presumed that Jews were cursed by God, their covenant with God either terminated or withered" (p. 187). These authors ground their break with this tradition in paradigm-shifting church statements. Beginning with *Nostra Aetate* and continuing with later documents, the Catholic Church radically revised its teachings about Jews. These provide a powerful impetus to the important and welcome theological work found here, as these authors venture beyond these church statements to explore daring new ground.

I review their essays with a sense of gratitude and appreciation, highlighting what I find most significant or important. Where I offer critical observations, I do so in a spirit of humility, recognizing my status as an outsider not only to the complexities of academic trinitarian thought, but to the Catholic tradition in general. I also raise some questions about the persuasiveness of their essays. I do this a bit uncomfortably, for as a Jew I of course strongly support their work, but hope that my comments might perhaps indicate ways that their arguments can be strengthened.

The authors' most creative and bold arguments are intended to affirm a trinitarianism that does not deny the Jewish covenant with God. Though there are some similarities in all their approaches, I want to begin with the essay by Cunningham and Pollefeyt. They offer a significant reevaluation of Jewish religious life grounded in two aspects of trinitarian thought. First, they consider God as creator and sustainer of all things, who invites Israel into a covenantal relationship and empowers Israel to perceive and accept this invitation. Therefore, God is the originator of the covenant that was made with the Jews. Cunningham and Pollefeyt use phrases that highlight the futurity and potentiality of this original act. God's call was "*an invitation to enter into* a permanent relationship" and "*an empowerment to become* a unique people*" (p. 196; italics added). This is faithful to the biblical message, which presents God's reaching out to the patriarchs and then the people of Israel at Sinai as momentous events of relationship-formation. These past events point forward in time to covenantal life with God. However, this is the less pathbreaking aspect of their model; even supersessionist Christians (unlike, say, Marcionites) historically affirmed God's past call to the Jews. Rather, what these earlier Christians denied was that the original relationship endured in the present and extended into the future. They argued that it had been abrogated, perhaps moments after Sinai following the sin of the Golden Calf or at the coming of Christ.

Therefore, it is the second trinitarian aspect that I see as more important and pathbreaking: the ongoing activity of "the Logos and the Spirit" in Israel's religious life. This has been taking place "since its [i.e., the covenant between God and Israel] inception" (p. 196) and, especially, "even after the time of Christ" (p. 197). This reflects a belief in the perpetual activity of the Trinity, namely, "God's constant outreach for relationship." It keeps alive the original, past experience of relationship-formation with the Holy One.

It is this present quality that represents a break with supersessionist theology and the belief that Jews were cast off once Jesus arrived. Not only in the past, but after the coming of Jesus, in the present, and into the future, Jews continue and will continue to experience "life-in-covenant." The authors here make a key temporal claim in their trinitarian theology: the call of God to the Jewish people was not limited to the past and did not end with the incarnation. Rather, Jews "continue to experience the indwelling of

God within their community and people." This rejection of a time-limited or past-only covenant distinguishes their approach from near-ubiquitous earlier (pre–Vatican II/pre-Shoah) approaches. This is a vital distinction and an important contribution to a revised trinitarianism.

Related to this are the authors' efforts to minimize any threat to this ongoing Jewish covenant because of the Jewish "no" to Christ. Contrary to many centuries of teaching, they claim that the Jews' refusal to accept Christian claims made about Jesus does not imperil the promises of the triune God to them. In my understanding, the authors, unlike earlier Catholics, minimize what Jews and Catholics disagree about (the incarnation of the Logos) and emphasize what Jews and Catholic agree about (the ongoing Jewish covenant). The latter is noteworthy because it reflects a welcome openness to that which was and is absolutely fundamental to Jewish religious identity.

Furthermore, the status of the covenant is also the topic that historically divided Jews and Catholics more than any other. These theological proposals come after a long history during which Christians refused any such affirmation of a "robust" Jewish religious life, typically because of the Jewish refusal to believe in Jesus. That is, the Jewish "no" ended the ongoing covenant. I therefore believe that the authors address a most painful divide: the need to see "the ongoing Jewish tradition on its own terms" (p. 186), a tradition that places the covenantal relationship with God at its center. I might suggest that this affirmation offers a helpful nuance to the church's demand that Catholics "learn by what essential traits the Jews define themselves."[1] Without minimizing the importance of Catholics learning about trait*s* (in the plural) of Judaism — and Jews learning about Catholic traits as well — I think it is fair to say that the covenant between God and Israel is the preeminent trait I would hope Catholics would recognize. The authors' trinitarianism is therefore a reversal of great significance, not even to be derailed by Jewish lack of belief in Christ.

On the other hand, none of the authors, despite some differences, deny that the incarnate Christ, whether recognized or not, is active even in this ongoing relationship between God and the Jews. Cunningham and Pollefeyt write that, in their experience of life in the covenant, "the People of Israel have been interacting covenantally with the Triune One" (p. 197). Jews just do not know it or experience it in a Christian trinitarian fashion.

---

1. Pontifical Commission for Religious Relations with the Jews, "Guidelines and Suggestions for Implementing the Conciliar Declaration *Nostra Aetate,* No. 4" (1974), preamble.

Likewise, Groppe, while insisting that Israel's bond with God is unique, holds that Christ is "infinitely related to every last creature" (p. 212; quoting LaCugna). Hoff's view is expressed in the more tentative language of paradox: the distinctly Christian utterable (i.e., Jesus) is also expressed in the non-Christian unutterable (i.e., "differing ecclesiological realizations" and even different religions). He too does not, however, actually sever the connection between the distinctly Christian and the non-Christian: "For by His Incarnation the Son of God has united Himself in some fashion with every person."[2] Rather, he defers the full revelation of the mystery of the unutterable to the end of days.

To summarize their varied discussions, for these Catholics it is impossible to conceive of divine activity — even God's covenanting with Jews — separate from the triune God, and specifically separate from the Logos incarnated in Jesus. This is a traditional affirmation, and one made repeatedly by the authors and in recent Catholic statements. It is, they write, in the nature of God to exist in three subsistents, and at all stages of this relationship with the Jews, as at all stages of human life generally. According to this model, Jews remain actors in a Catholic theological drama (Hoff borrows Rahner's term "anonymous Christians"). That is, their religious life, while presented positively and partly in terms a Jew would recognize, is ultimately seen in trinitarian terms.

To a Jew, it is at once scandalous and also — I recognize — unavoidable for Catholic authors such as Cunningham and Pollefeyt to say that "rabbinic Judaism and Jewish religious life up to today must therefore be seen as expressions of the divine Logos and Spirit" even if "Christ incarnates the divine Logos" (p. 197). The overall theological shifts the authors propose are enormous, but, in this regard, limited. They do not offer, and maybe cannot offer, an alternative way of conceiving of divine activity apart from trinitarian theology, even at the end of days, even among those who reject a Catholic understanding of it. While the historical areas of clash are minimized, and both Jews and Catholics have central aspects of their religious identities affirmed, the authors do not deny that Christ is somehow active in Jewish covenantal life. They naturally perceive religious reality in *their* "own terms." But those terms are not the terms that Jews use, though it should be observed that Jews also inevitably must seek to understand Christians through Jewish categories.

By ending the dispute over the legitimacy of the Jewish covenant, the

---

2. Second Vatican Council, *Gaudium et Spes* (1965), §22.

authors therefore go far, but only so far. They eliminate the most historically divisive issue for Jews, but still present the Jewish covenantal relationship in terms that remain at the core unrecognizable to Jews, for whom
there is no role for the Logos (as they understand it) in the covenant made
with the patriarchs or at Sinai.

Still, from my perspective, this is a signal improvement. There is a
huge difference between a refusal to grant legitimacy to Judaism (i.e., the
historical supersessionist position) and a refusal to understand Jewish
covenantal life as Jews do (i.e., apart from the Logos or Christ). The belief
that Jewish covenantal life is in "unity with the glorified humanity of the
Jew Jesus" (as Cunningham and Pollefeyt write; p. 198), while undoubtedly
not at all the way that Jews understand their covenant, is much less problematic than denying validity to Jewish covenantal life at all. In comparison to earlier supersessionist denunciations of Judaism, the terms of the
dispute have shifted massively. The shift, however, is still only partial.

From a historical perspective, then, there is much that is auspicious
about this endeavor. While Jews are not entirely "right" in their theological
understanding, the novel claim that the Jewish "no" does not imperil the
Jewish covenant with God undermines any motive to coerce Jews to
change their minds. Though the authors do not make this point, this theological model can also blunt traditional Catholic anger over Jewish stubbornness. The immensely distressing outbursts of rage that have disfigured
Catholic-Jewish relations and led to hostile acts are potentially stripped of
their motive-force. More broadly, there is no sense that the emergence of
two separate religious traditions in the first few centuries c.e. requires that
one yield to the other or disappear entirely. All these authors agree, in their
own ways, that present circumstances are religiously acceptable and do not
require human intervention to remedy a wrong, or even nonviolent polemics against the ignorant or stubborn other.

On this issue, all the authors agree. Cunningham and Pollefeyt see divine intentionality in this outcome: "The existence of two distinct communities in covenant with God is not the result of some sort of mistake.
Rather, it was God's will" (p. 200). In similar language, Groppe writes,
"God's personal providence allowed for the emergence of two distinct religious communities: Jewish and Christian" (p. 181). In the most formal language, Hoff notes that Jesus' incarnation was necessarily delimited "by
space and time" (p. 210) without denying any saving activity elsewhere in
the world. He therefore rejects an "exclusivist, singular theology of religion" that would render the Jewish covenant invalid or unrelated to God,

or to Christ. The implications of this belief in divine intentionality are therefore profound, for diversity is not just tolerated but affirmed. Again, however, this acceptance of religious diversity does not mean that such diversity is understood apart from trinitarian theology. Quoting Jacques Dupuis, Hoff insists that these different, non-Catholic traditions — including Judaism — remain "interdependent and complementary" (p. 209) because they all reflect the intentions of the triune God.

I do want to raise a concern about an argument that builds on the presence of these two distinct religions in the world today. The authors, especially because of their personal experiences (see below), see the existence of Judaism positively. Though the authors do not make the argument so simplistically, all are deeply impressed by, among other things, the continued presence of Jews. This idea is already found in the Vatican statements quoted by Groppe that "[t]he permanence of Israel . . . is a historic fact and a sign to be interpreted within God's design."[3] Though it does lead to a favorable view of Judaism in the case of the Vatican statement, such permanence need not necessarily do so.

That is, it is not necessary that this "is" (i.e., Jews' continuing to live as Jews) proves this "ought" (i.e., Jewish covenantal life is good and ought to continue). In fact, historically most Christians saw the continued existence of Jews very differently. Some were troubled or puzzled by it; Augustine famously believed Jews were preserved by God in order to endure divine punishment for disobedience. While these are not the only options, Jewish existence as such might just as easily contribute to a weakened supersessionist theology. We know this historically, and it is possible logically as well.

I therefore am wary of attempts to derive too much theologically from Jewish existence itself. The lessons it can offer are diverse and not all positive, especially when judged by worldly standards: there are comparatively few Jews at all; they have often faced exile and subjugation, etc. I much prefer the authors' emphases on what it is they learned in dialogue and friendship with Jews, rather than emphases on the presence of Jews itself. Ideally, the former might avoid the potential pitfalls of drawing theological conclusions from present reality.

As already noted, the authors' insistence on the validity of the Jewish covenant is repeatedly grounded in the personal and the relational. Their

3. Pontifical Commission for Religious Relations with the Jews, "Notes on the Correct Way to Present Jews and Judaism in Preaching and Teaching in the Roman Catholic Church" (1985), §25.

essays evince a profound respect for Jews and Jewish religious life that emerges not only out of theological reflection. By noting this, I do not want to minimize the significance of their analyses of trinitarianism and Judaism. However, they all highlight the significant influence contact with Jews and knowledge of contemporary Jewish life has on their theological views. They show that context influences us, and should influence us, deeply, especially when thinking theologically. Even on a topic as seemingly abstruse as trinitarianism, they demonstrate the relevance of lived experience, and it is important to recognize that this is at work here as well.

Cunningham and Pollefeyt, for example, admit that their "insight is possible because of the depth of dialogue and relationship that has provided opportunities for us to resonate with [Jews'] distinctive experiences of covenant with God" (p. 193). That is why "interreligious dialogue is an important touchstone for every theological enterprise" (p. 194). Likewise, Groppe's resistance to "dominant theologies" that deny validity to Jewish religious life is grounded in her own "direct personal encounter with Jews who have a deep spiritual life and practice." She mentions the example of her late teacher, Rabbi Michael Signer, and observes that "[t]he world would be spiritually poorer, not richer, were all Jews to stop hallowing the Sabbath, to cease grappling with the meaning of Torah" (p. 180). This affirmation of the positive spiritual significance of another religious tradition is a relative novum in world history, far beyond toleration. Such a view seems possible only in a diverse society that encourages contact with different others. It is also an essential feature of these reassessments of trinitarian theology.

Hoff expresses a similar idea. Again, in more formal language, he welcomes "joint theological discussions" and "open dialogue" between Jews and Catholics, to the same end: recognition of their differences along with affirmation of a "shared faith in the God of Israel" (p. 219). Helpfully, he identifies a tension that is present in all these essays, between doing theology from an "inner-logic of the church's revelation" and from "the exterior perspective of the world as it really is" (p. 204). In his case, he praises the second over the first. That is, he praises perspectives that reflect an awareness of the positive value of religious diversity (i.e., "the world as it is") rather than earlier Catholic theologies that *a priori* began by denying value to anything outside the church (i.e., outside its "inner-logic"). Like the two earlier writers, he believes that awareness of and personal exposure to the other require new ways of theological thinking.

It is nearly impossible to overstate the depth of the disjunction between centuries of Catholic anti-Jewish theology and these contemporary theologies. Few traditions have undergone such radical changes. For these changes to stick, they need to put forth deep roots. However, absent exposure not just to religious diversity generally but Jewish communities specifically, I wonder how deep-rooted such changes can be. To use Hoff's terminology, how lasting will a break with an "inner-logic" supported by centuries of both history and theology be? Catholicism's greatest growth is not in places where most Jews live, such as North America and, to a lesser extent, Europe, but in places where Jews are almost entirely absent, such as Africa and Asia. Memories of the Holocaust are inevitably fading in the West, and the sense of responsibility to alter religious teachings in its wake is fading as well. Perhaps more seriously, many perceive a growing conservatism in Catholic theology that, if not hostile to Vatican II, is at least somewhat skeptical about all its conclusions, including those regarding other religions. While the Catholic Church will, I believe, continue to support these welcome changes, the importance of personal contact with Jews leads me to question if changes in demography and conservative theological trends, and fewer opportunities for personal contact, may encourage backsliding on these issues.[4]

There is much that is complex and even elusive about trinitarian thought, not just for Jews but for Catholics (Groppe playfully describes this on p. 164). The authors frequently employ terms like "mystery," "limited understanding," "indeterminate," and "absence" when offering innovative trinitarian models that break dramatically with historic supersessionism. While these terms may indicate that which is inherently unknown, perhaps to be revealed at the end of days, they also hint at the unprecedented, maybe inexplicable changes taking place in Catholic theology. In millennia of Christian thought there has seldom been as radical a shift as that taking place in the last few decades; some lingering mystery seems appropriate. Even Paul, at the end of his tortured defense of the Jewish covenant with God in Romans 9–11, exclaimed, "How unsearchable are [God's] judgments and how inscrutable [God's] ways!" (11:33). These authors of course come much farther than Paul. However, his profound refusal to give up on the Jewish people offers a rare and heartening precedent for these important essays.

---

4. On these trends in general, see John L. Allen, Jr., *The Future Church: How Ten Trends Are Revolutionizing the Catholic Church* (New York: Doubleday, 2009).

"The Old Unrevoked Covenant" and "Salvation for All Nations in Christ" — Catholic Doctrines in Contradiction?

Christian Rutishauser, S.J.

1. Guidelines and Tasks Given by the Second Vatican Council

1.1. Reshaped Theology of Israel and of Salvation

The Second Vatican Council has dramatically changed the relationship of the church to the Jewish people. It laid the foundations for a new positive approach when it stated: "As the sacred synod searches into the mystery of the Church, it remembers the bond that spiritually ties the people of the New Covenant to Abraham's stock. . . . In company with the Prophets and the same Apostle [Paul], the church awaits that day, known to God alone, on which all peoples will address the Lord in a single voice and 'serve him shoulder to shoulder'" (Zeph. 3:9; *Nostra Aetate*, §4). Pope John Paul II internalized these guidelines, and took important steps for further developing the new relationship between the church and the Jewish people, particularly with his articulation of the "unrevoked Covenant."[1] The so-called Old Covenant God made with Israel at Mount Sinai retains its validity and effectiveness and the Jews' nonacceptance of Jesus as the messiah can — in the light of Romans 11:11-15 — even be regarded as positive since it enabled the forming of a New Covenant through Christ with people from other

---

1. Expressed in an address to Jewish leaders (Mainz, Germany, November 17, 1980). For further scholarly discussion, see Norbert Lohfink, *Der niemals gekündigte Bund: Exegetische Gedanken zum christlich-jüdischen Gespräch* (Freiburg/Basel/Wien: Herder, 1989); Hubert Frankemölle, *Der ungekündigte Bund? Antworten des Neuen Testaments* (Freiburg/Basel/ Wien: Herder, 1998); John T. Pawlikowski and Hayim Goren Perelmuter, eds., *Reinterpreting Revelation and Tradition: Jews and Christians in Conversation*, (Franklin, WI: Sheed & Ward, 2000).

nations.[2] This positive evaluation of Judaism by postconciliar Catholic theology signifies that Judaism up to the present day represents a legitimate continuation of the biblical tradition. When Judaism and the church face each other it means that faith meets faith, not heresy or false belief. Since the Council, a variety of Christian concepts and theologies of Israel have developed and many detailed aspects have been discussed, e.g., the understanding of the concept of the Promised Land, the relationship between New and Old Testaments, messianism, trinitarian monotheism, etc.

In addition to this new attitude toward Judaism, the Council has liberated Jesus' saving work from too restrictive an interpretation.[3] If the Roman Catholic Church had throughout her history repeated the well-known axiom *Extra ecclesiam nulla salus* ("Outside the church there is no salvation") by claiming the exclusivity of salvation, then the Second Vatican Council reinterpreted this claim in a threefold way:

First, it acknowledged that other religions and cultures "often reflect a ray of that Truth which enlightens all men" (*Nostra Aetate*, §2; see also *Gaudium et Spes*, §22; *Lumen Gentium*, §15; *Unitatis Redintegratio*, §13). By acknowledging that objective truth can reside in other worldviews and collective systems and by recognizing that the Holy Spirit and the grace of Christ are active in other religions too, Catholic theology has accepted an inclusivist understanding of her own truth. This has since been expressed in various theologies, liturgical texts, and the *Catechism of the Catholic Church*.[4] Thus, in addition to mission, it became possible for dialogue to

2. Hans Hermann Henrix, "Der kirchliche Christusglaube und die nicht vergebliche jüdische Messiashoffnung," in Hans Hermann Henrix, *Gottes Ja zu Israel: Ökumenische Studien christlicher Theologie* (Aachen/Berlin: Einhard, 2005), pp. 141-57.

3. See Karl Rahner, "Anonymes Christentum und der Missionsauftrag der Kirche," in Karl Rahner, *Schriften zur Theologie*, vol. 9 (Einsiedeln/Zürich/Köln: Benziger, 1970), pp. 498-515. For a historical overview about understanding salvation in tradition and the new formulation offered by the Council, see Franz Cserháti, *Eingliederung in die Kirche um des Heils willen: Eine Studie über die Vereinbarkeit der zwei katholischen Lehren: Heilsnotwendigkeit der Kirche und Heilsmöglichkeit ausserhalb ihr, mit besonderer Berücksichtigung der dogmatischen Konstitution Lumen Gentium des II. Vatikanums und des Axioms: Ausserhalb der Kirche kein Heil* (Frankfurt/Bern/New York: Peter Lang, 1984); Francis A. Sullivan, *Salvation Outside the Church? Tracing the History of the Catholic Response* (New York: Paulist Press, 1992); Molly Truman Marshall, *No Salvation Outside the Church? A Critical Inquiry* (Lewiston, NY: Edwin Mellen Press, 1993).

4. *Catechism of the Catholic Church* (Washington, DC: United States Catholic Conference, 1994), §§839-856. On the relevant recent controversy concerning the Good Friday intercession of Pope Benedict XVI for the Tridentine Rite, see Thomas Fornet-Ponse, "Die

be a paradigm of ecclesiastical "foreign policy."[5] However, the 2000 statement *Dominus Iesus* rejected a pluralistic theory of religion, according to which all religions represent more or less the same road to salvation, and also clearly emphasized the primacy of the Roman Catholic Church in relation to other Christian churches.[6]

Second, the Council differentiated the question of objective truth from the question of the individual's salvation even if he or she does not belong to a Christian church. Salvation also involves a person's ethical life and whether or not he or she ever had a real opportunity to get to know Jesus or the church and to decide for or against Christianity.[7]

Third, in addition, the position of the church was wisely reshaped even for formally baptized Christians who belong to the community of the church. It is not first and foremost the relationship to the church but to Christ that sets the decisive criteria of salvation, as is seen in the biblical tradition (John 14:6; 1 Tim. 2:3-6).

1.2. Emerging Tensions out of the Renewal

Both theological renewals, the one concerning the relationship to Judaism and the one referring to a refined concept of salvation, have been favorably received by the overwhelming majority of Catholics, and theologians have further developed and detailed these reforms. They form an irrevocable heritage for the future church, questioned only by small traditionalist circles. However, the Council's inclusivist approach to salvation, aiming at ultimately bringing all the nonbaptized to baptism, is in tension with the statement that Jews are already in an unrevoked covenant with God. Jews

---

'neue Karfreitagsfürbitte' für die Juden: Nüchterner Realismus oder enttäuschter Optimismus?" *Freiburger Rundbrief: Neue Folge* 16, no. 2 (2009): 93-104. For salvation inclusivism in the Good Friday liturgy in general, see Albrecht Gerhards, "Die Fürbitte für die Juden, in ihrem liturgischen Kontext," in Walter Homolka and Erich Zenger, eds., *"Damit sie Jesus Christus Erkennen": Die Neue Karfreitagsfürbitte für die Juden* (Freiburg/Basel/Wien: Herder, 2008), pp. 115-25.

5. Cf. Pontifical Council for Interreligious Dialogue, *Dialogue and Proclamation* (1991), p. 19. Available at http://www.ccjr.us/dialogika-resources/documents-and-statements/roman-catholic/vatican-curia/290-pcid-1991.

6. Unfortunately, this declaration of the Congregation for the Doctrine of the Faith does not take into consideration the special status of Judaism in relation to Christianity.

7. Karl Rahner, "Anonymes Christentum und der Missionsauftrag der Kirche," in Karl Rahner, *Schriften zur Theologie*, vol. 9 (Einsiedeln/Zürich/Köln: Benziger, 1970), pp. 498-515.

stand in a covenantal community with the God of Jesus Christ, even when they neither recognize Jesus nor belong to the church, a rather particular status presented by the Council. Is it to be understood that the universal claim of Jesus as Savior concerns all people except the Jews? Or does it nevertheless concern the Jews as well, since, for example, Jesus is the King of the Jews, as mentioned in the Gospel passion narratives (Matt. 27:29, 37; Mark 15:2, 9, 12, 26; Luke 23:3, 37f.; John 19:14, 19, 21)? What are the repercussions of the statement that Jesus is the messiah of the Jews? And how are we to regard the biblical verses describing Jesus as having fulfilled the covenant and as the aim of the law (Matt. 5:17; Rom. 10:4)?

It must be admitted that since the Council the definition of the relationship of the Old and the New Covenants is under discussion. Two-covenant theories stand side by side with concepts of one covenant constituted by a twofold people of God. The question has also been discussed as to whether there are one or two people of God, consisting of Jews and Christians.[8] With the question of salvation, whose understanding is itself evolving, these discussions about covenant(s) have reintensified. Has Judaism really established its own way of salvation? If so, then should not any organized Christian mission to promote baptism among Jews be given up? Has the Jewish messiah really come for the Gentiles only and not for the Jews? If that is the case, then what is one to make of the fact that Jesus of Nazareth lived as a true Torah-loving Jew, gathering his people under the covenant of Mount Sinai and reforming them from within? These questions have generated a number of controversial discussions because they require a fundamentally new conception of christology.

For many Jews, however, even asking such questions is an affront, for the historical memories of forced baptisms for Jewish salvation or of terrible persecutions are still present. Particularly the Christian sign of salvation, the cross, was often misused during Holy Week, bringing disaster to the Jews.[9]

---

8. John T. Pawlikowski, "Judentum und Christentum," in *Theologische Realenzyklopädie*, vol. 17 (Berlin/New York: De Gruyter, 1988), pp. 391-403; Johannes Oesterreicher, "Unter dem Bogen des Einen Bundes: Das Volk Gottes: seine Zweigestalt und Einheit," in Josef Pfammatter and Franz Furger, eds., *Judentum und Kirche: Volk Gottes* (Einsiedeln/Zürich/Köln: Benziger, 1974), pp. 27-69.

9. The explosive reawakening of old fears for a revived "mission to the Jews" caused by Pope Benedict's 2008 Good Friday intercession for the Tridentine Rite is considered by Hans Hermann Henrix as coming from a vital, existential layer of Judaism shaped more by the heavy burden of the past history between the church and the Jewish people than by any dogmatic claim. See Hans Hermann Henrix, "Bewahrung jüdischer Treue zum Bund und Liebe

We have to remember this tragic history and take its effects into consideration, even when we in this article are focusing on theological matters.[10] In any case, these systematical and theological questions have to be asked; otherwise the Jewish-Christian dialogue would lack truth and seriousness.

The following reflections are not about the salvation of individuals. This discussion is to be read in the context of grace and ethics. Our thoughts concern the salvific quality of the Jewish way after Christ's resurrection, its relationship to the Christian way, and the Christian claim of universal salvation through Christ. We start in part 2 with the elaboration of the difference in salvation history between God's people and other peoples, as well as its modification because of Jesus. Then in part 3 arguments against the classical form of a mission to Jews will be advanced even while simultaneously holding on to the claim of universal salvation through Jesus Christ. Part 4 will show that this claim in respect to Judaism also has to be redifferentiated with consequences for ecclesiological thinking, so that in part 5 it can be finally shown to what extent Jews and Christians together and individually are called to a relationship of dialogue and collaboration to bring the glory of God to the world.

2. Changes to the Unfolding of Salvation History Because of the Christ Event

2.1. Understanding the Universal Meaning of God's Covenant with the People of Israel

When Catholic theology speaks of "the unrevoked old Covenant," it accepts the intrinsic value of the Hebrew Bible and its continuation in the Jewish oral tradition. It also accepts God's special redeeming power and

---

zum göttlichen Namen: Zum kirchlichen 'Hauptgebet' und zur Karfreitagsfürbitte 2008," in Homolka and Zenger, eds., "Damit sie Jesus Christus Erkennen," pp. 141f.

10. The controversy following the publication of "No to Mission to the Jews — Yes to Jewish-Christian Dialogue" by the Jewish-Christian working group of the Central Committee of Catholics in Germany in April 2009 showed anew that those opposed to a mission to the Jews mostly present historical arguments, whereas the emphasis on universal salvation through Christ is supported with systematic and theological reflections. Once more, the pondering of historical and systematic arguments remains crucial for finding solutions for concrete acts. Exemplary are the articles in the *Frankfurter Allgemeine Zeitung* by the philosopher Robert Spaemann ("God Is No Bigamist," April 20, 2009) and the historian Michael Brenner ("God Is No Christian," April 28, 2009).

the human response to it present in the Jewish faith. Judaism is a grateful response to God's call and represents more than a "natural religion" born out of the human striving for transcendence. It is different from God's grace working in all cultures where human beings strive for truth, freedom, and justice. In the biblical narrative, God's special call to the Jewish people goes back to Abraham, but Judaism exists thanks to the divine liberation and safekeeping of the Exodus, delivering the Hebrews from slavery and leading them across the desert into the Promised Land. In this way the Jews have become God's special children, so that John Paul II could state: "You are our dearly beloved brothers and, in a certain way, it could be said that you are our elder brothers," elder brothers and sisters in faith.[11] They are the chosen property of the Lord and a sacred kingdom of priests (Exod. 19:5f.). The *halakhah* (the Jewish interpretive traditions of God's commands) is not a purely human ethic, but a road to salvation opened by God, although this particular salvation is subject — as is any other salvation by God — to being experienced in a fragmentary fashion. It is given in earthen vessels, which is also true of the new way Jesus opened.

An authentic "salvation history" way of thinking only becomes possible by accepting the covenantal structure from Mount Sinai because it marks the birth of the Jewish people. In this sense, the Sinai covenant is more fundamental for the Jewish-Christian dialogue than the covenant with Abraham, which is more relevant for the individual's belief.[12] The history of salvation is based on the fundamental difference between the chosen and specially separated people — as defined by the covenant (Lev. 20:24ff.; Deut. 7:6f.; 10:15; 1 Kings 3:8; 8:53; Ezra 6:21; Neh. 10:29) on the one hand and all the other people of the world, the so-called Gentiles, on the other hand. This differentiation, so essential for Jewish self-understanding, must be taken into account when dealing with a salvation-history way of thinking, but without lapsing into the judgment that God could not be active outside the covenantal community.

11. Address at the Great Synagogue of Rome, April 13, 1986: http://www.ccjr.us/dialogika-resources/documents-and-statements/roman-catholic/pope-john-paul-ii/305-jp2-86apr13.

12. The relation of the covenant of Sinai and that of Golgotha to the covenant with Abraham is discussed by Cardinal Ratzinger, "Das Erbe Abrahams," in Joseph Ratzinger, *Weggemeinschaft des Glaubens: Kirche als Communio* (Augsburg: Sankt Ulrich, 2002), pp. 235-38; Joseph Ratzinger, *Die Vielfalt der Religionen und der Eine Bund*, 4th ed. (Bad Tölz: Urfeld, 2005). See also Karl-Heinz Menke, "Zur Theologie des Judentums bei Joseph Ratzinger," *Communio* 38, nos. 3/4 (2009): 191-205.

It also is of capital importance to our quest. This separation of God's people, motivated by God's free will and pure love, is never to be considered preferential treatment. It is only intended to serve the salvation of the world. God creates the distinction between Israel and the Gentiles so that the Chosen will become a light to the Gentiles (Isa. 49:6), a covenant of the people (Isa. 49:8), and messenger for the nations (Jer. 1:10). This vocation, the fact of being chosen, and the resulting consequences affect the Israelites as a people and individual prophets as well. Paul considered himself in this tradition as Apostle to the Gentiles (Gal. 2:7). He assumed that the "chosenness" of the Jews was a permanent reality, and so in Romans 9–11 had to offer explanations of why he was finding many Jews reluctant to embrace Christ.

The Torah is the content of the "unrevoked covenant" that also sets a universal claim.[13] The universal aspect of Judaism up to today, however, does not include a missionary impulse. The Noahide commandments determine the righteousness of other people, not whether or not they become Jewish. Jewish tradition adds that in order to be righteous, Gentiles must observe certain ethical principles, have a legal structure in their societies, and respect the Jewish special covenantal relationship with God. The universal dimension of Judaism undergirds the logic of the ethical monotheism of the Bible, even if it can take different forms among different peoples. Christians have to take this universality of Judaism seriously, being especially challenged in their understanding of God's unique relationship with Israel, but in other ways as well, as in the ethical treatment of animals, for example.

2.2. The Doubling of the Covenantal Structure
Through the Christ Event

Jesus of Nazareth lived as a Jew within the defined reality of the covenant God established with the Israelites. Similar to his contemporaries, the Pharisees, he sought to bring the Torah more and more into all spheres of daily life. Thus he actually lived within the mission of the Torah, he taught

13. See the Jewish reflections in *Reflections on Covenant and Mission*, the 2002 dialogue statement published by the National Council of Synagogues and the Bishops' Committee for Ecumenical and Interreligious Affairs: http://www.ccjr.us/dialogika-resources/documents-and-statements/interreligious/517-ncs-bceia02aug12.

it profoundly, and he lived according to it even under the extreme condition of suffering on the cross. He personified the arrival of the kingdom of God and the completion of the road to salvation God had opened to his people. He embodied the Torah and he personified it himself: "the Torah became a person."[14] After he was resurrected from death, his followers definitively recognized him as the long-awaited messiah, even if his life, death, and resurrection were not entirely what they had expected.

The decisive event for the birth of Christianity consists in the modification of the basic difference between the people of God and the Gentiles that had shaped salvation history to that point. It happened not only as a result of the activity of Jesus, but because Jesus was also acted upon by God: realizing and embodying the goal of Jewish life, Jesus passed over out of the inner realm of Judaism into the hands of the Gentiles, as represented by the Romans. He was torn out of the core of Israel's covenant and handed over *(paradidonai)* to the Romans, by whom he was shamefully tormented and executed. Nevertheless, God placed him as a cornerstone for the covenant among the people (Mark 12:10; Matt. 21:42; Acts 4:11; Eph. 2:20; 1 Pet. 2:6ff.). Jesus' life consisted of crossing over the difference between the covenanted people and the nations. The word *paradidonai,* used fifty-nine times in the passion stories, expresses this transition and should be read from the point of view of salvation history. The standard translation, "betray," is tendentious.[15] In the "handing over" of Christ, Israel's God of the covenant intervenes for the salvation of all humanity, just as God had done for his chosen people in the Exodus. Here Judas is to be regarded as a person who hands over Israel's messiah to the priestly leaders and they deliver him on to the Romans.[16] This double handing-over starts with Judas. His name stands typologically for the people of Israel who "bestow" their complete existence, as embodied in the messiah, to the Gentiles, in the sense that the Gentiles can now participate in that existence. The Hebrew word *masar* corresponds to *paradidonai,* and is also used to designate the handing-over of God's Word to the next generation, something that never means a loss for the previous generation. It happens in a mysterious manner, not with clear intention and in a paradoxical way,

14. See Ratzinger, *Die Vielfalt der Religionen und der Eine Bund,* p. 72.

15. Wiard Udo Popkes, *Christus traditus: Eine Untersuchung zum Begriff der Dahingabe im Neuen Testament* (Zürich: Zwingli, 1967); Günther Schwarz, "Die Tat seines ersten Märtyrers: Die Judasfrage in aramaistischer Sicht," *Entschluss* 44, no. 5 (1989): 12-15; Pinchas Lapide, "Verräter oder verraten? Gerechtigkeit für Judas," *Entschluss* 44, no. 5 (1989): 32-38.

16. See "Im Schatten des Kreuzes: Judas Iskariot," *Entschluss* 44, no. 5 (1989).

so that nobody can boast about it but can only praise God for his providence and wisdom (see 1 Cor. 1:18-31). This act represents disaster and cross for Jesus, but he is resurrected by God for the redemption of all humankind. The category of *felix culpa* ("happy guilt") must be applied, according to which God guides the history of salvation independently of human failure or even by means of human failure.

If we have to examine the question of guilt as regards the extradition of Jesus, then we have only to deal with the actors in his immediate environment. And in any case, guilt stands on the side of those Jews involved, but even more on the side of the Gentiles. The latter are doing the crucifying. Judas and the Jewish priests are the characters on one side, Pilate the Roman governor on the other, as the Gospels variously narrate. But in all the Gospels, the Resurrected Jesus makes no reproach of guilt to anyone. This question of guilt is irrelevant. Although Jesus, the messiah, was betrayed by everybody — they all disobeyed: those under the Torah covenant as well as the Gentiles, as stated by Paul in Romans 2 and 3 — nevertheless, the most profound Jewish vocation was mysteriously and unexpectedly fulfilled: to be covenant and light to all people. The God of Mount Sinai lets the messiah of his people Israel become light and salvation to the world. Thus, he enables the God-fearing Gentiles to enter into the covenant and bestows the Holy Spirit.

The mediator from the Jewish people of the covenant to the nations, Jesus Christ, who was handed over and exiled through his crucifixion, "drew all people to himself" (John 12:32) after his death when Gentiles adhered to faith in the Crucified and Raised Messiah. The letters of Paul and the Acts of the Apostles (chapters 10 to 15) witness to this development. Through Christ, the separation between Jews and Gentiles is overcome, as extensively described in the Epistle to the Ephesians. One reconfigured covenant in Christ shall exist, a people from among Jews and Gentiles. However, even if the distinctions among peoples resulting from the covenantal structure is overcome, it does not mean it was actually suspended, but rather transformed: as in Jesus Christ there is neither male nor female, so there is neither Jew nor Greek (Gal. 3:28). But as in Christ the difference between men and women is not suspended, so the difference between Jew and Greek remains. Nevertheless a new constellation in salvation history is eventually created in which the people of the Sinai Covenant and the church of the Gentiles are standing side by side. From a Christian perspective, the messiah has become a bridge between Jews and the nations.

Thus, in the Holy Scriptures of the New Testament, Jesus figures in a double role; his meaning for Jews and Gentiles is differentiated: on one hand, Jesus is the King of the Jews, leading the way of the Jews to fulfill-ment (e.g., Matt. 5:18ff.; the passion narratives). Mark's Gospel shows this already at the beginning of Jesus' public appearance, presenting an exem-plary Sabbath with Jesus: he cures a man in the synagogue and a woman in her home, thus enabling them to fulfill their liturgical Sabbath role. Thus the order of the creation culminating in the Sabbath is able to be properly honored (Mark 1:21-34). In a similar way, John structures the beginning of the Gospel as the week of creation, marking the seventh day with the wed-ding at Cana and presenting it within an eschatological horizon. The cre-ation is completed; Israel is gathered anew, and the feast with delicious wines (Isa. 25:6ff.) can take place (John 1:19–2:12).

On the other hand, messianism, an eschatological phenomenon of Jewish history, mutates in the New Testament to christology, the founda-tion of the nascent church and the starting point of the covenantal life that brings the nations out of paganism. Jewish messianism is transformed into the christology of the church. The messianism of Jesus' time, aiming to gather and restore the Jewish people, is a pre-Christian phenomenon. It has to be respected as a reality of its own, different from ecclesiastical christology with its universal claim of salvation driven by the church's theological interpretation of Jesus' death and resurrection. But messianism and christology are inseparably linked to each other. From a Jewish per-spective messianism occurs at the end of time and the fulfillment of the Torah; from a Christian perspective Christ is the beginning, the origin of a new history of covenant for all people. This is a complete dialectical shift; messianism functions in Judaism differently than christology does in Christianity. Jesus Christ as the personification of the Jewish road to salva-tion becomes the road of salvation for all humankind through his handing over from within the covenant of Sinai to the pagan world and through his divine transition from death to resurrection. God himself here directs the history of salvation and makes Judaism fully enact its universal signifi-cance for the world without dissolving the covenant of Mount Sinai. To the contrary: when Jews live their vocation according to the Torah they pro-duce salvation for the Gentiles. This is the way of God's providence, of di-vine thoughts that are so different from human thoughts (cf. Isa. 55:8; Rom. 11:33-35).

Now the Gentiles have the Christ event as God's offer of redemption and liberation and can respond to it in faith, just as the Jewish people could respond to God's offer after the experience of the Exodus. The Christ proclaimed by Paul and the more "historical" messiah presented by the Synoptic Gospels, who seemed so different to many twentieth-century theologians, are actually both in continuity with the God of Israel who acts dialectically in the history of salvation. Now Jesus' death and resurrection modifies the borders of the covenanted community. As a consequence, the first century of the Common Era brought forth the church from among the Gentiles to stand side by side with Judaism. In the second century, the Christian Bible links the new church community and her New Testament to the Hebrew Bible, now read in the church as an Old Testament. The *ecclesia ex gentibus* ("church from the Gentiles") takes its position in difference but in proximity to Judaism as God's people. In this process, the *ecclesia ex Judaeis* — the community of the "church from the Jewish people" gathered by Christ (see Romans 9–11) — is the bond between the church out of the nations and nascent rabbinic Judaism, which was further interpreting and living out the Sinai Covenant.

3. The Claim of Jesus Christ as Universal Savior in the Context of the Salvation History of God

3.1. Rereading the Mission Command of Matthew 28:16-20

The Christ event had shifted the fundamental biblical difference between Israel as God's people and all the other peoples to a new border between the church and the Gentiles. From a historical point of view, the church first positioned herself among the God-fearing Gentiles near to Judaism and developed her missionary activity to a considerable degree among the same populations who had earlier been attracted to Judaism. Jesus, truly personifying Judaism and cornerstone of the extended and renewed process of salvation, became the gateway for the nations to the God of Israel. The command to evangelize and bring baptism, as formulated in Matthew 28:16-20, has this reconfiguration of salvation history as its immediate context. Accordingly, Matthew 28:16-20 is to be read as concerning all peoples, *except* the Jews, who are already people of God: "And Jesus came and spoke to them, saying: All power is given unto me in heaven and on earth. Go therefore, and teach *all nations*, baptizing them in the name of the Father, and of the Son, and of the Holy Spirit. Teaching them to observe all the things that I have commanded you and lo, I am with you always, even unto the end of the world" (Matt. 28:18-20). The command to baptize and evangelize is valid across the old borderline of the covenant and the nations, but not across the newly formed differentiation between the Jewish people and the church.

We can find in this short Matthean passage clear evidence for this interpretation: first, the Resurrected One appears to command this mission on a mountain that alludes, in the theology of Matthew, to the mountain of the first major sermon (Matthew 5–7) and to the mountain of Temptation (Matt. 4:8ff.). The Sermon on the Mount is followed by four additional discourses by Jesus in the Gospel of Matthew.[17] This organization by Matthew of the speech material of Jesus seems to refer to the five books of the Torah received on Mount Sinai. Thus, the command to baptize and the task to evangelize were pronounced from this standpoint and perspective. It can be read as reinforcing and intensifying the Sinai event through Christ to the Jewish people first, and secondly, he brings its message to the nations. Furthermore, as can be deduced from this allusion, it would be a temptation (see Matt. 4:8ff.) to bring the Judaism taught by the historical Jesus to the nations if this messiah had not first gone through crucifixion and resurrection.[18] That would effectively be laying all the nations before the Jewish messiah's feet. It is only the Resurrected One, who by going to the stake himself, became the cornerstone of the new covenant of salvation and grace. Without it, the Jewish message to the nations would be pure command and simple ethics. It would overburden the non-Jewish peoples because they wouldn't have the unconditional salvific experience of God that the Jews received by being saved from Egypt. This thinking is supported by the often-discussed "messianic secret" of Mark's Gospel, in which Jesus' death and resurrection is the precondition for perceiving Jesus as Christ and for proclaiming his message. For the question of salvation, this is the decisive point. The God of the Bible not only imposes ethics on people but first reaches out offering redemption, through the Exodus for the Jews and here through the cross for the Gentiles.

We have a second indication for this reading of Matthew 28:16-20: the text is talking about eleven and not twelve disciples. Judas has just "handed over" Christ to the Jewish authorities and through them to Gentiles. In Matthew's Gospel this is specifically described as an act guided by the logic

17. Commission of Disciples Discourse: 9:35–11:1; Discourse on the Kingdom of God: 13:1-53; Community Discourse: 18:1-35; Eschatological Discourse 24:1–25:46.

18. The historical Jesus taught Torah to Gentiles, e.g., the Syrophoenician (Mark 7:24-30) or Canaanite woman (Matt. 15:22-28), but the full meaning of his mission became evident only after his resurrection.

of salvation history, supported by a quote from the prophets: "Then was fulfilled what had been spoken by the prophet Jeremiah, 'And they took the thirty pieces of silver, the price of the one on whom a price had been set, on whom some of the people of Israel had set a price, and they gave them for the potter's field, as the Lord commanded me'" (Matt. 27:9-10).[19] Judas's action is understood within the horizon of God's providence. Now, one might say, the other disciples must, in an analogous way, hand over the messiah to the world, so that all the people can become his disciples.

Finally, the command to baptize as stated in Matthew 28 is to be read in parallel with chapter 10, a text that contains Jesus' command to go exclusively to the house of Israel (v. 5). The Gospel seems to put the two missions side by side and intentionally creates a tension. Whereas the mission to Israel takes place before Jesus' death and resurrection, the mission to the Gentiles comes afterward. In between, the actual event of the foundation of a renewed covenant comes into existence.

To summarize: in order to take the structure of salvation history seriously, the commands for mission and baptism given by the Matthean Jesus should be directed to all the peoples of the world, excluding the Jews. From a theological point of view, Christianity has to give up the traditional and classical "Jewish mission," not only for historical reasons but also out of a deeper understanding of Christ within the salvific economy of God.

Thus, *A Sacred Obligation,* the statement of an ecumenical group of Christian scholars, already emphasized in 2002: "In view of our conviction that Jews are in an eternal covenant with God, we renounce missionary efforts directed at converting Jews. At the same time, we welcome opportunities for Jews and Christians to bear witness to their respective experiences of God's saving ways. Neither can properly claim to possess knowledge of God entirely or exclusively." In addition, the statement continues with a subsequent point: "Affirming God's enduring covenant with the Jewish people has consequences for Christian understandings of salvation."[20] Of course, individual Christians should talk about Jesus Christ and witness him to everybody they meet, but not in a missionary sense toward Jews. Individual religious freedom is not curtailed by this basic theological grounding of the Jewish-Christian relationship. But the universal claim of Jesus Christ con-

---

19. The Gospel of Matthew explicitly refers with this quote to Jeremiah, but it seems to be a reference to Zechariah 11:12-13 according to the current Old Testament text.

20. http://www.ccjr.us/dialogika-resources/documents-and-statements/ecumenical-christian/568-csg-02sep1.

cerning Judaism, as traditionally taught in theology, needs to take a different form. One can only find it by rethinking Christian theology.

3.2. Jesus' Different Meaning for Jews and Gentiles in the Gospels

The command of the resurrected Christ to baptize "all the nations" is only directed toward the Gentiles. But we have to ask once more: What is the meaning of the claim that Jesus is universal savior? How do we understand such sayings as: "Jesus said to him, 'I am the way, and the truth, and the life. No one comes to the Father except through me'" (John 14:6); or "This is right and is acceptable in the sight of God our Savior, who desires everyone to be saved and to come to the knowledge of the truth. For there is one God; there is also one mediator between God and humankind, Christ Jesus, himself a human, who gave himself as ransom for all — this was attested at the right time" (1 Tim. 2:3-6). Are these declarations only for the nations but not for the Jews because they are already in a covenant with the God of Jesus?[21] It would be much too easy for Christian theology to answer with a simplistic, un-nuanced "Yes." This would distort the texts and contradict the whole tradition. It would also conflict with other central passages of the New Testament, e.g., Jesus is the King of the Jews according to the passion narratives. The theology of the Epistle to the Hebrews reinterprets the whole reconciling structure of the Old Covenant because of its theological understanding of Jesus' crucifixion. Pauline theology also reconsiders the Old Covenant from a new angle and offers a modified view of it. In addition, the Gospels give witness to a historical Jesus who taught his fellow Jews. They were his addressees. Jesus was there for his people and sent his disciples to gather the dispersed people of Israel (see Mark 6:6-34; Matt. 9:35–11:1; Luke 10:1-20).

The claim of Jesus Christ, as preached by the first believers in him after his resurrection, was truly a claim for Jews and also for other people, but in the differentiated way already seen in the Gospel of Matthew with its two different mission texts. This is also evident in the narrative theology of Mark: Mark relates two events of the multiplication of the loaves; in the

21. See the comment of Franz Rosenzweig: Although nobody comes to God except through Jesus Christ, the Jew, however, already is with God, whom Christianity calls "the Father of Jesus Christ." Letter to Rudolf Ehrenberg of November 1, 1913, in Franz Rosenzweig, *Der Mensch und sein Werk. Gesammelte Schriften,* vol. 1 (The Hague: Martinus Nijhoff, 1979), pp. 134ff. (http://www.ersterweltkrieg.eu/rosenzweig/rosenzweigichbleibealsojude.html).

first, bread remnants fill twelve baskets (6:35-44). Then the second occurs in the land of the Gentiles, on the other side of Lake of Galilee, and seven baskets of bread leftovers remain (8:1-9). Whereas the twelve baskets are meant for the twelve tribes of Israel, the Gospel seems to allude to the entire population of the nations with the seven baskets recalling the nations mentioned in Genesis 10:2; Deuteronomy 7:1; and Joshua 3:10.[22] With this eschatological action Jesus acts for the Jews and for the Gentiles as well. Precisely because Mark does not present only *one* large multiplication of the loaves but two indicates the extent to which the structure of the covenant with its difference and delimitation between Jews and Gentiles abides within the New Testament.

Following classical forms of poetic biblical parallelism, Luke also differentiates between Jesus' significance toward Israel and toward the Gentiles without separating them. Simeon, having met Mary and Joseph with the baby Jesus, declares: "Master, now you are dismissing your servant in peace, according to your word; for my eyes have seen your salvation, which you have prepared in the presence of all peoples, a light for revelation to the Gentiles and for glory to your people Israel" (Luke 2:29-32). Without deriving out of these poetic lines a whole dogma, they nevertheless show that the salvation by the messiah for all people is distinguished into "light for the Gentiles" and "glory for Israel."

Considering this differentiated meaning of Jesus in the New Testament, it seems appropriate to differentiate Jesus' impact according to the affected group. This is not a modern theological trick; it is much more the rediscovery of the ancient biblical difference between people of the covenant and peoples of the nations now reconfigured as the post-Christic twofold people of God's covenant: the church and Judaism.

4. The Differentiated Claim of Jesus Christ Toward Judaism

If the classical Christian "mission to the Jews" with the purpose of integrating them through baptism into the church — i.e., into the *ecclesia ex gentibus*, the church out of the nations as she is in fact — cannot really be an option, it is also true that the universal importance of Jesus to Christian eyes cannot be questioned. We therefore cannot avoid asking: In what way

22. See Jesper Svartvik, *Mark and Mission: Mk 7,1-23 in Its Narrative and Historical Contexts* (Stockholm: Almqvist & Wiksell, 2000), p. 300.

is Jesus significant for Judaism? If his significance for Jews does not include baptism and becoming Christian, then what could Jesus mean — from the perspective of Christian theology — for Jews?

In the Jewish-Christian dialogue of the late twentieth century we find a partial answer, which also appeared in connection with the controversy about the 2008 Good Friday intercession for the Tridentine Rite: in the eschatological time when all the nations, Christians and Jews, are led before God, then the messiah awaited by Jews and Jesus Christ will converge in a single individual. This was Walter Cardinal Kasper's interpretation of the new Good Friday intercession:

> The text proceeds once more from the 11th chapter of the Letter to the Romans. . . . Paul speaks in apocalyptic language of a mystery (11:25). . . . Paul sees the whole of his missionary activity among the Gentiles from this eschatological perspective. His mission is to prepare the gathering of the peoples which, when the full number of the Gentiles has entered, will serve the salvation of the Jews and bring forth eschatological peace for the world. So one can say: God will bring about the salvation of Israel in the end, not on the basis of a mission to the Jews but on the basis of the mission to the Gentiles, when the fullness of the Gentiles has entered. He alone who has caused the hardening of the majority of the Jews can dissolve that hardening again. He will do so when "the Deliverer" comes from Zion (Rom. 11:26). . . . Such petitions for the coming of the kingdom of God and for the realization of the mystery of salvation are not by nature a call to the church to undertake missionary action to the Jews. Rather, they respect the whole depth of the *Deus absconditus* ["hidden God"], of his election through grace, of the hardening and of his infinite mercy. So in this prayer the church does not take it upon herself to orchestrate the realization of the unfathomable mystery. She cannot do so. Instead, she lays the *when* and the *how* entirely in God's hands. God alone can bring about the kingdom of God in which the whole of Israel is saved and eschatological peace is bestowed on the world.[23]

Franz Mussner, in his consistent interpretation of the Epistle to the Romans, also looks at this particular passage, Romans 11, as if the saving of

---

23. "Striving for Mutual Respect in Modes of Prayer" in *L'Osservatore Romano*, April 16, 2008, pp. 8ff. For the whole text, see http://www.ccjr.us/dialogika-resources/themes-in-todays-dialogue/good-friday-prayer/446-kaspero8apr16.

Israel were the consequence of the *parousia,* or return of Christ. He recognizes for Judaism in humanity's unfolding history "a special place" because Jews are led on their way by God's grace, which should consequently be fulfilled at the end of time.[24] Heinz Günther Schöttler, when arguing against Cardinal Kasper's interpretation of the Good Friday intercession, points out that in Romans 11:25-36 there is no trace of a christological reference and, as a consequence, it would not be acceptable to pray for the Jews accepting Jesus as messiah at the end of time. At the time of the Final Judgment there will be neither christological nor ecclesiastic mediation, but God's kingdom will be established by God alone.[25] It is certain that at this moment the church will cease as a historical power, whereas the role of the eschatological messiah is shrouded in mystery.

In this regard, the Good Friday intercession for the ordinary rite is rather modest, leaving open the form of the salvation of Israel: "Listen to your church as we pray that the people you first made your own may arrive at the fullness of redemption." *Nostra Aetate* had earlier expressed this eschatological vision following vigorous discussions about the Jewish people being saved through Jesus Christ in historic time: "In company with the prophets and the same Apostle, the church awaits that day, known to God alone, on which all people will address the Lord in a single voice and serve him 'shoulder to shoulder' (Zeph. 3:9)" (see also Isa. 66:23; Ps. 65:4; Rom. 11:11-32).

In whatever way salvation may be manifested at the time of the Last Judgment, what is essential for us now is that the claim of universal salvation through Jesus Christ can and must be eschatologically suspended. Martin Buber from the Jewish side expressed similar expectations, saying that we can hope that the messiah Jews will recognize at the end of time might be the same as the Jesus of the church in his second coming.

This partial answer to the question of the significance of Jesus Christ for Jews may be an important basis for Jewish-Christian dialogue to function on the same wavelength and guarantee the integrity of both faith communities. However, this alone is not enough and leaves several questions open as Jews and Christians actually live in present-day history. It is hardly satisfying to simply refer to the last days, however justified and demanded it may be in the face of God's unsearchable wisdom.

---

24. *Traktat über die Juden* (München: Kösel, 1979), pp. 60f.

25. "Von Heilswegen und Holzwegen: Die Karfreitagsfürbitten für die Juden und ihre Theologien," in Homolka and Zenger, eds., "Damit sie Jesus Christus Erkennen," pp. 166ff.

So we are still faced with the question, what is Jesus' claim on Judaism in historic time? There could be a twofold answer:

First, perhaps it is about Jews trying to be more open to the self-definition of the church. Jews are right to insist time and again that dialogue could continue only on the basis of equality, that is, if Christians do not consider Judaism to be lacking in substance or to be stuck in a preliminary stage that Christianity fulfills. On the other hand, Jews could be expected to understand the church as being also in covenant with God and so ponder what their relationship to Jesus might be beyond historical controversy and polemic. In reality, the rabbinic tradition has not sufficiently considered how to judge as righteous the peoples coming from different nations according to the seven Noahide commands. This simple ethical judgment refers to some of the Gentiles, to individuals, but does not grapple with the specificity of their religious experience, including whether it is possible to view positively Christianity and the church. It is a challenge for both Jews and Christians to see each other as in covenant with God.

In order to realize the difficulties from the Jewish side, we can look at the controversy about *Dabru Emet: A Jewish Statement on Christians and Christianity* of the year 2000. In this document Jewish scholars invite their brethren to have a new look at Christianity and perceive the changes within the churches regarding Judaism.[26] The twelve Berlin theses proclaimed by the International Council of Christians and Jews in 2009 urge the same in order to revitalize the Jewish-Christian dialogue.[27] By drawing on thinkers such as Moses Maimonides, who attributed to Christianity a preparatory role for proper faith in God,[28] or Franz Rosenzweig, who saw Christianity as having a complementary function to Judaism,[29] and by heeding the encouragement of Rabbi Jonathan Sacks to the further devel-

26. Tikva Frymer-Kensky, David Novak, Peter Ochs, Michael Signer, and David Sandmel, eds., *Christianity in Jewish Terms* (Boulder, CO: Westview Press, 2000). Related publications in German are Rainer Kampling and Michael Weinrich, eds., *Dabru Emet — Redet Wahrheit: Eine jüdische Herausforderung zum Dialog mit den Christen* (Gütersloh: Gütersloher Verlagshaus, 2003); Erwin Dirscherl and Werner Trutwin, eds., *Redet Wahrheit — Dabru Emet: Jüdisch-christliches Gespräch über Gott, Messias und Dekalog* (Münster: LIT, 2004).

27. ICCJ/Konrad Adenauer-Stiftung, eds., *A Time for Recommitment: Jewish-Christian Dialogue 70 Years after War and Shoah* (Berlin: Sankt Augustin, 2009).

28. Maimonides, *Mishneh Torah*, Book 14, *Judges*. Section *Hilchot Melachim* ("Laws of Kings"), ed. Abraham M. Hershman, Yale Judaica series (New Haven: Yale University Press, 1949).

29. Part 3 of *Stern der Erlösung* (Frankfurt am Main: Suhrkamp, 6/1999); ET: *The Star of Redemption*, trans. Barbara E. Galli (Madison: University of Wisconsin Press, 2004).

opment of religious thinking,[30] Jews can move ahead on new roads. A key question is how far Jews can go in interpreting the christology that has become the basis of the New Covenant of the church. Is there a way to accept its function for Christians without having to consider it relevant in the same way for Jews? The significance of Jesus being handed over to the nations and the ensuing claim of his resurrection by some Jewish contemporaries needs to be discussed from a Jewish point of view today. In this way a spiritual depth to Jewish-Christian dialogue could be achieved, moving beyond the sociological and political agendas that define much Jewish-Catholic dialogue at the present time.

Second, in addition to a reconsidered Jewish view of Christianity, a claim of Jesus upon Judaism has also derived from Christian perspectives that are not authoritative for Jews. But might there not be a place for his interpretation of the Torah and his teachings in the Jewish tradition? As should be evident from this essay, this would involve neither a demand for baptism nor an ecclesiastical christology with its trinitarian image of God. The message and person of Jesus before his being handed over to the nations are pertinent for Jews, whereas the resurrection could function for Christians as their confirmation. Jesus' teaching could be included into the interpretation of the Torah and into the discussions about *halakhah.* Speaking in concrete terms: Could not Jesus' interpretation of the Sabbath, as mentioned in many debates in the Gospels, contribute to today's Jewish understanding of the Sabbath? And do not the words of the Sermon on the Mount (Matthew 5–7) about divorce or about the loving of enemies, have meaning for Jewish ears? Could not the parable of the Good Samaritan (Luke 10:25-37), which changes the question "Who is my neighbor whom I have to love?" to "Who proved to be the loving neighbor to the other?" also be for Jews a fruitful approach to the command to treat the stranger as one's kinsman (as in Lev. 25:23-28, e.g.)? As mentioned before, this is not about turning Jews into Christians, but that "the Jewish people, the first to hear the word of God, may continue to grow in the love of his name and in faithfulness to his Covenant," as has been formulated in the ordinary Good Friday intercession since 1970.

As Joseph Klausner, Leo Baeck, Pinchas Lapide, David Flusser, Shalom Ben-Chorin, and others have found, Jewishness can be discovered in the New Testament. Just as Catholics today profit by reading the Talmud and the

---

30. *The Dignity of Difference: How to Avoid the Clash of Civilizations* (London/New York: Continuum, 2002).

Midrashim of the Jewish tradition, similarly Jews could also benefit from Christian writings. Both religious communities are communities of learning, open to integrate wisdom from their surrounding cultures. Why should they not honestly admit that they have learned in history from each other?[31] Why can they not consciously be open to each other in the future?[32]

Beyond being an open learning community that finds a brother in Jesus, Jews cannot be expected to embrace the church's christology. Jews remain Jews even if some of them see in Jesus a messianic figure.[33] And if the death and resurrection of Christ are to be relevant for Judaism, it is not in the founding of a new religious identity. Jesus' death for sins (cf. Matt. 26:28 par.; 1 Cor. 15:3) would have to be interpreted in the categories of the Day of Atonement, and his resurrection by God as the confirmation of being one of the righteous among the Jews. In any case, Christians cannot tell Jews what Jesus means for them; it is a question for Jews to examine if at long last an era of peace between the two communities has arrived.

5. Being Open to the "Sacrament of Otherness"

In connection with a new, unprejudiced view of Jews and Christians, it is interesting to read the latest book of Michael Wolffsohn.[34] He points out that it is especially the rabbinic Judaism of Talmudic times that has taken

31. Michael Hilton, *"Wie es Sich Christelt so Jüdelt es Sich": 2000 Jahre Christlicher Einfluss auf das Jüdische Leben* (Berlin: Jüdische Verlagsanstalt, 2000).

32. On the meaning of Jewish tradition for the church, see my publication: *Christsein im Angesicht des Judentums* (Würzburg: Echter, 2008); also my article: "Jewish Christian Dialogue and the Theology of Religions," *Studies in Christian-Jewish Relations* 1, no. 1 (2005-6): 53-66, http://escholarship.bc.edu/scjr/vol1/iss1/7. Also see Paul Petzel, *Was uns an Gott fehlt, wenn uns die Juden fehlen: Eine erkenntnistheologische Studie* (Mainz: Grünewald, 1994); Gerhard Langer and Gregor Maria Hoff, eds., *Der Ort des Jüdischen in der katholischen Theologie* (Göttingen: Vandenhoeck & Ruprecht, 2009).

33. In the first centuries of the Common Era the *ecclesia ex Judaeis* was in existence, but it was destined to disappear. It is hard to imagine what kind of structure it could have today and how belief in Christ can be expressed, because the existing messianic community among Jews has not found its appropriate social expression. In any case, neither Jews nor Christians have the right to hinder or to have contempt for or even to attack "Messianic Jews." They do not menace Judaism, nor do they threaten the Jewish-Christian dialogue. The right to exist is the most important contribution Jews and Christians can give to the *ecclesia ex Judaeis* under the present historical circumstances.

34. *Juden und Christen — ungleiche Geschwister: Die Geschichte zweier Rivalen* (Düsseldorf: Patmos, 2008).

over, transmitted, and internalized the spirit of the historical Jesus even more than Christianity, which was more oriented toward the paradigm of the Old Testament. Indeed, Judaism was deprived of its Temple, and the lay movement of the Pharisees, who were particularly close to Jesus of Nazareth, provided its new form, whereas the church in interpreting the crucifixion of Jesus as a sacrifice and in bringing forth a priesthood adhered more to the old biblical tradition.[35] In such a paradoxical development in the centuries after Christ, Judaism had already resonated with many of Jesus' perspectives, as suggested above. But then we have the tragic history of contempt and persecution of the Jewish people by Christians. Today, an open and free dialogue is already a great achievement. The disastrous past history makes it understandable why one has to wait patiently for deep-seated wounds to heal in a process that may take generations. Above all, what separates Jews and Christians is history.[36]

If it has become clear that Judaism and Christianity stand in an "unwilling union"[37] in which they are chained together — asymmetrically in terms of demography, history, and theology, it is also evident that Jews and Christians are not just side by side, but they also share a genuine encounter and exchange. Together, they are on the way toward demonstrating their dialogical existence as people of God. Dialogical existence means that they need the other to understand themselves fully and to resist the tendency of monolithic self-definitions and identities.[38] Jews are the "Sacrament of Otherness"[39] for Christians and the other way round. These are the pa-

---

35. This thesis is supported, for example, by looking at the prayer of ordination of priests in the Catholic Church. Although it was pointed out in the New Testament that Christ was not of priestly descent and his service attributed to King Melchizedek (Heb. 7), the prayer of ordination retraces the Christian priesthood to the Aaronic order.

36. This conviction of Ernst-Ludwig Ehrlich was chosen for the title of a collection of his writings edited by Hanspeter Heinz and Hans Hermann Henrix, *"Was uns trennt, ist die Geschichte": Ernst Ludwig Ehrlich — Vermittler zwischen Juden und Christen* (München: Neue Stadt, 2008).

37. Hans Hermann Henrix, *Judentum und Christentum: Gemeinschaft wider Willen* (Regensburg: Topos, 2008).

38. See Dan Bar-On, *Die "Andern" in uns: Dialog als Modell der interkulturellen Konfliktbewältigung. Sozialpsychologische Analysen zur kollektiven israelischen Identität* (Hamburg: Koeber, 2003).

39. Alberto Melloni, *"Nostra Aetate* and the Discovery of the Sacrament of Otherness," in Philip A. Cunningham, Norbert J. Hofmann, and Joseph Sievers, eds., *The Catholic Church and the Jewish People: Recent Reflections from Rome* (New York: Fordham University Press, 2007), pp. 129-51.

rameters God established as the salvific road for both his people. While preserving their differences, Jews and Christians should jointly demonstrate that it is possible to travel together toward salvation by inviting other people to join them. Unfortunately, due to argument, competition, contempt, mistrust, and persecution it has not been possible to undertake this assignment in the past.

Nevertheless, a life of dialogue and exchange should now flourish in the divinely willed complementary community formed by Judaism and the church.[40] Judaism and Christianity remain intertwined in God's plan for salvation, a plan that has been revealed and can be recognized under the condition of this historical time. The Day will come when Jews and Christians stand shoulder to shoulder before God, both living in respect for each other and following God. That Day will see the salvation hoped for by all the nations.

40. From a Jewish point of view this exchange was again demanded because of a series of crises resulting from recent actions of Pope Benedict: "'Frage der inneren Nähe': Ein Gespräch mit Rabbiner Walter Homolka über den Jüdisch-Katholischen Dialog," *Herder-korrespondenz* 63, no. 4 (2009): 182.

The Jewish People at Vatican II:
The Drama of a Development in Ecclesiology
and Its Subsequent Reception in Ireland and Britain

Thomas J. Norris

1. Introduction

Though it is fashionable in certain contexts to describe the Second Vatican Council as essentially, even exclusively, a "pastoral" event, this is not the full truth. It is not even the vital truth. The Council is also an event of great theological import.[1] The time since the Council has demonstrated that, in fact, its undeniable pastoral focus *also* made it theologically innovative. In that way it vindicated Cardinal Newman's claim made in the nineteenth century that "theology is the fundamental and regulating principle of the whole Church system," for theology "is commensurate with Revelation, and Revelation is the initial and essential idea of Christianity."[2]

Perhaps nowhere is this more obvious than in the Council's chosen universal focus, its sustained desire to speak to all men and women of goodwill (see *Dei Verbum* [*DV*], §1; *Gaudium et Spes* [*GS*], §1; *Unitatis Redintegratio* [*UR*], §1). That very desire stands out in the range and variety of the sixteen constitutions and decrees emanating from the Council and promulgated by Pope John XXIII and Pope Paul VI. Subsequent reflection on these conciliar texts has tended to highlight increasingly the four great dialogues implicit in them. These dialogues are those within the Catholic Church, the Catholic Church in relation to the other churches

---

1. See Joseph Ratzinger, "The Ecclesiology of the Constitution *Lumen Gentium*," in *Pilgrim Fellowship of Faith: The Church as Communion* (San Francisco: Ignatius Press, 2005), pp. 123-52, esp. 123-26: "The Second Vatican Council certainly did intend to subordinate what it said about the Church to what it said about God and to set it in that context" (p. 125).

2. John Henry Newman, preface to the Third Edition of the *Via Media* (London: Longmans, Green & Co., 1891), p. xlvii.

and ecclesial communities, the church in relation to the great religions, and, fourth, the church in relation to men and women of goodwill. The subsequent reordering of the Roman Curia bears eloquent testimony to this fact, for it is at once obvious that the new curial councils emerged in order to serve *la théologie conciliaire*.

The relationship of the church of Jesus Christ to the people of the first covenant is a unique and mysterious one. It emerged at Vatican II with vigor, gaining the attention of the world and confirming the fact that "[t]he Church's relationship to the Jewish people is unlike the one she shares with any other religion." In spite of this divinely grounded relationship, however, "the history of the relations between Jews and Christians is a tormented one. . . . In effect, the balance of these relations over two thousand years has been quite negative."[3]

In attempting to evaluate the degree of reception of the Council's insight into the church's relationship to Judaism, it will be necessary to proceed in an orderly fashion. We shall first look at the standard theology of the church in the time leading up to Vatican II. Was there any attention given then to the relationship of Israel to the mystery of the church? In a second instance we shall briefly expound Vatican II's emerging teaching on Judaism and its implications for our grasp of the mystery of the church of Jesus Christ. Finally, we shall attempt to evaluate the actual level of reception of the conciliar insight in postconciliar ecclesiology in Britain and Ireland.

2. Preconciliar Ecclesiology

In the decades following the Council it was the trend to adopt a hermeneutic of rupture rather than of renewal in relation to the Second Vatican Council. In fact, "there exists a general impression that Vatican II accomplished a major revolution in ecclesiology."[4] Authors speak of a "Blondelian shift," of a "Copernican" or "Einsteinian" shift of perspective occur-

3. Commission for Religious Relations with the Jews, *We Remember: A Reflection on the Shoah*, Rome (March 16, 1998), in *Information Service* of the Pontifical Council for Promoting Christian Unity, n. 97, 19: text quoted in International Theological Commission, *Memory and Reconciliation: The Church and the Faults of the Past* (London: Catholic Truth Society, 2000), 5.4.

4. Avery Dulles, "Nature, Mission, and Structure of the Church," in Matthew L. Lamb and Matthew Levering, eds., *Vatican II: Renewal within Tradition* (Oxford: Oxford University Press, 2008), p. 25.

ring in the Second Vatican Council. Avery Cardinal Dulles described in vivid categories this "hermeneutic of rupture" when he wrote:

> Before the council, it is held, the Church was regarded as an institution founded by Christ with definite and immutable structures. After the council the Church was seen as a pilgrim community constantly restructuring itself to suit the times. Before the council the Church was regarded as necessary for salvation; after it, as one of many places in which people could live a life of grace. Before Vatican II, the Catholic Church saw herself as the sole legitimate Church; after it, as one of many realizations of the church of Christ, all imperfect. Until the council, the church was seen as a divinely instituted monarchy in which all authority descended from the pope; after it, as a People of God that governed itself through consensus.[5]

These "ecclesiologies" all have one thing in common: they are founded on serious exaggerations, and these exaggerations "overlook the nuances both in the preconciliar period and in Vatican II."[6] Furthermore, they insinuate a hermeneutic of rupture between the ecclesiology of the century leading up to Vatican II and the ecclesiology that emerged victoriously from the Council.[7] This brief description sets up a stark "then" and "now." However, there is another hermeneutic available, the hermeneutic of *ressourcement* (retrieval) and development that are indicative of genuine continuity.

Even a glance at the history of ecclesiology since the early nineteenth century is enough to detect the themes and the emphases beginning to enrich the treatise on the church. One sees that besides the very structural ecclesiology of the Counter Reformation, there began, in the nineteenth century, a movement of *ressourcement.* The truth is that

> there developed a movement for the restoration of ecclesiology through a return to the biblical, patristic and medieval sources. It originated with the Tübingen school (Sailer, Drey, Möhler, Kuhn) which brought out again the notion of the Body of Christ animated by the Spirit, in the

5. Dulles, "Nature, Mission, and Structure of the Church," p. 25.
6. Dulles, "Nature, Mission, and Structure of the Church," p. 25.
7. For two contrasting interpretations of Vatican II, the one of rupture, the other of continuity, see respectively John W. O'Malley, *What Happened at Vatican II* (Cambridge, MA: Harvard University Press, 2008), and Lamb and Levering, *Vatican II: Renewal within Tradition*, see n. 4.

perspective of a "kingdom of God" theology. The Church was not primarily a visible and hierarchical society endowed with a magisterium, but an organic fellowship with Christ. . . . The Church in all its fullness, became once more the object of theology.[8]

This movement of *ressourcement* inspired and expressed itself in the great theological developments of the nineteenth and twentieth centuries. It is enough to think of the biblical, patristic, and liturgical movements that prepared the ground for Vatican II. Many of the later contributors to these movements were actual *periti,* or expert advisors, at the Council: they enriched the drafts submitted to the council fathers and nourished the often dramatic debates unfolding in the aula of St. Peter's Basilica. At Vatican II, Newman's vision of theology as "the fundamental and regulating principle of the whole Church system" became fact.[9]

Still, the typical tract studied in Catholic seminaries and faculties between the First and the Second Vatican Councils was untouched by this recovery of themes. The standard ecclesiology was in fact a "hierarchology" more than an ecclesiology. This is the verdict of no less a theologian than Yves Congar.[10] To some extent this was inevitable though regrettable. "The Reformers questioned the whole system of ecclesial mediation (the primacy of the Pope, the powers of bishops and priests, the authority of tradition, the magisterium, the priesthood and the sacraments). This led theologians to concentrate in the definition of the Church on its juridical and visible reality and to give less prominence to the reality of grace."[11]

As a student of theology in Rome in the mid-1960s I came face-to-face with this juridical ecclesiology. There was little evidence of the rich *ressourcement* that the previous century and a half had effected. There was no sign, for example, of the idea of St. Augustine's *"Non est enim aliud Dei mysterium nisi Christus"*[12] ("There is no other mystery of God besides Christ"), no sign of the efficient causality by which "the Eucharist makes the Church" (Henri de Lubac), no sign of the church as the locus of the life of God, the Holy Trinity, whose life the church offers to humanity as the

---

8. Marie-Joseph le Guillou, "Church," in *Sacramentum Mundi* I (Bangalore: Theological Publications in India, 1968), p. 316.

9. See note 2.

10. See Kevin McNamara, ed., *Vatican II: The Constitution on the Church: A Theological and Pastoral Commentary* (London/Dublin/Melbourne: Geoffrey Chapman, 1968), p. 12.

11. Guillou, "Church," p. 316.

12. St. Augustine, *Ep.* 187,34, in CSEL, 57:113.

ground for humanity's eschatological hope, and no sign of the universal call to holiness of life as the ordinary expression of baptismal existence.

And the implications of this "hierarchology" were to be seen and felt in drastic and concrete fashion. The communities emanating from the Reformation, as well as the Anglican Church, were not connected to, and less still, "members" of the one, true church. Pope Pius XII's encyclical on the church, *Mystici Corporis*, published in 1943, seemed to support this ecclesiology,[13] holding that "non-Catholics could be spiritually united to the Church by desire and intention but could not qualify as members."[14] Accordingly, the only course open to them was the repudiation of their heresies and schisms followed by return to the Roman Catholic Church.

As for the Jews, the church as the new people of God had simply replaced them: they were no longer a chosen people. The "new covenant in the Lord's blood" (1 Cor. 11:25) had made the first covenant superfluous, in spite of St. Paul's words in the Letter to the Romans, "Let me put another question then: is it possible that God has rejected his people? Of course not. I, an Israelite, descended from Abraham through the tribe of Benjamin, could never agree that God had rejected his people, the people he specially chose long ago" (11:1-2a). The church as "the Israel of God" (Gal. 6:16; see 3:29; Rom. 9:6-8) had replaced the Israel "according to the flesh" (1 Cor. 10:18).

In the course of the Council this prevailing ecclesiology encountered the impulse toward rediscovery and retrieval, or *ressourcement*. The result was *Lumen Gentium*, which incorporated the abundant fruits of the various movements in Scripture, patristics, church history, and liturgy. The Council became the theater of a resulting dramatic debate, an encounter that was as vigorous as its fruits were to prove abundant. The church is a sacrament: that principle broadened out the definition of membership, a prime topic of *Mystici Corporis*, which had taught that non-Catholics could not be members of the church of Christ in the full sense of the word.

The recovery of the concept of sacrament for ecclesiology opened the way to a sacramental understanding of the church of God. This allowed the Council to think in terms of "realizations" of the church of Christ leading up to the famous teaching in *Lumen Gentium* §8 that "the Church of

13. See Karl Rahner, S.J., "Membership of the Church according to the Teaching of the Encyclical *Mystici Corporis*," in *Theological Investigations*, vol. 2 (Baltimore: Helicon Press/London: Darton, Longman & Todd, 1963), pp. 1-88.

14. Dulles, "Nature, Mission, and Structure of the Church," p. 27.

Christ subsists in [*subsistit in*] the Catholic Church." This permits, in other words, an understanding of the fact that the church founded by Christ and sent into the world *continues to exist.* However, it *also shows how* other churches or ecclesial communities participate in the one church of Christ in varying degrees.[15] In other words, "while the church is only one and really exists, there is being which is from the church's *being* — there is ecclesial reality — outside the church."[16] Both *Lumen Gentium* §16 and the *Decree on Ecumenism* §3 can now deal with the manner in which other Christians and their communities, who do not have full and visible union with the Catholic Church, may belong to the church by salutary bonds.

Furthermore, the church as the people of God is also related to the Jews. "In the first place there is the People to whom the covenants and the promises were given and from whom Christ was born according to the flesh (cf. Rom 9:4-5)."[17] The text proceeds at once to name the reason for their unique relationship to the church, "On account of their fathers, this people remains most dear to God, for God does not repent of the gifts he makes nor of the calls he issues (cf. Rom 11:28-29)." Significantly, the text draws on Paul's treatise on the issue in Romans 9–11. The way is being paved for what was perhaps the most spectacular *declaration* of the Council, that dealing with the relationship of the church with the religions, the first of which is Judaism.

3. Vatican II on the Jews

The interest of the Council in Judaism was both striking and original, particularly in view of the "ecclesiology of the Schools" that had preceded the great event. Perhaps the best way to enter into conciliar teaching is to study the emergence, development, and final formulation of that teaching in the course of the great Council.[18] *The history of the composition of that teaching*

---

15. See Thomas Norris, "*Subsistit in* — A Conciliar Formula and an Ecclesial Movement in Conversation," in Jean Ehret und Erwin Möde, eds., *Catholica. Einheit und Anspruch des Katholischen* (Freiburg/Basel/Wien: Herder, 2009), pp. 96-111.

16. Joseph Ratzinger, "*Deus locutus est nobis in Filio:* Some Reflections on Subjectivity, Christology, and the Church," in *Papers from the Vallombrosa Meeting* (Washington, DC: United States Catholic Conference, 2000), p. 28.

17. *Lumen Gentium,* §16.

18. John Oesterreicher's introduction to, and commentary on, the text of *NA* in Herbert Vorgrimler's *Commentary on the Documents of Vatican II,* vol. 3 (New York: Herder &

becomes the key way to interpret the texts of the Council addressing Israel's re-lation to the church. With its attitude of gospel openness, personified in Pope John XXIII and carried forward by Pope Paul VI, the Council was interested in the question of the Jewish people from the beginning.

A *kairos,* a moment of crucial decision, clearly covered the whole Council. A principal dimension of that grace was the emphasis on universality: What was the relationship of the Catholic Church to the other Christians, to Jews and the other religions, as well as to men and women of goodwill? Should the Jews, because of their religious uniqueness, historical vulnerability, and abysmal sufferings during the Shoah, be given distinct treatment or be included in the Decree on Ecumenism? This question was to occupy the Council with increasing urgency.

Not all were well disposed toward the thought of treating the topic at the Council. In general, the patriarchs from the Uniate churches of the Middle East were either critical or extremely cautious in approaching the subject. The minority status of Catholics, as well as the tensions between the fledgling state of Israel and the surrounding Arab nations, combined to cause a serious reserve concerning what ought to be done with the Jewish topic. It seemed as if "politics held theology in chains."[19]

As to the appropriate location in which to elaborate the Declaration, the initial decision at the Council was to include it in the Decree on Ecumenism. The arguments for this location were succinctly formulated by Fr. René Laurentin, the renowned French theologian and Mariologist. His summary of the debate and the arguments for including the Declaration in the Decree on Ecumenism may be read as typical of the central thrust of the theological debate. He wrote as follows,

1. We have common roots or, to put it more exactly, the same roots as Israel. . . . One could . . . speak of common roots in a quite special sense: "It is not you that support the root but the root that supports you," says St. Paul to the community that had arisen among the Gentiles (Rom 11:18). Indeed it is not enough to speak of a root, it is much more a question of a common stem. According to St. Paul, Israel is still "the

---

Herder/London: Burns & Oates, 1969), pp. 1-137 is particularly helpful in bringing out in fine detail the evolving debate on the topic during the Council. This context is essential to an exegesis of the text that is faithful to both the spirit of the Council and the decree itself.

19. Antoine Wenger, *Vatican II, Chronique de la Deuxième Session* (Paris: Editions du Centurion, 1964), p. 175.

true olive tree" into which we are grafted "contrary to nature." The "natural branches" are summoned to return to life (Rom 11:17-25).

2. There is a unity of goal and predestination. Israel is still the chosen people and "all Israel will be saved" (Rom 11:26, 32, etc.).
3. The split between Israel and the Church — which is, in any case, only partial — is nothing but a detour, an unnatural situation which at the deepest level forms part of the mystery of salvation and contributes to its realization (see St. Paul: Rom 11:14, 18-22, 30-31).
4. There is a deep solidarity and even a certain unity between Israel and the Church in their expectation of unity at the end of time. Christ has made Jews and Gentiles one "and has broken down the dividing wall of hostility . . . that he might create in himself one new man in place of the two" (Eph 2:14-15).[20]

In spite of this eloquent theological argumentation, the Council's Secretariat opted to produce a third draft as an appendix to the schema on Ecumenism. The draft acknowledged the beginnings of the church's faith in the patriarchs and the prophets, and that the church, though a new creation in Christ, continued God's covenant with Israel. Stressing the need to be careful not to misrepresent the Jewish people as accursed or deicidal, and the consequent imperative of avoiding anything that might ignite hatred toward them, the draft laid, according to John Oester-reicher, "a solid framework . . . , but only a framework. It lacked any links with Pauline theology."[21]

It fell to Cardinal Bea to introduce the draft to the Council fathers. He did so on September 25, 1964. "He began by saying that no other schema had so held the public in suspense and been so much written about. The interest was so deep that one could well say that many would judge the Council by the stand it took on this question."[22] What particularly worried the cardinal was the fact that the new draft still received bad press. The issues of deicide and of the eventual eschatological union of Israel and the church were going to cause much soul-searching both within and without the aula. The attendant difficulties in dealing with the misconceptions that threatened the Declaration from many quarters became the occasion of

20. R. Laurentin, *Bilan de la Deuxième Session* (Paris: Seuil, 1964), p. 150, as quoted in Vorgrimler, vol. 3, p. 52.
21. Oesterreicher, p. 60.
22. Oesterreicher, p. 62.

quality speeches on the twenty-eighth and twenty-ninth of that same September. They deserve our attention if we are to appreciate both the tone and the caliber of the emergent thought.

These speeches began with a statement from the German bishops' conference. "We German bishops welcome the Council's Decree on the Jews. If the Church in Council makes a statement concerning her own nature, she cannot fail to mention her connection with God's people of the Old Covenant. . . . We are conscious of the grave injustice done to the Jews in the name of our own people."[23] Cardinal Meyer of Chicago went to St. Thomas Aquinas for his insight in relation to the charge of "deicide."

> Is it not much more our duty in this connection to present the fullness of truth concerning the Jews, in the spirit of St. Thomas (*Summa Theologica*, III, q. 47, a. 5 ad c.)? . . . Following the teaching of Scripture, St. Thomas brings out these two points: (1) No single individual Jew of Christ's time was guilty, formally or subjectively, of deicide, since all acted in ignorance of Christ's divinity. That must be said explicitly in our text. (2) The bulk of the Jews should be acquitted of any formal guilt because they followed their leaders out of ignorance. As a proof of this, St. Thomas refers to St. Peter: "I know that you acted in ignorance" (Acts 3:17). Finally, it must also be said where the real guilt for the torments of Christ lies — "He died for us and for our salvation"![24]

It is surely legitimate to read in these interventions a new awakening among the bishops of the church to revealed dimensions of the church's being and, specifically, the relationship obtaining in the divine plan between the people of the first covenant and the people of the first and second covenants. "What is new is especially the statement that the Declaration on the Jews belongs essentially to the Church's self-realization, which was the principal task of Vatican II."[25]

This produces a stronger theological setting for the fourth draft. The expanding of the Declaration to include all the non-Christian religions shows indeed the importance of the subject in itself even as it now has to abandon all hope of inclusion in the Decree on Ecumenism. This fourth draft will include the Pauline teaching according to which the rejection of Jesus by a large part of Israel does not annihilate its special vocation. "It

23. Oesterreicher, p. 68.
24. Oesterreicher, pp. 70-71.
25. Oesterreicher, p. 96

continues to be the people loved and called by God. Thus it necessarily occupies a special place in the eschatological hope of the Church."[26] In presenting the new draft Cardinal Bea stressed the importance of the Declaration with the words, "What is at stake is to acknowledge the saving counsel of God and his benefactions, to condemn without exception hatred and injustice and to avoid them in the future. . . . No Council in the history of the Church, unless I am mistaken, has ever set out so solemnly the principles concerning them [non-Christian religions]. . . . We are dealing with more than a thousand million men who have never heard of, or never recognized Christ."[27]

Although the vote of the bishops was overwhelmingly in support, a new wave of opposition to the very idea of the Declaration appeared on the horizon. It came from the Middle East. Not even the good results emanating from the pilgrimage of Pope Paul VI to the Holy Land in January 1964 could dampen the vehemence of the reaction that threatened — so it seemed — the very existence of the already vulnerable Christian communities in the Arab lands. It was in this context in May 1965 that a number of bishops made important contributions that were to prove decisive for the unfolding debate. An outstanding instance was the intervention of Bishop Stangl of Würzburg. "The question is always: Has the Church been walking in the way of the children of this world who calculate and follow earthly considerations? . . . It is not only a question of the credibility of the Church but also of her claim to moral leadership."[28] This and similar interventions steeled the bishops, as it were, to proceed according to doctrinal correctness.

As to the delicate matter of "deicide," the Secretariat for Christian Unity opted for the idea behind the word but not for the word itself. Furthermore, the Secretariat was at pains to deny any collective guilt of the Jews for the crucifixion of Jesus. The text proposed and eventually approved in the Council stated the truth of the matter in this fashion: "What happened in Christ's passion cannot be blamed upon all the Jews then living, without distinction, nor upon the Jews of today." The Abbott edition of the texts of the Council in English provides a helpful footnote at this point, "The Secretariat recommended that the word 'deicide' be eliminated from the Christian vocabulary; it has given rise to false theological

26. Oesterreicher, p. 97.
27. Oesterreicher, p. 99.
28. Oesterreicher, p. 110.

interpretations that occasion difficulties in pastoral work and in ecumenical dialogue."[29]

4. The Reception of Vatican II in Postconciliar Ecclesiology

We will focus our attention at this stage on the work of ecclesiologists in Ireland and Britain in order to investigate whether or not they have "received" the teaching of Vatican II in relation to its unprecedented teaching on the Jews. A number of texts since the Council do in fact advert to the teaching of the Council. We will now look at a sample selection. A first text is to be found in a commentary on *Lumen Gentium (LG)* done by a team of Irish theologians three years after the Council and edited by Kevin McNamara, then a professor of dogmatic theology in Maynooth and later bishop of Kerry and archbishop of Dublin. It fell to the archbishop in fact to write the commentary on chapter two, which actually deals with the Jews. The text in *LG* §16, though a "brief statement," still "lays the theological foundation for the Council's Declaration on the same subject."

The truth is that "the Jews have a very special relationship with the Church." Then McNamara lists the foundations of that relationship. God gave this people the "testaments," as St. Paul reminds us (Rom. 9:4-5), and the promises. Furthermore, they enjoy "the incomparable privilege of having given birth to Christ, the founder and the head of the new people of God." As a result, "the grace of God is still active and fruitful among them." God still desires the "corporate acceptance of the kingdom" and that will one day become a reality. All this "invites Christians to repent of the wrongs inflicted on the Jews by Christians in the past." It also invites "Christians to acquire a lively sense of their historical debt to the people of Israel." The Constitution "proposes Christ's own attitude as the only true model for the Christian in his relationship with the Jews."[30]

A more recent Irish text comes from the Irish theologian, Fr. Christopher O'Donnell, O.Carm. In 1996 he published *Ecclesia: An Encyclopedia of Ecclesiology.* This very favorably reviewed study has a significant section titled, "The Church and Judaism."[31] Admitting that the history of the

29. Abbott, *Declaration on Non-Christian Religions,* note 23.

30. Kevin McNamara, ed., *Vatican II: The Constitution on the Church: A Theological and Pastoral Commentary* (London: Geoffrey Chapman, 1968), p. 154.

31. Christopher O'Donnell, *Ecclesia: An Encyclopedia of Ecclesiology* (Collegeville, MN: Liturgical Press, 1996), pp. 230-32.

church's relationship with the Jews is "not a glorious one," O'Donnell contends that "Vatican II spoke very positively about Jews in its Constitution on the Church (*LG* 16)." As for the Declaration on Non-Christian Religions, "its fifteen sentences indicate an irreversible turning point in the Catholic perception of Judaism." O'Donnell lists the facts underpinning the new Catholic perception as follows: "common roots in the covenant; God's gift and call to the Jews is without regret; the death of Jesus cannot be ascribed indiscriminately to all Jews living at the time or to those who came after; Scripture does not support the idea that the Jews are accursed; finally, the Church deplores feelings of hatred, persecutions and demonstrations of anti-Semitism directed against the Jews at whatever time and by whomsoever."[32]

The author highlights the fact that the Declaration has been instrumental in the drawing up of two documents since the Council, designed to implement the teaching of the Council. In 1974 *Guidelines for Implementing* Nostra Aetate made its appearance, while in 1985 there appeared *Notes on the Correct Way to Present Jews.* Some doctrinal points are highlighted. As for the Old Testament, it retains its perpetual value: thus the stance of the church against Marcion in the second century receives further confirmation. For the *Notes,* "the Church and Judaism cannot be seen as two parallel ways of salvation and the Church must witness to Christ as the Redeemer." O'Donnell identifies three areas as of particular importance in Jewish-Christian dialogue. These are the areas of liberation, spirituality, and the messianic, or "Christian Jews," movement.

In 1995 Professor Paul McPartlan, a priest of the Archdiocese of Westminster, London, published *Sacrament of Salvation: An Introduction to Eucharistic Ecclesiology.* The second chapter bears the title "Preparation of the Children of Abraham."[33] The author makes much of the Augustinian principle of the mutual indwelling of the Old and New Covenants, *"Novum in vetere latet, vetus in novo patet"* ("The New Testament in the old lies concealed, the old in the new is revealed").[34] He notices that this perception influenced medieval art as evidenced in the breathtakingly beautiful stained-glass windows of Chartres Cathedral, where the thirteenth-century artist

32. O'Donnell, *Ecclesia,* pp. 230-31.

33. Paul McPartlan, *Sacrament of Salvation: An Introduction to Eucharistic Ecclesiology* (Edinburgh: T. & T. Clark, 1995), pp. 14-29.

34. St. Augustine, *Questiones in Heptateuchum* 2, 73: PL 34,623; text quoted in Vatican II, *Dei Verbum,* §16; McPartlan, *Sacrament of Salvation,* draws our attention to further patristic sources in Henri de Lubac.

vividly depicts the links between the four evangelists and the four major prophets of the first covenant. McPartlan stresses that "it is important to see that the Old does not thereby become redundant; it is not cast off now that the New has come. On the contrary, *it remains as an indispensable preparation for the New*."[35]

The eminent English Dominican, Fr. Aidan Nichols, published in 1996 a text on Catholicism bearing the title *Epiphany: A Theological Introduction to Catholicism*.[36] While there is no reference to the Jews in the chapter dealing with the church, he dedicates the concluding chapter to the relationship of the church to the other religions. He turns to *Nostra Aetate* for the good reason that "while statements of this relationship are to be found scattered among individual Church Fathers and theologians, it has not previously come to expression at a theological 'place' so important as an ecumenical council."[37] Nichols stresses the fact that, following the Council, "we must begin with *Judaism*, the Church's own root and mother." He directs our attention to the fact of the loss of the Hebrew Christians in the *Catholica*. Had the Hebrew Christians survived, "the universal Church would have included . . . communities especially devoted to the meaning and observance of the Jewish ancestors of the Christian way." In other words, we would know the true meaning of Judaism *in and for* the church, especially since "there is a special inwardness or intimacy in the ways that Jews live with the Hebrew Bible and the other literature that made, or reflects, the world of the Gospels."[38]

Nichols stresses that "Judaism is not in the fullest sense a different religion from Christianity." This means that "there can be . . . such a thing as 'Hebrew Catholics,' Jews who have entered the church but with every intention of maintaining their Jewish heritage intact. They insist with Paul that 'God has not rejected his people whom he foreknew,' for 'the gifts and call of God are irrevocable' (Rom 11:29)." It has to follow that a simple supersessionist account of the church's relationship to Judaism is untenable. To opt for this would be "to ignore the tragic sense of loss, breathed in by so many pages of the New Testament, at Israel's failure to recognize the Christ." If "Judaism is not in the fullest sense a dif-

35. McPartlan, *Sacrament of Salvation*, p. 14. Emphasis added.

36. Aidan Nichols, *Epiphany: A Theological Introduction to Catholicism* (Collegeville, MN: Liturgical Press, 2006).

37. Nichols, *Epiphany*, p. 456.

38. Nichols, *Epiphany*, p. 460.

ferent religion from Christianity," then "a Catholic Christian can only be a qualified supersessionist."[39]

In 2007 Fr. Nichols published *Lovely Like Jerusalem,* whose subtitle is "The Fulfillment of the Old Testament in Christ and in the Church."[40] The topic is directly related to our inquiry. In his final chapter, he provides what he calls "A Thomist Finale: Thomas Aquinas on the Torah." There he expounds St. Thomas's treatise on the Old Law, which is "the longest of any in the *Summa theologiae.*"[41] Stressing the timeliness of Thomas's anti-Marcionite teaching even for our times, Nichols shows how Thomas used the categories of causality of Aristotle. "St. Paul declared in Romans, 'Christ is the end of the Law' (10:4). Consonant with the patristic interpretation of scripture, Thomas understands this to mean that Christ is the *goal* of the Law, taking 'goal' there in the strong Aristotelian sense — once more — (as) a final cause. Christ, the Messiah of God, is what the Law is ultimately *for.*"[42] For Thomas, the Torah spells out the precise "moral," "ceremonial," and "judicial" responsibilities of the Israelite, but "not just as any man but, more than that, as a *member of the people of the coming Messiah.*"[43] Nichols concludes, quoting the American Thomist scholar Matthew Levering, "In recognizing that Israel prefigures Christ, one does not therefore dismiss Israel as a reality in itself. Rather, as Aquinas explains, each aspect of Israel's history takes on importance in a way that no other ancient people's does."[44]

Throughout the volume Professor Nichols draws very often on an early work of Hans Urs von Balthasar called *Martin Buber and Christianity.* Prophetical for its time, this work had the purpose of opening a dialogue with Judaism even before Vatican II and through engagement with one of Judaism's most renowned philosopher-theologians. For Balthasar, "Israel's innermost nature implies a Christology."[45] But what is conspicuous by its

---

39. Nichols, *Epiphany,* p. 461.

40. Aidan Nichols, *Lovely Like Jerusalem: The Fulfillment of the Old Testament in Christ and the Church* (San Francisco: Ignatius Press, 2007).

41. Nichols, *Lovely Like Jerusalem,* p. 263. It is to be read in the *Summa Theologiae* at Ia IIae, qq. 98-105.

42. Nichols, *Lovely Like Jerusalem,* p. 266; italics in the original.

43. Nichols, *Lovely Like Jerusalem,* p. 268; italics in the original.

44. Matthew Levering, *Christ's Fulfillment of Torah and Temple: Salvation According to Thomas Aquinas* (Notre Dame: University of Notre Dame Press, 2002), p. 27.

45. Hans Urs von Balthasar, *Martin Buber and Christianity* (London: Harvill Press, 1961), p. 78.

very absence is any reference in this work of Nichols to either *Lumen Gentium* §16 or to *Nostra Aetate*. There is always positive reference to Israel and to the first covenant, but the surprise is that the more enterprising teaching of the Council is not mentioned in spite of its acknowledged importance. And with the omission of that teaching there is no significant theological engagement with the relevant Pauline teaching.

5. Conclusion

This investigation set out to study certain ecclesiological developments in the ecclesiology of Vatican II, particularly those concerning the place of Israel and the Jewish people in the mystery of the church of Jesus Christ. The concluding section looked at the reception of these breakthroughs in a sample of Irish and British theologians. In pursuit of this goal, we first looked at the standard ecclesiology actually taught in third-level treatises during the decades leading up to the Council. We then looked at the Council and discovered how this great stirring of hearts and minds engaged most creatively with the *ressourcement* that had been going on for almost one hundred years in Catholic theology but had had little or no influence on the ecclesiology taught in the schools during that time. This required some engagement, in a second moment, with the actual debate during the Council. The "order of invention" in that debate, protracted as we have seen over three of the four sessions of the Council, led to an "order of doctrine" of exceptional historical worth and theological significance.

Current scholarship in ecumenism and in New Testament studies has taken up and continued the conciliar insight. Thus Franz Mussner, the renowned New Testament exegete, stresses the fact that for the New Testament in general, and for Paul in particular, the churches "are inseparably and forever linked with Israel."[46] Following Mussner, Professor Hans Hermann Henrix takes up the concept of *sugkoinonos* ("co-participant") as deployed by Paul in Romans 11:17. He sees in this concept a ready tool to articulate the subtle but divinely intended rapport of the church and Israel. It expresses the nearness as well as the distance, otherness, and foreignness of Israel with respect to the church. It provides a kind of herme-

---

46. Franz Mussner, "Was haben die Juden mit der christlichen Ökumene zu tun?" *Una Sancta* 50 (1995): 333ff.

neutic, highlighting the Israel-church relationship as a singular instance of "the nearness of the different."[47]

The depth of the breakthrough in *Lumen Gentium* and *Nostra Aetate* must rank as an instance of that development of the "tradition which comes from the apostles." The Constitution on Divine Revelation continues, "For there is a growth in the understanding of the realities and the words which have been handed down. This happens through the contemplation and study made by believers, who treasure these things in their hearts (cf. Luke 2:19, 51), through the intimate understanding of spiritual things they experience, and through the preaching of those who have received through episcopal succession the sure gift of truth."[48] The achievements of *LG* and *NA* are enough to show that Vatican II was a great *theological* event also in relation to the relation of Jews and Christians. It is a fine illustration of Newman's principle that "theology is the fundamental and regulating principle of the whole Church system," being as it is "commensurate with revelation," as we have seen. For the Council articulated something largely untouched over two millennia, namely, an understanding of the mysterious abiding role of the Jews in the mystery of the church of Christ. An *Ecclesia ex circumcisione* and an *Ecclesia ex gentibus* (church from the circumcised, church from among the Gentiles) has received a surprising currency via an authentic development and not via rupture with the past.[49]

In the final section we looked at the reception of the conciliar teaching. Two distinguished ecclesiologists in Britain and two in Ireland did indeed acknowledge the teaching. Still, their acknowledgment needs to be built on by way of further theological elaboration in both theological terrains. As Pope John Paul II wrote in his Post-Synodal Apostolic Exhortation, *Ecclesia in Europa*, in June 2003, "there is need for acknowledgment of the common roots linking Christianity and the Jewish people, who *are called by God to a covenant which remains irrevocable (cf. Rom 11:29) and has attained definitive fullness in Christ.* Consequently, it is necessary to encourage dialogue with Judaism, knowing that it is fundamentally impor-

---

47. Hans Hermann Henrix, "Schweigen im Angesicht Israels? Zum Ort des Jüdischen in der ökumenischen Theologie," in Gerhard Langer and Gregor Maria Hoff, eds., *Der Ort des Jüdischen in der katholischen Theologie* (Göttingen: Vandenhoeck & Ruprecht, 2009), pp. 264-97.

48. Vatican II, *Dei Verbum*, §8, Abbott edition.

49. Perhaps the hermeneutic of rupture when set over against that of development-in-continuity has contributed to the slow adoption of the conciliar teaching.

tant for *the self-knowledge of Christians* and for the transcending of divisions between the Churches."[50] Theology in these islands now has the noble, but challenging, task of receiving the baton handed to it and then running for the glory of the God of Abraham, Isaac, Jacob, and Jesus the Lord and Christ (Acts 2:36).

50. Pope John Paul II, *Ecclesia in Europa,* June 2003, n. 56; italics added.

The Affirmation of Jewish Covenantal Vitality and the Church's Liturgical Life

Liam Tracey, O.S.M.

1. Introduction

Sometimes when liturgists get nostalgic about the reforms of the Second Vatican Council, they speculate about what might have happened differently. What if the Constitution on the Sacred Liturgy had come later in the work of the Council? What if it had come after the groundbreaking Constitutions on the Church and on Divine Revelation? What effects might a later placement in the Council's agenda have had? Might some of the unresolved questions that have troubled the reform in the nearly forty-five years since the Council's end have found a solution? It is hard to know and probably futile to indulge in such daydreaming. Of course, for all the writers of this book, *Nostra Aetate (NA)* is a key Council document. Yet I confess I have never heard liturgists wondering about this document's impact on the Constitution on the Liturgy. This is most unfortunate: there is no doubt that a greater awareness of the affirmations of *NA* could have enabled those who engaged in the reform of the liturgical books and those who authored books on liturgical renewal to move in a direction that acknowledged the ongoing vitality of Judaism and avoided some of the later pitfalls that will be discussed in this essay.

My own view is that the Constitution on the Liturgy would not have been very much different, as it represents a highpoint of the modern Liturgical Movement, a place of arrival and not so much one of departure.[1] It is

---

1. For a readable account of the modern Liturgical Movement, see John R. K. Fenwick and Bryan D. Spinks, *Worship in Transition: The Liturgical Movement in the Twentieth Century* (Edinburgh: T. & T. Clark, 1995).

for the Roman Catholic liturgy a summary of the work of several generations of liturgists, who sought to establish the theological nature of the liturgy and to locate the liturgical celebration at the heart of the life of the
church. In essence, they desired to show that liturgy was more than out-
ward ceremonial, or a science of rubrical concerns; rather, it is at the very
center of what it is to be church, a community of believers. Because it was
the first document of the Council, it is perhaps more inward looking than
other later documents. Certainly, its radical christocentric emphasis may
even border on christomonism, which was then carried over into many of
the general introductions to the reformed liturgical books.[2] As liturgists
have often noted, what is lacking is a coherent discourse on the role of the
Spirit in the celebration of the liturgy.[3] It is not at all clear that the reformed liturgical books have taken this critique seriously. Perhaps it may
even present a very high theology of the liturgy, but it is useful to recall the
context in which it was born and the battles that it sought to quell. A central thesis of this essay is that the liturgy can be mobilized as a power for
good or to communicate messages of denigration of others.

At the basis of my chapter is the assumption that the promulgation of
NA inaugurated a new era in the relationship between Judaism and the Roman Catholic Church. The various documents that have followed that
groundbreaking statement have sought to expand and deepen that new
openness. In speaking about the impact of *NA* and subsequent documents
on the liturgy, it is important to distinguish a number of different terms. In

2. The important General Introduction to the Lectionary for Mass is an example in
point; in §5 we read: "When in celebrating the liturgy the Church proclaims both the Old
and New Testament, it is proclaiming the one and the same mystery of Christ. The New Testament lies hidden in the Old; the Old Testament comes fully to light in the New. Christ
himself is the centre and fullness of all of Scripture; as he is of the entire liturgy. Thus the
Scriptures are the living waters from which all who seek life and salvation must drink. The
more profound our understanding of the liturgical celebration, the higher our appreciation
of the importance of God's word. Whatever we say of the one, we can in turn say of the
other, because each recalls the mystery of Christ and each in its own way causes the mystery
to be ever present." *Lectionary I* (Dublin: Veritas/London: Geoffrey Chapman, 1981), p. 2. See
also http://www.liturgyoffice.org.uk/Resources/Rites/Lectionary.pdf. A link with the work
of the Spirit of God in this number would help avoid what for some may be a promise/ful-
fillment approach to the Two Testaments. I do accept that the Spirit is mentioned further on
in the introduction.

3. Paradoxically, one of the strengths of the liturgy section of the *Catechism of the Cath-
olic Church* is its treatment of the role of the Holy Spirit in the celebration of the liturgy; see
Regis Duffy, *The Liturgy in the Catechism: Celebrating God's Wisdom and Love* (London:
Geoffrey Chapman, 1995), pp. 49-52.

particular, it is important to be clear on what is meant by the word *liturgy*. It is also vital to probe what implications would follow for the church's liturgical celebrations if the teaching of *NA* were to be taken seriously.[4]

In discussing liturgy it is useful to keep a number of distinctions or layers of understanding in mind. The first layer is a *theology of liturgy*, an overarching view of how liturgy is understood in the life of the Christian community. A theology of liturgy intersects with the doctrine of God, christology, ecclesiology, and relationships between Christianity and the world. Related to these areas of study are notions of salvation history, and covenant, both often cast in terms of promise and fulfillment with a christocentric focus. A second layer involves the impact on the *rites and prayers* of the church — what some traditions of Christianity call sacraments: the organization of time and the movements of seasons and feasts, the symbols used in the celebration, the nonverbal elements of the liturgy, and the use of music in the liturgical celebration. Still another layer concerns how *NA* and subsequent documents have impacted the *teaching of liturgy* in our theological faculties and seminaries. A fourth layer concerns *pastoral liturgy*, including what liturgical aids, especially for homily preparation, say about Jews and Judaism.[5] Pastoral practice itself also needs to be carefully examined. For example, the common practice of holding the Liturgy of the Word at the Easter Vigil in semi-darkness and only turning on the lights for the singing of the Gloria and the reading of Paul communicates something even when we are not aware of it.[6] This notion of liturgy

---

4. While the focus of this essay is the Roman Catholic liturgy, much of what is explored here can be applied to other Christian worship traditions. For a useful introduction, see Gail Ramshaw, *Christian Worship: 100,000 Sundays of Symbols and Rituals* (Minneapolis: Fortress Press, 2009).

5. The complex and multilayered nature of liturgy has been well expressed by Mary C. Boys, *Has God Only One Blessing? Judaism as a Source of Christian Self-Understanding* (New York: Paulist Press, 2000), p. 199: "Worship forms our Christian identity in powerful ways. The prayers we say, the psalms we chant, the hymns we sing, the texts we hear, the rituals we perform, the community that surrounds us, and the sacred space created — all these shape us profoundly. What ritual expresses is, as it were, 'impressed' upon those who participate in it. The more central a ritual is to a community's life, the more formative an influence it exercises."

6. J. Frank Henderson has noted in his essay, "Current Catholic Liturgical Options vis-à-vis Jews and Judaism": "In addition, the passages from the Hebrew Scriptures are read in relative darkness. After they have been proclaimed, 'the altar candles are lighted [and more lights often are turned on], and the priest intones the Glory to God, which is taken up by all present. The church bells are rung, according to local custom' [rubric of the sacramentary]. What messages are communicated by these nonverbal elements?" http://www.jfrankhenderson.com/pdf/currentoptions.pdf. Cf. "The Introduction to the *Lectionary for Mass*," which has

as practice is a crucial one. Whereas liturgy refers to the text and the book, what most worshipers experience and participate in is a liturgical celebration, which to a lesser or greater extent puts the ritual book into practice. Because of the power of liturgy to shape the world of the believing community and even beyond its confines, it is crucial to examine how it shapes our perception of "others" and in this case how it shapes the perception Roman Catholics have of Jews and Judaism.[7]

Each one of these levels of understanding can be further divided into the understandings of the worshiping community, the individual worshiper, the magisterial authority of a community at local and universal levels, and how the tradition of this community has understood the liturgical celebration.

Liturgy is central to the formation of a Christian; it is deeply significant in the formation of our Christian identity. It can be and is often deeply conservative, that is, it resists change. Many tend to regard liturgy as an unchanging expression of tradition, seeing it as a stable place in a changing world that brings uncertainty and confusion. They do not like their liturgy tampered with by these experts! Those charged with liturgical reform have not always been sensitive to this. Liturgy is rational but also deeply transrational. Liturgy takes place in time and space, but also changes and re-

---

the following comment: "On the holy night of the Easter Vigil there are seven Old Testament readings, recalling the wonderful works of God in the history of salvation" (§4a). In the same essay, Henderson asks: "The question is what is meant by salvation history? Does it recognize that Judaism has an ongoing living tradition since the birth of Christianity? It certainly seems to be open to supersessionist tendencies."

7. J. Frank Henderson, "Current Catholic Liturgical Options," writes about this perceptively, when he notes: "Furthermore, 'popular theology' is particularly influential during Advent, perhaps more so than the church's liturgy. There is Handel's Messiah, with its pastiche of passages from the Hebrew and Christian Scriptures, great artistic beauty and cultural popularity. There are the omnipresent Christmas (and Advent) carols, some of which are explicitly supersessionist and many of which use images of darkness and light to convey an implicit supersessionism. There are the common simplifications of Advent theology for children which tend to diminish the element of the future coming of Christ and the 'already but not yet' character of the incarnation. There are traditional messianic interpretations of the Hebrew Scriptures that seem to be embedded in our culture. There are the views and practices of other churches, which may be quite happy with supersessionism." The trouble is exacerbated with the disappearance of Advent from popular culture and now it is Christmas from sometime in October. One could also add concerns about some of the popular liturgical usages in the Advent season, the use of the Jesse Tree and some of the commentaries that accompany the use of the Advent wreath and calendar, which cast the story of salvation in a crude supersessionist mode.

names these spaces and times. It engages the head but also the heart, and thus any change in buildings or prayers or postures can evoke emotional responses. Changing the configuration of worship space, for example, frequently causes controversy.

2. The Liturgy and Documents of the *Nostra Aetate* Trajectory

Among the authoritative statements coming from Rome dealing with the impact of *NA* is the document titled *Guidelines and Suggestions for Implementing the Conciliar Declaration* Nostra Aetate *(no. 4),* published by the Secretariat for Christian Unity in 1975.[8] In the section dealing with liturgy, the document recalls the common bond existing between the Christian liturgy and the Jewish liturgy, which sees liturgy as a twofold activity — the service of God and the service of humanity out of love for God. This service is rendered effective in the celebration of the liturgy. Common elements in both traditions are noted and a special, indeed an essential place, is given to the Bible. Catholics are urged to understand that the "Old" Testament retains a "perpetual" value: "An effort will be made to acquire a better understanding of whatever in the Old Testament retains its own perpetual value (cf. *Dei Verbum,* §§14-15), since that has not been canceled by the later interpretation of the New Testament."

The section on liturgy in *Guidelines and Suggestions* has a brief paragraph on the preparation of translations of the Bible. While emphasizing that the text of the Bible cannot be altered, translations prepared for liturgical use should be concerned with bringing out the meaning of the text in its context. For example, while John's Gospel frequently speaks of "the Jews," in context the term may mean "the leaders of the Jews" or "adversaries of Jesus." Translators should avoid denigrating the Jews as a people.

Of particular concern, of course, is the homily, that is, how preachers break open the Word of God for their congregations, especially when they are dealing with difficult biblical texts. In the 2001 Instruction from the Congregation for Divine Worship, *Liturgiam Authenticam,* the Congrega-

---

8. I have taken the section dealing with the liturgy from the standard collection of liturgical documents, International Commission on English in the Liturgy, *Documents on the Liturgy 1963-1979: Conciliar, Papal, and Curial Texts* (Collegeville, MN: Liturgical Press, 1982), §1064. *Guidelines and Suggestions* was published by the Secretariat for Christian Unity (Commission for Religious Relations with the Jews), dated December 1, 1974, and published in January 1975.

tion for Divine Worship instructs: "Similarly, it is the task of catechists or of the homilist to transmit that right interpretation of the texts that excludes any prejudice or unjust discrimination on the basis of persons, gender, social condition, race or other criteria, which has no foundation at all in the texts of the Sacred Liturgy."[9] Surely this task is also directed to those who prepare commentaries on the readings, write the prayer of the faithful, or prepare general worship aids for the use of the Sunday assembly.[10]

In 1985, the Commission for Religious Relations with the Jews published a document titled *Notes on the Correct Way to Present the Jews and Judaism in Preaching and Catechesis in the Roman Catholic Church*. The liturgy is mentioned in two articles of these *Notes*. Again the Bible as used in Christian and Jewish celebrations is placed at the center of the discussion on the liturgy. Passover is seen as a common celebration of Jews and Christians,[11] and the concept of "memorial," while different in content, is seen as having a similar dynamism, linking past, present, and future. One wonders how this squares with the exclusion of readings from the Hebrew Bible during Eastertide and reading some of the more controversial passages from the Acts of the Apostles during this season.[12]

---

9. As others have noted, *Liturgiam Authenticam* seems to be particularly unaware of the impact of *NA* on how the liturgy is understood in the context of the Christian-Jewish encounter. It reiterates a christological and unified reading of the scriptures. A similar criticism can be leveled at the liturgical section of the *Catechism of the Catholic Church*, which has been characterized by some liturgists as overtly typological and supersessionist in its approach to the liturgy.

10. I have taken this section of *LA* §29 from the Vatican website: http://www.vatican.va/roman_curia/congregations/ccdds/documents/rc_con_ccdds_doc_20010507_liturgiam-authenticam_en.html. The Guidelines of 1975 state clearly that "The preceding remarks (about the Homily) also apply to introductions to biblical readings, to the Prayer of the Faithful, and to commentaries printed in missals used by the laity."

11. The *Notes* state: "This is particularly evident in the great feasts of the liturgical year, like the Passover. Christians and Jews celebrate the Passover: the Jews, the historic Passover looking towards the future; the Christians, the Passover accomplished in the death and resurrection of Christ, although still in expectation of the final consummation (cf. supra §9). It is still the 'memorial' which comes to us from the Jewish tradition, with a specific content different in each case. On either side, however, there is a like dynamism: for Christians it gives meaning to the eucharistic celebration (cf. the antiphon *'O sacrum convivium'*), a paschal celebration and as such a making present of the past, but experienced in the expectation of what is to come" (§24). See http://www.vatican.va/roman_curia/pontifical_councils/chrstuni/relations-jews-docs/rc_pc_chrstuni_doc_19820306_jews-judaism_en.html.

12. For instance, during the Third Week of Easter the readings are from the homily of Peter on the Feast of Pentecost and the martyrdom of Stephen (Acts 2 and 7).

To these two important documents, one should add that of the Pontifical Biblical Commission, *The Jewish People and Their Sacred Scriptures in the Christian Bible* of 2001. Although it does not focus specifically on the liturgy, nevertheless, much of what is discussed in that document has a direct influence on the liturgy, since interpretation of Scripture is fundamental to the church's liturgical life. A central issue for this discussion is the role of Scripture. How is Scripture used in the worship of the church? What readings are chosen for use and how are readings from the Hebrew Bible used along with readings from the New Testament?

3. Issues with the Lectionary

Until recently, scholars had confined their attention to the Sunday lectionary, with perhaps a cursory glance at the *Lectionary for Weekdays*.[13] Scholars rightly pay attention to the Sunday lectionary because it is the one most familiar to worshipers. Liturgists are commonly agreed that this lectionary still requires further revision.[14] Especially important is the way the first reading (typically from the Hebrew Bible) is interpreted; now it typically functions as a proof-text or a crude promise/fulfillment reading, especially during Ordinary Time.[15] Two issues are important here: (1) for

13. For a helpful survey of this issue, see Michael Peppard, "Do We Share a Book? The Sunday Lectionary and Jewish-Christian Relations," in *Studies in Christian-Jewish Relations* 1 (2005): 89-102. This e-journal can be accessed at http: //escholarship.bc.edu/scjr/vol1/iss1/art9.

14. Of particular concern is the way in which the three readings on a Sunday are placed together. As has been noted by liturgical scholars, there is little support for this position in the liturgical tradition; see Adrian Nocent, "The Roman Lectionary for Mass," in *The Eucharist: Handbook for Liturgical Studies III*, ed. Anscar J. Chupungco (Collegeville, MN: Liturgical Press, 1999), p. 183: "The starting point for choosing the readings was the choice of gospel. In other words, beginning with the gospel pericopes, the council fathers wished to choose corresponding readings. They wished to restore the ancient practice of three readings for Sundays and feasts: from the Old Testament, from the writings of the apostles and from the gospel. But they meant to choose so as to create a certain link among the readings. This desire cannot be supported by tradition. We know that, except in a few special cases, the book of readings and the book of Gospels were composed independently."

15. I have already mentioned earlier in this paper some of the problems associated with the Easter season. This is not to ignore preoccupations with the seasons of Advent and Lent, ably shown by J. Frank Henderson. The selection of readings for the Sundays of Lent seems to follow a particular view of salvation history, whereas the use of Isaiah in Advent follows a rather crude promise/fulfillment motif. He writes: "Finally, it may be suggested that, at the

the first time in many centuries Roman Catholics are reading in the celebration of the Eucharist from the Hebrew Bible; (2) there is an increasing call in some parts of the Roman Catholic world to return to two readings on a Sunday. The rationale for this second issue seems to involve the length of the readings; alternatively, it is often claimed that the people do not understand them. Were such calls to be heeded, it would inevitably lead to the dropping of the first reading. This would lead us back to the situation before the liturgical reforms of Vatican II, where many Catholics never heard the Hebrew Bible proclaimed in their liturgical celebrations.

Because of the central role of scripture in the liturgy and beyond, its uses and abuses have tended to be the central focus in any discussion of liturgy in the Jewish-Christian encounter. That it is indeed crucial is not to be doubted, but it can mean that other elements of the liturgy are overlooked, elements that need reflection and discussion. The scriptures are held in a liturgical context; indeed within the Roman Catholic context, it is the lectionary and its hermeneutics that shape many believers' view of the scripture.[16] Roman Catholics have a liturgical Bible that is surrounded with rituals and words, prayers and movements, all of which enrich and interpret that scriptural Word.[17] Some attention has been paid to preach-

---

popular level, some passages from the Hebrew Scriptures have simply been 'christianized.' That is, their source, biblical context and Jewish use have been forgotten and they are treated as if they were part of the Christian Scriptures. This category would seem to include the suffering servant passages of Isaiah and the prophetic passages associated with Advent and Christmas." See "Current Catholic Liturgical Options," http://www.jfrankhenderson.com/pdf/currentoptions.pdf.

16. Andrew D. Ciferni, "Scripture in the Liturgy," in *The New Dictionary of Sacramental Worship*, ed. Peter E. Fink (Dublin: Gill & Macmillan, 1990), p. 1146: "The ordering of pericopes employed in the celebration of the church year is itself an interpretive element — even before the act of preaching. Moreover, the assignment of particular pericopes, their use in relationship to others, the chapters and verses chosen or omitted and their employment in conjunction with various liturgical actions or objects is rooted in the hermeneutical stances of the arrangers of the lectionary and the redactors of the liturgical rites." The relationship between the lectionary and the shaping of time is an important one to note; the readings chosen for a particular season or feast color how that time is lived by the worshiper.

17. One liturgical book that has been overlooked by scholars in this field — one that I believe is deeply problematic — is the *Collection of Masses of the Blessed Virgin Mary* of 1986; see *Collection of Masses of the Blessed Virgin Mary, Volume 1: Sacramentary* (New York: Catholic Book Company, 1999). I find this problematic in that the biblical readings used for these Masses of the Blessed Virgin Mary in the accompanying lectionary also contain readings from the Hebrew Bible, a departure from post–Vatican II practice, we note in the *General Introduction* 39: "Within this biblical corpus it is possible to distinguish three types of read-

ing and music, especially hymnody. What has not been examined in any real way are the prayers of the liturgy and how liturgy is taught. The recent controversy over the Good Friday prayer written by Pope Benedict XVI has shown us how prayer texts can become points of dispute and even lead to rupture between Jewish and Roman Catholic dialogue partners.[18] In this part of the paper I would like to focus on these two elements: how liturgy is taught and some official liturgical prayers.

In examining some current work on this topic, I note with some concern how Keith F. Pecklers deals with the issue of the origins of Christian liturgy. Pecklers, an American Jesuit who teaches at both the Pontifical Gregorian University and the Pontifical Liturgical Institute, is the author of the volume *Worship* in the popular New Century Theology series published by Continuum.[19] In dealing with the development and decline of Christian liturgy, he has a section titled "The Apostolic Period," where we read the following: "Since Christianity emerged from Judaism, it follows logically that the origins of Christian worship are to be found within Jewish cult. A defining moment was the destruction of the Jerusalem temple in 70 C.E. which brought with it the end of sacrificial worship of the old covenant."[20]

This seems at best a simplistic reading of Christian origins, offering lit-

---

ings: (a) readings from both the Old and New Testaments that relate to the life or mission of the Blessed Virgin or that contain prophecies about her; (b) readings from the Old Testament that from antiquity have been applied to Mary. The Fathers of the Church have always regarded the Sacred Scriptures of both the Old and the New Covenant as a single corpus that is permeated by the mystery of Christ. Accordingly certain events, figures, or symbols of the Old Testament foretell or suggest in a wonderful manner the life and mission of the Blessed Virgin Mary, the glorious daughter of Zion and mother of Christ." Section B of this number seems to me to fall in the worst kind of promise/fulfillment reading of the Hebrew scriptures and a kind of proof-text reading of these events. Certainly words like events, figures, and symbols recall a typological reading. Not all typological readings are supersessionist, but they must be used with care and nuanced; see the useful discussion by Mary Boys in her study of typology and the liturgy, Boys, *Has God Only One Blessing?* pp. 219-22.

18. Hans Hermann Henrix, "The Controversy Surrounding the 2008 Good Friday Prayer in Europe: The Discussion and Its Theological Implications," in *Studies in Christian-Jewish Relations* 3 (2008). This article can be accessed at http://escholarship.bc.edu/scjr/vol3/iss1/24/. While attention has focused on the Good Friday prayer, the wider restoration of the 1962 ritual books envisaged by Pope Benedict XVI in *Summorum Pontificum* also needs further consideration and study.

19. Keith F. Pecklers, *Worship,* New Century Theology series (London/New York: Continuum, 2003).

20. Pecklers, *Worship,* p. 34.

tle nuance on the complex world of first-century Judaism(s) and the Jesus movement. Nor does it remind readers that the ongoing relationship and separation between Christianity and Judaism went on in some places for several centuries and in many places well after 100 c.e.[21] The New Testament is clear that the earliest followers of Jesus did not reject the Temple or its worship (e.g., Acts 3:1).[22] For many, the characterization of the covenant as "old" is also deeply problematic. To be fair to Pecklers, he does note later on in this section: "Christianity did not emerge in the first century as what we would today regard as a formal religion: there were no shrines or temples, no sacrifices or public cult, no celebration of public feasts."[23]

He goes on to note the many Jewish elements that were carried into Christian worship, but then notes:

> That being said, we must be careful not to perceive too intimate a relationship between Jewish and Christian liturgical practice. For while early Christians wanted to maintain the traditions of their past, they were also keen to demonstrate how they were ritually different from their spiritual forebears as they had now become followers of Christ. Jesus himself embodies this balance between the old and the new: "I did not come to abolish the law and the prophets but to fulfill them" (Matthew 5:17).[24]

On describing the religious practice of Jesus, Pecklers notes:

> As a faithful Jew, Jesus observed the Sabbath but he was not enslaved to it. True worship necessarily included service of others — even on the Sabbath when Jews were to refrain from all activity, thus his conflict with the Pharisees (Mark 2:27). People and their needs came before any slavish interpretation of the law. Jesus also participated liturgically in the great

21. Boys, *Has God Only One Blessing?* pp. 150-51: "The partings of the way were neither orderly nor sequential. For instance, Mark's Gospel, which most date at approximately 70 c.e., implies more separation from Judaism than do the later Gospels of Matthew and John, whose hostility toward the synagogue indicates their continuing engagement — and argument — with it."

22. For a useful discussion of Jewish worship at the time of Jesus and his first disciples, see Paul F. Bradshaw, *The Search for the Origins of Christian Worship: Sources and Methods for the Study of Early Liturgy*, 2nd ed. (London: SPCK, 2002), pp. 21-46. As Bradshaw notes, there was not just great variety in patterns of early Christian worship but also in that of Judaism.

23. Pecklers, *Worship*, p. 35.

24. Pecklers, *Worship*, p. 34.

feasts of the Jewish liturgical year: Passover (Matt 26:17-19); Pentecost (John 5:1); the Feast of Tabernacles (John 7:10); and the Dedication of the Temple (John 10:23). Jesus also distinguished between worship that was purely ceremonial or superficial, and true worship (and "true worshippers") who worshipped God "in spirit and truth" (John 4:23-24).[25]

Similar sentiments can be found in the influential history of liturgy by the former president of the Pontifical Liturgical Institute, the Filipino Benedictine, Anscar Chupungco, where he concludes his section on the Jewish Roots of Christian Liturgy as follows:

The attitude of critical fidelity should accompany the study of Christian worship. Jesus did not abolish the traditions of his people, though he critiqued them in order to bring them to perfection. And the first disciples kept much of their religious traditions, though they saw in them the foreshadowing of Christ's mystery. The shape of Christian worship which we inherited from the past is part of our tradition, but its human components need always to be critiqued and, if necessary, purified. It can happen that liturgical norms and practices become another form of sabbath that ignores the basic law of love and service and forgets that it has been instituted to respond to human needs.[26]

At least these writers deal with the Jewish roots of Christian worship. Some other standard and respected liturgical histories do not even mention or barely acknowledge the Jewish roots, e.g., Adolf Adam and Robert Cabié.[27] Rarely in histories of liturgy or of the sacraments is Judaism pre-

25. Pecklers, *Worship*, pp. 34-35. This view contrasts with that of Nathan Mitchell, another highly respected liturgist, in his recent study *Meeting Mystery: Liturgy, Worship, Sacraments* (Maryknoll, NY: Orbis, 2006), p. 73, where he notes: "It is true, of course, that in their sacraments, Christians often claim to 'do what Jesus did.' Yet their literature has often presented him as an anti-ritualist who disputed or despised the liturgies of the Temple and synagogue. Recent scholarship, however, resists the conclusion that Jesus' religious attitude was one of anti-ritualism. On the contrary, there is good reason to think that a Jewish male of Jesus' background (the northern Galilean countryside, where the uncomplicated 'basics' of Jewish faith and life were emphasized) would have taken regular participation in the synagogue for granted."

26. Anscar J. Chupungco, "History of Liturgy until the Fourth Century," in Anscar J. Chupungco, ed., *Introduction to the Liturgy: Handbook for Liturgical Studies* 1 (Collegeville, MN: Liturgical Press, 1997), pp. 101-2.

27. Adolf Adam, *Foundations of Liturgy: An Introduction to Its History and Practice* (Collegeville, MN: Liturgical Press, 1992). While this one volume aims to be the standard in-

sented as a living reality beyond the confines of the Christian New Testament and early Christian communities. Jewish prayer formulae and liturgical services are often presented out of context or with no context at all. Allied to this can be the tendency to collapse Jewish feasts and holy days into their Christian "equivalent" and fail to note that these holy days continue to be celebrated by a living community.

4. Issues with the Sacramentary and Liturgy of the Hours

Roman Catholic liturgical worship is a given one; that is, the structure of the liturgical celebration is specified to worshiping assemblies and codified in liturgical books. The scriptural readings are held in the framework that is called the lectionary, and the prayers of a particular liturgy, called the *euchology*, are to be found in the ritual book (sacramentary). These prayers are filled with scriptural citations and allusions and indeed offer a hermeneutic of the scriptures themselves.[28] I would like to examine briefly two

---

troduction to the nature and history of liturgy, there is no sustained introduction to Jewish worship and just some passing references to Judaism.

28. The Italian liturgist and scripture scholar Renato De Zan has noted Scripture being present in liturgy both as an *underlying structure* (signs, symbols, and gestures taken from the scriptures), and as *reformulations* in prayer and as *proclamation* in the Liturgy of the Word; see Renato De Zan, "Bible and Liturgy," in *Introduction to the Liturgy: Handbook for Liturgical Studies 1*, ed. Anscar J. Chupungco (Collegeville, MN: Liturgical Press, 1997), pp. 39-40: "When *Sacrosanctum Concilium* says that the prayers draw their inspiration and their force from Scripture, there is much more to this statement than might appear at first glance. The texts, after all, are made up not only of expressions, sentences, and pericopes. They also have a consequentiality that follows certain logical patterns of structural schemes. Beneath the succession of texts lies a recurring 'model,' an 'archetype,' a 'plan,' an 'example to imitate,' that transforms and orders both the individual prayers and the entire celebration. Indeed, the structure for celebration and the structuring of liturgical texts are derived from certain prayer and celebration schemes that are biblical in nature. The Fundamental structure linking the foundational saving Event to Celebration, Scripture, and Fulfillment, is an overall framework within which every subsequent celebration is inserted and from which it derives meaning. Various elements make up this fundamental structure, the most important being the covenant, the Passover meal, and blessings." Another distinguished Italian liturgist, Enrico Mazza, in his influential book on Eucharistic origins, makes the following remarks regarding typology: "The Old Testament can be used in several ways to shed light on the Christian Eucharist. These ways are reducible to two different methods, the typological and the historical. With the help of the typological method, it can be shown how the old law prefigures the new and, consequently, how the old has its fulfillment in the realities of the New

prayers that refer to the Hebrew Bible and the New Testament. The first is the blessing of water for the celebration of Christian baptism:

Prayer over the Water

Father,
you give us grace through sacramental signs,
which tell us of the wonders of your unseen power.

In baptism we use your gift of water,
which you have made a rich symbol of the grace
you give us in this sacrament.

At the very dawn of creation
your Spirit breathed on the waters,
making them the wellspring of all holiness.

The waters of the great flood
you made a sign of the waters of baptism
that made an end of sin
and a new beginning of goodness.

Through the waters of the Red Sea
you led Israel out of slavery
to be an image of God's holy people,
set free from sin by baptism.

In the waters of the Jordan
your Son was baptized by John
and anointed with the Spirit.

Your Son willed that water and blood should flow from his side
as he hung upon the cross.

Testament. In this perspective, even the eucharistic celebration will be seen as a fulfillment of Old Testament types, such as Melchizedek, the manna, and the various kinds of sacrifice. This method is particularly suited to shedding light on the salvific power of the Eucharist." See Enrico Mazza, *The Celebration of the Eucharist: The Origin of the Rite and the Development of Its Interpretation* (Collegeville, MN: Liturgical Press, 1999), p. 9. The issue of typology is a particularly difficult one as a method of reading scripture, since it has ancient roots; however, when it becomes an allegorical reading, it can become a mere promise/fulfillment reading, which does not acknowledge the ongoing reality of the original text.

After his resurrection he told his disciples:
"Go out and teach all nations,
baptizing them in the name of the Father, and of the Son,
and of the Holy Spirit."

Father,
look now with love upon your church
and unseal for it the fountain of baptism.

By the power of the Holy Spirit
give to this water the grace of your Son,
so that in the sacrament of baptism
all those whom you created in your likeness
may be cleansed from sin
and rise to a new birth of innocence
by water and the Holy Spirit.

The celebrant touches the water with his right hand and continues:

We ask you, Father, with your Son
to send the Holy Spirit upon the waters of this font.

May all who are buried with Christ in the death of baptism
rise also with him to newness of life.

We ask this through Christ our Lord.
Amen.[29]

The three events of the Hebrew Bible are followed by three events from the life of Christ. However, this is not a typological reading. Rather, the natural use of water, scripture, and the meaning of baptism are woven together in a rich tapestry of what Christians understand by baptism.

29. Prayer over the Water, in *Rite of Baptism for Children* (Dublin: Veritas/London: Geoffrey Chapman, 1992), p. 48. For a commentary on this prayer, which is also used in a longer version at the Easter Vigil, see Mark Searle, "*Fons Vitae:* A Case Study in the Use of the Liturgy as a Theological Source," in *Fountain of Life,* ed. Gerard Austin (Washington, DC: The Pastoral Press, 1991), pp. 217-42. J. Frank Henderson notes that this prayer is an example of how "[c]ertain Roman Catholic liturgies contain prayers that refer to stories from the Hebrew Scriptures through allusion to biblical persons and events, for example the thanksgiving over water in liturgies of baptism/Christian initiation. In general these prayers show respect for the Hebrew Scriptures, whose stories are taken as models for Christians" ("Current Catholic Liturgical Options," p. 4).

Staying with an Easter theme, I turn now to a collect from the Easter Vigil. This is "Easter Vigil Prayer Three," which is prayed after the reading from the Book of Exodus. My translation is taken from the Sacramentary.

> Let us pray:
> Lord God,
> in the new covenant,
> you shed light on the miracles you worked in ancient times:
> the Red Sea is a symbol of our baptism,
> and the nation you freed from slavery
> is a sign of your Christian people.
> May every nation
> share the faith and privilege of Israel
> and come to new birth in the Holy Spirit.
> We ask this through Christ our Lord.

Whereas the Red Sea is presented as a symbol of baptism, the call is to the nations so that they come to share the faith and privilege of Israel. Earlier in the prayer, however, Israel is presented as a sign of the Christian people. Now let us look at the translation of this prayer in the Liturgy of the Hours, where it appears in the Office of Readings:[30]

> Lord God,
> you have revealed, in the light of the New Testament,
> the meaning of the miracles you did in former days.
> The Red Sea was to be a symbol of holy baptism,
> and the race set free from captivity
> was to prefigure the sacraments of the Christian people.
> Let all the nations who, by their faith
> have succeeded to Israel's privilege,
> be regenerated by sharing in your Spirit.
> Through Christ our Lord.

It certainly is a different prayer and reflects a different view of Jews and Judaism. This prayer reflects much more strongly a promise/fulfillment motif and, one could argue, it tends to a supersessionist theology. The miracles wrought by God in the Hebrew Bible are seen to find their meaning in the miracles performed now. Other nations have succeeded to

---

30. The Liturgy of the Hours has yet to be studied from the perspective of the Jewish-Christian encounter and more specifically how Judaism is presented in the prayer texts.

Israel's position and privilege; one wonders what the role of Israel is now. The liberty achieved by escaping from Egypt is reduced to prefiguring Christian sacraments.

Certainly, greater attention needs to be paid to the euchology (prescribed prayers) not just of the Eucharist but of other liturgical celebrations of the church, like the various sacramental celebrations, the Liturgy of the Hours, and the movement of the liturgical year, without going on to explore popular piety and hymnody.[31] It underlines the importance of the translation of the third edition of the Roman Missal that is now being finalized and is a source of considerable controversy.[32] Will this new translation be attentive to *NA* and the other documents flowing from it? If not, we could well end up with prayer texts that do not reflect the values and teachings of this dialogue.

5. Conclusion

The theological underpinnings are still crucial for any real progress in this field. As long as the nature of liturgy is seen in an exclusively christocentric way, little progress can be made into seeing the liturgy as the celebration of all of God's marvelous works. Key to all of this will be a more expansive reading of the concept of the paschal mystery. The liturgy as a realization of the paschal mystery of Christ has been central to a renewed liturgical theology; it has served liturgical reflection well as a means to understanding the saving nature of the liturgical celebration. But perhaps now is the time to widen our grasp of this paradigm, to see how the paschal mystery in the liturgy is a celebration and presence of the whole saving work of God from creation to its fulfillment. Closely allied to this task is the teaching of liturgy in seminaries and theological centers. Those entrusted with teaching the history of liturgy must be conversant with what is a basic revolution in the Christian understanding of Judaism. The deepened grasp of Judaism and a more complex understanding of the emergence of Christianity from Second Temple Judaism have affected how Jesus and his disciples are seen in

31. See Rita Ferrone, "Anti-Jewish Elements in the Extraordinary Form," *Worship*, forthcoming.

32. On the controversy, see Keith Pecklers, *The Genius of the Roman Rite: The Reception and Implementation of the New Missal* (New York: Burns & Oates, 2009), and Michael G. Ryan," What If We Said, 'Wait'?" http://www.americamagazine.org/content/article.cfm?article_id =12045.

their historical context. They shine new light on the formation of the Jesus movement, the partings of Judaism(s) and Christianity(s). Greater attention to the inherent plurality of both faiths in these early formative years reminds us how their identities were fluid and their boundaries porous.

Christian liturgy must never be used to denigrate or offend Jews, not simply out of politeness or a reluctance to offend, but because this is part of our fidelity to the gospel message. Yes, our traditions differ, and we hold very differing beliefs, but we also descend from a common heritage that is respected and cherished in the ministry of Jesus. Liturgical histories need to integrate some of the recent insights about the complexities of Second Temple Judaism and Christian origins; these histories must include a greater attention to the pluralism of both.

Further clarity is needed regarding the documents of the magisterium that deal with the reading of scripture. The message seems at times confusing or even contradictory. It leads one to suspect that NA and the documents following from it have had little impact on the magisterium except when it is dealing directly with Jews and Judaism. How Roman Catholic liturgy uses the "Old" Testament in its worship needs continual conversation. This is true for the composition of the lectionary, but especially for the hermeneutical underpinnings of that book. Of particular concern to many scholars in the Jewish/Christian dialogue is the use of the passion account of John on Good Friday. I would also add here the use of the "Reproaches" as well, or the use of the prophets in the season of Advent, where the prophetic proclamations of the messiah are seen as all fulfilled in the first coming of Christ at Christmas.[33] Forgotten is that the season of Advent also pre-

33. The Reproaches, or *Improperia*, are sung during the veneration of the Cross on Good Friday and are used widely throughout the Christian world on that day. They can be understood by some as accusing Jews of culpability for the death of Jesus, and thus fostering anti-Jewish sentiment. Others see them as condemning all. See the excellent study by J. Frank Henderson, "Critical Reflections on the Reproaches of the Good Friday Liturgy," http://www.jfrankhenderson.com/pdf/goodfriday2.pdf. John Allen also wrote about this topic, "Good Friday's Can of Worms," *National Catholic Reporter* (March 17, 2000), *HighBeam Research* (February 19, 2010). http://www.highbeam.com/doc/1G1-61184931.html. He notes that "[d]ebate over the reproaches raises issues of Judaism and the meaning of suffering. Each year Good Friday opens the memory of the suffering and death of Jesus to renewed Christian contemplation. For many Catholic liturgists, it also opens a can of worms. Among the most difficult judgments for those planning Good Friday liturgies is whether to use the so-called 'Reproaches,' a litany of accusations placed on the lips of Jesus and directed at 'his people.' Also called the Improperia, the reproaches are part of the rite for the veneration of the cross. They are customarily sung or chanted. For some, the reproaches recall the

pares for the coming of Christ at the end of time and indeed at each present moment. Shortening some readings will address some of the issues raised, but this is only an intermediate step.[34] My own sense is that until the basic hermeneutical question is addressed, little progress will be made on these fronts. As long as the church's account of itself assumes the role of Israel and writes out the people of Israel, there will be continuing problems. This leads us far beyond the issue of liturgy and into some of the basic and fundamental questions of covenant, mediation, and salvation.

The pastoral formation of the laity must be a priority for all involved in this conversation. As the number of priests declines in some parts of the world and the numbers of Catholics increase, many other forms of liturgy will be used on a Sunday besides the celebration of the Eucharist. This will lead to new kinds of leadership of the prayer of the church within these communities. The issues of the Christian-Jewish relationship must be kept to the fore in the training of these new leaders. As Roman Catholicism becomes less and less European and North American, and grows in other parts of the world, there is a danger that attitudes toward Jews are seen as something belonging to the past and not essential to one's Christian identity. Often these communities will never have experienced Judaism as a living and vital tradition. Paradoxically, the drive to inculturation can also mean a "forgetting" of the Jewish roots of Christianity. Others have pointed out how the lack of contact with living Jewish traditions can lead writers and communities to stilted viewpoints of Judaism. One way forward may be to invite Catholic communities to pray for the Jewish people on other days besides Good Friday, especially on the occasion of Jewish feast days and holidays.

Education is still needed for those who prepare pastoral aids of all

---

troubled history of Christian anti-Judaism, especially the accusation of deicide — blaming all Jews for the death of Christ. While that position was officially disavowed at Vatican II, some believe the reproaches (elements of which date back to the ninth century) are a holdover of that ancient prejudice."

34. While I have not dealt with it in this chapter, caution needs to be exercised regarding the dramatization of readings, not just on Good Friday but also during other times of the year. The same caution can be applied to devotional materials of dubious kinds that are often filled with inaccurate presentations of Jews and Judaism and even worse. See Bishops' Committee for Ecumenical and Interreligious Affairs [of the United States Catholic Bishops], *Criteria for the Evaluation of Dramatizations of the Passion* (Washington, DC: United States Catholic Conference, 1998); also available at http://www.ccjr.us/dialogika -resources/documents-and-statements/roman-catholic/us-conference-of-catholic-bishops/ 480-bceia1988.

kinds, especially in the area of preaching. But education is required beyond this as well for musicians and lyricists, artists and architects, catechists and teachers. Most of all, education is required for the people in the pew, those who serve their communities as readers and parish council members, those who lead prayer services and are members of liturgy groups, and all those who have a responsibility for the prayer of the church. The inappropriate appropriation of Jewish symbols and feasts by Christian congregations is still a cause of concern and requires constant vigilance.

If the ultimate aim of theology is doxology and it is the truest kind of theology, it is essential that our doxological praise is rooted in a dialogue that is true and integral.

Exploring the Interface of Dialogue and Theology: A Jewish Response to Christian Rutishauser, Thomas Norris, and Liam Tracey

Ruth Langer

Jews and Christians engaged in dialogue have moved past the preliminary stages of forging interpersonal relationships and exchanging information to the point of challenging each other with deeper questions. Projects like that of this book are products of dialogue, but this process also requires a stepping back from conversation in order to do internal soul searching. This then provides a coherent groundwork for moving the dialogue forward in a substantive and compelling way. The three essays to which I have been asked to respond provide us with a picture of precisely this dynamic. Thomas Norris and Liam Tracey review the state of contemporary official teachings about Jews and Judaism in the realms of Catholic ecclesiology and liturgical theology, areas whose specialists have for the most part not been directly involved in dialogue. As a consequence, most have not been challenged to engage in the difficult work of thinking carefully through the implications of the new thinking about Jews and Judaism for the fundamental teachings and practices of their own disciplines. Thus, these two essays function as wake-up calls. They are able to point to some directions for the future, but within the confines of a short essay, only begin to survey the extensive work that is still needed.

Christian Rutishauser's essay, in contrast, is a direct outgrowth of a very specific and focused question raised by the dialogue. Catholics deeply engaged in dialogue have come to realize that understanding the place of Jews' covenant with God today is critical to the full implementation of *Nostra Aetate*. Indeed, the kind of theological work his essay (and this book's driving question) represents may be the key step in moving the new relationship between Christians and Jews from one of superficial friendship to one of deeper and enduring understanding. Especially because

Rutishauser concludes by moving back into dialogic mode, I will comment only briefly on Norris's and Tracey's essays, devoting most of my response to Rutishauser's proposals.

Thomas Norris asserts that the previous century's theological rethinking of the nature of the church enabled the Second Vatican Council to teach a formulation that was universal in scope, acknowledging the existence, in some form, of ecclesial reality outside of the Catholic Church. This in turn allowed the church to begin theologizing seriously and positively about the role of other religions in the world, especially Judaism. Because this new thinking had not yet become an element of standard theological education, this aspect of the Council's work appeared revolutionary and discontinuous with previous teachings. This made it more difficult to implement in the actual life of the church. Indeed, were it easy, there would be no need for the project whose work is reflected in this volume. Norris points to a handful of Irish and British theologians who have integrated these teachings into their writings on ecclesiology. I am struck by how limited his examples are and how little they seem to have developed their theologies beyond the terse teachings of the Council. In this he intimates that the integration of the new thinking and its elaboration into a more robust set of teachings remains at a very preliminary stage.

Liam Tracey's essay reinforces this impression. As he asserts, through its verbal and nonverbal (or extraverbal) elements, liturgy is a primary vehicle for communicating the teachings of the church. At the same time, liturgy tends to be very conservative. People relate to it at emotional, precognitive levels; they want it to operate in expected ways, creating echoes and activating memories from one occasion to the next. Thus, implementing actual liturgical change successfully and in a way that is theologically coherent is extremely challenging. In addition, as Tracey points out, the liturgical vision of the Council was also a product of the emerging thinking of previous decades. However, the preconciliar liturgical work did not engage directly with questions that addressed the status of Jews and members of other religions and the Council's own Constitution on the Sacred Liturgy *(Sacrosanctum Concilium);* its initial document, promulgated in December 1963, so far predated *Nostra Aetate* that it does not integrate its insights. Thus, the implementation of the Council's liturgical directives was frequently done without contemplation of how the teachings of *Lumen Gentium* and *Nostra Aetate* challenged many of the liturgical presuppositions of the church. Tracey too can point to only a handful of theologians who have worked to integrate the new thinking about Jews and Judaism into the liturgy, and his long list of areas of the liturgy that require serious examination from this perspective speak for themselves.

Thus, these two essays at a basic level present us with a single message: regarding the nature of the church and its liturgy, the Second Vatican Council established as doctrine what theologians had been teaching over the previous century. However, this preconciliar thinking had not challenged existing presuppositions about the role of Jews in the official and unofficial teachings of the church, meaning that the earlier documents of the Council, especially that on the liturgy, had no discussion pointing to the need to integrate the teachings of *Nostra Aetate* into their particular concerns or suggesting how to do so coherently. Implementation of the teachings about Jews and Judaism into these specific disciplines of ecclesiology and liturgical theology (and into other areas of Catholic teaching as well) is an extremely complex process, not one yet well achieved. Achieving this goal requires hard work and a willingness to challenge both popular expectations and theological presumptions in order to discover the path to a reintegration that will accommodate all the necessary principles.

Christian Rutishauser's essay responds to this challenge. He offers a focused exploration of one of the many topics on which such hard work is needed, looking directly at the question of the Christ Jesus and the Jewish People Today project and its primary question: How can one understand the assertion that the Jewish people are in eternal covenantal relationship with God theologically and simultaneously maintain the church's fundamental understandings about the universal salvation offered through Christ? Full evaluation of the theological value of Rutishauser's proposal must be made by members of his own Catholic and wider Christian community. From a specifically Jewish perspective, I will comment on a selection of his points and then conclude by turning to his challenges to the Jewish community. I offer these observations in the hope that they may be helpful for the inner-Christian discussion.

First, Rutishauser writes as a person experienced in dialogue, for whom Jews are not abstractions but real human beings. Therefore, he recognizes that the fundamental questions of this inner-Christian discussion of the role of Christ for Jews are an affront to many Jews given the history of Christian attempts, many successful, to undermine Judaism's integrity and bring Jews to baptism (§1.2). Other than the few Jews engaged in high-level dialogue and conversant with Christian theological issues, most Jews will indeed easily misunderstand the entire discussion and purpose of the

Christ Jesus and the Jewish People Today project. Its presentation must therefore be extremely carefully nuanced if it is to contribute to future understandings. The presence of Jewish auditors throughout the process leading to this book and of Jewish respondents to the book's essays has been an important methodological tool helping this inner-Christian conversation to achieve this aim.

In his theological proposals, Rutishauser makes a series of important points. Most fundamental, perhaps, from a Jewish perspective, is his recognition that it is the Sinai Covenant, Torah itself, that needs to be the focus of this discussion, including its specific commandments to Israel of how to live a life in relationship with God (§2.1). This reflects reasonably well Jewish self-understanding that the Sinai revelation is the most important manifestation of God's covenantal relationship with Israel, and that response to its halakhic directives — not just the Ten Commandments, but all of God's commandments — is the essence of Jewish covenantal living.

Judaism does not have Christianity's reasons to enter into a single-covenant versus multiple-covenant debate. Indeed, the Bible portrays God as entering into multiple covenants with Israel, representing different aspects of the divine relationship with her. Nevertheless, once one understands Torah in a broader sense that encompasses all divine revelation to Israel, it can also include all these various covenants (or manifestations thereof). Rutishauser's turn to the Sinai Covenant is coherent, with careful readings of recent papal language about the Jewish covenant with God.[1] Those suggesting, unlike Rutishauser, that the popes are referring only to God's covenant with Abraham create an understanding that is problematic from a Jewish perspective. Beginning with Paul, Christian understanding of God's relationship with Abraham has stressed God's promise that Abraham's descendants would be a blessing to all the peoples of the earth and has ignored the parts of these promises key to Jewish self-understanding: the particular covenants of circumcision and of the land. Indeed, Judaism understands God's covenant with Noah to be universal (and distinct from the Sinai Covenant); the other biblical covenants it sees as particular, with Israel.

Where I have more difficulty is in Rutishauser's assertion that Israel's

---

1. See the texts of Pope John Paul II's speeches in Mainz in 1980 and at Mount Sinai in 2000, and Pope Benedict XVI's speech in the synagogue in Rome in 2010. All are available in the papal archives on the Vatican's website (http://www.vatican.va/holy_father/index.htm). The English translation of the Mainz speech is somewhat problematic on this point and does not transmit the ideas of the German original well. English texts are all available from http://www.ccjr.us/dialogika-resources/documents-and-statements/roman-catholic.

status as God's chosen ". . . is *only* intended to serve the salvation of the world. God creates the distinction between Israel and the Gentiles *so that* the Chosen will become a light to the Gentiles (Isa. 49:6), a covenant of the people (Isa. 49:8), and messenger for the nations (Jer. 1:10)" (p. 235; emphases mine). Coherent with the Christian emphasis on the universal aspects of the Abrahamic covenant, this understanding reduces Israel's purpose to being part of the Christian universal agenda and denies any role to God's particular relationship with Israel except as it serves that universal agenda.

Particularism is not necessarily exclusivism, as it can mean a recognition and valuing of every nation's particularism. There is no question (in my mind) that Israel's chosen status does not imply superiority. It is a calling to a particular service, one that is often not an easy one. But this is a service of God for God's mysterious reasons and it is particular to Israel. The theme of being a light of the nations or a blessing to them is only *an* element of this service and not even necessarily the most important one. An American analogy would be today's preference for cultural diversity over the "melting pot." The "melting pot" of course really represented an expectation that immigrants would lose their national particularisms and come to conform to an Anglo-Saxon or at least a Eurocentric, generally Protestant, set of norms.[2] Jews do serve God by serving the world, but this universal horizon comes from within Judaism's particularity and returns to it as well.

Rutishauser's explicit turn to the Sinai Covenant also opens a door that could be helpful for his argument. He presents Jesus as the embodiment and personification of Torah. This could well be what John means when he refers to Jesus as Logos. We know all too little about theologies of Logos in late Second Temple Judaism, but the sense that God's Word had an existence and presence in people's lives seems to have been part of at least Greek-influenced Judaism. Daniel Boyarin argues that rabbinic Jews ceased to speak in these terms in the course of the process of Jewish and Christian self-differentiation, but that remnants remain in targumic discussions of God's *memra'*, i.e., Word.[3] Thus, the conception that Torah

---

2. Similarly, the next paragraph is problematic, as it builds on this presumption of Judaism's universalism. I find the Jewish discussion to which Rutishauser refers, in "Reflections on Covenant and Mission," to be itself one that lacks clarity. Indeed, I do not read it the way that Rutishauser seems to.

3. Daniel Boyarin, "The Gospel of the *Memra*: Jewish Binitarianism and the Prologue to John," *HTR* 94, no. 3 (2001): 243-84; and his *Border Lines: The Partition of Judaeo-Christianity* (Philadelphia: University of Pennsylvania Press, 2004), Part II, "The Crucifixion of the Logos: How Logos Theology Became Christian."

might be embodied within a particular manifestation of God has some roots in Judaism.

I am intrigued by the implications of Rutishauser's suggestion that the Gospels' *paradidonai* be read not as an act of betrayal by the Jews, but as God's positive act literally of handing his Word over to the Gentile Romans. I leave evaluation of this biblical reading to New Testament scholars. Rutishauser suggests an analogy with the Hebrew root *m-s-r*, but misses that this word, like the Greek, carries two opposite valences. He refers to its positive meaning as *mesoret*, that which is handed down as a tradition; however, the verb can also indicate betrayal. A *moser* is an informer, one who hands things over (inappropriately) to someone else, i.e., one who betrays others. Thus, the analogy with the Hebrew is less helpful than he suggests, but this should not negate his argument for the benign meanings of the concept.

As a Jew, I can be quite satisfied with the argument that God's handing his Word over to the Gentiles opens the covenant to the Gentile world without affecting God's Sinai-based relationship with Judaism. This explains how both communities can fit into the divine covenantal framework. However, I am not at all certain that a Christian theologian would find that this ultimate differentiation between Jew and Gentile answers the question of how Christ functions for Jews. Rutishauser seems dissatisfied with his own answer. He is critical of the response that pushes a solution off to the eschaton, but also sees no alternative.

From a Jewish perspective, the eschatological solution is a nice piece of *pilpul,* a mental manipulation that allows us to achieve our immediate goal of living as two communities side by side in friendship today. In practice, Jews can accept an expectation that we will discover at the eschaton whether Jews or Christians have been correct about the person of the messiah, as this defers the issue indefinitely. However, there are several problems with this solution to the Christian theological conundrum. The obvious one is that this is a practical solution, not one that is philosophically rigorous. More seriously, in the case that Rutishauser references, Cardinal Kasper's explanation of the revised Tridentine Rite Good Friday prayer, we are confronting a practical impossibility. If the church's approved liturgical texts have a potentially harmful plain-sense meaning that can be obviated only through complex acts of interpretation, then the community in the pews is being misled. Liturgy does not operate this way.

Rutishauser concludes his essay with a move back to dialogue, calling on Jews to engage in a parallel process of theological thinking about Christianity. These points demand some preliminary responses. He asks that perhaps Jews "could be expected to understand the church as also being in covenant with God and so ponder what their relationship to Jesus might be beyond historical controversy and polemic" (p. 246). He is correct in pointing out that the rabbinic tradition has not developed a discussion of how other religions in their specificity are in relationship with God. However, traditions like the Noahide commandments or the concept that the righteous of the nations have a place in the world to come (i.e., they are saved)[4] do present opportunities for a theological inclusivism that could be formulated in terms of the particulars of different religions. They also begin with the presumption that God is indeed in covenantal relationship with other peoples, albeit a different covenant than Israel's. To claim otherwise would be to limit God. Indeed, resources for such discussions are being developed and this discussion is beginning within the Jewish world.[5]

The second half of Rutishauser's challenge is more problematic. Does dialogue with Christians require that Jews have a relationship with Jesus? Rutishauser's request goes beyond the historical to ask that Jews find meaning for themselves in the understanding of early Christians that the man they handed over to the nations was resurrected (and manifest as divine). Understanding the role of the historical Jesus within his Jewish world is something that more and more Jews are doing. Similarly, increasing numbers read the New Testament as an important witness to the Jewish world of the first century. It is even possible to understand Jewishly that God created Christianity to bring knowledge of God to the Gentile world.[6]

However, Rutishauser's request goes beyond the intellectual to the affective or faith-based and is thus much more difficult. Jews who have a "relationship" with Jesus cross the sociological boundary between our two communities, a boundary that has been well established by Jewish resistance to Christian missionary activities. Rutishauser writes, "Jews remain Jews even if some of them see in Jesus a messianic figure" (p. 248; see also

---

4. This precise formulation is medieval. See, for instance, Maimonides' *Mishneh Torah*, Laws of Repentance 3:5, Laws of Kings 8:11, and the supercommentaries on these that point back to a discussion in B. Sanhedrin 105a, which touches on this topic only in a very abstract way.

5. See, for example, Alan Brill, *Judaism and Other Religions: Models of Understanding* (forthcoming, Palgrave-Macmillan, 2010); or a forthcoming volume edited by Eugene Korn and Alon Goshen-Gottstein, *Jewish Theologies of the Religious Other* (Littmann).

6. Cf. Maimonides, *Mishneh Torah*, Laws of Kings 11:4, though the full passage is more problematic.

n. 33). This is the claim today of Messianic Jews, Jews for Jesus, and other similar missionary groups. From the perspective of rabbinic Judaism, Jews who accept Jesus exclude themselves from the life of the Jewish community. Technically, one's Jewishness is indeed irrevocable (as is baptism in Catholic theology), so they may rejoin the Jewish community without formal conversion and their contractual relationships like marriage remain binding.[7] As a demographic minority on the world's stage, Jews are extremely uncomfortable with this attempt to blur communal boundaries, and do not permit the reverse phenomenon of Christians becoming Jews but maintaining key elements of Christian faith.

Rutishauser's suggestion that there be a place for some of Jesus' teachings in Jewish tradition is less complicated since most of these teachings, in their origins, were very much questions of how to apply the teachings of Torah in the first-century world. These teachings help us to understand the path that rabbinic Judaism chose or did not choose to take. It is increasingly clear that rabbinic Judaism did define itself in dialogue, not with Jesus himself, but with the emerging Christianity of subsequent centuries. Christianity thus is not a deviation from Judaism, but a partner in the emergence of our separate paths. Rutishauser's suggestion that we see these two paths as the separate paths of Jews and Gentiles allows us to preserve the authenticity of both to admit freely, as he says, that we "have learned in history from each other" (p. 248).[8]

In his final section, Rutishauser speaks of Jews and Christians being "sacraments of otherness" for each other and in this, demonstrating their "dialogical existence as people of God" (p. 249). He is explicit that this is a mutual relationship. Again, a Jewish perspective challenges this. Christianity has to deal with the Judaism from which it has emerged; Islam engages with both Christianity and Judaism. But Judaism has no internal theological need to engage with Christianity and Islam, only historical ones, and

---

7. This is an extremely complex topic, developed in the crucible of the reality of medieval mission and resultant conversions. For a brief synthesis of the issues, see my forthcoming book on the *birkat haminim,* chapter three, in the discussion of the *meshummad* (apostate).

8. As I write this, I have received by email a pdf of Zev Garber's introduction to a volume of the journal *Shofar* 28, no. 3 (2010), dedicated to examining the question of what the understanding that Jesus lived and died a faithful Jew means to contemporary Jews. He calls on Jews to undertake a parallel process of introspection to that undergone by the Catholic Church, and to "cleanse the People Israel of any conceived and/or perceived anti-Christian bias" (p. 9). I have not yet been able to examine the volume itself. He also announces a book-length publication on the same topic.

Christians need to remember that significant Jewish communities engaged primarily with Islam. Even today, in Israel, developing a dialogic relationship with Islam is a more urgent, if difficult goal. Thus, the relationship that Rutishauser suggests responds to a much deeper theological need in Christianity than it does in Judaism. Jews have historical reasons to desire a repaired and improved relationship with Christians, but the theological need applies equally to all of the world's religions. An expectation that Jews give priority to Christianity, especially over Islam, arises from a christocentric perspective on the world that Jews cannot share.

These three essays demonstrate that documents alone are not enough; they are only as good as their implementation. Otherwise they remain mere words. Norris's and Tracey's essays illustrate areas where implementation has barely raised the difficult questions that need to be addressed before there can be a coherent expression of liturgical theology or ecclesiology that incorporates the teachings of *Nostra Aetate*. Rutishauser's essay, on the other hand, offers a step forward on one of the complex theological questions that have emerged for Catholics. I am not certain that his answer brings us to a solution that will be satisfactory to all theologians, but it is a substantive proposal that deserves further discussion. My observations are those of a Jewish participant in dialogue, a supporter of this process. God willing, the time will come soon when Catholic participants in dialogue will have the privilege to be auditors to parallel Jewish discussions.

About the Contributors

Also served as: 1 = editor; 2 = steering committee member; 3 = project coordinator

MARY C. BOYS, S.N.J.M., ED.D. is the Skinner and McAlpin Professor of Practical Theology at Union Theological Seminary in New York City, USA.[1,2]

PHILIP A. CUNNINGHAM, PH.D. is Professor of Theology and Director of the Institute for Jewish-Catholic Relations of Saint Joseph's University in Philadelphia, USA.[1,2,3]

TAMARA COHN ESKENAZI, PH.D. is Professor of Bible at Hebrew Union College-Jewish Institute of Religion in Los Angeles, USA.

ADAM GREGERMAN, PH.D. is the Jewish Scholar at the Institute for Christian & Jewish Studies in Baltimore, USA.

ELIZABETH GROPPE, PH.D. is Associate Professor of Theology, specializing in Catholic systematic theology, at Xavier University in Cincinnati, USA.

DANIEL J. HARRINGTON, S.J., PH.D. is Professor of New Testament at the Boston College School of Theology and Ministry, USA.

REV. HANSPETER HEINZ, PH.D. is Professor Emeritus of Pastoral Theology, University of Augsburg, and chairs the discussion group "Jews and Christians," *Zentralkomitee der deutschen Katholiken*, in Germany.

HANS HERMANN HENRIX, DR. PHIL. H.C. is Honorary Professor of the University of Salzburg, Austria, and Director Emeritus of the Episcopal Academy of the Roman Catholic Diocese of Aachen, Germany.[1,2]

GREGOR MARIA HOFF, PH.D. is Professor of Fundamental Theology and Ecumenism at the University of Salzburg, Austria, and Chairman of the Salzburger Hochschulwochen.

WALTER CARDINAL KASPER, TH.D. served as President of the Pontifical Council for Promoting Christian Unity and of the Pontifical Commission for Religious Relations with the Jews at the Vatican from 2001 to 2010.

EDWARD KESSLER, PH.D. is Executive Director of the Woolf Institute of Abrahamic Faiths and Fellow of St. Edmund's College, Cambridge, UK.

RABBI RUTH LANGER, PH.D. is Associate Professor of Theology (Jewish Studies) and Associate Director of the Center for Christian-Jewish Learning, Boston College, USA.[2]

REV. BARBARA U. MEYER, PH.D. is Adjunct Professor for Christian Thought and History at the Hebrew Union College Jerusalem (The Israeli Rabbinical Program), Hebrew University Jerusalem (Faculty of Law), and the Interdisciplinary Center Herzliya (IDC).

REV. THOMAS J. NORRIS, D.S.T. is Professor of Systematic Theology at Saint Patrick's College, Maynooth, Ireland, and a member of the Holy See's International Theological Commission.

JOHN T. PAWLIKOWSKI, O.S.M., PH.D. is Professor of Social Ethics at the Catholic Theological Union in Chicago, USA.[2]

DIDIER POLLEFEYT, PH.D. is Professor in Theology of Jewish-Christian Relations and Post-Holocaust Theology and Vice-Dean of the Faculty of Theology, Katholieke Universiteit Leuven, Belgium.[2]

CHRISTIAN RUTISHAUSER, S.J., PH.D. is Head of the education sector in the Lassalle-House Bad Schönbrunn, Switzerland, and lecturer for Jewish Studies at the Munich School of Philosophy, and the Gregorian University, Rome.

RABBI MARC SAPERSTEIN, PH.D. is Principal of Leo Baeck College, London, UK, and Charles E. Smith Professor Emeritus of Jewish History at the George Washington University, Washington, DC, USA.

REV. JOSEPH SIEVERS, PH.D. is Professor of Jewish History and Literature at the Pontifical Biblical Institute and former Director of the Cardinal Bea Centre for Judaic Studies at the Pontifical Gregorian University in Rome, Italy.[1, 2, 3]

REV. JESPER SVARTVIK, TH.D. is the Krister Stendahl Professor of Theology of Religions at the Centre for Theology and Religious Studies at Lund University, Sweden, and the Swedish Theological Institute in Jerusalem, Israel.[1, 2]

LIAM TRACEY, O.S.M., S.L.D. is Professor of Liturgy and Director of Post-Graduate Studies at Saint Patrick's College, Maynooth, Ireland.

Index of Subjects

Antisemitism: Christianity and the roots of, 14, 15, 21, 22, 74, 117; church's role in, 14-15, 17-18, 64, 69-71; contemporary scholarship on, 15; Nazism and, 73; negative depiction of the Jews and, 39, 42-43, 54; popes' statements on, 21, 24; Shoah relation to, xxv

Christian-Jewish relations: biblical understanding of, 81; church's different attitudes toward, 170, 196; controversies and, 47; Epistle to the Hebrews and, 77, 79n.1, 83; historical context and, 47; historical memory and, 14; new historical and theological research on, xxx, 28, 47, 78, 248; New Testament texts and, 17, 77n.1, 79; "old" and "new" covenant and, 78-79; pastoral formation and, 285; theological dimensions of, 30; theology and church's teaching on, 114; Trinitarian theology and, 168. See also Jewish-Christian dialogue

Conversion, xxx, 71, 93, 94, 156, 186, 294

Covenant: differently experienced by Jews and Christians, 191-93; relation of old and new, xiv, 11, 78, 185n.11, 186, 232, 246, 255, 262, 276; robust understanding of, 187, 189-91. See also Covenant, New; Covenant, Old; Salvation

Covenant, New: Christology as the basis of, 247; Easter Vigil Prayer, 282; Letter to the Hebrews and, 81, 83, 86, 197, 187; Jeremiah and, xiv, 82, 90, 187, 190; Cardinal Kasper on, 186; *Nostra Aetate* and people of, 229; people of God of, 79n.8; Resurrected One as the cornerstone of, 240; through Christ with people from other nations, 229

Covenant, Old: church's connection with God's people of, 259; end of, 17, 91, 169; end of sacrificial worship of, 276; German bishops' statement and, 259; God's rejection of, 107; Epistle to the Hebrews and, 80n.14, 85, 87, 91, 107, 242; Jeremiah and, 107; Judaism as, 83; never revoked, xxviii, 79n.8, 183, 186, 233; obsolescence of, xiv, xxvi, 79, 83, 107, 187-88; Pauline theology and, 242; permanent validity of, 188, 229; people of God of, 79n.8; perspective in biblical texts on, 80, 107, 242; transformation not annulment of, 161

Death of Jesus. *See* Jesus, death of

Deicide charge, xxv, xxvii, 45, 46n.40, 258, 259, 260, 285n.33

Dominus Iesus: Jesus Christ as unique mediator in, 183n.1; and Jewish-

Christ, xxiii, 103; church is the new, 46, 47, 160, 255; covenant terminology of, 79n.8; dialogical existence of Jews and Christian as, 249, 294; Epistle to the Hebrews and, 86n.30, 88; followers of Christ had become, 35; Gentiles as part of, 94-96; God's rejection of the former, 35; Hebrew Bible and, 160; Matthew 28:16-20 and, 239; membership in, 94, 95, 97; never revoked by God, 183; one or two peoples, 232; Paul on, 95; proximity of church from Gentiles to Judaism as, 239; relation of the church to the Jews as, xxxi, 253, 256; relationship of Jews with Christ, the founder of, 261; salvation history and, 233; separation of, 235; sinners belonging to, 215; a twofold, 232, 243

Persecution: anti-Jewish sentiment and, xxv; Christian separation from Judaism includes, 179; church deplores, 262; committed by medieval Christians, 71; gospel and Christian, 76; of the Jewish people by Christians, 249; for Jews still present memories of, 232, 250; and the massacre of six million Jews, 76n.16; Matthew 27:25 and potential antisemitism, 109; passion narratives and, 40, 54

Pontifical Biblical Commission (PBC), *The Jewish People and Their Sacred Scriptures in the Christian Bible:* and Albert Cardinal Vanhoye on Epistle to the Hebrews, 188; and church's liturgical life, 274; and the death of Jesus, 52; focus on exegesis of, 48; and Jewish messianic expectation, 180, 199; and the Jews in the New Testament, 48-52; on Old Testament as Word of God, 138n.62; pastoral orientation in, 51-52; on validity of the rabbinic exegetical traditions, 171-72

Popes: antisemitism, statements on, 21, 24; Benedict XVI on the Holocaust, 20-23; Benedict XVI on the Jewish-

ness of Jesus, 121; Eugene IV on salvation, 184n.7; John XXIII and *Nostra Aetate,* 16; John Paul II on the Holocaust, 18; John Paul II on the Messiah, 117; John Paul II on salvation history, 117, 118

Proselytism. *See* Missions to convert Jews

Reconciliation, xxvi, 2, 11, 32, 102, 120n.11, 144, 145, 148, 150

Salvation: already/not yet, 190, 191; Athanasius and question of, 154; Christ as the definitive way to, 205; Christ event and theology of, xxii, xxix, 137, 141, 231, 236, 259; Christian mission and forced baptisms for Jewish, 232; Christology and universal claim of, xxviii, 233, 233n.10, 238, 245; church and Judaism not as two parallel ways of, xxviii, 185, 262; church necessary for, 253; connection between covenant and, xxii, xxviii, 189, 232; Council of Chalcedon on, 125, 126; Decree on Ecumenism on, 258; *Dominus Iesus* on, 198, 231; economy of, 166, 169, 173, 174, 205; eschatological climax of, 191, 193, 245; exclusivist view of, 138, 184, 230; God's plan of, 167n.12, 185n.11, 190, 209, 250; Good Friday intercession and Israel's, 244-45; *halakhah* and, 234; history of, 116, 124, 238, 239; inclusivist approach to, 200, 231; interpretations of the passion and, 40, 44; Israel's way to, 138n.62, 206, 219, 232; Jewishness of Jesus and, 144, 150, 153; liturgy and, 177; multiple facets of, xxvi-xxx; *Nostra Aetate* and, 47; Pope Eugene IV and, 184n.7; post-conciliar ecclesiology and, 262, 269n.2, 271n.7; and reconciliation, 148, 150; *Redemptoris Missio* and, 204; reinterpreting of biblical texts on, 102, 190, 239, 240, 241, 243; religiously plural